THE CATHOLIC CHURCH
AND NAZI GERMANY

the catholic church and nazi germany

GUENTER LEWY

McGRAW-HILL BOOK COMPANY

New York
Toronto

The Catholic Church and Nazi Germany

Library of Congress Catalog Card Number: 64-21072

First Edition

37627

Acknowledgment is made to the following sources for permission to use material previously published:

The American Jewish Committee, for the article "Pius XII, the Jews and the German Catholic Church" in the February 1964 issue of *Commentary*.

Parts of Section 2 of Chapter VII are from the article "The German Roman Catholic Hierarchy and the Saar Plebiscite of 1935," reprinted from the *Political Science Quarterly* Volume LXXIX, No. 2, June 1964.

TABLE OF CONTENTS

PREFACE

Rolf Hochhuth's play *The Deputy* has caused new attention to be focussed upon the relationship of the Roman Catholic Church and Hitler's Third Reich, a subject which for many years has been obscured by what may justifiably be called an extensive mythology. One reason for the emergence of such comforting legends is the human tendency to suppress unpleasant memories, and this in turn inhibits scholarly research into the dark corners of the recent past. "It is safe to assume," predicted the German Catholic writer Theodor Haecker in 1939, in the diary which he kept during the tragic days of Nazi rule, "that the Germans will do everything, consciously and unconsciously, in order to forget as quickly as possible all that is now said, written and done. The memory of a guilt weighs heavy, it 'depresses.' If he can, man throws it off." Haecker's prediction came true; to a large extent it explains also the often fierce reaction to Hochhuth's play, especially from the ranks of German Catholicism. Obviously, a raw nerve has been touched.

This book, work on which was begun in 1960, tells the story of the relations between the Catholic Church and German National Socialism. It seeks to elucidate the historical record, which we can now reconstruct with considerable accuracy as the result of the capture by the Allies of large quantities of German State and Party documents and the opening of some Church archives. The known inaccessibility of the Vatican archives concerning the more recent past can be compensated for in good measure by careful combing of the archives of the German Foreign Ministry and German diocesan archives, all of which contain a large number of communications from and to the Holy See. While the passage of time may broaden the perspective with which we can analyze events that happened a relatively short time ago, much of the more direct knowledge we can gain through talking to people still living today will be lost to future investigators. Hence the decision to proceed with such an inquiry now, not quite twenty years after the downfall of the Third Reich, appears justified.

I have resisted the temptation of making comparisons between the behavior and fate of the Catholic Church and the Protestant churches under Hitler. That is a story of great complexity, deserving of its own book-length treatment; any brief allusions to it, I concluded, would be more misleading than informative. Also in the interest of a treatment in depth, this study is limited to the Old Reich, exclusive of Austria and other territories later acquired by Nazi Germany. The emphasis throughout is on the German episcopal hierarchy and the Papacy. Such a frame of reference largely alleviates the necessity of deciding who is to be seen as speaking for the Catholic Church, for there cannot be any doubt as to the official standing of Pope and bishops. According to Catholic teaching, of course, the Church is a *corpus Christi mysticum* and includes more than hierarchy and clerics. But policy and pastoral pronouncements are made by bishops, not laymen.

These decisions, delimiting the breadth of this work as they do, have required me to treat quickly many instances of truly heroic individuals in the lower ranks of the Church who acted out of conscience and paid dearly for it. I trust, however, that my mention of such incidents and names, no matter how brief, will add to the reverence due them.

Needless to say, leadership even in a hierarchically organized religious body is not simply a one-way track. The Pope's actions—or lack of action—were to a considerable extent influenced by the behavior of the Papacy's "constituencies," especially the German Church. In turn, in order to understand the positions assumed by the German episcopate we must take into account not only state policy and external conditions in general, but also the political attitudes of the rest of the clergy and of rank-and-file Catholics. Hence, I have given attention not only to the official pronouncements of the episcopate, acting individually or collectively, but I have examined Catholic newspapers, periodicals, and the writings of individual Catholics of stature. I have also tried to talk to as many men and women who lived through the events in question as proved feasible, for, especially because of the repressive character of the Nazi state, there is much to be known that is not recorded in documents or other written records.

This discussion of the Church's relationship with the Third Reich at first glance may seem to encompass only what might be called the temporal or political life of the Church. Seemingly untouched remains what many regard as the essential function of the Church—her existence as the spiritual community of the faithful and custodian of sacramental mystery. This is the Church which lives beyond the confines of time and nations. But this apparent dichotomy, at least in theory, is a false one. The Christian lives in this world and his Church does not confine herself to ritual and to providing spiritual comfort. She seeks to permeate all aspects of life with the truth of Christian teaching and considers herself responsible not only for faith but also for morality. Here lies one of the important roots of that conflict of jurisdictions between Church and State which in one form or another has been with us since the earliest history of Christianity.

In practice the Church has frequently stressed her spiritual role only and has cloistered herself within the walls of her churches and monasteries. In this way she has prevented many clashes with temporal rulers and has been able to perpetuate the Church as a visible institution. To some extent, as we shall see, this also happened during the era of the Third Reich. But this concern with maintaining historical continuity raises some basic questions to be dealt with in this study.

The subject matter of this book is controversial. Even among German Catholics important facts are disputed and opinions are divided on such questions as the wisdom of the Concordat of 1933, the bearing of the episcopate during the war period, the role or absence of a role played in the extermination of the Jews of Europe. The vehemence with which many Catholics reacted to an article by Dr. E. W. Böckenförde on German Catholicism in the year 1933, published by the Catholic periodical *Hochland* in 1961, and, more recently, the bitter response to Hochhuth's *Deputy* bear witness to the emotion-laden character of the problem. It is part of the past with which contemporary Germany continues to grapple and with which it seeks to come to terms.

I have made the deliberate effort not to fit this work into any preconceived scheme. At the same time, I cannot claim to have remained impartial. This could have been achieved only as a concomitant of moral indifference. To the best of my ability I have adhered to the canons of scholarship and intellectual honesty. More none may demand.

The debt which I owe to individuals and foundations is great. The Social Science Research Council awarded me a Faculty Research Fellowship which, supplemented by a grant from Smith College, made possible research in Germany during the academic year 1961–62. There I was granted the privilege of working in the diocesan archives of Passau, Regensburg, Eichstätt, Hildesheim, Paderborn, Aachen, Trier, Mainz, and Limburg/Lahn (officials in the dioceses of Bamberg, Cologne, Freiburg/Breisgau, Rottenburg, and Speyer, for reasons best known to themselves, declined to cooperate). Dr. Franz Rödel put at my disposal the rich collection of the *Katholische Judaeologische Institut* in Jetzendorf/Ilm. I had all the co-operation a scholar might hope for from the staff of the *Bundesarchiv* in Koblenz, of the archives of the Foreign Office and the Ministry of Justice in Bonn, of the *Hauptstaatsarchiv* and the *Geheime Staatsarchiv* of Bavaria in Munich, of the *Hauptarchiv* in Berlin, and the American Berlin Document Center. The Bavarian State Library was most helpful in supplying books from its own collection or from the holdings of other libraries. The *Institut für Zeitgeschichte* and the library of the Franciscan monastery of St. Anna in Munich, as well as the Caritas Library in Freiburg/Breisgau, were generous in meeting my unending requests. I am obliged to Professor Eric Voegelin, head of the Institute of Political Science at the University of Munich, who put at my disposal a place to work, and to the staff of the Institute for their help and advice. I

spent several weeks in the Wiener Library in London and benefited from the fine collection on Nazi Germany put together by a
group of dedicated workers. The number of individuals who gave
of their time to tell me of their experiences during the Nazi period
are far too numerous to list individually and I can merely record
here my thanks to all those who must remain unnamed. Finally,
the Rockefeller Foundation awarded me a grant after my return
from research abroad which gave me another year free from teaching
duties during which some further research in the National Archives
in Washington and most of the writing of this book were done. I
would like to express my gratitude to all whose help I have enjoyed.

I am also indebted to many friends and colleagues who read
all or part of the manuscript in draft, though I should add the
customary caveat that this book's analyses and interpretations remain for better or for worse my own responsibility. In particular
I must mention George Kateb, Cecelia M. Kenyon, Alan Mitchell,
and Beate Ruhm von Oppen, who gave me the benefit of detailed
criticisms and suggestions.

The patience of my children and the encouragement and assistance of my wife I also gratefully record, even though this acknowledgment hardly does justice to their part. I dedicate this book to
them.

Guenter Lewy

NORTHAMPTON, MASS.
MARCH 16, 1964

The Course Is Set **I**

The Encounter With National Socialism Before 1933 **1**

On January 30, 1933, Hitler became chancellor of the German republic. With his appointment by the aging president, Hindenburg, National Socialism had arrived at its long-sought goal of political power, even though temporarily the party only shared the reins of government. Within a week the first measures intended to muzzle any opposition had been passed. After February 27, memorable for its Reichstag fire, the Nazi machinery, adept at both legal suppression and outright terrorization, swung into high gear. New elections held on March 5 now brought the Nazis a sizable plurality over any other party, but no absolute majority. Thus the final consolidation of power had to wait a little longer for the death of the German parliament. On March 23 Hitler gave a policy statement in which he promised, among other things, to work for peaceful relations between Church and State; the Reichstag in turn approved the Enabling Act, which for a period of four years transferred the power of legislation from parliament to the cabinet. Five days later the German Catholic episcopate, organized in the Fulda Bishops' Conference, withdrew their earlier prohibitions against membership in the Nazi party and admonished the faithful to be loyal and obedient to the new regime.

The significance of the Fulda declaration, which will occupy us more fully in our next chapter, was undoubtedly weighty. Some Catholics were surprised and confused, for only a few weeks earlier they had been told to vote *against* Hitler and *for* the Catholic-led Center and Bavarian People's parties. Essentially the declaration was a recognition of the new facts of political life, a reversal which some Catholics had predicted would occur once Hitler succeeded in heading a government. Moreover, in some ways the bishops' withdrawal of the ban on participation in the Nazi movement was a logical outgrowth of the ambivalence that had characterized the episcopate's attitude to National Socialism during the preceding twelve years. It can be fully understood only in the context of the political attitudes held by German Catholicism during the Weimar period.

1. The Position of German Catholicism in the Weimar Republic

The Catholic Church had prospered under the republic. The Weimar constitution had liquidated all vestiges of Bismarck's restrictive legislation, imposed during a conflict in the 1870s known as the "Kulturkampf," and it had guaranteed the free and unhindered exercise of religion. Despite a formal separation of Church and State, financial subsidies to the churches had been continued. Organized in twenty-five dioceses, the Catholic Church by the end of the twenties numbered over 20,000 priests for 20-million Catholics, as against 16,000 pastors for 40-million Protestants. Soon one spoke of a "monastic spring": new monasteries were built and the religious orders founded new houses and established new schools. Catholic organizations of every kind multiplied. The *Volksverein für das Katholische Deutschland* (People's League for German Catholics), founded in 1890 by Ludwig Windthorst as a parent organization for various peasants', workers' and artisans' associations, grew into a mass organization of over 500,000 members and 4,300 branch associations. The *Katholische Jugend Deutschlands* (Catholic Youth of Germany) by 1933 reached a membership of over 1,500,000 and embraced 33 subsidiary societies.[1] There were also *Katholische Arbeitervereine* (Catholic Workers' Associations), *Katholische Beamtenvereine* (Catholic Civil Servants' Associations), a *Katholischer Deutscher Frauenbund* (Catholic League of German

Women) and many more, all in addition to a multiplicity of local parish societies and clubs. In 1931 Karl Bachem, the historian of the Center party, noted with pride, "Never yet has a Catholic country possessed such a developed system of all conceivable Catholic associations as today's Catholic Germany."[2]

Catholic intellectual life flourished and men like Max Scheler and Romano Guardini and Catholic publications such as the *Allgemeine Rundschau, Hochland* and *Stimmen der Zeit* enjoyed high prestige among non-Catholics too. The Catholic daily press was strong. Moreover, German Catholics were able to strengthen their political influence, for the Catholic Center party, founded in 1870 as a counterforce to widespread anti-Catholic sentiments in Bismarck's Germany, now assumed a key role.

The leaders of the Center party as well as many individual Catholic bishops at first condemned the revolution of 1918. Opening a national gathering of Catholics in Munich on August 27, 1922, Cardinal Faulhaber characterized the November revolution as "perjury and high treason."[3] Similarly, the chairman of the Center party deputation in the National Assembly in his first speech on February 13, 1919, declared that the party could not approve of the revolutionary upheaval that had overthrown the monarchy, though he added that the party now, "after all that has happened, takes its stand on the grounds of the accomplished facts."[4] In time, the Center party became one of the mainstays of the Weimar republic. Consistently polling 12 to 13 per cent of the national vote, the Center became an ally of the Socialists, and Catholic leaders at various times assumed important government positions. Members of the Center party held the chancellorship in eight of the fourteen cabinets between 1918 and 1933. To be sure, friction developed here and there over such questions as the recognition of confessional schools, the regulation of divorce and subsidies for unmarried mothers, the free distribution of literary works considered morally offensive and the unhindered agitation of freethinkers, but by and large the integration of German Catholicism into the mainstream of German life progressed steadily and the old denominational cleavage had lost much of its former importance.

But with the new strength resulting from the "return from exile" came a concomitant weakness. German Catholicism, and the

Center party too, had always been characterized on the one hand by divergent views on political, social and economic matters and on the other by an impressive cohesiveness and unity in defending the freedoms of the Church against Bismarck and like-minded enemies. With the rights of the Church secured by the Weimar constitution, the external threats holding German Catholicism together had all but disappeared and the political divisions now became more prominent. Whereas at the time of the Kulturkampf the percentage of Catholics voting for the Center party had exceeded eighty per cent, the figure now stood at about sixty per cent.[5] Some Catholics supported the left-wing parties; others, resentful of the Versailles peace settlement, were attracted by the aggressively nationalistic politics of both the German Nationalists and the new Nazi party. This sizable minority resented the way parish priests and clerical school teachers pressured the faithful to support the Center party and its ally, the Bavarian People's party.

As early as 1920 a small and little-noticed group of Catholics in Berlin had founded a *Katholikenbund für nationale Politik* (Catholic League for Patriotic Politics) which aimed at achieving a synthesis between right-wing radicalism and Catholicism. In 1924 a branch organized in Munich participated in publishing the periodical *Der Rütlischwur,* a section of which was entitled *"Der Völkische Katholik."** The *Katholikenbund* called for a fight against the three forces of evil which it considered the enemies of Germany as well as of the Church: Marxists, Jews and Freemasons. This struggle, it was argued, could be fought successfully only by an alliance of Catholics and *Völkische.*[6] A regular contributor to the *Rütlischwur* was the Catholic assistant priest, Josef Roth, later to become an official in Hitler's Ministry for Ecclesiastical Affairs. Curate Roth specialized in anti-Semitic tirades, which repeated what he had had to say on this subject in a pamphlet distributed by the Franz Eher firm of Munich, the young Nazi party's official publishing house.[7] Another early Catholic supporter of the National Socialist movement was Abbot Albanus Schachleiter, the former head of the Benedictine monastery of Emmaus (Prague). He had met

---

* The word *Völkisch* is difficult to translate. It derives from *Volk* (folk) and has strong connotations of racism and nationalism. The *Völkische* represented the extreme right wing of the German political spectrum.

Hitler for the first time in 1922 and during the following years he engaged in much public lecturing on behalf of the Nazi party.[8]

In the early twenties the Hitler movement was small in numbers and Catholic membership in it was smaller still. By 1930 the Nazi party had made sizable gains and many more Catholics had made common cause with it, including a number of priests like Karl König in Berlin, Dr. Philipp Haeuser in Augsburg and Wilhelm Senn in Flehingen. These men were attracted by the Party's anti-Communism, its fight against liberalism, parliamentarism, pacifism and other allegedly un-German ideologies, and by its militant program of liberation from the Versailles treaty. The German hierarchy had as yet made no pronouncements on the teachings of the growing Nazi movement. Abbot Schachleiter and a few other priests engaged in pro-Nazi propaganda had been warned to exercise more restraint in their public appearances, but this was all. Cardinal Faulhaber, speaking of Hitler and his movement before a meeting of Catholic students and academicians in the Löwenbräu Beer Cellar in Munich on February 15, 1924, saw a great tragedy in the fact that the "originally pure spring had been poisoned by later tributaries and by Kulturkampf."[9] Hitler, he said, knew better than his underlings that the resurrection of the German nation required the support of Christianity. This theme of the good and well-intentioned Führer and his evil advisors was to recur periodically after the Nazis came into power in 1933.

It was true, of course, that Hitler himself had repeatedly disavowed any interest in religious warfare and that he had left most of the sniping against the Church and "political Catholicism" to the editors of the *Völkischer Beobachter,* the party's official paper. *Mein Kampf* said little about religion or Christianity, perhaps out of a shrewd awareness of the political risks involved in antagonizing Bavaria's predominantly Catholic population. Article 24 of the program of the National Socialist Workers' Party, adopted on February 20, 1920, had demanded "liberty for all religious denominations in the state, so far as they are not a danger to it and do not militate against the morality and the moral sense of the Germanic race. The Party, as such, stands for positive Christianity, but does not bind itself in the matter of creed to any particular confession."[10]

This religious program did not draw any episcopal criticism

until the Nazi party, benefiting from the economic collapse of 1929, had made impressive headway in the elections of September 1930, returning a Nazi contingent to the Reichstag nine times the size of that of 1928. The NSDAP now occupied close to one fifth of all the seats (18.5 per cent). The rise in strength was smallest in the predominantly Catholic constituencies, where the vote for the Catholic parties had even shown an increase. But the gains of the Nazis, even there, could give rise to concern.[11] Also, 1930 had seen the publication of Alfred Rosenberg's *Myth of the Twentieth Century* which interpreted the Party's "positive Christianity" in an ominous way: it called for the doing away with the "Jewish" Old Testament, for a purging of the New Testament from "obviously distorted and superstitious reports"[12] and for the creation of a German Church anchored not in abstract dogma and denomination, but in the forces of blood, race and soil.

2. The Warnings of the Bishops Against Nazism

The first bishop to sound the alarm was Cardinal Bertram of Breslau, where the Nazi vote between 1928 and 1930 had jumped from 1.0 to 24.2 per cent.[13] In a widely publicized statement issued at the close of the year 1930, Bertram criticized as a grave error the one-sided glorification of the Nordic race and the contempt for divine revelation increasingly taught in all corners of Germany. He warned the faithful against the ambiguity of the concept of "positive Christianity," which, he said, "for us Catholics cannot have a satisfactory meaning since everyone interprets it in the way he pleases." There is room for nationalism, Bertram granted, but a fanatic nationalism logically leads to mutual hatred and to a worship of race which the Church could never recognize. "Here we are no longer dealing with political questions but with a religious delusion which has to be fought with all possible vigor."[14]

Several months earlier the Vicar General of the diocese of Mainz, Dr. Mayer, answering an inquiry, had informed the Nazi party's district office in Offenbach that Catholics could not be permitted to be members of the NSDAP. The inquiry had been prompted by the sermon of Father Weber, a parish priest, in the small hamlet of Kirschhausen, in which he had told his parishioners

(1) that Catholics were forbidden to belong to the Nazi party, (2) that members of the Nazi party would not be allowed to attend funerals or other church functions in group formation and (3) that a Catholic acknowledging his adherence to the teachings of that party could not be admitted to the sacraments. The Vicar General confirmed that Father Weber had acted on the basis of instructions given out by the diocesan chancery, and he proceeded to explain that this action had been necessitated by the incompatibility of Catholic doctrine and the Nazi program, specifically Article 24. The guarantee of religious freedom in the Nazi program, Dr. Mayer pointed out, was qualified by conditions which seemed aimed at denying religious liberty to the Catholic faith. The Christian moral law is valid for all times and for all races and "it therefore is a great error to demand that the Christian creed be made to conform with the ethical and moral sense of the Germanic race." The concept of "positive Christianity," under which the Nazi leaders demand a German God and a German Christianity, in effect involved the establishment of a German national church. None could fail to realize, he ended his letter, "that the religious policies of National Socialism contradict Catholic Christianity."[15]

The Nazi press quickly picked up the challenge and sharply attacked the Bishop of Mainz. But Bishop Ludwig Maria Hugo stood by his Vicar General. When the *Gauleiter* (regional party leader) of Hesse sought permission for the laying of wreaths on November 9 at the graves of soldiers fallen in World War I and buried in Catholic cemeteries, his request was denied on the ground that political parties whose ultimate outlook on life conflicted with the doctrine of the Church could not be allowed to hold such ceremonies on Catholic soil.[16] On the other hand, Bishop Schreiber of Berlin, during the same month, indicated that Catholics were not forbidden to become members of the Nazi party.[17] Clearly the German episcopate had not worked out a common stand on this subject. In early December 1930 Cardinal Bertram had attempted to formulate a joint statement but no agreement had been reached on its wording.[18] Instead the various church provinces published statements of their own formulation.

On February 12, 1931, the eight bishops of Bavaria, organized in the Bavarian (Freising) Bishops' Conference under the chairmanship of Cardinal Faulhaber, the Archbishop of Munich and Freising, issued their instructions to the clergy regarding the problem of National Socialism. A number of incidents had occurred shortly before which called for a clarified ruling. On May 18, 1930, for example, units of the local storm troopers (S.A.) had attended services in the cathedral of Regensburg, bringing with them their flags and banners. When the press throughout Germany reported the event under sensationalist headlines like "Swastika in the Cathedral," the chancery in a press release denied that it had allowed the Brownshirts to bring along their banners. Such permission could not have been granted, it was pointed out, since only consecrated flags may in principle be brought into churches. The chancery statement conceded that the S.A. had asked and received permission to attend the services.[19] In another instance, on December 14, 1930, a Catholic priest, Dr. Haeuser, had given the principal address at the Christmas celebration of the Nazi party of Augsburg.

The pastoral instructions now issued to the Bavarian clergy aimed to prevent such embarrassing occurrences. The bishops denied any intention of passing judgment on the political aims of the National Socialist movement, but as guardians of the faith they felt called upon to warn against National Socialism "as long and insofar as it adheres to a religious and cultural program which is irreconcilable with Catholic teaching." The bishops strictly forbade Catholic priests to take any part whatsoever in the National Socialist movement, and they prohibited the attendance of National Socialist formations with flags at divine services "since such parades in churches would make people think that the Church has come to terms with National Socialism." The question of admitting National Socialists to the sacraments should be decided on an individual basis depending on whether the Catholics in question were mere fellow travelers or active members of the party having full knowledge of its anti-Catholic orientation. "Should National Socialism, against our hope, adopt the methods of Bolshevism, we then, of course, could no longer assume the existence of good faith (*bona fides*)."[20]

A more restrained statement was made public by the six bishops of the Cologne church province on March 5, 1931, which called the errors of the National Socialist movement similar to those of the

Action Française, condemned by Pope Pius XI. The bishops expressed their regret that the admonitions issued earlier by Cardinal Bertram and the bishops of Bavaria had not been heeded by the leaders of the Nazi movement. The expectation that these leaders would clarify the aims and principles of their party in such a way as to alleviate the misgivings of Catholics had not been fulfilled. Now a serious warning could no longer be delayed, "especially since our policy of waiting and watching the development of the National Socialist movement has already been misinterpreted."[21] The bishops of the Cologne province did not raise the question of the permissibility of membership in the Nazi party or the other pastoral problems discussed in the instructions of the Bavarian episcopate.

Membership in the Nazi party was ruled impermissible for Catholics by the three bishops of the Paderborn province in their pronouncement published on March 10. The proviso inserted was the same as that made by the Bavarian bishops: this ruling holds "as long and insofar as it [the NSDAP] adheres to a religious and cultural program, which is irreconcilable with Catholic teaching."[22] The bishops disavowed any political motivation. Their concern, they insisted, was entirely religious. But "National Socialism is not only a political party, it also represents a total world outlook. As such it involves an attitude toward religion and it poses demands in the area of religion."[23] The hope was expressed that the many Catholics who had joined the Nazi party out of dissatisfaction with the prevailing difficult political and economic conditions would heed the warnings of their pastors. In similar manner the bishops of the Upper Rhenish church province (Freiburg, Mainz and Rottenburg) on March 19 came out against the anti-Catholic views of the NSDAP and they forbade Catholics "to acknowledge their adherence to them by word and deed."[24]

From August 3 to August 5, 1931, the Bishops' Conference of Fulda convened for its yearly deliberation. The conference had been meeting more or less regularly since 1867; it was usually attended by all the Prussian bishops and the bishops of the Upper Rhenish province. The Archbishop of Munich and Freising sat in as a representative of the Bavarian bishops, organized in the Freising Bishops' Conference, thus giving the assembly the character of an all-German gathering. However, the decisions of the conference were advisory in nature and not formally binding. This lack of organizational unity was to continue to plague the German episcopate throughout the Hitler period, despite the fact that attendance after 1933 included all twenty-five German bishops and even though a permanent secretariat was later set up to provide continuity of deliberation and action.

The background of the bishops was notably similar. Though some were sons of noble families and others were of more humble origin, all of them had distinguished themselves during their studies for the priesthood and many had engaged in advanced theological study in Rome. Nearly all had then become professors or heads of seminaries before being appointed church officials and eventually bishops. Only one, Bishop Preysing of Eichstätt (later Berlin), had also studied a secular subject, law, and had come to the priesthood at a more advanced age. Preysing later became one of the most consistent opponents of Nazism and stands out as the one bishop with insight into the totalitarian aspirations of the Nazi regime. Most of the other members of the episcopate were excellent theologians or administrators but possessed only limited understanding of political matters. Their average age was slightly above sixty; their outlook on politics had been shaped by life in imperial Germany before World War I. Many were still convinced monarchists; all had a basically conservative outlook and were distrustful of liberalism and democracy.

The Fulda Conference of August 1931 took up the challenge posed by the growing Nazi movement. It had before it a proposal to amend the guidelines for the clergy in their dealings with organizations hostile to the faith, adopted in 1921. According to the earlier statement Catholics were strictly forbidden to belong to or support organizations which pursued policies hostile to Christianity and to the Catholic Church whether operating under a Socialist, Freemason or any other name. Membership in such organizations was forbidden also in the case of parties which "in addition to objectionable aims pursue others of fully acceptable character," for "membership cannot be limited to certain specifically permissible endeavors."[25] Those who persisted in belonging to these organizations even after warning were to be denied admission to the sacraments. Now in 1931 it had been suggested to make these rules applicable to the Nazi party, for which purpose the conference had before it the following draft of an amendment:

> Obviously the foregoing principles are to be applied to the National Socialist party, which pretends to be no more than a political party with justified national goals, but which in fact stands in clearest conflict with fundamental truths of Christianity and with the organization of the Catholic Church of Christ's founding. . . .The issue is not one of blunders by individuals but rather the over-all effect of pronouncements and events which determine the character of the party. In the face of these, occasional denials are of no significance.[26]

The draft failed of adoption. Inasmuch as it equated the NSDAP with the Socialists, Communists and other freethinkers, the resolution apparently went beyond the consensus that had formed with regard to the Nazi party. Many bishops probably were unwilling to give up hope that the party might forswear its brand of "positive Christianity" and presumed that it might yet be possible to convert the Nazi movement into an ally against the threatening left-wing radicalism. An emissary of the Nazi party, Hermann Göring, had recently in Rome assured Monsignor Pizzardo of the Papal Secretariat of State that the leaders of the movement did not approve of the anti-Catholic utterances of certain of its members.[27] It seemed encouraging that recently some members of the NSDAP had demonstratively resigned from the party on the grounds that it was not sufficiently bold in its opposition to Catholicism.[28]

The bishops at Fulda probably also felt some hesitation over being drawn further into the arena of partisan politics. With an increasing number of Catholics aligned with the right-wing parties came increasing pressure on the bishops to relinquish their support of the Center party and to adopt a more neutral attitude. Typical of this sentiment was the letter by 100 Catholics addressed to Archbishop Klein of Paderborn on July 20, 1931, complaining about the difficult position of those not belonging to the Center party. A copy of this letter had been formally submitted to the Fulda Bishops' Conference.[29]

There probably was little hope of driving a permanent wedge between hierarchy and Center party, if only because of the extensive involvement of high-ranking clergy in the leadership of the

Catholic parties. But the existence of this minority sentiment could help defeat a strongly worded resolution condemning the Nazi party by name. Instead the Conference voted for the following ambiguous statement:

> The fight against radicalism, that is against extreme national-ism as well as against Socialism and Communism, should be carried out from the standpoint of the faith but not from that of partisan politics. Inasmuch as the whole foundation of the faith is called into question, considerations of what is possible or useful for the moment must yield. *Quaerite primum regnum Dei* [Seek first of all the kingdom of God.][30]

The National Socialists were quick to perceive that the Catholic episcopate was far from united on the question of how best to handle the Nazi problem. Exploiting the bishops' fear of the left-wing parties, they continued to stress in their agitation that only the assumption of full political power by National Socialism could protect Christianity from its mortal enemy, Marxism.[31] The Nazi propagandists also noted that even those bishops' declarations most critical of National Socialism had paid their respect to the national-istic aspirations of the Nazi party, and they proceeded to put these utterances to good use. National Socialism, one of them wrote, welcomes "the gratifying fact that the German bishops warmly acknowledge the importance of the national cause and that they approve and even support with religious arguments national aims which represent a main part of the National Socialist program of liberation."[32]

The bishops had indeed thought it necessary to accompany their warnings against National Socialism with affirmations of their intense feeling of national solidarity. "We love the fatherland, the country of our cradle, the country of our language, the country of our forefathers, the country of our graves," the bishops of the Paderborn church province had written. "Indeed we consider the fulfillment of the citizen's duties towards the fatherland and his par-ticipation in the development of the individuality and greatness of our people a command of God. . . ."[33] The bishops of the Cologne province had insisted that their rejection of the idea of a national church should not be interpreted as minimizing the importance of love of *Volk* and fatherland: "We understand and welcome it from the standpoint of our holy religion, indeed just because of it, when in our poor fatherland, humiliated and reduced to servitude, the sense of unity of all Germans and countrymen [*Stammes- und Volksgenossen*] is everywhere given new life."[34] The bishops of the Upper Rhenish province had regretted that Germany alone "unjustly and for so long had had to bear the heavy burden of the war guilt. . . ."[35]

To be sure, the hierarchy's expressions of patriotism were accompanied by warnings against overlooking the good traits of other peoples and against arrogance and extreme nationalism in the relations between nations. These qualifications were left out by the Nazis when they argued that the Catholic episcopate supported their nationalistic drive; when the National Socialist propaganda machine wanted to paint "political Catholicism" as subservient to Rome and responsible for a policy of meek national surrender, the passages warning against chauvinism were played up.

All in all, it is doubtful that the nationalistic confessions of the bishops prevented many Catholic would-be Nazis from joining the party. The Nazis always were able to outdo the bishops' patriotism. Indeed, the fanning of the nationalistic spirit undoubtedly contributed to the atmosphere of crisis, which more and more enveloped the fragile political institutions of the Weimar republic and which was increasingly exploited by those elements purveying the most rabid brand of chauvinism. Instead of taking the wind out of the sails of the extreme right, the constant stress on devotion to the fatherland helped make nationalism more respectable without really convincing those who questioned the Church's devotion to the national cause. The same tragic fate was to meet the continuation of this line after 1933.

3. The Strategy of Nationalism

The emphasis on the deep national roots of German Catholicism was not, of course, merely political in nature, nor was it new. The Kulturkampf of the 1870s had left German Catholicism, a minority in a predominantly Protestant country, burdened with a deep-seated national inferiority complex. Bismarck and his anti-Catholic supporters had attacked the Catholics as being ultramontanists, subservient to Rome, and in league with the Catholic countries, that is, Austria, France and Poland. The Catholics had reacted to these charges with a superheated patriotism. They had sought to prove that they were good and reliable citizens of the German fatherland, and these professions of loyalty and dedication to the German nation had continued into the Weimar era. There they drew new strength from the nationalistic currents of opinion that were widespread in a country defeated in war and humbled by a harsh peace settlement. The Catholic youth movement in particular was given to a romantic brand of German nationalism, in which the idea of a revived German empire (*Reich*) guided by Christian principles occupied an important role.[36] Addressing a large meeting of Catholic youth in Berlin at the end of March 1932, Bishop Bares of Hildesheim commended their dedication to the national cause. He went on to say, "We are patriotic to the core, German through and through, prepared to make every sacrifice for *Volk* and fatherland."[37]

What was here undoubtedly the expression of deeply felt sentiment was sometimes also used as part of political strategy. After the smashing election victory of the Nazis in 1930, representatives of all important Catholic organizations met under the auspices of the *Volksverein für das katholische Deutschland* to discuss ways of halting the threatening brown tide. The results of this deliberation were published in 1931. In a manner mindful of the periodically re-emerging National Bolshevik course of the German Communist party, the Catholic organizations decided upon a program of "dynamically" overcoming National Socialism. As the first and most important aim they listed the creation of a great popular movement supporting liberation from the shackles of the treaty of Versailles. Historical and national values were to be put into the center of all educational activity. More attention was to be given to the German minorities in Central Europe, which were predominantly Catholic. A foreign policy was to be worked out which would bring about the political unification of Central Europe and which would be based on strong resistance to "the West." "We must learn again that politics involves combat and strife between peoples and states."[38]

If this came dangerously close to supporting the pan-German aims of the extreme right, some of the language of the rest of the program sounded even more like the demagoguery of the Nazis. The German people should organize their liberation from subjugation by "plutocracy and finance capitalism," the state should be freed from domination by the party bureaucracies, the economy should be based on organically ordered corporate self-rule. At the same time the program called for the recognition of National Socialism as fascism and a mortal enemy of German Catholicism. It seems not to have occurred to these Catholic leaders that perhaps they were attempting to exorcize the devil with the help of Beelzebub.[39]

The stress of many Catholic publicists on the "dynamic" defeat of National Socialism led logically to a certain ambivalence in evaluating the Nazi movement. They pointed out the anti-Christian elements in the Nazi program and declared these incompatible with Catholic teaching. But they went on to speak of the healthy core of Nazism which ought to be appreciated—its reassertion of the values of religion and love of fatherland, its standing as a strong bulwark against atheistic Bolshevism. Many expressed regret that National Socialism had assumed the character of a *Weltanschauung,* a philosophy of life, instead of achieving its potential—a patriotic movement "which every friend of the fatherland in principle could have supported."[40] Not that things were hopeless as yet. In January 1932 the highly esteemed Jesuit Friedrich Muckermann, later to become one of the most outspoken enemies of the Nazis, declared it a duty to influence National Socialism in order to develop its positive nucleus and help it become a true reform movement.[41] And Father Nötges in his important quasi-official study of the Nazi problem reminded the reader that the condemnation of National Socialism by the episcopate was conditional—"as far as . . . as long as . . ."—because of the expectation "that National Socialism, notwithstanding everything, might succeed someday in eliminating from its program and its activities all that which conflicted in principle and in practice with Catholicism."[42]

One could, of course, hear other voices also. The Catholic weekly *Der Gerade Weg* in Munich, edited by Dr. Fritz Gerlich and the Franciscan Ingbert Naab, subjected all aspects of the Nazi program to a devastating critique;[43] the *Allgemeine Rundschau* of Georg Moenius kept up a warning voice against the Catholic flirtation with nationalism and militarism; and similar sentiments were voiced by the liberal *Rhein-Mainische Volkszeitung.* But most of the Catholic polemical literature that appeared during these years just prior to the Nazi assumption of power directed its fire at the Nazis' quasi-religious teachings, at their opposition to confessional schools and similar matters, with only occasional references to the Brownshirts' glorification of violence, their anti-semitism and their demand for dictatorial rule.[44]

If one reason for this state of affairs, as we have seen, was the affinity for the nationalistic aims and the anti-Communism of the Nazi movement; another was the lack of strong democratic conviction on the part of many segments of German Catholicism. There were those in the clergy who were openly hostile to the revolutionary origin of the Weimar republic and who, like the future Bishop of Münster, Count Galen, sharply criticized the acknowledgment of popular sovereignty made by a constitution that had omitted God.[45] Many harbored resentments against a regime that had extended legal recognition to all religious denominations and thus, as Archbishop Faulhaber put it in 1920, had "granted the same rights to truth and error."[46] Even more widespread was an attitude of indifference to the democratic institutions. This attitude had roots in the continued popularity of the authoritarian and organic ideas of the state propagated in the nineteenth century by Catholic romanticists such as Adam Müller and Joseph Görres and enunciated in conscious opposition to the "un-German" ideas of the Enlightenment and the democratic ideals of the French Revolution. It drew strength from the persistent identification of liberalism with atheism. Last but not least, concern for the maintenance of political liberty was further weakened by preoccupation with the protection of the rights of the Church and religion. This "narrowing of political consciousness,"[47] another of the traumatic effects of the Kulturkampf of the nineteenth century, meant that many Catholics regarded the continuation of state subsidies to the Church and the protection of the confessional schools as more important than the defense of democracy.

4. The Policy of the Center Party

The Center party had always been divided into a conservative right wing, largely though not exclusively based in Bavaria, and a more progressive wing, frequently referred to as the *Kölner Richtung* because its chief support was in the Rhineland. Attempting to bridge the increasingly sharp divisions, the Party in December 1928 elected a priest to the chairmanship, Monsignor Ludwig Kaas. A former professor of canon law at Trier, since 1920 a member of the Center party's Reichstag delegation and a brilliant speaker, the forty-seven-year-old Dr. Kaas was known as a conservative with authoritarian leanings. A year later, with Kaas's help, the financial expert Heinrich Brüning became leader of the parliamentary party, and thereupon the right wing assumed control. The Party now increasingly relinquished its earlier strong commitment to the republic, giving up the role of a party supporting the constitution (*Verfassungspartei*) as the progressive leader Matthias Erzberger had approvingly characterized it. The rise of many other clerics to positions of leadership that followed the elevation of Monsignor Kaas increased the always latent tendency in a confessional party to become an organizational bulwark for the prerogatives of the Church rather than a political party committed to the defense of the rule of law and democracy, the prerequisite of any free political activity.

The breakup of the so-called Great Coalition with the Social Democrats and the People's party in the spring of 1930 and the rule of Brüning from 1930 to 1932, who claimed to be responsible to the nation rather than to the Reichstag, further weakened the Center party's attachment to the principles of parliamentary government. The frequent resort to the presidential emergency decrees provided by Article 48 of the constitution, coupled with the leadership cult built up around Brüning, created a pattern of authoritarian power soon to be imitated and enlarged by others less attached to republican principles. Brüning's nationalistic foreign policy was in keeping with the strategy of dynamically overcoming the Nazi threat. It failed, however, to win back those Catholics estranged from the Catholic parties. In the Reichstag elections of July 1932, the National Socialists polled 37.4 per cent of the popular vote and elected 230 deputies. This more than doubled their representation and made them the largest single party in the Reichstag. The Center party and the Bavarian People's party again slightly increased their strength, but their combined vote still represented less than half of the Catholic vote of almost 13-million. The number of Catholics voting for the Nazis in 1932 may have exceeded 2-million.

The Catholic bishops, as always, had encouraged the faithful to vote for the two Catholic-led parties. A statement issued by the episcopate of Prussia on July 12, 1932, stressed the great importance of the forthcoming elections "not only in political respects but also because of the influence of the legislative branches of the government on the promotion and protection of religious interests and on the position of the Church in public life." Catholics were exhorted to elect representatives "whose character and proven attitudes give evidence of their stand for the peace and the social welfare of the people, for the protection of the confessional schools, the Christian religion and the Catholic Church. Beware of agitators and parties that are not worthy of the confidence of Catholics."[48]

Shortly after the July elections the Fulda Bishops' Conference convened and again took up the problem of National Socialism. The number of voices calling on the bishops to retract their opposition had been growing. Thousands and hundreds of thousands of deeply religious Catholics, one writer had argued, were members of the National Socialist movement and were caught in a most serious conflict of conscience, a crisis many resolved by leaving the Church. The hierarchy ought to re-examine its position. "Why should it be impossible to achieve in Germany, what in Italy has proven so beneficial for country, people and Church?"[49]

The Bishops' Conference seems not to have remained uninfluenced by considerations of this nature. To be sure, the episcopate took notice of the fact that by now all dioceses had declared membership in the Nazi party to be inadmissible. The resolution adopted expressed fears that the seizure of power by the National Socialists would seriously jeopardize the interests of the Church and declared it "inexcusable that many join the party pretending to want to support only the economic and other secular political aims of the party."

All this seemed to represent a toughened attitude. But the bishops, in laying down guidelines for the handling of individual cases, considerably softened their stand and made their ban of Nazi party membership as flexible as conditions might warrant it. "It is left to the determination of the clergy," the same resolution went on to say, "whether in a particular case the act of formally belonging to the party, without specifically promoting its cultural aims and without participating in its propaganda activity, could be excusable.

This might be so in the case of membership because of an innocently mistaken interpretation, because of the influence of a kind of mass psychosis, because of terroristic compulsion or because of the intention to prevent disastrous consequences."[50]

On May 30, 1932, President Hindenburg ousted Brüning and installed the ultra-conservative Franz von Papen. Thus came to an end the last government that at least from time to time had been able to obtain a parliamentary majority. Papen, a Catholic nobleman and member of the Center party, had only hours before promised Monsignor Kaas that he would not undertake the formation of a new government. The Center party promptly censured him and Papen declared his exit from the party a day later.

The leaders of the Center party were angered by Brüning's dismissal and, hoping to tame the Nazi movement, they now started negotiations with the National Socialists aimed at the formation of a coalition government. Building upon earlier contacts between Brüning and Hitler from the years 1930 and 1931,[51] formal talks started on August 13 and dragged on for weeks, without leading to positive results. A practical consequence of the Center's desire for a government of "national concentration" was the election of Göring to the presidency of the Reichstag on August 30.[52] For another, the negotiations surprised and deeply confused many rank-and-file Catholics who for years had been warned by these same leaders against the anti-Christian aims of the Nazi movement. The move also seemed to undercut the authority of the bishops, who since the previous year had expressed the same sentiments. The talks had started a few days after Hitler had sent a telegram of solidarity to five of his storm troopers who had been condemned to death for the particularly brutal murder of a Communist worker in the Upper Silesian village of Potempa near Beuthen. This prompted the editor of *Der Gerade Weg* to write:

> We are convinced that Hitler represents the incarnation of evil. It is for us a most shocking experience that . . . at a time when Hitler and his fellow leaders of the party in their statements about the assassins of Beuthen make an unequivocal confession in the principles of wickedness, the leaders of the Christian Bavarian People's party and of the Center sit down to negotiate with him and his comrades and even dare to call them suitable "guardians of right."[53]

The clergy, too, followed the negotiations with dismay. The instances multiplied when National Socialists, who now regarded themselves as again in the good grace of the Church, ostentatiously attended church services in S.A. uniform. The archdiocesan chancery of Cologne on October 10 found it necessary to remind the clergy that the wearing of party uniforms and the prominent display of party badges by parishioners during divine services was inadmissible, whether in the case of closed formations or individuals.[54]

Clearly matters had reached a state of considerable confusion. The Reverend Senn, one of the first Catholic priests to have become a National Socialist, who in October 1931 had promised to submit all future writings to the censorship of the archdiocesan chancery of Freiburg, had recently published another pro-Nazi pamphlet without first obtaining the *Imprimatur*. Hitler and "the wonderful movement for the liberation of Germany created by him," he had written, were "instruments of divine providence."[55] For the violation of ecclestiastical discipline Senn had been suspended in July, but he was reinstated on December 14 after he had apologized and declared that he, of course, condemned any anti-Christian views to be found in National Socialism.[56] His newly appointed archbishop, Dr. Konrad Gröber, told a gathering of clergy that the time had come for the Church gradually to assume a more conciliatory and "prudent" attitude toward National Socialism.[57]

The dissolution of Weimar democracy was in the final stage. In the elections of November 1932 the strength of the National Socialists declined slightly but so did that of the Socialists. No one could delude himself into thinking that the cause of democracy was on the upswing. Unemployment was rampant, the mood of desperation deepened. The coalition of democratic forces that might have saved the republic was not to be found. The Communists considered an assumption of political power by the National Socialists a prelude to a proletarian revolution, and they put the fight against the Socialists ahead of the struggle against the Nazis. The leaders of the Center party, fearful of a Communist uprising against rule by reactionary elements, considered Papen a greater threat than Hitler and they urged the admission of the National Socialists to the responsibility of ruling. In this hour of crisis individual Catholics received little meaningful guidance from their bishops who continued to support the Catholic parties, while at the same time the door was left ajar to peace with the Nazis if and when the latter saw fit to modify their espousal of a German church.

Writing at the end of the year 1932, Walter Dirks, the editor of the Catholic *Rhein-Mainische Volkszeitung,* expressed the fear that in the event of the establishment of a Nazi dictatorship German Catholicism might retreat from the political into the religious sphere and make its peace with the totalitarian state. This had happened in Italy and it might happen in Germany too. The natural law ethic of the Church, Dirks felt, was flexible enough to come to terms with such a dictatorship just as it had earlier settled down to peaceful coexistence with the democratic republic; this ethic did not include an affirmation of democracy based on principle. The end of Walter Dirks's article today reads like the prediction of a prophet:

> Should Catholicism be prepared to forego political resistance, should the German bishops be prepared to exhort the Catholics loyally to co-operate with the new regime, as the Pope in fact does in Italy, then it can be assumed that the regime will know how to restrain those elements bent on a Kulturkampf. Indeed, it will have much to offer to the Church. Conflicts between the totalitarian state and the demands of the Church would be unavoidable even in such a case, but these conflicts would be skirmishes taking place around the rims of a broad common base. Full religious freedom, far-reaching Christianization . . . of education and of public life in general, the fight against irreligiosity and immorality without the restrictions of a liberal regime—these must exercise a profound attraction upon the unpolitical elements within the Catholic camp.[58]

To be sure, the Hitler regime in practice did not reveal itself to be quite so generous. Religious liberty was frequently curtailed and the confessional schools eventually were destroyed. But Dirks's fears basically came true in 1933. The temptation of accepting at face value Hitler's promises of friendly relations between Church and State proved too strong. Here was the opportunity to set Hitler against Rosenberg and to withdraw without a loss of face the Church's warnings against National Socialism, which threatened to constitute a serious liability now that the Nazi movement had achieved political power. The adoption of the Enabling Act had eliminated the Reichstag as a possible brake and had all but done away with the ability of the Catholic parties to protect the interests of the Church. After March 1933 the establishment of a working relationship with the new dictatorial regime was therefore urgent.

The coming to terms was facilitated by the ambivalence which had characterized the hierarchy's opposition to National Socialism. For a long time the bishops and many Catholic politicians had expressed appreciation for the patriotic motives of the Nazis; they had welcomed the anti-Marxism of the National Socialists; they had called for more authority in the state. Had the hour perhaps come when the healthy and positive core of National Socialism had finally asserted itself? To be sure, ugly things were still going on. Many leading Socialists, Communists and other enemies of the Nazis had been arrested, mistreated and thrown into concentration camps, and in the cellars of S.A. barracks old accounts were being squared. But these, perhaps, were only transitory phenomena, part and parcel of change. Hitler was going to establish order and eliminate the threat of Communism. The state was being strengthened. Why cry after the parliamentary shenanigans and the political instability of the preceding years? The episcopate had stressed all along that the political aims of the Nazi movement were none of its concern. Was this commendable restraint, keeping intact the boundaries between Church and State, or was it opportunism and indifference in the face of injustice and evil? This was the question increasingly to be posed by the events beginning to unfold after the March days of 1933.

The First 120 Days of Hitler's Rule 2

1. Hitler Promises Confessional Peace

In his first radio address to the German people after becoming chancellor, Hitler on February 1 declared that the members of the new government "would preserve and defend those basic principles on which our nation has been built up. They regard Christianity as the foundation of our national morality and the family as the basis of national life."[1] As far as Hitler's own views were concerned, his statement was propagandistic and designed to cultivate good will. It formed part of Hitler's strategy to pass off the new National Socialist–Nationalist coalition, in which the Nazis occupied only three of eleven posts and in which the Catholic Papen was vice-chancellor, as a government of "national concentration." As policy Hitler had already in *Mein Kampf* stressed the importance of not interfering with the religious doctrines and institutions of the German people. In fact, until the very end of his reign Hitler maintained a shrewd awareness of the political risks involved in a head-on collision with the established churches. He often reacted with ill-concealed scorn to Rosenberg's scheme of a German Christianity. Schacht recalls Hitler's saying, "I have always told Rosenberg one doesn't attack petticoats or cassocks . . ."[2] and similar expressions are reported by many others.[3]

From this apparent divergence of views within the Nazi inner circle, churchmen, in the early years of the regime especially, deduced that Hitler did not approve of the attacks upon the churches made by various party functionaries occupying state positions. But this was not necessarily a correct conclusion. The truth seems to be, rather, that whenever Hitler did stop restrictive measures, it was usually for tactical reasons. Hitler's ridicule of Rosenberg's role as prophet did not arise out of sympathy for either the Christian churches or their teachings. If anything, Hitler privately had even less use for Christianity than Rosenberg. "A German Church, a German Christianity, is a distortion," Rauschning reports him saying early in 1933. "One is either a German or a Christian. You cannot be both." A National Socialist Germany would have no use for the Christian mentality of keeping an eye on the life in the hereafter. "We need free men who feel and know God in themselves."[4]

Until the day when such men were readily at hand the process of re-education would be lengthy. Meanwhile Hitler thought of tolerating the churches, for he believed that a citizen's loyalty to the state had to be anchored in religious belief. As he had written in *Mein Kampf*, "For the politician the estimation of the value of a religion must be decided less by the deficiencies which it perhaps shows than by the presence of a visibly better substitute. As long as there is no apparent substitute, that which is present can be demolished only by fools or by criminals."[5] Bismarck, he told Rauschning, had been stupid in starting a Kulturkampf: this only made martyrs of the clergy. Far better to make the priests ridiculous and contemptible, though even such steps would most probably not be necessary.

> We should trap the priests by their notorious greed and self-indulgence. We shall thus be able to settle everything with them in perfect peace and harmony. I shall give them a few years' reprieve. Why should we quarrel? They will swallow anything in order to keep their material advantages. Matters will never come to a head. They will recognize a firm will, and we need only show them once or twice who is master. They will know which way the wind blows.[6]

Hitler's strategy of winning the support of German Catholicism by promises and concessions was helped to success by the desire of the Center party leadership, still pursuing their strategy of attempting to tame the Nazis, to be included in Hitler's cabinet. Hitler did not agree to chairman Kaas's terms and nothing, therefore, came of the talks held on January 30 and 31,[7] but clearly the Center's leadership was in principle open to Hitler's overtures. There also were rumors afloat that the Vatican was anxious for German Catholicism to come to terms with Hitler on the grounds that National Socialism represented an important bulwark against Communism.[8] George N. Shuster recalls that the Papal Nuncio in Berlin, Monsignor Cesare Orsenigo, was of this opinion and that the latter "was frankly jubilant" about Hitler's accession to power. "He felt that the new government would soon be offering the same concessions to the Church as Mussolini had deemed it expedient to make in Italy."[9] According to Father Robert Leiber, a man close to Cardinal Pacelli, then Papal Secretary of State, the Vatican during those days scrupulously refrained from interfering in the affairs of the German Church; Pacelli even omitted private letters to Germany in order to eliminate any suspicion that the Holy See sought to influence the course of events.[10] This may well have been so. But members of the Papal Curia were less discreet, and very soon high German Church dignitaries visiting the Vatican were to bring back word of the Holy See's attitude toward the new developments.

After the talks with the Center party had failed to secure a parliamentary majority for the new government, Hitler obtained Hindenburg's permission to dissolve the Reichstag and to call for new elections. There is little doubt that this had been Hitler's aim all along and that the negotiations on his side were not carried on in good faith. The new elections, conducted with appropriate use of the newly gained positions of power, were expected to bring about a sharply increased representation of the Nazi party. The passage of an Enabling Act would then do away with the despised parliamentary system and make it possible for the National Socialist revolution to proceed without undue obstacles.

The Nazis did not keep secret that the elections scheduled for March 5 might be the last ones, that all political parties besides the Nazis and Nationalists had lost their reason for existence and might as well disband. Nevertheless, in the electoral campaign that now got under way the Center party persisted in seeing as its main enemy Hitler's conservative partners, Hugenberg and Papen. Hitler himself and his movement were treated somewhat more circumspectly. The Center line still consisted of emphasizing the struggle against Marxism, liberalism and atheism, and of stressing patriotism and recognizing the "good" in the National Socialist movement.[11] Not even the wave of Nazi terror against the Catholic parties' headquarters and newspaper offices all over Germany, the prohibition of meetings, the confiscation of election posters and the wholesale dismissal of civil servants who were members of the Catholic parties brought about a change in the Center party's orientation, though the rank and file became increasingly restive. A manifesto, to which the thirteen most important Catholic organizations subscribed, called for vigorous defense of civil rights guaranteed by the constitution and warned against the threatening dictatorship. The right-wing extremists, they said, claimed to fight Bolshevism and atheism. But "Bolshevism can make its appearance also in a patriotic garb."[12]

On February 11 Cardinal Bertram addressed a letter to the members of the Fulda Bishops' Conference in which he suggested the issuance of a statement before election day. "Unpleasant as it is to publish a pastoral letter dealing with political elections, I find weighty reasons to satisfy the expectations of people, who are face to face with atheism, the danger of Kulturkampf and systematic attempts at terror and deception. This could be done in a manner similar to those declarations issued at several previous elections which found a good reception among the most faithful segments of our people."[13] Cardinal Bertram included the draft of such a pastoral statement and, after general consent had been obtained, this declaration was made public on February 20. In language identical with the exhortations issued before the elections of July and November 1932, the faithful were again admonished to participate in the forthcoming important elections, to vote for representatives "whose proven character and proven attitudes" give evidence of their concern for the rights of the Church and to be aware of "agitators and parties not worthy of the confidence of Catholics."[14]

That the declaration called for the election of candidates worthy of Catholic support without mentioning the Catholic parties by name was promptly put to use by Catholic Nazis. A group in Koblenz, for example, thanked their bishop, Bornewasser, for not [sic!] having supported the Center party and for urging the election of Catholic National Socialists, for only those were truly dedicated to the defense of the Church.[15] Such interpretations caused several bishops to issue explicit endorsements of the Center party. Thus on February 25 Bishop Kaller of Ermland released a statement in which he made it clear that only the Center party could be relied upon to stand up for the rights of the Catholic faith. "Even though National Socialism displays certain attractive features, we must refuse to support it as long as it still adheres to those principles which the German bishops have rejected as being heresy."[16] Archbishop Faulhaber of Munich, on the other hand, in his pastoral letter of February 10 refrained from any direct reference to the elections and simply discussed in very general terms the rights and duties of the state toward its citizens and those of the citizen toward the state.[17] The book of a Catholic author that appeared a year later (with the *Imprimatur*) attributed the losses incurred by the Bavarian People's party during the elections of March 1933 to this neutral attitude of the Archbishop. "Had the Cardinal not indirectly pointed out the path to be followed in the future?" he asked rhetorically.[18]

New ways of lessening the hold of the confessional parties on the Catholic population now began to be sought by a group of Catholic National Socialists in Berlin, organized under the name *Arbeitsgemeinschaft katholischer Deutscher*. On February 19 they submitted a memorandum to Hitler. The most important task—the chairman, Georg Lossau, argued—was to obtain a revocation of the bishops' ban on membership in the Nazi party. To achieve this aim he proposed that Nuncio Orsenigo be urged to issue a public declaration invalidating the episcopate's prohibition of participation in the Nazi movement on the grounds that the declaration of heresy was reserved to Church councils and the Pope. The Nuncio should declare that "the Catholic Church, in agreement with the hitherto adopted attitude of the Vatican and in order to further its own interests, was prepared to fight alongside the new nationalist Christian German government against Bolshevism and its supporters," and that according to canon law there existed no impediments to a Catholic voting for the National Socialist or similar patriotic parties. The bishops themselves, Lossau suggested, should be asked to retract their ban and Catholic papers mentioning it should be confiscated.

Copies of this memorandum went to Minister of the Interior

Frick and a number of other leading party members, but no action was taken. The one copy preserved bears the handwritten notation, dated February 23, "Beginning of struggle against the churches not possible before the elections."[19] A few weeks later the German bishops, without having their hands forced by higher authority, would do just what this band of Catholic Nazis had set as a major Nazi goal.

On February 27 the Reichstag building went up in flames. Whether this spectacular deed was an act of the Nazis themselves or whether it was done by the Dutchman van der Lubbe alone may never be known with certainty. Whoever the arsonist, the event enabled Hitler to obtain from Hindenburg a "Decree for the Protection of People and State" which suspended civil rights and liberties and made it possible for the Nazis to step up repressive measures against their political opponents. The charge that the Reichstag fire was a signal to set off a Communist uprising was widely believed and caused millions to swallow the Nazis' claim that only they could prevent a Communist take-over.

The elections held on March 5 amid an atmosphere of terror brought the Nazi–Nationalist coalition a narrow majority of 52 per cent. The Center party, its strength buttressed now by the votes of many non-Catholics, again held its own; the Bavarian People's party suffered some losses, especially among the rural population.[20] In a meeting of the cabinet held two days after the elections Hitler expressed the view, propounded earlier by Lossau in his unsuccessful memo, that the parties of the coalition would be able to make further headway among the supporters of the Center and the Bavarian People's party only "if the Curia dropped both parties."[21] In due course that plum, too, was to fall into Hitler's lap.

A few days after the elections Cardinal Faulhaber left for Rome on his *ad limina* visit* and used the opportunity to discuss the new situation in which the Church found herself. The Holy Father, Pius XI, Cardinal Faulhaber reported a month later to a conference of the Bavarian bishops, during a consistory on March 13 "publicly praised the Chancellor Adolf Hitler for the stand which the latter

---

* A visit to the Pope for the purpose of reporting on the state of their diocese required of all archbishops and bishops every five years (every ten years from outside Europe).

had taken against Communism."[22] At the same time reports were circulating again that the Vatican was anxious for the friendly co-operation of German Catholics with the Hitler government and that both the Center party and the bishops were about to take steps leading to a reconciliation.[23]

New pressure on the bishops to re-examine their positions came from the Nazi press but also, and perhaps more significantly, from within the Catholic camp. The election victory of the National Socialists was regarded by many Catholics as confirmation of the legal character of the Hitler regime. The determined propaganda of the Nazis, reinforced by constant street demonstrations and strong-arm methods, had had considerable effect; the feeling spread that a forceful movement of national regeneration was underway in which all could and should join. The Nazis' call for the burial of con-fessional differences found a ready echo in a society in which the longing for the religious unity of the German people had been strong ever since the inter-confessional comradeship experienced in World War I. Quite a few leaders—later referred to as the "March casual-ties"—now left the Center party, and several influential Catholic newspapers like the *Augsburger Postzeitung* called for support of the new Reich that was being created by the National Socialist movement. "We want to be inside the German community, for we love Germany. And it is unworthy especially of the Catholic attitude of mind to persist in negativistic opposition, when the hour calls for work and positive goals."[24]

The pressure to seek an accommodation was reinforced by the wholesale dismissals of Catholic civil servants known as adherents of the confessional parties. There was also the problem of the numerous Catholic organizations and the many thousands of men and women employed by them, for which a place in the new order had to be found before they dissolved of their own accord or as the result of the acts of violence that were occurring daily. In these circumstances the bishops had reason to fear that the Catholic ranks were breaking up and that a re-examination of their attitude to the National Socialist movement was imperative.[25]

Cardinal Bertram, chairman of the Fulda Bishops' Conference, had already written to President Hindenburg shortly before the elections expressing the Prussian bishops' concern over the threats to a free vote. On March 10 he again addressed the aged President, this time in even stronger language. A day earlier the Bavarian government, headed by Heinrich Held of the Bavarian People's party, had been forced out of office. News of acts of intimidation and terror were multiplying. Cardinal Bertram expressed the fear that the freedom of legitimate and loyal organizations was put in jeopardy by the events of the last few days. "We bishops, moreover, are faced with the momentous question whether the movement now in possession of political power will respect the sanctity of the Church and its position in public life."[26] President Hindenburg on March 14 acknowledged Bertram's letter and stated that he had forwarded it to Hitler. He also promised personally to take up with the Chancellor the issues raised.[27] Copies of Hindenburg's letter were circulated by Cardinal Bertram to all the German bishops, but this reply did not go very far in allaying their fears.

On March 19 Cardinal Bertram sent a confidential inquiry to the members of the Fulda Bishops' Conference in which he asked whether a revision of the Church's attitude to National Socialism was indeed necessary. The diocesan chanceries, he remarked, were receiving urgent requests for clarification from the clergy, and some instructions, he agreed, were definitely indicated. But the time for a public proclamation, Bertram maintained, had not yet come. For that the situation was not sufficiently clear. The change in political conditions did not constitute a reason to revise the Church's position adopted as part of its pastoral concerns. In his letter Bertram also reported that Papen had visited him on the previous day (March 18) and that the Vice-Chancellor had inquired whether the Church would not revise its stand on Nazism. "I pointed out: The act of revising has to be undertaken by the leader of the National Socialists himself."[28] He had given Papen a copy of his memo of March 10 to Hindenburg and had added that he still hoped for a truly satisfactory reply.

As far as instructions to the clergy were concerned, Bertram proposed to point out that the episcopate's earlier rulings remained in force only insofar and for so long as the erroneous teachings in question continued to be subscribed to by the leaders of the Nazi party. Should this state of affairs cease to exist, the rulings would no longer be valid, but "such a change of attitude has not yet convincingly taken place." The question of how to handle individual party members had already been discussed in the instructions adopted at Fulda in August 1932, in which allowance had been made for serious dissatisfaction, deception, economic pressures, etc. "The events of recent times confirm the correctness of these suggestions and demonstrate that on occasion they can be applied even to leading members of the National Socialist party who refrain from displaying aggressive defiance of Church authorities and who adopt a correct attitude rather than one of hostility toward the Church."[29] The clergy also was to be reminded that demonstrations in churches were undesirable. Bertram ended his letter by asking for speedy comment on his proposals.

The pastoral instructions proposed by Cardinal Bertram in effect amounted to a quiet withdrawal of the ban on membership in the Nazi party. If even "leading members" of the party now were acceptable to the Church, clearly only very few obstinate and tactless diehards would run afoul of the old prohibitions. We have no exact information on how the members of the episcopate reacted to these suggestions. A number of them, as is apparent from a letter of Cardinal Bertram, did suggest issuing a public declaration and several of them sent in drafts.[30]

Meanwhile a series of new events had changed the situation. Negotiations had started on March 20 between Hitler and Frick on one side and the Center party leaders—Kaas, Stegerwald and Hackelsberger—on the other: under what conditions would the Center party vote for the Enabling Act desired by Hitler? The consent of the Catholic parties was necessary if this act was to receive the required two-thirds majority. In these talks, which were concluded on March 22, Hitler comported himself in a conciliatory manner and agreed to practically all the demands of the Center party negotiators. He promised to continue the existence of the German states, not to use the new grant of power to change the constitution and to retain civil servants belonging to the Center party. Moreover, Hitler pledged to protect the confessional schools and to respect the concordats signed between the Holy See and Bavaria (1924), Prussia (1929) and Baden (1932). He also agreed to mention these promises in his programmatic speech to the Reichstag on March 23 to be delivered before the vote on the Enabling Act.[31]

Was Kaas in touch with members of the German episcopate during these days? Clearly such promises were of greatest importance to them. We do not know. However, when Hitler announced them on March 23 the bishops were to give the final push to a proposal, contemplated for some time, to withdraw formally and publicly the proscription of the Nazi party. That this step on their part was expected was underlined by the pointed absence of Hitler and Goebbels from the special Catholic services held in Potsdam on March 21 on the occasion of the ceremonial opening of the new Reichstag. An official communiqué explained that the two Catholic ministers had felt obliged to absent themselves because the bishops in a number of recent declarations had called the leader and members of the NSDAP renegades of the Church who should not be admitted to the sacraments. "To this day, these declarations have not been retracted and the Catholic clergy continues to act according to them."[32]

In this manner the strained relations between the Catholic head of the government and the Church were held up publicly for all to see, and the bishops once more were reminded what was expected of them. Hitler had no intention of disavowing Rosenberg and his teachings, nor was he prepared to revise any other party doctrine. But he surmised that the Church might settle for some generalized promises to respect the existing concordats, the confessional schools and other similar matters. This, he already knew, would also secure the support of the Center party for the Enabling Act.

On the afternoon of March 23 Hitler announced the program of his government in a policy speech delivered before the new Reichstag. It included his own carefully worded version of the promises made to the Center party leaders. The government, he declared, would undertake the political and moral purification of public life and thus secure the conditions for a really profound religiosity. "The national government regard the two Christian confessions as the weightiest factors for the maintenance of our nationality. They will respect the agreements concluded between them and the federal states. Their rights are not to be infringed. . . . The national government will allow and secure to the Christian confessions the influence which is their due both in the school and in education. . . . The government of the Reich, who regard Christianity as the unshakable foundation of the morals and the moral code of the nation, attach the greatest value to friendly relations with the Holy See and are endeavoring to develop them."[33]

In a bad case of wishful thinking the lay and spiritual leaders of German Catholicism grossly overrated and misunderstood Hitler's smooth talk. He did not promise to guarantee "the existing rights of the Christian confessions in the areas of school and education," as the Center party negotiators had demanded, but rather he spoke of granting them the influence which was "their due." But who would decide their due? Similarly, the rights of the churches were to be left intact, but this promise was tied in with Hitler's expectation that the Christian confessions in turn would treat with respect the government's striving for the national and moral regeneration of the German people. Moreover, his promise followed the section's preamble in which the Christian confessions were declared to be an important support for the maintenance of the German nationality. In the spirit of Machiavelli and true to his earlier pronouncements, Hitler here had openly made the continued free existence of the churches dependent upon their usefulness to the state. As one astute scholar, well versed in Hitler's policy toward the churches, has recently said, "Even in the face of the worst measures taken in later years against the churches, one cannot reproach Hitler for having broken his policy statement; whoever had ears to listen on March 23, 1933, ought not to have indulged in any illusions."[34]

In the evening session of the Reichstag, which followed a dramatic afternoon meeting of the Center party fraction, Monsignor Kaas rose to announce that the Party, despite certain misgivings, would vote for the Enabling Act. The English historian Bullock calls this fateful step "a fitting close to the shabby policy of compromise with the Nazis which the Center party had followed since the summer of 1932."[35]

The Center's surrender to Hitler was a result, in part at least, of the Party's one-sided concern for the protection of the prerogatives of the Church. Once these seemed assured, the majority was willing to try the authoritarian rule proposed by Hitler. Also, once again, in this hour of supreme crisis, they were afraid to have the Catholics' patriotism questioned. Any understanding that a democratic party without democracy was like a fish out of water was lacking. To be sure, had Hitler not been able to obtain the required parliamentary sanction, he undoubtedly would have used force; suspecting this, many members of the Center party, in addition to everything else, may have been primarily concerned with preventing bloodshed. But blood was to flow anyway, and it would have made all the difference for later developments if Hitler had been forced at this time into an open violation of the constitution, thus depriving his rule of the prestige resulting from a legal assumption of power.

2. The Bishops Withdraw Their Ban

On March 24 Cardinal Bertram again addressed the members of the Fulda Bishops' Conference. The style of this letter and of those written during the following days reveals the haste in which they were composed. The various drafts received in response to his letter of March 19, the head of the Fulda Bishops' Conference pointed out, were out of date in view of the Chancellor's programmatic speech before the Reichstag on the previous day. "A public proclamation now is definitely advisable, even though views will differ on how to formulate it. A draft is enclosed. Such a joint proclamation will be especially effective if it can be issued in the next few days." Comments, therefore, should be sent in quickly. A draft of instructions to be issued to the clergy would follow.[36]

These proposed instructions to the clergy were mailed a day later. At the suggestion of Cardinal Faulhaber they also went to the members of the Bavarian Bishops' Conference. In his covering letter Bertram emphasized the urgency of issuing these pastoral instructions without delay, for inquiries from the clergy on how to handle the National Socialist movement in its present stage were pressing and numerous.

1. To wait until it can be known whether the government will implement the generous promises contained in the Chancellor's programmatic speech can mean a delay of years. Nothing would be worse than that. Hence I think that we should use this moment to go as far as is reconcilable with faith and canon law.

2. In the predominantly Catholic big cities, where closed formations of the S.A. at present are not admitted to the Catholic

services, attendance at church services is made mandatory by command of the leaders. The result is that the Catholic members of the S.A., especially since this is the only way for them to obtain clothing and bread, in full force flock to the Protestant churches. This will increase.

3. Nothing in the enclosed draft ought to be in conflict with faith and canon law. The disciplinary rules aim at the better promotion of the salus animarum [salvation of souls].

The letter concluded with the request to send answers by telegram.[37]

Cardinal Bertram now had joined the camp of those bishops who were in favor of withdrawing the various prohibitions imposed on the Nazi party. His change of position seems to have been the result of the impression made by "the generous promises" of Hitler, which Bertram may well have considered a response to the hint he had given to Papen on March 18. It may also have been caused by mounting concern over the threatened apostasy of Catholics already in the Nazi party. The leadership of the Party during those early days, hoping to paralyze the churches, was encouraging its members to join churches. If the doors of the Catholic Church remained shut, perhaps Cardinal Bertram reasoned, the Protestants would reap the benefit of this officially inspired religiosity.

The question whether the Vatican had any share in Bertram's decision to urge a public pronouncement making peace with the Nazi movement cannot be answered yet with any accuracy. Monsignor Kaas had left Berlin on March 24 for a brief visit to Rome.[38] In view of Kaas's important part in the negotiations soon to begin for a concordat between Germany and the Holy See, it is tempting to speculate that here too the prelate had a role to play. But since Bertram's letter to the episcopate announcing his new position was sent out on the day of Kaas's *departure* for Rome, this hypothesis is not very persuasive. On the other hand, we know that the German ambassador to the Vatican, Bergen, in a dispatch of March 16, had suggested that Bishop Schreiber of Berlin be consulted and that "in *strictly confidential* talks the possibility of removing the existing conflicts be explored."[39] It is not very likely that this idea represented Bergen's personal initiative; far more plausible is the assumption that the proposal stemmed from a suggestion made by a member of the Curia. But we know neither whether anything came of this proposed peace talk nor whether Cardinal Bertram in this manner perhaps received a confirmation of the rumors afloat that the Vatican was interested in a reconciliation between the Church and the new regime. It is also possible that such word was relayed to him by Cardinal Faulhaber after the latter had returned from his *ad limina* visit to the Vatican early in March. According to the well-informed Father Leiber, the Papal Secretary of State, Cardinal Pacelli, upon hearing of the episcopate's proclamation exclaimed, "Why did the bishops have to meet the government half way that fast? And if they had to do it, could they not have kept them waiting for another month?"[40] But the utterance, even if indeed made in this form, mainly concerns the timing of the announcement and does not in and by itself rule out Vatican interest in such a reconciliation.

Equally inconclusive is the evidence available today concerning a possible connection between the Center party's consent to the Enabling Act and the Bishops' proclamation on the one hand and the consent of Hitler's government to start negotiations aiming at a concordat with the Holy See on the other. Ambassador Bergen, in the note of March 16 just referred to, had suggested that Hitler in his speech before the Reichstag emphasize the great interest of the new government in maintaining friendly relations with the Holy See. Bergen thought that such a statement would help in changing the attitude of the episcopate towards the movement, and here again one is inclined to see a Vatican initiative. Hitler not only adopted the suggestion, but he went even further and spoke of the great importance attributed by his government to the continuation of "cultivating and developing" friendly relations.[41] Did the word "developing" adumbrate the negotiations for a concordat which indeed started soon thereafter? The complex pre-history of the Concordat will be taken up in our next chapter, but we must note here that even if the Bishops' proclamation was in no way directly connected with these early diplomatic feelers, it certainly prepared the ground for them.

On March 27 Cardinal Bertram was able to inform the German episcopate that the members of the Fulda Bishops' Conference had reacted to his draft with "gratifying accord." He had disregarded, he wrote, a few minor amendments that had been suggested, for any further changes would have required further time-consuming correspondence. Such a delay seemed inadvisable: several bishops had "requested not to wait another hour." He particularly asked for the forbearance of the Bavarian bishops, for, not being sufficiently well acquainted with the special conditions in the Bavarian dioceses, he had not found it possible to take these into consideration.[42] Bertram had suggested March 29 as the date of publication for the final text of the declaration he had drawn up, but the haste was great and most bishops made it public on March 28. The Bavarian bishops at first wished to issue a separate declaration stressing somewhat more explicitly the defense of the Catholic parties and organizations, but after some prodding, their head, Cardinal Faulhaber, agreed on March 30 to accept the text proposed by Bertram.[43] Thus this important proclamation could appear with the backing of all the German bishops.

The text as finally made public on March 28 differed somewhat from Bertram's draft. The changes, on the whole, somewhat toughened the tone of the declaration.[44] It began by stating that in the last few years the German bishops, out of concern for the purity of the Catholic faith and for the protection of the tasks and rights of the Church, had taken a negative attitude toward the National Socialist movement. The prohibitions and warnings issued were to have remained in effect as long and insofar as the reasons prompting their promulgation existed.

> It has now to be recognized[45] that public and solemn declarations have been made by the highest representative of the nationalist government,* who at the same time is the authoritative leader of that movement, through which due acknowledgment has been made of the inviolability of Catholic doctrinal teaching and of the unchangeable tasks and rights of the Church. In these declarations the nationalist government has given explicit assurances concerning the validity of all provisions of the Concordats concluded by individual German states with the Church. Without repealing the condemnation of certain religious and

* The National Socialist–Nationalist coalition government was often referred to as the *nationale Regierung*. Since "national government" can also mean the central government in a federal system, I have translated *nationale Regierung* as "nationalist government."

moral errors contained in our earlier measures, the episcopate
believes it may trust that the above-mentioned general prohibitions
and warnings need no longer be considered necessary.[46]

Catholic Christians, to whom the voice of their Church is sacred, do not require at this time a special admonition to be loyal to
the lawful authorities and to fulfil conscientiously their civic duties
while rejecting on principle all illegal or subversive conduct.[47]

The admonition to all Catholics, the declaration continued,
to work for the tranquility and well-being of the people, for the
protection of the Christian religion, the rights of the Church, the
confessional schools and youth organizations remains in force. "In
effect remains the admonition addressed to political and similar
associations and organizations to avoid in the house of God and at
church services, out of reverence for their sanctity, whatever can
give the appearance of a political or partisan demonstration and
therefore may cause offense." The appeal, so often and urgently
made before, continues in force to stand up for the growth and
effectiveness of the Catholic organizations whose work is so full of
blessing for "Church, people and fatherland."[48]

The pastoral instructions to the clergy were issued by the
bishops of the Fulda Conference on March 29 essentially as proposed by Cardinal Bertram on March 25. Members of the National
Socialist movement and party may be admitted to the sacraments
"without being harassed on account of such membership," the
clergy was told, "provided that there exist no general objections
to their worthiness and that they are resolved never to agree to
views or acts hostile to faith or Church. Similarly, the mere fact
of belonging to that party does not constitute ground for refusing a church burial. . . . Members in uniform may be admitted to
divine services and to the sacraments even if they appear in larger
numbers." It should be arranged through friendly understanding
that flags of the various party organizations not be brought into
the churches, since this has the character of a political demonstration. But if this should happen anyway, scandals which usually
are caused by insisting on immediate removal are to be avoided.
The appropriate quiet and dignified explanations are then to be
repeated. Special services for political organizations in general are
to be omitted, but this remark does not affect patriotic occasions
of general nature. Secular organizations not hostile to the Church

may be admitted to burial services, and their flags, as is usual outside the churches, may be brought along. The instructions ended by emphasizing that it remains the task of the Church, especially in times of political upheaval, to direct the eyes of the faithful upon the higher spiritual aims of man as taught by the Christian religion.[49]

The Bavarian bishops, on April 10, issued differently worded instructions, but with essentially the same content. An added point was the insistence that, on the occasion of patriotic celebrations ordered by the state, church bells were to be rung only by order, or at least by permission, of the diocesan authorities. Priests should not let themselves be intimidated on this point. In the realization that the earlier prohibitions had by no means been popular and generally accepted, the bishops praised the "exemplary discipline which the clergy had shown in most difficult times with regard to the episcopal instructions of February 1931." They called for Christian obedience to the new Bavarian government, though they insisted that error and injustice would have to be criticized, especially the violent acts carried out by lower echelons and against the will of the highest authorities in Berlin. "We have confidence that our clergy will avoid, in word and in conduct, in sermons and in burial addresses, whatever could be interpreted as disrespect for the government or as undignified obeisance." The Catholic priest should by all means of pastoral care available to him "oppose the godlessness and immorality of the times and thus in his way support the plans of the nationalist government, which by means of governmental measures has promised to work for the spiritual renewal of our national life."[50] At a meeting of the Bavarian Council of Ministers on April 24 the Premier was able to report that Cardinal Faulhaber had issued an order to the clergy to support the new regime in which he (Faulhaber) had confidence.[51]

3. A Policy of Co-operation Takes Shape

With such instructions and pronouncements by the hierarchy, working relations had finally been achieved. The condemnation of certain erroneous teachings, it is true, was explicitly left standing, and the Bavarian episcopate is supposed to have let it be known "that the decree of the German bishops by no means constitutes an invitation now to join the National Socialist party."[52] But essentially peace had been made and, as some saw it, practically unilaterally too,[53] for Hitler and his movement had not retracted or revised any point of their program. Irrespective of whether one assumes naïveté or opportunism on the bishops' part, or some other motive, the episcopate's declaration repesented a formal recognition of the legitimacy of the new regime and of the acceptability of Catholic membership in the movement increasingly dominating the affairs of state.

This, certainly, was the interpretation drawn in the spring of 1933. The declaration of the bishops had ended a condition which many Catholics had gradually felt to be intolerable, wrote Alphons Nobel, the editor of the Catholic *Augsburger Postzeitung*. The withdrawal of the prohibitions imposed earlier meant that from now on "the positive attitude of the German Catholics to the new state is no longer impeded by religious scruples." The declaration, he said, confirmed the correctness of this positive attitude, which his paper had urged from the very first days of the new regime.[54] For many leaders and rank-and-file members of the Catholic parties and other organizations the declaration of the bishops signified the beginning of a new epoch.

One of the marks of this new epoch would be the speed in which the *permissibility* of a positive attitude to the new state was superseded by the affirmation of the Catholics' *duty* to adopt such an attitude. The leader of the Center party in Baden, Monsignor Föhr, on March 30 called the co-operation of Catholics in the new Reich a duty; the same day similar sentiments were expressed by the Party's leaders in Cologne.[55] A declaration of the Catholic teachers' organization, published on April 1, noted with approval that Adolf Hitler and his movement had overcome the un-German spirit which had triumphed in the revolution of 1918. It exhorted its members to participate in the building of the new order, to be "helper and friend of the nationalist movement, which today has the power and the honor to bring to life all that at this time is new and healthy in our people."[56] The Catholic workers' movement on April 2 declared its readiness to co-operate in the creation of a strong national state and in the building of an order at once

Christian and German;[57] the Association of Catholic Young Men on April 4 similarly offered to join the forces that were now working for national renewal and unity. The circular reserved the right to oppose injustice whenever it might show itself.[58] The Central Association of Catholic fraternities on April 4 withdrew the ban on membership in the Nazi party.[59]

All these affirmations of loyal co-operation would be mistakenly regarded as caused by the declaration of the episcopate. The bishops acted, at least in part, in response to the growth of just such sentiments within German Catholicism. With the public reversal undertaken by the episcopate, it now became possible to express these ideas freely. Many people in the country during those days indubitably experienced a genuine feeling of national enthusiasm and exhilaration. Within this context of widespread relief from crisis and frustration many Catholics, moreover, were favorably impressed by the forced dissolution of the leftist-dominated freethinkers' associations, by the suppression of the Communist party and by the promulgation of a number of ordinances favoring religious education. The Prussian government on February 22 had decreed the gradual abolition of the interdenominational schools and had reintroduced religious instruction in the vocational schools.[60] None knew at the time that Göring had obtained the consent of the Prussian Cabinet for this measure with the argument that is was necessary "for political reasons."[61] A law announced on February 27 recognized seven Catholic feast days as legal holidays.[62] Small wonder that many Catholics tended to overlook the terror which at this point fell mainly upon the shoulders of their Marxist, Communist and liberal enemies. When Jehovah's Witnesses were suppressed in Bavaria on April 13 the Church even accepted the assignment given it by the Ministry of Education and Religion of reporting on any member of the sect still practicing the forbidden religion.[63] The nascent totalitarian state was leaving intact the special group interests of Catholicism; under the circumstances it was not hard for the Church to make peace with it.

A few dissenting voices still were to be heard. Two articles in the April 1933 issue of the Jesuit periodical *Stimmen der Zeit* stressed the importance of defending the democratic freedoms and the rule of law.[64] Father Stratmann, the head of the pacifist German

Catholic Peace Union (*Friedensbund deutscher Katholiken*), called for the courageous and unerring maintenance of principle, warning against compromises.[65] The prominent Catholic theologian Konrad Algermissen of Hildesheim, writing to Cardinal Bertram on March 31, told of a widespread feeling of dejection that he had encountered among priests and laymen.[66]

Some Catholics felt that the Church had yielded ground; acts of violence against Catholic organizations were continuing, yet the bishops had admonished the faithful to be obedient and to refrain from any illegal conduct.[67] Then, as later, active resistance to Hitler's state was discouraged by the bishops; there were those who regretted this fact. Disappointment was aggravated by the reports from Rome. It was not known that the visit of Papen and Göring to the Vatican on April 10 had laid the groundwork for negotiations aiming at a concordat, though a few rumors to this effect had begun to appear. But when it was openly reported that the two German ministers had been received with great honors, it was apparent to all that the Vatican certainly did not take a hostile attitude towards the new regime. The Catholic *Allgemeine Rundschau* concluded, "The bishops cannot fight where Rome concludes peace."[68]

But such reactions were relatively few in number. In the eyes of most Catholics, it would seem, the declaration of the bishops had cleared the air. For the members of the Center party, moreover, the declaration also provided the guidance which their party leaders were no longer willing or able to give. Monsignor Kaas left for Rome on the evening of April 7, never again to set foot on German soil. From now on the leadership role of the episcopate became ever more important.

It was hoped, especially, that the bishops would be able to do something to halt the unabated dismissals of Catholic civil servants. Coming at a time of widespread unemployment, this purge caused much suffering. On April 6 Cardinal Bertram again turned to Hindenburg. He pointed out that the German bishops responding to the President's answer to the presentations of the episcopate, and trusting the generous declarations of the Chancellor, had on March 28 issued a public proclamation aimed "at establishing a relationship to the new organization of public life." Still, and despite very commendable measures which the new government had taken in order to eliminate rebellious elements and to protect public morality, the Cardinal said, the Catholic public was deeply concerned and depressed. This feeling, Bertram asserted, was caused by the dismissals of veteran Catholic civil servants who had faithfully served their country and who were sincerely prepared to work with equal dedication under the new government.[69]

The threat of dismissal for all those earlier opposed to the National Socialists was increased by the promulgation of the new Civil Service law on April 7. The bishops of the Cologne church province now issued a public statement similar in portent to Bertram's letter to Hindenburg. "Filled with burning love for the fatherland, whose national strength they always support with all means at their command, the bishops nevertheless witness with deepest regret and concern that the days of national exultation for many loyal citizens, and many conscientious civil servants among them, undeservedly have become days of heavy and bitterest sorrow."[70]

A few days later Cardinal Bertram, in his capacity as head of the East German church province, and Archbishop Gröber, head of the Upper Rhenish province, published similar proclamations. Archbishop Gröber began his statement with a nationalistic confession of the kind soon to preface all criticisms by the German bishops of government policy: "Intimately bound up with the German people through language and blood and grown gray in the work of decades in and for the people, the bishops of the Upper Rhenish church province deplore the slanderous attacks made against our people by those beyond the German borders." At the same time, he went on to say, we regret whatever can diminish the nation's prestige and can give the appearance of injustice as in the case of the removal of loyal citizens from their positions.[71] Outside Germany had arisen the voice of protest against the Nazi terror against Jews and political opponents. Reports on brutalities in the new concentration camps had begun to leak out. Archbishop Gröber rejected these criticisms as slanderous and found injustice exemplified by the dismissals of Catholic civil servants. During 1933 he became a "promoting member" of the S.S., a status involving regular monthly financial contributions, and soon began to be known as the "brown bishop." He retained his membership until he was excluded in January 1938. By then he had begun to realize that his earlier confidence in the Nazi regime had been misplaced, though he continued his affirmations of national solidarity and refused voluntarily to give up his promoting membership.[72]

A desire to help construct the new Third Reich was in the air. Among Catholics it led, on April 3, to the founding of an organization of conservatives that took the name *Kreuz und Adler* (Cross and Eagle). This frame of mind, which in the case of Archbishop Gröber probably was the result of a combination of conviction and tactics, here very clearly was an outgrowth of conscious identification with the aims of the new government. The initiative for the formation of the group had been taken by Papen, who assumed the title of Protector. Among the members were to be found a number of well-known Catholic professors of theology like Otto Schilling and Theodor Brauer, newspapermen like Emil Ritter and Eugen Kogon[73] and several other men and women of diverse professions. A widely publicized appeal called on German Catholics to join enthusiastically in the creation of the Reich that personified the God-given mission of the German nationality. The purpose of the new organization was declared to be the deepening of Christian–conservative thinking among the German people. It would function in a non-partisan manner and its "success is not tied to the existence of political parties, which according to conservative thinking are, anyway, ephemeral structures."[74] At the first public meeting sponsored by *Kreuz und Adler*, held in Berlin on June 15, Papen called for the overcoming of liberalism and characterized the Third Reich in the making as a "Christian counterrevolution to 1789"[75]

Similar ideas were expressed by other Catholic individuals and organizations. The general secretary of the Catholic Journeymen's Association (*Katholischer Gesellenverein*), Nattermann, on May 18 invited Hitler to a national congress of apprentices to be held the following month in Munich, a gathering that would aim at winning the hearts of the members for Hitler's work. We see in you, he wrote, "not only the authority appointed from above, but the leader who has accomplished through political power what Adolf Kolping, our founder and leader, tried to achieve by way of an intellectual transformation, namely the overcoming of liberalism and socialism."[76] For Hitler's forty-fourth birthday on April 20 Monsignor Kaas sent a telegram of congratulations from Rome that was published in the press: "For today's birthday sincere good wishes and the assurance of unflinching co-operation in the great enterprise of creating a Germany internally united, enjoying social peace and externally free."[77] The effect of this call for "unflinching co-operation" by the leader of the Center party was further to accelerate the movement of Catholics into the Nazi camp.

Kaas' call for co-operation, as we know now, expressed the wishes of the Holy See where he resided. Baron von Ritter, the Bavarian ambassador at the Vatican, reported on April 24 that Kaas and the Papal Secretary of State were in constant touch with each other. "There can be no doubt that Cardinal Pacelli approves of a policy of sincere co-operation by the Catholics within the framework of the Christian *Weltanschauung* in order to benefit and lead the National Socialist movement. From the mouths of other prominent Cardinals, too, I have heard utterances which pointed completely in the same direction."[78] The German episcopate received new and explicit information about this Vatican policy at a conference called by the heads (metropolitans)* of the German church provinces that met in Berlin on April 25 and 26. It was attended by the Bishops Berning (Osnabrück), Schreiber (Berlin), Kaller (Ermland), Vicar General David (representing the Archbishop of Cologne), the Prelates Föhr (representing the Archbishop of Freiburg) and Gierse (representing the Archbishop of Paderborn), Provost Riemer (representing the Archbishop of Munich), Canon Negwer (representing the Archbishop of Breslau) and Vicar General Steinmann of Berlin.

The conference, with Bishop Berning as chairman, had the purpose of preparing the ground for talks with various members of the government and of making proposals for the all-German bishops' conference scheduled to convene on May 30. Provost Riemer reported on the conference of the Bavarian episcopate held on April 20 in Regensburg, at which Cardinal Faulhaber had given an ac-

---

* The title "metropolitan" is carried by archbishops who preside over a church province containing a number of sees. The bishops heading these sees, or dioceses, are called "suffragans." The authority of the metropolitan over his suffragans is strictly limited by canon law, making him essentially a *primus inter pares* (first among equals).

count of his talks at the Curia in Rome. Faulhaber had left a lengthy memorandum with the Papal Secretary that stressed the differences between the German and Italian fascist movements.[79] Prelate Föhr relayed information concerning the visit of Papen and Göring to the Vatican: the two ministers had made a good impression there. "One wants everything avoided that could make the relationship between Church and State more difficult. One appreciates the movement particularly because of its fight against Bolshevism and immorality." Archbishop Gröber, in response to an inquiry at the Vatican, had been told that a concordat between the Reich and the Holy See had been discussed in the talks with Papen and Göring.[80] No longer could there be a question as to what kind of basic attitude the Holy See wanted the German episcopate to adopt towards the Hitler regime: the episcopate now knew that an attempt to reach a formal agreement at the highest level in the form of a concordat was underway.

But there was, of course, no assurance that these negotiations would be successful. In fact, Bishop Berning, while the conference was in progress, received word from someone fresh from Rome that Kaas considered Papen and Göring unreliable.[81] Hence, for the time being one would have to chart a course built on the *de facto* situation of the day. It was finally recommended that the bishops organized in the Fulda and Freising Bishops' Conferences meet jointly as soon as possible, preferably in Berlin, in order to let the German people know that the episcopate had established contact with the government. The public proclamation decided upon by the Bavarian bishops should be converted into one to be issued by all the German bishops. In the meantime an attempt should be made to get in touch with the government "in order to express, along with due appreciation for its striving for morality and the building of the state, the concern felt by Catholics for the freedom of the Church, the confessional schools, the Catholic organizations and the continued participation in the state machinery of Catholic civil servants."[82]

The fears for the confessional schools again came to the fore when the conference took up point four of its agenda: problems of school and education. The assurances given by the Chancellor and others were questioned, especially since the National Socialist teachers' association openly called for the establishment of inter-denominational secular schools. The Catholic teachers' organizations, it was decided, by all means should maintain their existence, though individual members could also join the National Socialist organization. Bishop Berning was to take up these matters with the appropriate minister.

Apprehension within the Berlin conference was also voiced about the future of the other Catholic organizations. Monsignor Kaas was supposed to have been extremely pessimistic on this score. It was regretted that in some instances Catholic organizations had voluntarily joined the NSDAP and its affiliated formations. The episcopate should publicly admonish the faithful to maintain the independence of their organizations as long as practicable. Simultaneous membership in the Catholic and National Socialist organizations could be acceptable if it proved necessary to guarantee one's livelihood. As far as membership of the clergy in the Nazi party was concerned, it was felt that, after the episcopal ban had been withdrawn, a direct prohibition would probably not be feasible, but the conference suggested "that at the present time the clergy maintain special caution in any political activity."[83]

In view of the uncertain future of the Catholic organizations, a lengthy discussion took place over the reorganization of Catholic Action. This "participation and collaboration of the laity with the apostolic hierarchy," as Pope Pius XI had defined it, had never been very popular in Catholic Germany, which instead had built up a network of strong nationwide organizations largely independent of episcopal control. It was now proposed to strengthen the supervision of the bishops over the existing organizations and to establish a new *Katholische Volksbund* (Catholic People's League) that should try to enlist those Catholics estranged from the older organizations.[84] This plan, together with all other suggestions agreed upon by the conference, was to be submitted for formal action to the all-German bishops' conference.

While this gathering of representatives of the German metropolitans was going on, other talks were being held with members of the government. On April 25 Bishops Berning and Kaller called on Vice-Chancellor Papen, who was very reassuring. Papen felt confident that the freedom of the Church, of the Catholic organizations and of the confessional schools would not be harmed. Hitler, he hoped, would be able to restrain those lower party echelons harboring anti-Catholic sentiments. The Center party, it seems, was already written off, for neither Papen nor the bishops raised the question of its continued existence. Papen told his visitors that no ban on the political activity of the clergy was contemplated. That the Vice-Chancellor's assurances ought to be received with great skepticism was reported to the conference by Monsignor Wolker, the president of the Association of Catholic Young Men, who claimed to have knowledge of a plan of Papen to suppress all Catholic organizations.[85] This suspicion was to prove well-founded.

On the following day, April 26, Bishop Berning, accompanied by an assisting prelate, paid a visit to Dr. Rust, the Prussian Minister of Public Worship and Education. The latter, too, did not see any danger to the confessional schools as long as they instilled patriotism in their pupils and adopted a positive attitude to the state. Bishop Berning replied, "For the Catholic Church as well as for Catholics that goes without saying." The Bishop expressed concern over the rumored introduction of uniform textbooks for all schools, including those of the confessional type. He agreed, of course, that the textbooks used in the Catholic schools would have to be revised and "would have to treat positively the National Resurgence [*Nationale Erhebung*] and the attitude toward the state." Dr. Rust replied that a decision on this question had not yet been made. He also promised that Catholic teachers would not be dismissed just because of their being Catholic.[86]

Throughout the Hitler regime only a few talks took place between Hitler and any of the Catholic bishops. One of these rare face-to-face meetings occurred on this same day, April 26, when Bishop Berning and Monsignor Steinmann were received by the Chancellor. Bishop Berning later characterized the talk, lasting one hour and a quarter, as "cordial and to the point." He began the conversation by stating the Church's basic position:

> The bishops, it goes without saying, rendered the state and the authorities what according to God's command is their due. The Church has done this under earlier forms of government, and she would do the same under the present one; she would urge the faithful to be obedient and respectful. The bishops gladly recog-

nized that the new state promoted Christianity, raised the level of morality and fought the battle against Bolshevism and godlessness with vigor and success. But the bishops, at the same time, shared the fears which existed in many Catholic circles and which made the confident cooperation with the state more difficult. . . .[87]

Bishop Berning then listed the Church's apprehensions over its right to handle its own affairs in full independence (some of the measures taken against the Protestant churches had caused alarm), the freedom of the confessional schools, the rights of the Catholic organizations and the dismissal of Catholic civil servants. He asked for a clarifying statement that perhaps could be brought to the attention of the public at large.

Hitler began a lengthy and somewhat unsystematic speech by answering the last point, saying that his views could be communicated to the other bishops but that the public should only be informed of the fact that the visit had taken place.[88] He welcomed the opportunity to explain himself to a Catholic bishop, for he had been reproached with being an enemy of Christianity and this reproach had hurt him deeply. He was convinced that without Christianity one could neither run a personal life nor a state, and Germany in particular needed the kind of religious and moral foundation only Christianity could provide. But Hitler also had come to realize that the Christian churches in the last centuries had not mustered enough strength to overcome the enemies of both state and Christianity unaided. They had falsely believed that liberalism, Socialism and Bolshevism could be defeated by way of intellectual arguments. Hence he had decided to come to the Church's help and he had undertaken to destroy godlessness and Bolshevism. Occasional harshness might accompany this fight but that could not be avoided. After relaying this last sentence, Bishop Berning commented, "He spoke with warmth and equanimity, here and there temperamentally. Not a word against the Church, for the bishops nothing but appreciation."

Hitler then touched upon the Jewish question and, again stressing the fundamental agreement between National Socialism and Catholicism, pointed out that the Church always had regarded the Jews as parasites and had banished them into the ghetto. He was merely going to do what the Church had done for 1,500 years.

Altogether, Hitler affirmed, he was personally convinced of the great power and significance of Christianity and he therefore would not permit the founding of another religion. For this reason he had parted company with Ludendorff, and Rosenberg's book was no concern of his—it was a private publication.[89] Being a Catholic himself, he would not tolerate another Kulturkampf and the rights of the Church would be left intact.

Concerning the school question, Hitler declared that he would never accept an entirely secular school system. Character could be built only on the basis of religion. We must have believers, Bishop Berning reports him saying. "Trouble with Poland is on the horizon. We need soldiers, devout soldiers. Devout soldiers are the most valuable, for they risk all. Therefore we shall keep the confessional schools in order to bring up believers," and in this task Church and State must co-operate closely. Hitler also promised to continue the Catholic organizations if they promoted Christian ideas and at the same time maintained a positive relationship to the state and were public-spirited. But all residues of liberalism and Marxism would have to be eliminated. The Chancellor expressed the hope that it would continue to be possible to employ civil servants who were members of the Center party, though economy measures and the need to make room for National Socialists might lead to some hardships. Hitler ended the talk by stressing the great importance he attributed to working closely with the Catholic Church.[90]

Much the same note was struck by Hitler in a letter addressed on April 28 to Cardinal Bertram in reply to the memos submitted by the latter to Hindenburg and Frick, as well as to a communication of April 16 to the Chancellor himself. Bertram in all of these had pleaded for the Catholic civil servants and those organizations under attack. In his letter to Hitler he had emphasized that neither the bishops nor the Catholic organizations had any intention of intervening in purely secular political affairs. The Catholic organizations had always done their share in raising Christians who were strong spiritually as well as physically and who were prepared to make sacrifices for the fatherland. This striving they would continue, but such work required a measure of independence without which nothing would come of that happy and successful co-operation these organizations were prepared to render.[91]

Hitler replied by telling at length of the acts of violence and the hardships which members of his movement had experienced in the years prior to 1933. The resulting feeling of bitterness might have caused occasional acts of retribution after the accession to power. Still, justified as these undoubtedly had been, he regretted it if any priest had been inconvenienced or harmed. He asked for details and promised an investigation. Concerning the Catholic organizations, he assured Bertram "that, insofar as such organizations do not entertain any partisan tendencies hostile to the present regime, there is also no intention to proceed against them. The government would be happy if it should develop that these conditions exist. For it does not desire conflicts with the two churches in Germany but a sincere co-operation for the good of the state as well as for the good of the churches."[92]

Reading today these accounts of Hitler's utterances and his letter to Cardinal Bertram of April 28, we are struck by the open and unconcealed avowal of the entirely political reasons that prompted him to seek and maintain a policy of peace with Christianity. Just as in his speech before the Reichstag on March 23, Hitler here completely subordinated the rights of the churches and their organizations to the claims and interests of the state. They would be left undisturbed on condition that they played the role of inculcating loyalty and patriotism desired by the new regime. The German Catholic bishops seem not to have noticed where Hitler's priorities stood, or, if they did, they felt that a *modus vivendi* could be established if only they stressed continually their love of the fatherland and an intention to stay out of politics. But in Hitler's totalitarian aspirations the political arena encompassed all aspects of human life, whereas the episcopate still thought of politics in the completely outdated categories of political partisanship. This was their basic misunderstanding and one of the main roots of all future conflicts.

Adherence to their promise to stay out of politics to the bishops meant giving no further support to confessional parties. They wanted the Catholic organizations to continue to rally the faithful, they hoped to keep their hold on the young generation through youth organizations that engaged in sports, camping and other pleasant pastimes attractive to the young. But Hitler, as it was to become more obvious every day, was not prepared to brook any such competition for the minds and souls of the German people. He wanted the undivided allegiance of everyone, their uttermost loyalties, irrespective of and unhampered by religious ties. The National Socialist party with its various affiliated formations was to be the single instrument for achieving this total control. In the failure to recognize the totalitarian goals of Hitler's state, which was regarded by the Church, as by many other Germans, as just another anti-Communist authoritarian regime that had its good as well as its bad sides, lay the basic error and tragedy of the leadership of German Catholicism in 1933.

On May 6 Cardinal Bertram acknowledged Hitler's letter of April 28. He recognized with thanks, Bertram wrote, that the serious misgivings hitherto held by the German episcopate had been eliminated by the Chancellor's declaration before the Reichstag and by the recent talk with Bishop Berning. It was now hoped that genuine co-operation on the basis of mutual confidence could follow. The Church, as always, and irrespective of the forms of government, was "aware of its sacred duty to deepen in the hearts of the faithful that respect and obedience towards the constituted authorities which was a religious virtue, and to lead all segments of the people to make sacrifices and to participate in the promotion of the common good." He pleaded, however, that the Church could not play its proper role as a people's church if its work was limited to the sacristy. The Church needed its organizations, the confessional schools, the possibility of ministering to those inducted into the Labor Service. Bertram ended by once again expressing appreciation for all the measures already taken by the government against Bolshevism and godlessness.[93]

In statements addressed to the Catholic public, meanwhile, the episcopate displayed optimism. Cardinal Bertram, who in his above-cited letter to Hitler still expressed fears regarding the future of the Catholic organizations, told a conference of clergy at Beuthen on May 3 of the desire of the new government to enlist the help of the Church in the struggle against Marxism, atheism and immorality. "The Church is not to be pushed back into the sacristy, but it is expected to accomplish through its own intellectual and spiritual resources what the state seeks to do for the recovery of the nation by way of the political power at its command. To do such Catholic work no new invitation is necessary for us."[94]

Similarly, a joint pastoral letter of the Bavarian episcopate dated May 5 called for the support of the government's program of "spiritual, moral and economic rejuvenation." The pastoral letter also included some critical comments about the implementation of the recent *numerus clausus* decree (but not against the principle as such of setting a quota for Jewish students at institutions of higher learning) and on the threats to the free press. It defended equality before the law and it called for adherence to the principles of justice and love. But the main thrust of the letter clearly lay in the invitation to join forces. The past should be forgotten. "Nobody now may because of discouragement and embitterment stand aside and be resentful; nobody who is sincerely prepared to participate may because of narrow-mindedness and lack of generosity be put aside."[95]

In view of these and similar episcopal pronouncements and in line with the general climate of *Gleichschaltung* (synchronization) local branches of Catholic organizations here and there began to declare their dissolution, or members, with or without pressure, were joining the NSDAP. The chanceries of most West German dioceses during the second half of May spoke out against this trend. "Our Catholic organizations accept the present government and participate in the popular movement of national renewal even if they do not put themselves under the command of formations of the NSDAP. The government of the Reich has agreed to the independence of our Catholic organizations and institutions. Individual Catholic organizations have no right to decide on their own to join National Socialist formations, rather they must conform to the directives of their central boards and of the diocesan authority."[96] In a further effort to deter the trend the spiritual adviser of the Central Association of Catholic Fraternities suggested to Cardinal Faulhaber that all Catholic organizations from now on be led by clerics appointed by the bishops. Otherwise, he warned, there existed the danger, especially in the case of the Catholic university fraternities, "that these Catholic organizations will completely disperse."[97]

Individual Catholics, on the other hand, now could join the

NSDAP. The central board of the Association of Catholic Young Men, for example, on May 2 and 3 decided that "the fact of belonging to the *Jungmännerverein* in principle does not rule out membership in the NSDAP, including its various formations (S.A., S.S., etc.)." Those so joining should receive special training for their apostolic task.[98] Soon the Nazi party was to bear down on this practice by forbidding simultaneous membership in Catholic and National Socialist organizations.

This, then, was the situation when the bishops convened for their first all-German conference at the end of May 1933. The future of the Catholic organizations, despite repeated assurances, was in serious doubt. The destruction of the Socialist trade unions consummated on May 2 and the confiscation of the property of the Social Democratic party on May 10 were an ominous foreboding, indicating that the regime had no intention to limit its repressive measures to Communists. The *Gleichschaltung* of bureaucracy, judiciary, educational and cultural institutions and press was proceeding at full speed. Pressure was being applied on all fronts. Still, the Church had hopes that it would soon be able to gain a more secure position. Informal negotiations had been under way for some weeks now for the conclusion of a concordat between the Reich and the Vatican. The need for such a treaty in the eyes of the Church seemed more urgent after Hitler on April 7 had appointed Reich governors (*Reichsstatthälter*) in all the states, superseding the regular, elected governments. The question loomed large whether this act of usurpation did not undermine the validity of the existing concordats with Prussia, Bavaria and Baden. By the time the German episcopate convened in Fulda on May 30 the possibility of a concordat with Hitler had become a near-certainty, and the joint pastoral letter issued by that conference needs to be considered in that context. We therefore turn now to the Concordat negotiations of the spring and early summer of 1933 and to their prehistory during the Weimar republic.

The Concordat Between Germany and the Holy See of July 20, 1933 **3**

When the world learned on July 9, 1933, that a Concordat had been initialed by Nazi Germany and the Holy See, public opinion generally regarded the event as a great diplomatic victory for Hitler. Actually, one could with equal justice have looked upon the pact as an important achievement for the Papal Secretary of State, Eugenio Pacelli, who had worked toward it ever since his appointment as Papal Nuncio in Germany in 1920.

1. Prehistory

The political upheaval of 1918, the adoption of the Weimar constitution for the Reich and of the new constitutions in the German states in 1919 had made a formal realignment of the relations between Church and State seem imperative. Questions such as the state's financial subsidies to the Church, the legal status of the clergy, the appointment of bishops, support for the confessional schools and the imparting of religious instruction in the public schools all called for resolution. The government of the Reich, for its part, was interested in friendly relations with the Holy See for reasons of foreign policy. It sought to prevent the establishment of new diocesan boundaries for the predominantly Catholic Saar and the ceded German territories in the east (Danzig and Upper Silesia). Such diocesan reorganization would have strengthened the French and Polish claims and jeopardized the eventual return of these areas to Germany. Both sides thus had an interest in a treaty.

Negotiations for a concordat took place from 1919 to 1922, and later new feelers were put out by the German government and the Vatican periodically. The story of these negotiations has been told and need not delay us here.[1] They failed primarily because both the Reichstag and the Reichsrat (the Weimar republic's upper house representing the *Länder*) were dominated by non-Catholic majorities, which for various reasons opposed a formal pact with the Vatican. The extreme left and extreme right, liberals and Socialists as well as the Protestant churches, all were unwilling to make the required concessions, especially with regard to the school problem. Instead, the Holy See had to be content to conclude concordats with three states: namely, Bavaria (1924), Prussia (1929) and Baden (1932), where the great majority of German Catholics lived.[2]

One of the problems not taken care of by these *Länderkonkordate* was the regulation of pastoral care in the armed forces of the Reich (the *Reichswehr*). This issue provides an important link between the earlier abortive negotiations and the Concordat of 1933. Negotiations over this matter began in 1921 and dragged on for years. The government wanted military chaplains to have exempt status; that is, to be subject to their own army bishop only, and not to the local ordinaries (bishops). The German hierarchy, fearful of losing control over the military clergy, opposed such exemption. Finally, in October 1929, *Reichswehrminister* General Groener forced the Foreign Ministry to take up the problem directly with the Holy See. A resolution of the issue was pressing since the military chaplains lacked most of the powers of regular priests; for example, they could not administer the sacraments of baptism or matrimony without first obtaining the permission of the local priest or bishop.

The Vatican now tried to use the urgent desire of the German government on this matter as a bargaining point in its continuing attempt to negotiate a concordat with the Reich. The Bavarian ambassador to the Vatican reported on March 9, 1930, that Monsignor Kaas, who sojourned in Rome in order to negotiate some matters related to the implementation of the Prussian concordat, had also discussed the appointment of a German army bishop with Cardinal Pacelli, the new Papal Secretary of State. Cardinal Pacelli, Baron von Ritter surmised, seemed interested in obtaining a concordat with the Reich as reassurance for the interests of the Church in case a reform of the Reich's quasi-federal constitution should call into question the independent existence of the states and the validity of their concordats with the Holy See.[3]

In this way Kaas entered the picture, eventually to become one of the key figures in the negotiations leading to the realization of Pacelli's old wish. Kaas had been a close friend of Pacelli ever since 1925, when he had been appointed by Cardinal Bertram as advisor to the Nuncio in Berlin. The prelate, after December 1928 head of the Center party, had made an important contribution to the successful conclusion of the Prussian concordat in 1929. He was to render similarly useful services in the achievement of the Concordat with Hitler in 1933. In fact, Monsignor Kaas eventually became one of the key advisors to the Papal Secretary of State, later Pope, on all matters pertaining to Germany.[4]

In the negotiations during 1931, mainly conducted for the German government by Diego von Bergen, the ambassador to the Holy See, the Curia was prepared to yield to the government's desire for the appointment of an army bishop, if, in return, the government would agree to certain demands of the Holy See. These included three main points: (1) the abolition of the penalty provided by the civil law for priests who in the case of a moral emergency conducted a religious marriage ceremony without a preceding civil marriage, (2) a promise that the financial subsidies to the Church would not be terminated without prior agreement with the Holy See, (3) a guarantee of the rights of Catholics concerning the confessional schools and religious instruction in the state schools.[5]

The government, on the other hand, insisted on separating the question of the military chaplaincy from the demands of the Holy See. It was known in Berlin that the chances for obtaining the approval of the Reichstag and of the states for a concordat containing these provisions were virtually nil. The deadlocked negotiations therefore came to a standstill in July 1931, to be revived about

a year later when the German bishops took the initiative and renewed their proposal of a non-exempt military clergy. Writing to
Archbishop Klein of Paderborn, the new *Reichswehrminister,* General von Schleicher, once more turned down this scheme. This letter
was drafted with the help of Monsignor Kaas and Counselor Fritz
Menshausen of the Foreign Ministry's Vatican desk. Schleicher told
Klein that only the opposition of the German episcopate prevented
the settlement of this vexing problem. The Vatican was prepared
to grant Germany the right to appoint an army bishop, which
prerogative it had conceded to most other states. In Italy the
episcopus castrensis was even an archbishop. Germany, he wrote, if
only for reasons of political prestige, would settle for nothing less,
and if the bishops did not change their recalcitrant stand, the government would begin to liquidate the military chaplaincy.[6]

On instructions from the Fulda Bishops' Conference of August
1932, Archbishop Klein wrote Schleicher on September 12 that the
German bishops would, of course, accept any solution agreed upon
in direct negotiations between the government of the Reich and the
Holy See. Klein mentioned that he had informed Nuncio Orsenigo
of this decision of the Fulda Conference and that he had asked him
to communicate it to Rome.[7] At this point probably Papen first
heard of these negotiations, when Counselor Menshausen personally
informed the new Chancellor of the willingness of the German
bishops to bow to the Vatican's wishes.

Shortly thereafter the Papal Secretary of State reopened the
negotiations by submitting a memorandum to the Foreign Ministry
that once again noted the willingness of the Holy See to let the Reich
appoint an army bishop, if the government would co-operate in
the satisfactory solution of questions covering certain interests of
the Catholic Church in Germany not included in the concordats
with various German states. In addition to the three demands listed
in the memorandum of April 23, 1931, Pacelli now asked for binding assurances that in case of a change in the constitution or laws of
the Reich, the rights of the Church recognized in the concordats
with the states would not be impaired. Pacelli, who during his years
in Germany had had an opportunity to become well acquainted
with the aims of the National Socialist movement, may have
thought here of the Nazis' professed goal of a more centralized

Reich, which Hitler indeed was to begin implementing as soon as the Enabling Act had been passed. The Papal Secretary of State ended the memorandum by observing that if the Italian *episcopus castrensis* had the rank of archbishop, this obviously was related to the fact that Italy had entered into a comprehensive concordat with the Holy See. What the Vatican expected as a *quid pro quo* could hardly be stated more bluntly.[8]

A copy of this memorandum was sent by Pacelli to Chancellor Papen. In his covering letter the Cardinal expressed the hope that the Chancellor would show understanding for the wishes of the Holy See.[9] Shortly before, Nuncio Orsenigo had called on Papen and had been told that the Chancellor considered the demands of the Vatican to be reasonable. The State Secretary of the Foreign Ministry, Bernhard W. von Bülow, in a handwritten memorandum, noted that "the Chancellor, for reasons of domestic politics, would gladly meet the demands which Pacelli had stated in his letter concerning the military chaplaincy." Von Bülow added that he pointed out to Papen the difficulties that stood in the way of such a stand.[10] The State Secretary also dispatched a copy of Pacelli's memorandum to the Ministry of the Interior and asked for comment. In a letter sent on the same day to *Reichswehrminister* Schleicher, Von Bülow proposed that the government of the Reich, in the interest of a speedy settlement of the military issue, agree to parallel negotiations on both the military chaplaincy and the four wishes of the Vatican involving domestic affairs.[11]

The Ministry of Interior thereupon prepared the draft of a note to be submitted to the Vatican in response to Pacelli's memorandum of October 25. The government of the Reich here again insisted on separating the two problem areas. Concerning the school question (point 3) the note promised to continue to respect the interests of the Catholics; with regard to the issue of state subsidies (point 2) the government declared its willingness to consult the German episcopate and representatives of the Holy See before proceeding to enact any drastic change. Pacelli's demand that the government also obtain the agreement of the Vatican was turned down. The same fate met demands 1 and 4, which involved a requested change in the marriage law (the penal provision of Article 67 of the *Personenstandsgesetz*) and the guarantee that the Reich would always be bound by the concordats concluded by the Holy See with the states. No government, the draft note declared, could make concessions on these two points "since there is no chance of obtaining the necessary majorities approving of these basic changes in either the Reichstag or the Reichsrat, no matter what their ideological or political makeup."[12]

This draft note was probably prepared late in 1932 or in the early days of 1933. It was discussed at a meeting of representatives of the affected ministries held on February 25, 1933. Though Hitler had become Chancellor four weeks earlier, the deliberations do not seem to have been affected thereby. The result of these talks was the decision to submit two separate notes to the Vatican, one again to insist on an exempt military chaplaincy and the other to reject most of the Holy See's demands.[13] On March 3 Menshausen informed Ambassador Bergen that he would discuss the entire problem complex with Monsignor Kaas. The latter, Menshausen added, right after the elections was scheduled to travel to Rome in order to take up with Pacelli the hostile treatment accorded by Belgium to pro-German Catholic priests in the former German territory Eupen-Malmedy.[14]

Neither of the projected notes was ever dispatched to the Vatican.[15] For in the meantime the political realities had undergone a radical change, culminating in the passage of the Enabling Act of March 23. On April 5 Menshausen prepared a memorandum, classified secret, that surveyed the negotiations concerning a concordat with the Reich since 1920, and submitted it to the Foreign Minister, Freiherr Constantin von Neurath. Menshausen summed up the new state of affairs in these words: "The situation has been completely altered by the new composition of the Reichstag and especially by the passage of the Enabling Act. There now exists the possibility to comply fully with the wishes of the Holy See without also involving the Reichstag. Above all, it is now possible to conclude a *Reichskonkordat,* the realization of which until now has always failed because of the objection of the Reichstag."[16] Two days later, on April 7, Menshausen was told by Vice-Chancellor Papen that he (Papen) during his forthcoming visit in Rome would suggest to the Vatican the conclusion of a concordat.[17]

2. Negotiations (April-July 1933)

Our knowledge as to who in this new set of circumstances was the first to offer a concordat is fragmentary. Papen himself, a man not noted for his modesty, has always maintained that the idea was exclusively his. In his memoirs, published after World War II, he recalls that early in 1933 he was greatly worried over the anti-clericalism of the Nazi Party's radical wing. Even Hitler's reassurance of peaceful intentions toward the Church, he wrote, failed to allay his fears. "I decided to pay an Easter visit to Rome to study the possibility of reaching some firm agreement."[18] Back in 1934 Papen gave a somewhat different acount of the motives that had moved him to seek a concordat:

> Considering the state of affairs in Europe and in view of the social disintegration proceeding in Germany, the rescue effort of National Socialism was inevitably the last chance of saving Germany from the abyss of social annihilation. It therefore went without saying that all energies had to be concentrated upon overcoming as far as possible the ideological differences between German Catholicism and the National Socialist movement. This was the basic conviction inspiring my ardent desire to reach, as quickly as possible, a new arrangement of affairs between the Reich and the Holy See, a desire which I also discussed with the Chancellor immediately after the 30th of January 1933.[19]

This 1934 version is more in keeping with what we know about Papen in 1933, the "Protector" of the pro-Nazi Catholic organization *Kreuz und Adler*. But common to both renderings is the assertion that he, Papen, acted on his own initiative, animated only by his personal convictions of Germany's and/or the Church's needs in that crucial hour. This claim is made credible by the numerous statements of both Pope Pius XI and Pius XII in which they always speak of the Concordat sought in the spring of 1933 by the German government with Vice-Chancellor Papen as spokesman.[20] Similarly, according to Father Leiber, then private secretary of Cardinal Pacelli, the impetus for the Concordat of 1933 was given by the German government acting through Papen. The Papal Secretary of State in 1933 would have preferred a mere *"modus vivendi"* that guaranteed the continued validity of the *Länderkonkordate*.

In fact, Father Leiber recalls, Pacelli made rather far-reaching demands in order to dissuade the Reich from its desire for a concordat.[21]

But the Vatican version leaves open the question whether Papen was only the government's spokesman or also the originator of the plan. It is clear that he was aware of the earlier negotiations for a concordat. We have seen how in 1932, Papen, then Chancellor, had received a copy of Cardinal Pacelli's memorandum of October 25, 1932, and how he had expressed himself in favor of meeting the Vatican's demands. The Foreign Ministry, on the other hand, knew of Papen's intention to travel to Rome before his departure on April 7. Counselor Menshausen speaks of getting in touch with Papen "in accordance with instructions" and of Papen "*confirming* to me his intention to suggest in the Vatican . . . the conclusion of a concordat with the Reich" (my italics).[22] How did the Foreign Ministry hear of Papen's plans? Was Hitler informed about them? How does Göring's presence in Rome fit into the picture?

Papen's own testimony on the chain of events is unclear if not contradictory. In his memoirs he implies that he gained Hitler's consent to negotiations for a pact with the Vatican only after his return from Rome. But according to Papen's note to Bergen in 1934, quoted earlier, he discussed his ideas for a concordat with Hitler "immediately after the 30th of January 1933." And in 1949 he testified before a German denazification tribunal that in April 1933 he had proposed to Hitler to secure the rights of the two Christian confessions by way of treaties. "He indicated his agreement. I traveled to Rome by his order."[23] Finally, in a deposition made in 1956, Papen states that it was President Hindenburg who gave him a formal commission to arrange for treaties that would protect the Christian churches.[24] From this it has been deduced that it was Hindenburg, and not Hitler, who sent Papen to Rome. The aged President, it has been surmised, was moved to suggest this step because of Cardinal Bertram's repeated submissions in March that the future of the Church was in danger.[25]

All these conjectures overlook the one person who may well have played the decisive role. That man is Monsignor Kaas. For many years Kaas had been a valuable troubleshooter and trusted intermediary between the German government and the Vatican. He had played an important role in the conclusion of the concordats with Prussia and Baden and, as we have seen, he had also been involved in the negotiations over the military chaplaincy. Early in 1933 he had been scheduled to visit Rome to conduct top secret talks with Cardinal Pacelli about conditions in Eupen-Malmedy. This trip was postponed because of the uncertain political situation in Berlin,[26] and did not take place until March 24.

In the meantime relations between Kaas and Papen had improved. On March 6, one day after the Reichstag elections, he called on the Vice-Chancellor and offered to put an end to the old animosities.[27] According to the account we have of the talks between Kaas and Hitler, prior to the Center party's consent to the Enabling Act, the question of a concordat was not discussed. Hitler in his speech to the Reichstag on March 23 mentioned the willingness of his government "further to cultivate and develop" friendly relations with the Holy See, and some later writers speak of Kaas having made the consent of his party to the Enabling Act dependent upon Hitler's willingness to start negotiations for a concordat with the Reich.[28] Such an understanding is not impossible, though at this point it remains unverified. A day after the vote on the Enabling Act, on March 24, Kaas left for Rome to discuss Eupen-Malmedy. At that opportunity Kaas in all likelihood also touched upon the old question of a concordat. But before any of these matters could be clarified Kaas was recalled for talks with Hitler.[29] He was back in Berlin by March 31.

During Kaas's stay in Rome the German bishops had withdrawn their ban on membership in the Nazi party. On March 30, the *Tägliche Rundschau,* a paper close to Schleicher, hailed the episcopate's declaration but insisted that a final reconciliation would come only in a *Reichskonkordat,* for which, the paper pointed out, the preparations were already under way.[30] On April 2, following a meeting of a number of Center party leaders with Hitler, Frick and Lammers (head of the Reich Chancellery) about the continuing dismissals of Catholic civil servants, Kaas had a private talk with Hitler.[31] On April 7 he left Berlin, whether of his own volition or at the request of another cannot yet be determined. On the following morning he met Papen in Munich and they traveled to Rome together.[32] There, as we shall see, he participated actively in the talks about a concordat.

None of the above information provides any conclusive proof

that it was Kaas who brought about Papen's mission to the Vatican. But a number of factors support the hypothesis that Kaas pointed out to Hitler the willingness of the Holy See to conclude a concordat. The kind of reassurance for the *Länderkonkordate* that Pacelli had been concerned about for a long time now clearly was more urgently needed than ever. Reports about violence against Catholic organizations, newspaper offices and even priests undoubtedly created grave apprehension. It is not very likely that Papen would have undertaken his trip to Rome at Easter time without some prior soundings and without at least some indication that the proposal of a concordat would find a friendly reception.[33]

A tentative reconstruction thus makes the following sequence of events plausible: On February 25, 1933, it had been decided to answer Cardinal Pacelli's memorandum of October 1932 in two separate notes which, as drafted by Foreign Ministry Counselor Menshausen, insisted on an exempt military chaplaincy and turned down most of the Curia's other demands as politically unrealizable. These notes were never dispatched, though Kaas apparently was informed about their content by Menshausen and probably discussed them with Pacelli during his visit to Rome in the last week of March. After his return from the Vatican, or at the latest on April 2, Kaas drew Hitler's attention to these preliminary negotiations, and told him of the willingness of the Holy See to sign an accord on the basis of Pacelli's note of October 25. The Chancellor may also have been informed of this by Ambassador Bergen, who returned to Berlin from the Vatican at the end of March and was received by Hindenburg, as well as Hitler, on March 30.[34] The Reichstag's opposition having been cleared away by the elections of March 5 and the passage of the Enabling Act of March 23, Hitler decided to explore the possibility of a concordat with Rome. In the meeting of the cabinet on March 7 he had already talked of the importance of getting the Curia to drop both confessional parties. This, he soon learned, the Vatican was prepared to do. Such a treaty with the spiritual center of world Catholicism, he figured, in addition to benefits for the internal situation in Germany, would undoubtedly bring for his regime a considerable increase in prestige in the world at large. He therefore ordered Papen to go to Rome and instructed the Foreign Ministry to get in touch with the Vice-Chancellor before his departure to familiarize him more completely with the results of the earlier negotiations. Menshausen in his memorandum of April 7 notes that, as instructed, he got in touch with Papen and informed him especially about "the pending negotiations concerning pastoral care in the armed forces."[35]

The Catholic Papen was the obvious choice for this mission. It is quite possible also that Papen had already indicated to Hitler his interest in working for a rapprochement between National Socialism and the Holy See. In order to underline the good will and seriousness of the new government Hitler sent along Hermann Göring, minister without portfolio and an important party dignitary, who had been on a mission of peace to the Vatican in 1931. To keep the entire venture secret Papen met Kaas only in Munich and Göring flew directly to Rome. We know—and with this we return to verified facts—that Papen asked Menshausen to keep the purpose of the trip secret and indicated that he would inform the press that he had gone to Rome for a vacation over the Easter holidays.[36]

When Counselor Menshausen got in touch with Papen on the day of his departure on April 7, he put in his hands copies of several documents: specifically, a draft of a concordat from the year 1924, guidelines for a concordat drawn up in 1926, the memorandum of Pacelli of October 25, 1932 and the two draft replies agreed upon on February 25, 1933, together with his own memorandum of April 5. To Menshausen's question whether Papen had a definite draft ready for the new Concordat, the Vice-Chancellor replied in the negative. "He added in strict confidence that he intended, as one of the chief counter-demands, to include a provision contained also in the Italian concordat, to the effect that the clergy are forbidden to register and be active in any political party. As requested I sent the Vice-Chancellor a copy of the corresponding Article 43 of the Italian concordat."[37]

That either Papen or someone else must have talked about his intention to get the clergy out of politics before April 7 becomes clear from the fact, to which Menshausen drew the Vice-Chancellor's attention, that the Paris *Journal* on the preceding day had published a story to this effect, sent in by its correspondent in Berlin. Germany, the *Journal* reported, had made overtures to the Vatican concerning a concordat, one of the main points of which was a provision forbidding Catholic priests to be candidates for political office.[38] The *Tägliche Rundschau* wrote on April 7 that Papen and the Center party were actively working for a concordat with Rome.[39] Apparently some person or persons had been less than discreet.

The diary of Kaas gives us a fairly detailed account of the instructive conversation that took place between the prelate and Papen during their joint trip from Munich to Rome. Touching on Hitler's speech of March 23 and the changed situation created by it, Kaas, according to his own summary, told Papen:

> In the interest of the nation as well as from the standpoint of German Catholicism, I would be only too happy if the direction chosen by these declarations would continue to be followed. Nothing would contribute more to the inner consolidation of the authoritarian regime. Therefore, and out of inner conviction, I have chosen also an attitude of positive co-operation. It would be a source of sincere satisfaction for me if I could render some good services for the alleviation of the tensions, particularly in the area of cultural and religious policies. These tensions have existed for a long time and probably could be considered finally eliminated only when an understanding has been reached on the basis of incontestable provisions.[40]

In this connection, as Kaas's diary continues, he especially mentioned the confessional schools and the Catholic organizations, the future of both of which was still unclear. Papen replied that all these problems could be solved in the form of a concordat between the Reich and the Holy See. As a counter-concession, Papen went on, one would have to think primarily of "a far-reaching de-politicizing of the clergy." After the satisfactory protection of the interests of the Church had been achieved, the Center party, relieved of this task, should become a purely political party which would have to share the sympathies of Catholics with all other groupings. Kaas here notes:

> I did not rule out the acceptability of this idea, but I pointed out that above all one would first have to bring proof that sufficient guarantees of the cultural and religious interests [of Catholics] had been indeed created. If that were the case, I would surely not be ungenerous. On the contrary, nothing would personally please me more than the possibility of winning the great National Socialist movement to such a policy. It above all, as well

as the state, would clearly gain strength; a process which until now, unfortunately, had not fully come to fruition.[41]

Papen's desire to deal the Center party a serious blow does not come as a surprise. Ever since June 1932, when he had practically been read out of the party and especially after September of the same year, when the Center party deputies in the Reichstag had voted for the Communist-sponsored no-confidence motion against Papen's government, he had been eager to obtain revenge. Moreover, following his own political inclinations, he fully agreed with Hitler's plans to destroy all political parties as soon as practicable. The forced withdrawal of all priests from the Catholic parties, where they occupied important positions of leadership, would go a long way toward this end.

But that Monsignor Kaas, who until two days earlier had been the esteemed leader of the Center party, should so readily see eye to eye with Papen on the "de-politicizing of the clergy" is not so understandable. The explanation lies, probably, in Kaas's preoccupation with the protection of the educational and religious interests of the Church, for which he was willing to pay a price. Moreover, on the occasion of his visit to the Vatican in March he had undoubtedly been told what soon became an open secret; namely, that the Curia too regarded the German Catholic parties as expendable. A certain tension between the Center party and the Holy See had always existed and, as in the case of the *Popolari* in Italy led by Don Sturzo, the Curia had also been suspicious of the Party's essentially political commitment. It had supported the Center party as long as it served as the bulwark for the Church's demands in the realm of education, marriage and divorce legislation.[42] The successful conclusion of the concordat with Mussolini had strengthened the view in the Vatican that a concordat was a far better way of dealing with Hitler than relying on Catholic political parties. Finally, with the emasculation of the Reichstag by the Enabling Act, the usefulness of the Party was definitely terminated.

In this connection Sir Robert H. Clive of the British Legation to the Holy See reported about this time on a conversation with the Papal Under-Secretary of State, Monsignor Pizzardo: "The Holy See were far more interested in the mass of Catholic voters in Germany than in the Deputies who had represented the Party in the Reichstag. They doubted the possibility of recreating the Center Party as a political party and were not greatly interested in the question."[43] Just as earlier the *Popolari* had been disavowed, now the Center party was to be abandoned.

After the arrival of the two Germans in Rome on April 9, the first to be received by Cardinal Pacelli was Monsignor Kaas. According to Father Leiber, Kaas had not come to Rome at the invitation of the Vatican, and Papen too has maintained that Kaas's trip to Rome was in no way connected with his own mission.[44] If both men are right, this would mean that Kaas left Germany out of concern for his personal safety or, which is more likely, in order to be at the one spot where his services might be most useful.[45]

On the morning of April 10 Papen called on the Papal Secretary of State, and on the same day he and Göring were received by Pope Pius XI. The Holy Father, Papen writes in his memoirs, "remarked how pleased he was that the German Government now had at its head a man uncompromisingly opposed to Communism and Russian nihilism in all its forms."[46] The Bavarian ambassador at the Holy See reported two days later that the Pope had been favorably impressed by the two German statesmen and that he felt relieved of earlier concerns.[47] Talking to German reporters, Papen denied that the subject of a concordat had been raised during the audience with the Pope.

During the next few days Papen and Kaas, as well as Göring, met several times to prepare matters for the second talk with Cardinal Pacelli.[48] Kaas mentions in his diary that, among other provisions, he also drafted the article for the de-politicizing of the clergy. On April 15 Papen and Kaas both met with Cardinal Pacelli, and Kaas subsequently was instructed to prepare the draft of a concordat. More talks followed between Kaas and Pacelli during the next two days, and on April 18 the Papal Secretary of State had a lengthy conversation about the Concordat with Pope Pius XI. A number of leading German Catholics, among them Dr. Joseph Wirth of the progressive wing of the Center party, were also in Rome during this time and urged the Vatican to come to the help of German Catholics. They were told that only a concordat with the Reich could be of any use at this point.[49]

On the evening of April 18 Papen left for Berlin. On the same day Ambassador Bergen reported that "the visit of the Reichstag President [Göring] and the Vice-Chancellor came off, as scheduled, to the complete satisfaction of those concerned, particularly the audiences with the Pope, who stated to third persons that from the explanations and impressions he had received, he entertained the best hope of a continuance of friendly relations between the Holy See and Germany."[50]

From this point on, the files of the German Foreign Ministry give us a fairly complete picture of the ensuing negotiations. They were conducted in the main by Monsignor Kaas, who maintained written contact with Papen in Berlin[51] and was in constant touch with Ambassador Bergen in Rome. The Foreign Ministry, too, now began to share in the deliberations and Counselor Menshausen prepared comments on several drafts for the Foreign Minister. Article 31, concerned with the political role of the clergy, quickly became one of the main bones of contention and the Vatican eventually decided to solicit the reaction of the German episcopate to this provision as well as to the rest of the draft agreement before finally committing itself.

Papen, when informed of the delay, expressed his impatience. Nothing good could come of this consultation, he observed, for "the episcopate is still too much under the influence of the ideas of the Center party." He regretted that Brüning, who on April 6 had succeeded Kaas as leader of the Party, still wanted to preserve it. "Parties as understood by the liberal thought of the past epoch will no longer have any place, if only for the reason that coalitions or majority decisions will in the future be inconceivable." German Catholicism should lend its support to the new conception of the state, but not in a partisan manner. The association *Kreuz und Adler* pointed in the right direction here. Even Catholic Action in Germany unfortunately had a political tinge and it worked hand in glove with the Center party. "I believe that if the Vatican could decide, in accordance with the Italian model, to comply with our wishes as regards Article 31, the purely religious life of Catholic Germany would at the same time experience an extraordinary strengthening."[52]

The Fulda Bishops' Conference met from May 30 to June 1.

The resultant joint pastoral letter, published on June 10, did not mention the negotiations in Rome; we will return to it in the next chapter. The Conference, however, in its first meeting did hear a report on the talks by Archbishop Gröber. The episcopate also discussed the draft of the Concordat submitted to it by the Vatican, and it made a number of suggestions.[53] As foreseen by Papen, the bishops did not accept the government's draft of Article 31, though, as Cardinal Faulhaber subsequently informed the Vice-Chancellor, "they did not at all want to let the conclusion of the Concordat break down over that."[54] Faulhaber also proposed, "in order to avoid having Kaas appear openly in connection with our negotiations," to have a member of the German episcopate go to Rome and participate officially in the conclusion of the talks. He suggested Bishop Preysing of Eichstätt for this task, but Papen proposed and obtained Archbishop Gröber of Freiburg instead.[55] It is not clear why Faulhaber wanted Kaas to remain in the background. Perhaps he feared unfavorable repercussions among the German Catholics, many of whom felt that Kaas had deserted them.

On June 16 Papen informed Bergen that Hitler had agreed to his going to Rome to complete the negotiations in person. "My journey only has point, however, if enough is done by the Vatican to meet our wishes regarding Article 31."[56] Other issues, too, were holding matters up, and it was not until June 29 that Papen could go to Rome.

When the Vice-Chancellor, accompanied by Ambassador Bergen, went to see Cardinal Pacelli on the evening of his arrival, he found the Papal Secretary of State visibly upset over the latest reports from Germany. An all-German meeting of Catholic Journeymen held in Munich from June 8 to 10 had been broken up by force. In the second half of June, as part of the Nazis' stepped-up striving for a one-party state, the regime had opened a systematic campaign of terror against the Center party and its counterpart in Bavaria, accompanied by a new wave of arrests and dismissals from public office. The Congress of Christian Trade Unions was dissolved on June 24. On June 28 Goebbels, threatening force, publicly demanded the dissolution of the Center party.[57] In Bavaria, in particular, a large number of priests had been taken into custody, many had been mistreated, the premises of Catholic organizations had been searched and their possessions confiscated. Cardinal Faulhaber on July 5 complained that almost one hundred priests had been arrested in the last few weeks.[58] Whether these measures were actually intended to put pressure on the Vatican to comply with Hitler's demands, in particular the liquidation of the Catholic parties, is not yet fully proven, but they certainly had this effect.

The Nazi terror against the German Catholics had not gone unnoticed by the European press,[59] yet Papen tried to convince Pacelli that the attacks of the foreign press were part of a scheme by enemy powers to dissuade the Vatican from concluding a treaty with Germany. "The Vice-Chancellor," Bergen reported to the Foreign Ministry, "gave a vivid picture of the development and reasons why National Socialism is being attacked today by all the world. He urged the Cardinal Secretary of State to contribute to the general pacification by quick conclusion of the Concordat."[60] Within three further days of negotiations, carried on under the impact of the news from Germany, all earlier difficulties were solved and final agreement was reached on the evening of July 2. Bergen, writing to von Neurath, praised the negotiators:

> Herr von Papen conducted the negotiations with skill and verve; to finish official negotiations for a Concordat in four sessions is a record and something new; without the excellent preliminary work of Prelate Kaas this would not have been accomplished. Prelate Kaas was present at the last three sessions, and Archbishop Gröber of Freiburg was also present at those on Saturday and Sunday; he was summoned by telegram at the desire of the Cardinal Secretary of State. The Archbishop displayed full understanding for the wishes of the government and the necessities brought about by the new situation. . . . The Cardinal Secretary of State was visibly influenced by reports, letters and telegrams constantly being received concerning the arrest and maltreatment of the clergy, etc., as well as the latest foreign press propaganda.[61]

The draft agreement had also been approved by Pius XI. According to Papen, the Pope had received objections to the conclusion of a concordat with Nazi Germany from "all sorts of sources." One of these may have been Brüning.[62] However, as Papen explained later, Pope Pius XI "had insisted on the conclusion of the Concordat because he wanted to come to an agreement with Italy and Germany as the countries which, in his opinion, represented the nucleus of the Christian world."[63] Even if we assume that this summary of the Pope's motives includes some embellishment by Papen, it essentially coincides with what we know from other sources about the great anxiety felt by Pius XI about the threat of atheistic Communism.

The text of the Concordat agreed upon was sent by Papen to Berlin for Hitler's approval. In a covering letter the Vice-Chancellor explained the most important changes. The controversial Article 31 had now become Article 32. This was done, as Ambassador Bergen put it in his note to Neurath a day later, "in order to place at the end the discussion of removing the clergy from politics, a very difficult question for the Vatican, and to confront the Curia with the difficult decision whether it could take the responsibility for sacrificing all the concessions attained with difficulty in the earlier articles solely on account of Article 32."[64] Article 31 now regulated the activity of various Catholic organizations while Article 32, as Papen told Hitler, "finally brings the solution which you have wished, Chancellor, whereby the Holy See issues regulations excluding membership and activity in political parties for all members [of the clergy] and the people belonging to orders [*für alle Mitglieder und Ordensleute*]."[65]

The leaders of the Center party in Germany realized that the end had come for their party that had now alienated friend and foe alike. The second half of the month of June had seen the consolidation of the totalitarian state proceed at a stepped-up tempo. On June 22 the Social Democratic party had been outlawed, on June 28 the Democrats (*Staatspartei*) dissolved themselves and a day later the leader of the German Nationalists, Hugenberg, dramatically resigned from the government while his aides liquidated the party. In these circumstances Brüning and the other leaders of the Center party, the members of which increasingly were leaving the sinking ship, realized that they could not hold the party together. The Nazi terror against "Political Catholicism" continued unabatedly, while the news from Rome seemed to indicate that the Vatican had decided to drop the Catholic parties.

On June 29 Brüning told the British Ambassador in Berlin, Sir Horace Rumbold, that the Center party would probably dissolve itself the next day: he no longer could count on the support of his own followers. "He also had good reason to believe that Cardinal Secretary of State was hostile to existence of the Center party in its present form."[66] Comments of Archbishop Gröber, made just prior to his departure for Rome to participate in the negotiations for the Concordat, to the effect that a positive attitude to the state was essential, were understood by the leaders of the Center party as a further hint not to obstruct the negotiations by recalcitrance.[67]

Whether the Vatican actually put pressure on the leadership to liquidate the Center party cannot be determined, though most probably such outright interference was not necessary. The Center leaders, it appears, agreed with Rome that the dissolution of their party was a price worth paying for a concordat from which one expected a safeguard for Catholic interests. A refusal to comply with the Nazis' pressure to dissolve the Party, moreover, would have meant an open clash and would have called for the kind of resistance which the German bishops had repeatedly spoken against. The historian of the Center party, Karl Bachem, no doubt expressed the views of many when he wrote in his diary, "After the bishops unanimously have professed their recognition of the new government, such resistance for us would have been morally unjustifiable and impossible. We have no choice but to follow the example of the bishops. . . ."[68]

Father Leiber argues that the Vatican did not sacrifice the Center party in order to obtain the Concordat, while the political scientist, K. D. Bracher, considers the negotiations in Rome a "stab in the back" for the Party.[69] Both are partially right. Strictly speaking, Leiber may be correct, for the forced dissolution was already under way and with or without a concordat it obviously could have been prevented only by open defiance. But the Curia knew the meaning of Article 32, and it certainly did not exert itself in trying to save the Party. On the contrary, on July 3 Papen was able to cable Neurath, "In the discussion which I had with Pacelli, Archbishop Gröber, and Kaas this evening, it developed that with the conclusion of the Concordat, the dissolution of the Center party is regarded here as certain and is approved. Again, however, conclusion is being made dependent on an early statement by the Chancellor that peace will thereby finally be restored and the interference

of subordinate officials checked. Such a statement would also facilitate psychologically the decision of the Center party."[70]

Hitler, in a telephoned instruction on July 1, had authorized
Papen to tell Pacelli that after the conclusion of the Concordat he
would "arrange for a thorough and full pacification between the
Catholic portion of the people and the Reich government or the
Länder governments," and that he "would be willing to put a finish
to the story of past political developments." Papen had relayed this
promise,[71] in return for which Pacelli had agreed to the Concordat,
including Article 32. The end of the Center party was regarded as
"certain"; it was taken for granted, as it had probably been all
along. Even if Papen never explicitly demanded the liquidation of
the Catholic parties during the negotiations, there could be little
doubt that it was just this that he and Hitler had in mind. On
either July 2 or 3 Kaas talked to the Center leader, Joseph Joos,
by telephone from the Vatican and asked him in a tone of impatience, "Have you people not yet disbanded?"[72] What Rome expected of the political leaders of German Catholicism was indeed
unmistakable. The Bavarian People's party dissolved itself on
July 4, the Center party published its decree of dissolution in the
late evening of July 5.

The negotiations for the Concordat had now entered the final
phase. In a series of meetings on July 4 and 5 Hitler, together with
Neurath, Frick, Count von Schwerin-Krosigk (Minister of Finance)
and Gürtner (Minister of Justice), examined the draft treaty and a
number of changes were made. The Ministry of the Interior, much
to the surprise of its officials, was only now involved in the discussion. Most of the alterations entered by Neurath on the draft were
based on suggestions made by Rudolf Buttmann, head of the department *Kulturpolitik* in the Ministry of the Interior, in a memorandum prepared in great haste on Hitler's order.[73] Buttmann then
was sent to Rome to get the changes accepted by the Vatican, but
did not succeed in all instances.

These last negotiations were again conducted by Papen, Pacelli,
Kaas and Gröber, in addition to Buttmann. The question as to which
of the Catholic social and professional organizations would be protected by Article 31 caused prolonged discussion. It was finally decided to insert a sentence to the effect that the government of the

Reich and the German episcopate would determine these organizations "by mutual agreement."[74] This agreement, we can note, anticipating a bit, was never reached. In the late hours of July 8 Bergen informed the Foreign Ministry in a telegram, "Concordat was initialed this evening at 6 o'clock by the Vice-Chancellor and the Cardinal Secretary of State."[75]

A public statement to be made by Hitler upon the announcement of the initialing of the Concordat had been drafted by Buttmann and approved by the negotiators for the Holy See. But Hitler objected to certain phrases, especially one that involved the promise to settle the question of the protected Catholic organizations within a month's time. After a series of telephone calls to Rome, a new statement was agreed upon that was released to the press on July 9:

> The conclusion of the Concordat between the Holy See and the government of the Reich appears to me to furnish sufficient guarantee that the German citizens of the Roman Catholic faith will from now on place themselves unreservedly in the service of the new National Socialist state. I therefore issue this order:
>
> 1. The dissolution of those Catholic organizations which are recognized by the present treaty and which were dissolved without instructions by the government of the Reich, is to be rescinded immediately.
>
> 2. All coercive measures against priests and other leaders of the Catholic organizations are to be annulled. A repetition of such measures in the future is inadmissible and will be punished in conformity to the existing laws.
>
> I am happy in the conviction that a period has now been concluded in which religious and political interests unfortunately all too often were locked in seemingly unsolvable contradictions. The treaty concluded between the Reich and the Catholic Church will serve to bring about also in this area the peace which all need.

The statement ended with an expression of hope that the problems involving the Protestant churches would also soon be solved.[76]

Papen recalls that Goebbels, Heydrich and other radical anticlericals in the party objected vigorously until the last moment to the conclusion of the Concordat and tried to sabotage the agreement by creating violent incidents involving the clergy and Catholic organizations. "But Hitler still had authority to tell his radical colleagues that his reconstruction plans could only be carried out

in an atmosphere of harmony in religious matters," and he consequently issued the above order revoking all such measures.[77] It
appears that Papen at the time really believed in the good intentions of Hitler, for in several letters from the Vatican he implored
the Chancellor to stop the terror against Catholics, especially in
Bavaria. The fact that Hitler waited until the Concordat was initialed before he actually ordered a halt to these coercive measures
makes a really basic split over the church issue between Hitler and
his radical followers in 1933 seem somewhat unlikely. In later years,
too, Hitler was to show himself adroit at using coercion against the
Church, switching it on and off according to political expediency.

At the meeting of the Cabinet on July 14, Vice-Chancellor
Papen reported on the negotiations that had ended so successfully.
He reviewed the key provisions of the Concordat and mentioned
that Mussolini had urgently supported the treaty with the Vatican
"because he felt that this would represent a considerable strengthening of the German position."[78] Hitler then took over. Rejecting a
debate on points of details, he stressed the great success that had
been achieved and the significance of the Concordat, especially "in
the urgent fight against the international Jews. Possible shortcomings
in the Concordat could be rectified later when the foreign policy
situation was better." The Chancellor, according to the minutes of
the cabinet meeting, saw "three great advantages":

> 1. That the Vatican had negotiated at all, while they operated,
> especially in Austria, on the assumption that National Socialism
> was un-Christian and inimical to the Church;
> 2. That the Vatican could be persuaded to bring about a good
> relationship with this purely National German State. He, the
> Reich Chancellor, would not have considered it possible even a
> short time ago that the Church would be willing to obligate the
> bishops to this State. The fact that this had now been done was
> certainly an unreserved recognition of the present regime;
> 3. That with the Concordat, the Church withdrew from activity
> in associations and parties, e.g. also abandoned the Christian labor
> unions. This, too, the Reich Chancellor would not have considered
> possible even a few months ago. Even the dissolution of the Center
> could be termed final only with the conclusion of the Concordat,
> now that the Vatican had ordered the permanent exclusion of the
> priests from party politics.

The objective which he had always striven for: namely, an agreement with the Curia, had been attained much faster than he had

imagined even on January 30, and "this was such an indescribable success that all critical misgivings had to be withdrawn in the face of it."[79] The Cabinet, thereupon, approved the treaty.

Misgivings about the concessions made by the Reich had indeed been voiced. Bernhard Rust, the Prussian Minister for Education, Science and Culture, had complained before the meeting that the *Reichskonkordat* had enlarged the rights of the Church, and that in comparison to the Prussian concordat the position of the state had been worsened.[80] But Hitler brushed aside such objections. He was not unduly worried over the fine print of the treaty, which he had no intention of keeping. His eyes were on the political effect at home and abroad, and nothing else mattered.

On July 18 Archbishop Gröber and Bishop Berning held another round of talks with Buttmann in the Ministry of the Interior which put to rest the fears of the episcopate regarding the future of the Catholic organizations. The government promised that these could, but would not be forced to, join National Socialist formations and that their members would not be subjected to any disabilities on account of such membership.[81] That the Vatican declared itself satisfied with these assurances and approved of the treaty even though the list of the protected organizations had not been agreed upon, was to prove a grave mistake. On July 20 at the Vatican the Concordat was formally signed and sealed by Papen and Pacelli in an elaborate ceremony. Presents were exchanged amid expressions of mutual recognition and joy. The rapprochment between Nazi Germany and the Holy See had become a fact.

3. Terms

The text of the Concordat was released on July 22. The preamble stated that the two contracting parties, "led by their common desire to consolidate and enhance the existing friendly relations between the Catholic Church and the State in the whole territory of the German Reich in a stable and satisfactory manner," had decided to conclude a solemn agreement that would supplement the existing *Länderkonkordate* and would secure for the other states uniform treatment of the questions involved.[82] Article 1 guaranteed "freedom of profession and public practice of the Catholic religion" and the right of the Church "to regulate and manage her own affairs independently within the limits of laws applicable to all and to issue—within the framework of her own competence —laws and ordinances binding on her members." The phrase "within the limits of laws applicable to all" was taken over from Article 137, Section 3, of the Weimar constitution where, according to one widely accepted interpretation, it had been intended to give the churches equal status with other private associations and to rule out discriminatory legislation of the Kulturkampf type. Very soon this provision of the *Reichskonkordat* was interpreted by the Nazi government as a clause limiting the rights guaranteed in the treaty, qualifying especially the right of preaching the moral principles of the Catholic religion.[83] This was merely one of the many sections of a hurriedly drafted instrument that allowed for contradictory interpretations.

Article 2 confirmed the continued validity of the existing *Länderkonkordate,* and Article 3 reaffirmed diplomatic representation for the two parties by an Apostolic Nuncio in Berlin and an ambassador at the Holy See. Article 4 secured full freedom of communication for the Holy See with the German clergy and for the bishops with the faithful "in all matters of their pastoral office." They could issue and publish freely ordinances, pastoral letters, official diocesan gazettes and other enactments for "the spiritual guidance of the faithful" and could make these known to the flock "in the ways heretofore usual." But all this was qualified by the phrases "in all matters of their pastoral office" and "within the framework of their competence (see Art. 1, para. 2)"; this competence was soon interpreted by the Nazi government in a most narrow manner, essentially limiting the Church's function to matters of worship and ritual.

The next six articles (5-10) concerned the legal status of the clergy. Priests were guaranteed protection against malicious slander or other interference with their spiritual activity and against the misuse of clerical dress. They were granted exemption from jury duty and similar obligations; the secrecy of the confessional was affirmed. A member of the clergy could accept an appointment by the state only after receiving the *nihil obstat* from his bishop, and the Church could withdraw this permission "for important reasons" at any time. Articles 11 and 12 laid down that changes in diocesan boundaries could be made subject to government approval only, but ecclesiastical offices could be freely established if no subsidy from state funds was involved. Catholic parishes, episcopal sees, religious orders, etc., were guaranteed juridical personality by Article 13 and they were granted the same rights as any other publicly recognized corporation "in accordance with the general laws applicable to all." Here again the Church's prerogatives were made subject to legal regulation by the civil law, and while such a provision might be considered harmless in the case of a state basically friendly to the interests of organized religion, it clearly established a Pandora's box of troubles when the law was in the hands of a regime intent upon subjecting the churches to its control.

The appointment of bishops was dealt with in Article 14. The government here was able to obtain the inclusion of a so-called political clause which made the appointment of a bishop by the Pope conditional upon the absence of "objections of a general political nature" against the appointee on the part of the state. Such a right of veto had originally been granted by the Holy See to a number of German Protestant princes in the early nineteenth century, had been omitted by the Weimar constitution, but had reappeared in the *Länderkonkordate*. The political clause was also included in the concordats with a number of other countries such as Poland (1925), Rumania (1927), Portugal (1928) and Italy (1929).[84] This article had been accepted by the Holy See only after the government had agreed to insert a number of clarifying provisions in the Additional Protocol appended to the Concordat. Here it was laid down that the state's objections had to be presented within twenty days and that Article 14 "does not establish for the State a right of veto." As later experience in connection with the diocese of Aachen was to show, the state had achieved just such a power, for it could object to candidate after candidate without even revealing the nature of the political objections involved and thus block the filling of a vacant see. The same article also limited the clergy to German citizens. Article 15 guaranteed the religious orders full freedom for their pastoral, charitable and educational work.

In Article 16 new bishops, already selected with the consent of the government, were tied even more closely to the state by being required to take an "oath of loyalty." They had to swear to respect the government and cause their clergy to do the same. "In the due solicitude for the welfare and the interests of the German Reich," they were, while performing their spiritual office, "to prevent anything which might threaten to be detrimental to it."

Article 17 guaranteed the property of the Church "according to the common law of the state." In the next clause, the Concordat fully met the old demand of the Vatican that the Holy See be consulted and an amicable agreement be reached in the case of a discontinuance of the state's payments to the Church. Much to the surprise of all concerned, the Nazi regime, despite all its feuding with the Catholic Church, continued paying these subsidies, albeit in somewhat reduced amounts, until the very end. It has been argued that the Church might have felt freer to criticize Hitler if the latter had decided to cut off all financial support as some of his politically less adroit, anti-clerical followers repeatedly demanded.

The Catholic educational system was protected by Articles 19 to 25 of the Concordat. These provisions probably represented the biggest single concession to the interests of the Church in the entire document, though Hitler in due course disregarded them. The continuance of the Catholic theological faculties at the state-supported universities and the affirmation of the right of the Church to establish theological seminaries, provided by Articles 19 and 20, did not represent any great advance. But the recognition of religious instruction in the public primary, vocational, secondary and higher schools as a regular subject "to be taught in accordance with the principles of the Catholic Church" (Article 21) marked an improvement over existing provisions. Therefore, the assumption of the obligation to stress and cultivate "the patriotic, civic and social consciousness and sense of duty" of pupils in such religious instruction seemed a negligible price to pay. As Bishop Berning had told Dr. Rusk in April of 1933, for Catholics the fulfillment of this patriotic duty was axiomatic.

The Church next was given the right of veto over the appointment and continuation of Catholic teachers of religion by the requirement of Article 22 that teachers have the *missio canonica* (ecclesiastical license) from the local bishop, a privilege the Church had unsuccessfully sought for a long time. Finally, the biggest triumph seemed achieved in Article 23, guaranteeing "the maintenance of the existing Catholic confessional schools and the establishment of new ones" wherever parents requested it and the number of prospective pupils was sufficiently large. Papen remarks on this provision with justification, "Only those who [in the twenties] had lived through the ceaseless struggle to obtain this concession can realize what a victory it represented in the mind of Germany's Catholics."[85] Articles 24 and 25 protected the professional training of teachers for the Catholic confessional schools and the right of religious orders "to establish and run private schools." These rights were qualified, however, by the omnipresent phrase, "within the limits of the general legislation and conditions laid down by law."

All in all, Articles 19-25, concerning Catholic education, seemed to have brought the Church the fulfillment of several important and long-sought demands.

Another point was scored by the Church in Article 26, where the Reich accepted the old demand of the Vatican for a revision of the matrimonial law. It was conceded that "a church wedding may precede the civil marriage ceremony not only in case of a grave illness of one of the fiancés which does not permit any delay, but also in case of great moral emergency," confirmed by the episcopal authorities. This provision was used later by a few enterprising and daring Catholic priests to perform religious marriage ceremonies in cases where the civil code, as for example in the Nuremberg racial laws, prohibited a civil marriage.

In Article 27, on the other hand, the government achieved its wish for an "exempt pastoral ministry" for the German army, headed by an army bishop to be selected by mutual agreement of the Reich government and the Holy See. The German episcopate was given some control over the military clergy by the provision that only priests who had the approval of their local bishop for such pastoral work could be appointed as military chaplains. An Apostolic Brief, to be formulated in co-operation with the Reich, was to regulate these matters in detail.

Article 28 guaranteed the Church the right of pastoral care in state-run hospitals, prisons and similar institutions. This provision was soon violated when the regime refused the offer of the Church to hold services in the concentration camps. Catholic members of national minorities by Article 29 were granted the same rights in respect to the use of their mother tongue in divine services as were enjoyed by the German population in the corresponding foreign state. Article 30 required that a prayer be said "for the welfare of the German Reich and its people" after every High Mass.

The next two articles concerned the all-important issue of the Catholic organizations, which, as we have seen, had held up the conclusion of the Concordat for some time. Those organizations "devoted exclusively to religious, cultural and charitable purposes" had not presented any problem; Section 1 of Article 31 provided for their protection without any qualifications. Organizations having political aims, such as the Catholic Peace Union, no longer had any place in the new Germany; this went without saying and was not even mentioned. The impasse over organizations having social or professional purposes had been "solved" by postponing the drawing up of the lists of protected organizations. The second section of Article 31, therefore, simply spoke of affording them protection "provided they guarantee to develop their activities outside political parties." Section 3 empowered the Reich government and the German episcopate "to determine, by mutual agreement, the organizations and associations which fall within the provisions of this article."

Article 32, finally, gave Hitler what had been one of his main reasons for concluding the Concordat: the exclusion of the clergy from politics. "With regard to the special conditions existing in Germany and with regard to the provisions of the present Concordat . . . guaranteeing the rights and privileges of the Catholic Church . . . the Holy See will issue ordinances by which the clergy and the religious will be forbidden to be members of political parties or to be active on their behalf." By the time the Concordat was signed and published, the one-party state had become reality. In fact on July 14, the day that Hitler's cabinet approved the Concordat with the Holy See, a "Law against the Formation of New Political Parties" had outlawed all parties save the NSDAP, thus legalizing what terror had in reality achieved in the preceding weeks. Article 32 was therefore rather gratuitous, but the very bruiting of it during the negotiations had helped to send the Catholic parties into oblivion. (The ordinance of the Holy See forbidding priests to be members of a political party was never issued.

This meant, in effect, that members of the clergy could remain in or join the NSDAP without violating church discipline. The Nazi state allowed such membership with the reasoning that "the movement sustaining the state cannot be equated with the political parties of the parliamentary multi-party state in the sense of Article 32 of the *Reichskonkordat*."[86])

A clause inserted into the Additional Protocol stated that "the same provisions, regarding activity in political parties, will be enacted by the Reich for the non-Catholic confessions" and it furthermore confirmed that Article 32 did not impose upon the clergy "any restriction on their preaching and exposition of the dogmatic and moral teachings and principles of the Church, as it is their duty to do." As in the case of Article 1, this provision was largely nullified by narrow interpretations of the duty and competence of the clergy.

The Concordat ended on the same conciliatory note as the preamble. Article 33 provided that should any divergence arise regarding the interpretation or application of any provision of the treaty, "the Holy See and the German Reich will arrive at an amicable solution by mutual agreement." The last article (34) called for ratification as soon as possible.

In a spirit of co-operation the two parties agreed to keep secret an annex to the Concordat governing the treatment of the clergy in the event that Germany should introduce universal military training. Students studying for the priesthood were declared exempt therefrom except in the case of general mobilization. In that event most of the diocesan clergy were to be exempt from reporting for service, while all others were to be inducted for pastoral work with the troops or into the medical corps.[87] These provisions, as we know from a letter of Kaas to Papen, were inserted at the request of the Fulda Bishops' Conference.[88] So well was the clause kept secret that even a man in such an elevated office as Ernst von Weizsäcker, State Secretary in the Foreign Ministry from 1938 on, did not know of its existence until appraised of it by Nuncio Orsenigo on August 29, 1939, a few days before the outbreak of World War II.[89]

While this request of the German episcopate did not necessarily signify an approval of Hitler's policy of rearmament, it nevertheless reflected considerable foresight. The privileges here promised the clergy in the event of war may also have provided an additional reason why Pope Pius XI, despite his anger at the repeated gross violations of the Concordat by the Hitler regime after 1933, refrained from renouncing the Concordat as many suggested he do.[90]

4. Ratification

On his way back to Berlin after the signing ceremonies Papen attended a meeting of the Association of Catholic Academicians (*Katholischer Akademikerverband*) at the noted Benedictine monastery of Maria Laach. In a speech delivered there on July 22 the Vice-Chancellor hailed the Concordat as "the final conclusion of the Kulturkampf in Germany." The Holy Father, he related, had been warned against concluding a treaty with so unworthy a partner as the German Reich led by Adolf Hitler, but Pope Pius XI had agreed to the treaty "in the recognition that the new Germany had fought a decisive battle against Bolshevism and the atheist movement." The Pope had told him that he had full confidence in the assurances of the Reich Chancellor that the national renaissance would be carried out upon the sole foundation of Christianity. The Curia, Papen continued, accustomed to thinking in the perspective of long periods, had been prepared to give up trustfully what in the age of liberalism perhaps had seemed necessary and important. Now the German Catholics, too, Papen suggested, should realize that the Concordat provided full opportunity for the Church's development and that they, therefore, could forego the old political ties. "As a matter of fact, there also exists, of course, an undeniable inner connection between the dissolution of the German Center party that has just taken place and the conclusion of the Concordat." Papen ended his talk with a call to German Catholicism to forget all former resentments and to rally to the building of the Third Reich.[91]

The *Völkischer Beobachter*, two days later, went a step further and saw in the Concordat a most solemn recognition of National Socialism by the Catholic Church. "The provocative agitation which for years was conducted against the NSDAP because of its alleged hostility to religion has now been refuted by the Church itself. This fact signifies a tremendous moral strengthening of the National Socialist government of the Reich and of its reputation."[92]

Similar statements appeared in the official party organ *National-*

sozialistische Korrespondenz, probably attempting to pacify anti-Catholic diehards; and even some Catholic papers made somewhat extravagant claims concerning the political significance of the Concordat. They were answered by two articles in the quasi-official organ of the Vatican, *L'Osservatore Romano,* on July 26 and 27, which Eugen Klee, the Chargé d'Affaires of the German Embassy to the Holy See, termed "undoubtedly inspired by the Papal Secretariat of State."[93] The articles stressed the advantages accruing to the Church from the various provisions of the Concordat and insisted that the Church had not abandoned thereby her traditional neutrality toward various forms of government. The Concordat did not represent "a confirmation or recognition of a specific trend of political doctrines and ideas." The Holy See negotiated with states, as such, in order to guarantee the rights and liberties of the Church. The question of a state's constitution concerned the nations alone.[94]

The Vatican's reply, in turn, brought about a retort by Buttmann of the Ministry of Interior, which the German press was forced to publish on July 30 as a reply "from a well-informed source." The German expert corrected a number of allegedly false interpretations of the Concordat and concluded by reminding the Vatican that the Concordat had been concluded with the German Reich which, "as Rome should know, is completely dominated by the National Socialist 'trend.' The conclusion of the treaty therefore means the *de facto* and *de jure* recognition of the National Socialist government."[95]

The Vatican at first demanded that the German government disavow these press commentaries. Apart from the insults to the Vatican's self-esteem caused by the harping on the great victory achieved by Nazi Germany, such statements could only damage the Holy See's standing in the rest of the world, which did not always look favorably upon occurrences in the Third Reich. Pacelli, in a talk on August 19 with a member of the British Legation to the Holy See, tried to meet the reproach that the Concordat meant an approval of the National Socialist mode of governing by expressing his disgust and abhorrence of the reign of terror to which Hitler's government had subjected Germany.[96] Eventually, however, the Papal Secretary of State agreed to forget the whole matter on condition that the German press refrain from any further discussion of the Concordat.[97]

Last-minute obstacles also arose in connection with other even more basic issues. On September 5 a discussion took place between Klee and Pacelli in the course of which the Cardinal brought up the disquieting reports that had reached him from various parts of the German Reich, especially from southern Germany, concerning the continuing harassment of the Catholic clergy, the Catholic press and Catholic organizations. These reports indicated, he argued, that the Concordat was being interpreted in a manner most detrimental to the Catholic interests. It was most important, therefore, that the list of Catholic organizations to be protected under Sections 2 and 3 of Article 31 be agreed upon before ratification and that assurances be provided for the right of Catholic organizations to function publicly. The press controversies regarding Article 32 also made it urgently necessary "that the concepts and spheres of activity of party politics, politics in general and public life be defined in relation to each other." Pacelli stressed that his remarks were not meant to evade ratification, but had as their only object an amicable agreement "on the sense and implementation of the Concordat."[98]

The German episcopate, meanwhile, had been consulted by Pacelli on the question whether ratification should indeed be postponed pending the satisfactory resolution of the most important difficulties. Cardinal Bertram answered on September 2 in the name of the German bishops, who had discussed the matter at their second plenary conference within the span of three months, held at Fulda from August 29 to 31. Bertram urged that ratification of the Concordat take place as soon as possible. It was widely believed, he wrote, that in entering into a concordat Hitler aimed merely at an increase in prestige for reasons of foreign policy and that the government had made too many concessions. "Such voices will get louder, if ratification is delayed. This causes disquiet among the Catholic population." Moreover, only after the ratification of the treaty had taken place would it be possible for the Church to proceed more energetically against the numerous anti-Catholic actions. Any further delay would weaken the position of the episcopate. At the time of ratification, the head of the German episcopate suggested, one should also demand that the existing grievances be remedied at once.[99]

These grievances were listed by Bertram in the second part of his letter: Catholic organizations everywhere were being publicly denounced as politically unreliable, their members were being subjected to economic sanctions, the Catholic press was subjected to severe reprisals whenever it dared to express an independent opinion and Catholic civil servants continued to be dismissed. He also inquired whether the Vatican might not be able to put in a good word for Jewish converts to the Catholic religion, who were being made destitute because of their non-Aryan descent.[100]

The wish of the German episcopate for speedy ratification appears to have been the main reason Pacelli waived his earlier demand that the problems listed in the note of September 5 be first resolved. After new talks with Klee the Vatican declared itself satisfied with a joint communiqué that was to be released at the time of ratification. The communiqué would announce that the German government was prepared to enter into consultations with the Holy See on the points raised in the discussions on September 5, "as well as on all those Concordat matters which need to be clarified and definitely settled immediately in order to bring about an understanding that is genuinely in harmony with the letter and the spirit of the Concordat and that will ensure a fruitful cooperation of Church and State."[101]

The last roadblock had thus been overcome by an important concession of the Holy See. The Concordat became final in the afternoon of September 10, when documents of ratification were exchanged between Cardinal Pacelli and Chargé d'Affaires Klee. The same evening Pacelli addressed a letter to Cardinal Bertram. He informed him of the events of the afternoon and told him that if the Holy See had gone along with the wishes of the German government for prompt ratification without first insisting on removal of the numerous gravamina, "the determining factor had been the highly esteemed views of the Fulda Bishops' Conference."[102]

5. Significance

The reaction of German Catholicism to the conclusion of the Concordat will occupy us in the following chapter. Here it remains to assess once more the reasons that prompted both sides to enter into this treaty and to discuss its import for later developments.

There is general agreement that the Concordat increased substantially the prestige of Hitler's regime around the world. As Cardinal Faulhaber put it in a sermon delivered in 1937: "At a time when the heads of the major nations in the world faced the new Germany with cool reserve and considerable suspicion, the Catholic Church, the greatest moral power on earth, through the Concordat expressed its confidence in the new German government. This was a deed of immeasurable significance for the reputation of the new government abroad."[103] True, the Concordat was not the first diplomatic victory for Hitler; it was preceded five days earlier by the Four Power Pact with France, Great Britain and Italy. But the difference in prestige was tremendously on the side of the Concordat.

It is also not to be denied that the Concordat had a certain usefulness for the Church by creating a legal base for protests against the regime's hostile measures. Though the spirit and the letter of the treaty were to be violated by Hitler practically from the day of its conclusion the Church at least had a way to support itself against these encroachments by legal arguments.

But the achievement of this legal vantage point also had its disadvantage. In the days of persecution that soon set in, the existence of the Concordat, as Gerhard Ritter has observed, "acted as a brake since it could legitimately be feared that over-loud protest would endanger the rights that were left untouched."[134] The pact with Hitler in effect, then, dictated a policy of caution when a more vigorous opposition was called for or desired. An open conflict or break with the regime had to be prevented at all cost, for either might jeopardize those privileges the Concordat still protected. To make matters worse, the Concordat was virtually no deterrent at all against the Nazis' attacks. At the same time, it very definitely broke the back of any latent Catholic resistance to the Hitler regime before it could develop. The fact that the Holy See had concluded a pact with the National Socialist state paralyzed the will to resist of those Catholics who, despite this diplomatic rapprochement, did not consider the Nazis reformed and rehabilitated.

Doubtless, the number of Catholics prepared to do battle with the Nazi regime was small. Therefore, a Vatican refusal to go along with the German offer probably would have been viewed by most

German Catholics as an unfriendly act toward their country and deplored as an unrealistic stand preventing the desired reconciliation with the Hitler regime. "The capitulation," as Carl Amery has pungently observed, "was carried out primarily not by the bishops or prelates of the Center party or the monsignori, but by the *juste milieu* of German Catholicism."[105] No leader, lay or clerical, can for long oppose widely accepted values and modes of thinking in the group he is heading and expect to maintain his position of leadership and influence. The leadership of the Holy See over world Catholicism forms no exception to this rule.

It is also true, as Father Leiber suggests, that it was not the Concordat that made resistance to the Nazi regime impossible from the start, but the affirmative vote of the Center party to the Enabling Act, and the German bishops' declaration of peace of March 28. The conclusion of the Concordat, he correctly notes, was a logical outgrowth of these two prior decisions.[106] But Leiber's argument has two great weaknesses. First, it minimizes the share, direct or indirect, of the Vatican in both of these earlier events. Secondly, it fails to come to grips with the important motivating force common to all three of these accommodations to the dictatorship-in-the-making. The consent of the Center party to the Enabling Act, as well as the bishops' formal withdrawal of the ban on the Nazi party, and the Concordat especially, represented an attempt to find a *modus vivendi* with the new Germany. It was hoped that this state would become just another authoritarian regime, one which would protect the Church against the threat of Communism and create more-or-less acceptable conditions for its pastoral functions. If these could be secured, other matters counted but little.

The fact that the Concordat lent the sanction of the Church to the destruction of the Center party and its ally, the Bavarian People's party, stands out in perspective as one of the milestones in the consolidation of the one-party state. The consent of the Curia to the liquidation of all Catholic organizations having a political program also helped strengthen the emerging totalitarian regime. But for the Church at the time, these were unintended side effects.

For the Nazis, on the other hand, the destruction of the confessional parties and the exclusion of the clergy from politics was extremely important. Article 32, therefore, frequently was referred to by the German negotiators as the *conditio sine qua non* for Hitler's approval of the Concordat. But while this aim, as Bracher correctly notes, makes the Concordat very definitely a political instrument of the National Socialist seizure and consolidation of dictatorial power,[107] it does not thereby make the pact entirely *sui generis*. Secular powers have always signed treaties primarily to obtain political benefits for themselves. Also, as we have seen, there exists a very definite continuity between the Vatican's striving for a concordat with the Reich in the twenties and the successful conclusion of this treaty in 1933, when the old obstacles had been cleared away by Hitler's assumption of power and his destruction of the parliamentary government. Even if our hypothesis that the Holy See made the first move in 1933 could be refuted, this would still not destroy the inner connection between the earlier abortive and the later successful negotiations for such a pact. The stakes for the Church remained essentially the same, and she was prepared to sign a concordat with whoever promised to enhance and safeguard essential interests like state subsidies to the Church and the confessional schools.

In a sense it is accurate to say that both sides in 1933 played with false cards. For Hitler the political effects of the Concordat at home and abroad were decisive; he had no intention of keeping all the promises he made. Most of these, moreover, were listed in such ambiguous language, encumbered by so many qualifications, that an interpretation conveniently in keeping with Hitler's aims was not very difficult. As in the case of Hitler's declaration before the Reichstag in March 1933, warning signs were distributed all over the text of the Concordat that should have drawn attention to his motives for affixing his signature to it. But the Church, too, had ulterior motives. Hitler's regime, it was widely believed in those days, would not last very long. "A Concordat might therefore be signed with Hitler safely, and it would be useful under whatever regime ensued as a legal basis for determining the Church's position. A Concordat with the Reich, favorable to the Church, would be in existence, and it would serve as the starting point for all future negotiations."[108] Such long-range thinking was given as one of the Church's reasons for concluding the Concordat by an astute observer and friend of the Church, Waldemar Gurian, in 1938. It was also a view voiced by Himmler's *Schwarze Korps*.[109] And the correctness of this strategy—if a strategy there was at all—was confirmed on March 26, 1957, when the West German Federal Constitutional Court upheld the continued validity of the Concordat for the German Federal Republic.[110]

The Concordat had results that were unintended and that probably could not be clearly foreseen in 1933 by either of the contracting parties. Archbishop Gröber, in a pastoral letter read after the end of the Second World War, reflected that the Concordat had deceived the German Catholics and the whole world.[111] Back in 1937, on the other hand, a handbook edited by him and published with the recommendations of the entire German episcopate, regarded the Concordat as "proof that two powers, totalitarian in their character, can find an agreement, if their domains are separate and if overlaps in jurisdiction become parallel or in a friendly manner lead them to make common cause."[112] The harmonious co-operation anticipated at that time did not quite materialize. But the reason for this, as we shall see later, lay less in the lack of readiness of the Church than in the shortsighted policies of the Hitler regime. If the German National Socialist state was prepared to treat the Church as Mussolini's Fascist government did in Italy, the gate to friendly relations stood open. This, as far as the Church was concerned, was the essential message of the Concordat concluded between Nazi Germany and the Holy See in July of 1933.

4 The Great Reconciliation

1. The Fulda Bishops' Conference of May 30-June 1, 1933

The representatives of the German metropolitans, meeting in Berlin at the end of April, had called for the early convening of a plenary conference of all German bishops, the first such meeting since 1848. This conference met in Fulda on May 30. The opening session discussed problems related to the *Reichskonkordat* being negotiated at Rome and dispatched the customary message of greeting to the Supreme Pontiff. Next, to draft a joint pastoral letter, a committee was appointed, consisting of the three German cardinals—Bertram, Faulhaber and Schulte—Archbishop Gröber, and Bishops Ehrenfried and Preysing.[1]

The committee had before it a draft composed by Cardinal Bertram, but the final copy included only two passages from Bertram's text. The draft by Bertram was primarily theological in content;[2] the other members of the committee apparently considered a more direct confrontation of the political issues of the day essential. This point had also been made in the suggestions forwarded to Bertram. Two of these letters are preserved, though their authorship is not known.[3] One of them proposed that the pastoral letter include a call to the Catholic press not to desert Catholic principles. Some

94

Catholic newspapers, the writer pointed out, as a result of pressure exerted by the National Socialist movement and in an attempt to keep up their circulation, had become uncertain and compromising in their appraisal of National Socialism. The danger of a national Church, separate from Rome, should also not be underestimated. Many Catholics, especially among the youth, were affected by the National Socialist propaganda, and their power of resistance was being sapped, if not destroyed, by the fear of losing their livelihood. The threats to the existence of the Catholic organizations should be clearly pointed out.[4]

The other writer suggested that the pastoral letter affirm the importance of creating and maintaining "a legal order, based on natural and divine law" and that it call for "the revival of confidence in the impartial administration of laws and regulations for every citizen." Protective custody should be resorted to as little as possible and care should be taken "that the concentration camps not become seedbeds of hate dangerous to the future development of the state." The government of the Reich, the writer maintained, was possessed of good will in this regard, but not all other authorities in the state were following the same line. It was also suggested that the bishops create a committee of experts from the various Catholic organizations to handle questions of *Gleichschaltung* in a uniform manner. Efforts should be made, in co-operation with the state authorities, to bring about the realization of the corporate social and economic order envisaged by the encyclical *Quadragesimo anno* (1931) of Pope Pius XI.[5]

Only a few of these suggestions found their way into the text of the pastoral letter as finally adopted. The joint pronouncement did not reflect any new attitude toward the National Socialist state or movement, but it provided a detailed justification of the line of co-operation that had been decided upon in March, and therefore is of considerable importance. The letter began by pointing out the seriousness of the times, in which old institutions were disappearing and a new state was being formed. The German people, it said, now were increasingly reflecting upon and stressing their own values and strengths. "We German Bishops are far from underestimating or even preventing this national awakening." They had always regarded love for the fatherland and for their own people as a divinely granted creative power. "Therefore, neither do we German Catholics need a new attitude toward people and fatherland, but to continue, at most in a more conscious and emphatic manner, what until now we have recognized and fulfilled as our natural and Christian duty." Of course, the bishops insisted, this love for the fatherland did not make the Catholics forget their Christian ties with other peoples of the kingdom of God, through which Christ saves all men without distinction of language, nation or race.[6]

The second section, too, began with affirmations of loyalty and remarks favorable to the Nazis' political outlook, followed by some qualifying and more critical comments. The times, the bishops observed, were characterized by a strong emphasis on authority and by an unyielding demand for the incorporation of the individual and all groups into the state. This was in conformity with Catholic thinking. "The value and meaning of authority attain particular importance especially in our Holy, Catholic Church and have led to that complete determination and victorious strength of resistance which even our enemies admire. We Catholics, therefore, do not find it at all difficult to appreciate the new, strong stress on authority in the German state." On the other hand,[7] the episcopate stressed, they expected that the state, following the example of the Church, would "limit human freedom only as much as the common good demanded." Any abuse of authority and injustice weakened and damaged the state.

In section three the bishops welcomed "the goals which the new state authority pursues in order to achieve liberty" for the German people. "Our German nation, after years of bondage, disregard for our national rights, and shameful interference with them, must again receive that freedom and place of honor in the family of nations which is its due on account of its numerical size and its cultural ability and performance."[8] The bishops did not speak here of an un-Christian policy of vengeance or even of a coming war, the pastoral letter continued, but merely demanded justice and living space (*Lebensraum*).

Such a breaking of chains, as well as all measures aiming at the rejuvenation of the people, were entirely in keeping with Catholic ideas. The bishops expressed the hope that the physical invigoration of the youth would not involve the neglect of the soul or danger to the Catholic religious life by encouraging disdain for the holy Sunday. If the state sought to promote the unity of the German people, the Catholics would have full understanding for that also. But this compactness should be realized not only through equality of blood, but also through common ways of thinking. "The exclusive stress on race and blood leads to injustices which burden the Christian conscience, especially when they affect fellow men who through the holy sacrament of baptism have been reborn and renewed in Christ." Justice had also to be meted out to former enemies, who should not be exterminated, but reformed and won for service in the new state.[9]

The rest of the pastoral letter was devoted to an enumeration of certain misgivings over the position and treatment of the Church. The bishops welcomed the declaration of the leaders of the new state that their work of renewal would be anchored in the foundations of Christianity. Disbelief, immorality and Bolshevism thus would no longer threaten the German soul. But Christianity could not be allowed to express itself in the framework of a national church, divorced from the Vicar of Christ in Rome.[10] Also, the Church could fulfill her role only if allowed to function unhindered and with complete liberty. It was not enough if the Church was merely free within the house of God while administering the sacraments. "For her task consists of permeating all aspects of human life, the private as well as the public." The Church must be allowed to work for the Christianization of the people, especially the young, and this ruled out the utilization of interdenominational schools.[11] She should be allowed to keep the Catholic press, the Catholic youth and other organizations, the existence of which strengthened rather than weakened the body politic. "The Catholic press, in particular, has always and everywhere proven itself as a force that upholds the state. It exhorts its readers to make themselves a part of the nation and calls on them willingly to submit to the lawful authorities."[12]

In closing, the bishops repeated that their demands did not result from hidden reservations toward the new state. "A temporizing standing aside or even hostility of the Church toward the State would have disastrous consequences for both Church and State." The German leaders, the bishops hoped, would be able to stamp out those sparks which certain elements here and there wanted to fan into an anti-Catholic conflagration. "Only then will the new state attain its irresistible strength and that unity free of tensions that will gain for us the esteem of the other nations and their appropriate willingness to co-operate, as well as the blessing of God from above."[13]

The French Catholic historian Robert d'Harcourt has characterized this pastoral letter as consisting of "professions of loyalty, seasoned with drops of vinegar." The bishops, he says, "were trying to reconcile the irreconcilable, to flatter the hangman and console the victim."[14] The episcopal pronouncement, indeed, went rather a long way toward accepting certain basic principles of "the new state" which, it was stressed, the bishops supported without any hidden reservations. The real nature of this state, and its aims, the bishops misunderstood almost completely. Hitler did not seek a new "stress on authority," but a dictatorship. He wanted for Germany not "a place of honor in the family of nations," but unchallenged hegemony over Europe. His cult of race and blood did not aim at restoring German unity, but at the domination of the "Aryan race" and the extermination of inferior peoples. Hitler's regime stood for all that the bishops saw merely as threatening aberrations or as the unauthorized excesses of subordinates.

The Catholic episcopate was, of course, not alone then in failing to perceive the totalitarian goals of the Nazi movement or to foresee the aggressive aspirations of Hitler's foreign policy. The Protestant churches, most of the intellectuals and many people abroad showed no more political acumen. But the fact that the German bishops continued, as we shall see, to fail to penetrate the myth of the Nazis' patriotic and noble intentions even in later years, suggests that this misunderstanding of the essence of Nazism in June of 1933 was based on more than Hitler's deceptive words. The bishops, in concert at least, found no harm in Hitler's one-party state. Their pronouncement expressed little concern over the suppression of civil rights and liberties except insofar as they touched the special freedoms of the Church, its schools, newspapers and organizations. They spoke of moral renewal while the brown terror tortured and murdered. The banning of the freethinkers' and nudists' magazines and the destruction of the godless Communist movement in Germany were welcomed, even if achieved as part of the liquidation of all political opposition. What the bishops had already regarded before 1933 as the healthy core of National Socialism was now being realized, and they found reason to characterize it as consonant with Catholic thinking. It is hard to resist the conclusion that it was the attraction felt for certain elements in the Nazi ideology more than anything else that prevented the German episcopate from apprehending the true inhumanity of National Socialism in 1933 as well as in later years.

The call for the loyal co-operation of the Catholics with the new state, in June 1933, was undoubtedly related also to the hope for a concordat. Pending its signing the boat was not to be rocked. German Catholicism had always attributed great importance to its many organizations, and the episcopate now was most anxious to placate the state in order to obtain written safeguards for the threatened Catholic associations. German Catholics had never been used to supporting their priests and schools, and the fear of losing state subsidies therefore was another important factor making for submissiveness. Later the desire not to jeopardize the Concordat and the Church's institutional structure dictated a continuation of the same line. Finally, the exhortation to be obedient was part of an old tradition and of a total inability to envisage the possibility of a break between Church and State. The alliance between throne and altar had lasted too long: seemingly no amount of persecution could deflect the Catholic episcopate from their conviction that it was the task of the Church to sustain the state at all cost. No matter what the regime did, therefore, the Nazi state remained the lawful authority that had to be obeyed in accordance with God's command.

In addition to the joint pastoral letter, which was read in most dioceses on the first and second Sundays of June 1933, the Fulda Conference also issued pastoral instructions to the clergy. These followed, frequently verbatim, the instructions handed down by the Bavarian bishops on April 10 and need not be gone into again. A new paragraph entitled "Criticism of the Attitude of the Episcopate" is interesting because it asked the clergy to correct mistaken interpretations of the bishops' declaration of March 28. Inasmuch as a footnote directs attention to the work of Father Nötges on National Socialism and the report of the *Volksverein* conference dealing with the same problem, both published in 1931, apparently these criticisms mainly involved the earlier ban on the Nazi party. In this connection the clergy were told to point out that the Church, despite its rejection of all error, "always practices far-reaching leniency toward those Catholics who have tended to accept the economic and political aims of National Socialism, while at the same time adhering to staunch Catholic views and conduct."[15]

2. German Catholicism Enters the Third Reich

The joint pastoral letter of the Fulda Bishops' Conference of May 30, according to the Bavarian ambassador to the Holy See, was welcomed by the Curia.[16] In Germany, too, it was generally well received and helped relieve tension. Professor Hans Peters, a prominent Center party politician, summed up its significance in these words: "The German bishops at their recent meeting at Fulda have stated in clear language the ideas and goals we have in common with the National Socialist movement. They have thereby worked out the positive foundation for our participation in the work of the new state."[17] This theme of active participation was expressed also by individual churchmen. Bishop Bornewasser addressed a gathering of Catholic youth in the Cathedral of Trier and declared, "With raised heads and firm step we have entered the new Reich and we are prepared to serve it with all the might of our body and soul."[18]

On June 25 the *Katholikentag* (annual Catholic congress) of the diocese of Berlin rallied 45,000 Catholics in the Grunewald Stadium. The mass meeting was attended by the Papal Nuncio, who was accompanied to the altar to the sound of ringing bells and fanfares, and, probably for the first time, by an S.A. contingent carrying swastika flags. Hitler had been invited but had declined with regrets.[19] Dr. Erich Klausener, head of Catholic Action, addressed the rally and stressed that "the momentous awakening of the German nation posed great tasks for the German Catholics."[20] Almost exactly one year later Klausener was murdered in the blood purge of June 30, 1934. His affirmations of patriotism and co-operation with the new regime proved unavailing.

The Nazis, even in 1933 placing no trust in the newly displayed amity of organized Catholicism, did not respond in kind. They had no intention to, for the National Socialist regime aimed at the destruction of all rival centers of loyalty. It therefore was not interested in the co-operation of Catholics *qua* Catholics. During the month of June, as noted in the last chapter, the pressure for the *Gleichschaltung* of all political parties and professional and other associations greatly increased, and the Catholic parties and organizations, accused of "political Catholicism," came under severe attack. The situation was particularly serious in Munich and Upper Bavaria, where in May the Church had been put under heavy pressure by Seidler, who exercised quasi-legal police powers as the special delegate of the S.A. to the government of Upper Bavaria. In a talk with Vicar-General Buchwieser of the Archdiocese of Munich, Seidler had demanded that the Archbishop issue an order prohibiting the political activity of the clergy, and he had asked for the rehabilitation of Abbot Schachleiter as the price for stopping further arrests of priests.[21] Following the publication of a pro-Nazi article in the *Völkischer Beobachter* of February 1, 1933, Schachleiter had been suspended by Rome for violation of Church discipline, and this act of censure had angered Nazi circles. Another sore point for them was the continuation of Dr. Emil Muhler, a man of well-known anti-Nazi sentiments, as head of Catholic Action in Munich. Cardinal Faulhaber, anxious not to jeopardize the negotiations for the Concordat in Rome, retreated on both issues. Dr. Muhler was asked to resign his office,[22] and Faulhaber promised the S.A. leader that he would do his utmost at the Vatican to obtain the speedy lifting of Schachleiter's suspension.[23]

But these concessions did not satisfy the Nazis. On June 11 the Bavarian Minister of the Interior, Adolf Wagner, demanded that the Cardinal keep the Catholic organizations off the streets, restrict their activity to purely religious purposes and disavow the Bavarian People's party.[24] The urgency of the situation was underlined by the maltreatment of the Catholic journeymen meeting in Munich at this time. On June 12 Faulhaber protested to Hitler and various Bavarian state officials against these acts of violence. The fact that the journeymen had been prevented from holding their concluding service was an unheard-of interference in the religious freedom of the Church. All this had happened, he wrote, even though "the *Gesellentag* had expressed in its speeches and its general make-up a flaming confession to the state of the nationalist coalition and to willingness to participate in it."[25] On the same day Faulhaber wrote Wagner that once again he had issued instructions to the clergy "to avoid in sermons and private talks everything that could destroy confidence in the nationalist government or damage the peaceful co-operation of Church and State." He had full confidence that Chancellor Adolf Hitler would protect Germany against the threat of Bolshevism and, if only for that reason, would support his work by prayer and deed. However, he did not have the same confidence in all the lower-ranking state authorities. Referring to the joint pastoral letter of the German episcopate, Faulhaber turned down the demand that the Catholic organizations limit themselves to purely religious activities.[26]

Other bishops, too, concerned about the Concordat negotiations, counseled restraint. Bishop Sebastian of Speyer on June 20 had imposed the interdict on the town of Hexheim, where a priest and his curate had been subjected to particularly undignified treatment and forced to flee their home.[27] A few days later peace talks were held with a representative of the Nazi party's *Gauleitung* (regional leadership). The *Gauleitung* promised to bring about the release of all arrested priests, in return for which the Bishop issued an instruction to the clergy to exercise special restraint and to refrain from criticism.[28] Archibshop Gröber, on June 28, advised his clergy "to stress especially those truths of Catholic doctrine which are suited to promote peace and unity, strengthen the authority of the state and contribute to the spiritual support of our people. In the interest of the priests themselves and of the Church, we find reason to issue the admonishment and instruction to avoid in sermon, catechetical instructions, as well as in organizational activity and in private talks, everything that could be interpreted as criticism of leading personalities in state and community or of the political views held by them."[29] Similarly worded instructions were issued in the dioceses of Würzburg, Passau and Paderborn.[30]

Despite these gestures of good will, the Nazi terror against the Catholic parties and organizations intensified until the dissolution of both the Center and Bavarian People's party had been achieved.

A new wave of arrests in Bavaria began on June 28 and led to the imprisonment of 1,917 persons, many of them leading Catholic personalities. Cardinal Faulhaber, who earlier had urged the Bavarian People's party to continue its work on behalf of the Church, now refrained from any active support. The Bavarian People's party declared its dissolution on July 4, whereupon most of the prisoners were released. The main purpose for which they had been taken into "protective custody" had been accomplished.[31] The "voluntary" disbandment of the Center party was announced a day later. As Morsey observed, the protracted haggling prior to dissolution over the absorption of the Center's representatives in the Reichstag by the Nazi delegation did not contribute to a dignified departure from the political scene.[32] An unsigned statement released in the late evening hours of July 5 announced that the Center party had dissolved itself. Three days later in Rome the Concordat was initialed. German Catholicism as an organized political force had ceased to exist.

The announcement of the conclusion of the Concordat between Germany and the Holy See gave rise to a new wave of hopefulness in the Catholic camp that affected even those not entirely happy about the dissolution of the Catholic parties. On July 10 Bishop Vogt of Aachen sent a telegram of thanks and congratulations to Hitler in which he promised that "diocese and Bishop will gladly participate in the building of the new Reich."[33] A day later Bishop Berning of Osnabrück was appointed by Göring (Prime Minister of Prussia since April 11) to membership in the reorganized Prussian Council of State. This body did not wield any power, but the fact that a Catholic bishop had been called to and accepted a state office of considerable prestige contributed to the general feeling of optimism and accelerated the movement of former Center party supporters into the Nazi camp.[34]

The formal signing of the Concordat on July 20 was similarly greeted with much applause. In the name of the Fulda Bishops' Conference, Cardinal Bertram addressed a letter of "recognition and thanks" to Hitler that received wide publicity. The Catholic episcopate, Bertram pointed out, as soon as the Chancellor's declaration had made it possible, had expressed their sincere and joyous preparedness to co-operate as best they could with the government

now ruling that had set itself the tasks of promoting the Christian
education of the people, repelling ungodliness and immorality, developing readiness to make sacrifices for the common good and protecting the rights of the Church." The harmonious co-operation of
Church and State for the achievement of these lofty aims had now
been confirmed by the Concordat. The episcopate expressed the
hope that the implementation of the treaty would come about
quickly so that the Church could bring to bear the forces of the
Catholic religion upon the promotion of the belief in God, morality and faithful obedience to the state authorities.[35]

Cardinal Faulhaber, too, sent a handwritten letter of congratulations to the Chancellor:

> What the old parliaments and parties did not accomplish in 60
> years, your statesmanlike foresight has achieved in six months.
> For Germany's prestige in East and West and before the whole
> world this handshake with the Papacy, the greatest moral power
> in the history of the world, is a feat of immeasurable blessing.[36]

Faulhaber went on to state his hope that the Concordat would be
adhered to by all the various echelons of the state, and he suggested that the momentous hour be celebrated by an amnesty for
all those in protective custody for no crime but their political convictions. The Cardinal ended his letter with the wish "coming from
the bottom of our heart: May God preserve the Reich Chancellor for our people."[37]

Others were no less enthusiastic. A joint telegram of Bishop
Bornewasser and Vice-Chancellor Papen, occasioned by the ceremonial exhibition of the holy frock of Christ in the cathedral of
Trier on July 24, assured Hitler of their "steadfast participation in
the work of resurrecting the German Reich."[38] Addressing a pil-
grimage of Catholic journeymen to the holy frock on August 13,
Secretary General Nattermann affirmed that Hitler and Kolping, if
alive, could now shake hands. The *Gesellenverein* and the NSDAP,
Natterman declared, had the same aim, the unity of the German
people, and he would be happy "if the staunch and loyal sons of
Kolping would turn into equally loyal S.A. and S.S. men."[39] Vicar
General Steinmann, taking the place of the sick Bishop Schreiber
of Berlin, told a meeting of several thousand Catholic youths:
"What we all have longed and striven for has become reality: we

have one Reich and one leader [*ein Reich und einen Führer*] and this leader we follow faithfully and conscientiously . . . For us this is not a question of personality. We know that he who stands at the head is given us by God as our leader."[40]

The affair went further. The *Völkischer Beobachter* published a picture showing Steinmann, surrounded by other clerics, replying with raised right arm to the Hitler greeting of the Catholic youth organizations marching by before him.[41] When a German-American paper in New York, *Aurora und Christliche Woche,* criticized Steinmann for having supported the Hitler government in an undignified manner, the latter replied in an open letter that the German Catholics did indeed regard the government of Adolf Hitler as the God-given authority. However, they owed fidelity and obedience to it not only for such formal reasons, but because this government had defeated Bolshevism, annihilated the Marxist atheist movement and liberated the German people from the plague of trashy and dirty literature. "The future will some day gratefully acknowledge that Germany, situated in the heart of Europe, has erected a bulwark against Bolshevism and thereby saved the occident from the Red tide."[42] Steinmann did not live to see the day when the Red Army, provoked by an abortive attack of the alleged savior of Western civilization, deeply penetrated central Europe and occupied Berlin itself, the place where he had made his ill-fated prophecy.

After the ratification of the Concordat on September 10 special services of thanksgiving were held in all the Catholic churches of Germany. Arrangements for a big service in Berlin were made by the regional National Socialist propaganda department, which promised itself, from this celebration, the conversion of many Catholics still skeptical about the Nazi movement. The program, as proposed by the *Gauleitung,* was approved by Nuncio Orsenigo and the diocesan chancery. It consisted of a special High Mass in the Cathedral of St. Hedwig, attended by uniformed formations of all Catholic S.A. and S.S. men in Berlin with their flags and banners, members of Catholic organizations and many government officials, as well as the Papal Nuncio. The service was carried by loudspeakers to the many thousands on the adjoining square who could not be accommodated in the cathedral itself. The preacher

celebrated the epochal reconciliation just concluded between the
Holy Father of all Catholics and the leader of the great German
people's movement, "a man of marked devotion to God and sincerely concerned for the well-being of the German people that will
be governed in accordance with the will of the Divine Creator."
After the service the huge crowd sang the national and party
("Horst Wessel") hymns.[43] A telegram of thanks to Hitler, signed by
Steinmann and Klausener, promised to rally all forces for *Volk*
and fatherland.[44]

The Catholic organizations, too, hurried to affirm their loyalty
to state and movement. Monsignor Ludwig Wolker, president of
the *Jungmännerverband,* reminded his men that the Concordat imposed upon all of them the duty not only of respecting and obeying
the laws of the state, but also of "recognizing the new state of National Socialist character, its ideas, its leadership, its forms and of
putting ourselves at its disposal with complete readiness and fidelity."[45] At the same time, the Catholic young men were ordered
from now on to use the new *Deutschen Gruss,* that is, to raise their
right arm in salute, and to display the swastika flag along with the
flags of their own organization.[46] A programmatic statement of the
Catholic youth organization *Neudeutsche Jugend,* also published
in September, welcomed the new organically and hierarchically
ordered state, based on the German leadership principle instead of
on Western abstract ideas, and called for the full and close co-
operation between the totalitarian state and the totalitarian
Church.[47] The inherent difficulties of any coexistence of two totalitarian powers were not perceived.

Among the episcopate two bishops in particular showed great
zeal in promoting the acceptance of German Catholicism as a trustworthy partner of the new state. One of these was Bishop Berning
of Osnabrück, Göring's appointee to the Prussian Council of State.
Already in June Ambassador Bergen in Rome had reported that the
"Bishop of Osnabrück, during his recent stay in Rome, showed a
gratifying understanding of the wishes of the Government and of
the needs of the new times."[48] At his inauguration as a member of
the Council Berning declared that the German bishops not only
accepted and recognized the new state but served it "with ardent
love and with all our strength." At the end of the festive opening of

the Council of State, Göring led three hurrahs (*Sieg-Heil*) for the Führer; the assembly, including Bishop Berning, with raised right arms sang the German and "Horst Wessel" hymns.[49]

The other bishop in good rapport with the Nazi regime was Archbishop Gröber. On October 9, addressing a meeting of Catholic organizations in Karlsruhe, Gröber declared amid great applause that he gave "his complete and wholehearted support to the new government and the new Reich."[50] As Cardinal Bertram a little earlier had written in a letter to Catholic students of theology, none should any longer doubt the sincerity of the Church in accepting and standing up for the new order.[51]

The episcopate, of course, was again to some extent merely mirroring the sentiments of large segments of German Catholicism, which after the successful conclusion of the Concordat with Rome were in a true state of euphoria. This was also the hour of the opportunists who excelled in discovering numerous affinities between National Socialism and Catholicism. A number of well-known Catholic scholars and theologians now sought to find a theoretical justification for the reconciliation of Church and State. The church historian, Professor Joseph Lortz, saw basic similarities between the Nazi and the Catholic *Weltanschauung*. Both were opposed to Bolshevism, liberalism, relativism, atheism and public immorality, and had in common the espousal of corporatist principles, return to the Germanic sources of the German people and the importance of faith as something grand and heroic.[52] The German Catholics, according to Lortz, were obligated in conscience to support National Socialism wholeheartedly, as it represented not merely the legal authority, but, to an overwhelming degree, Germany itself.[53]

Michael Schmaus, Professor of Dogmatic Theology at Münster, reminded his readers that the German bishops would not have revoked the ban on membership in the Nazi party if they had thought that Catholic and National Socialist ideas were in conflict. Whereas Catholic and liberal thinking could never be reconciled, Catholicism and National Socialism could and should march hand in hand. The new stress on authority in the state represented the counterpart in the natural sphere to the Church's authority in the supernatural realm.[54] Catholics had always regarded the fate of the people, anchored in blood and soil, as a manifestation of divine providence and for that reason they would also have to share "the just concern for maintaining the purity of the blood, the basis for the spiritual structure of the people."[55] Both of these books by Lortz and Schmaus appeared in a new series, *"Reich and Kirche,"* that was published with ecclesiastical permission and anounced the following aims:

> *Reich und Kirche* is a series that has the purpose of serving the building of the Third Reich by uniting the forces of the National Socialist state and Catholic Christianity. The series is motivated by the conviction that no basic conflict exists between the natural renaissance of our people to be witnessed today and the supernatural life of the Church. In fact, the restoration of the political order calls for its completion through the resources of religion. To awaken and deepen the understanding for this undertaking is perhaps the biggest spiritual task of contemporary German Catholicism, and its best contribution to the success of that great work of German renewal to which the Führer has summoned us. . . . Being entirely German and entirely Catholic, the series will examine and promote the relations and encounter between Catholicism and National Socialism and it will point the way toward the kind of fruitful co-operation that is outlined in the *Reichskonkordat*.[56]

The world-renowned theologian, Karl Adam of Tübingen, argued that not only were National Socialism and Catholicism not in conflict one with the other, but belonged together as nature and grace.[57] In Adolf Hitler Germany at last had found a true people's chancellor. "Now he stands before us, he whom the voices of our poets and sages have summoned, the liberator of the German genius. He has removed the blindfolds from our eyes and, through all political, economic, social and confessional covers, has enabled us to see and love again the one essential thing: our unity of blood, our German self, the *homo Germanus*."[58] Professor Theodor Brauer from Cologne stressed that the appreciation of national essence must also include the approval of racial purity. Catholics had to participate in the new Germany, even if at first they were given a cold shoulder.[59] The theologian, Karl Eschweiler of Braunsberg, pointed out that the National Socialist *Weltanschauung* and Catholic truth were not opposites and that the ideas which the bishops had condemned in earlier years did not constitute the official program of the Party.[60] When he went as far as to approve the compulsory sterilization law enacted on July 14, 1933, Eschweiler was suspended and barred from teaching until he submitted to censure by Rome. After his death in 1936 an obituary in Alfred Rosenberg's gazette called him a "martyr to the Roman system."[61]

A number of new periodicals, too, dedicated themselves to the task of reconciliation. The weekly *Zeit und Volk,* edited by Axel Emmerich (today writing under the name Edgar Alexander) and published by the Catholic firm, Kösel und Pustet, made its first appearance on July 20, 1933. Taking note of the de-politicizing of German Catholicism, the editor called upon Catholics to find new ways of participating in the building of Germany's future and to accept the new state out of inner conviction.[62] The monthly *Deutsches Volk* was similarly devoted to promoting the unity of will between Catholicism and National Socialism. Writing in its columns, Dr. Jakob Hommes pointed out that Catholics should find it easy to embrace the world of ideas of National Socialism, since Catholicism too was essentially conservative, opposed to individualism, liberalism, rationalism and materialism.[63]

There can be little doubt that these calls for ideological *Gleichschaltung* did much to facilitate the acceptance of National Socialism by the German Catholics. The fact that prominent men like Adam, Lortz and Schmaus aligned themselves with the new regime and movement was seen by many Catholics as proof that National Socialism, despite some superficial faults, could not really be so bad.[64] Furthermore, practically all these books and periodicals appeared with the approval of Church authorities and thus carried the stamp of orthodoxy.

Again reflecting the new climate of opinion came the reorganization of several pro-Nazi Catholic groups. Both Papen's *Kreuz und Adler* and Lossau's *Katholische Vereinigung für Nationale Politik* now disbanded, and a new *Arbeitsgemeinschaft Katholischer Deutscher* (AKD) was founded in early October, led by Papen and a number of veteran Catholic National Socialists. In addition to continuing to work for the mobilization of Catholics for the National Socialist cause, the group set itself the task of collecting complaints regarding the treatment of Catholics and taking care of the removal of difficulties in the relations between Church and State.

On October 3 the AKD was recognized and confirmed in this

function by Rudolf Hess, Hitler's deputy.[65] The same day Papen wrote to Cardinal Bertram informing him of the purposes of the new organization and asking for the support and co-operation of the episcopate.[66] Bertram replied that he could not obligate the remaining members of the episcopate, especially in view of the fact that the organization had been founded without prior consultation with the bishops. The Catholic associations already showed great zeal in mobilizing Catholics for the new Reich and he hoped that the AKD would not try to hinder their work. Negotiations about existing problems were also best carried out by way of direct contact of the bishops with the authorities.[67] When another member of the AKD made a second attempt a little later to obtain ecclesiastical approval (the *Placet*) for the AKD Bertram again answered in the negative, stating that the declared purpose of the organization made it appear as if only Catholics lacked the necessary patriotic consciousness.[68] The AKD, thereupon, had to be content with a recommendation from Archbishop Gröber, who welcomed the founding of the new organization as proof of the usefulness of Catholic men who had the ability to lead and were dedicated to the new Reich.[69]

Papen later recalled that some members of the episcopate viewed the founding of the AKD "with the most intense suspicion" and as an interference in their sphere. They also felt that after the conclusion of the Concordat the Vice-Chancellor had done nothing to achieve an implementation in keeping with the interests of the Church.[70] In this appraisal Papen was no doubt correct. Many bishops still looked unkindly upon Papen because of his feuding with the Center party in 1932; they also resented his attempt to play the mediator between Church and State. Bishop Bornewasser, on November 24, complained to Bertram that Papen's emissaries traveled from bishop to bishop and caused considerable confusion. "I believe the moment will come when the episcopate, acting in unity, must put the AKD in its place."[71]

There is no evidence, however, to indicate that the bishops were opposed to Papen because of his political views. Papen's frequent references in his speeches to the happy harmony between the corporatist principles of *Quadragesimo anno* and National Socialism, and his appeal to the Catholics' hostility to liberalism and Communism[72] differed in no important point from the public pronouncements of the hierarchy and lesser Catholic spokesmen. To cite an example of the latter, the Catholic journeymen's associations of Berlin were told by their president at an hour of commemoration in November that they must give proof of their ability to fight shoulder to shoulder with the movement that was building the new Reich. The similarities in the Papal encyclical *Quadragesimo anno* and the plans of the government of the Reich were pointed out and a swastika pennant was affixed to the banner of the assembled associations. Vicar Capitular Steinmann, leading the diocese of Berlin after the death of Bishop Schreiber, declared, "Gladly and joyously the Catholic journeymen's associations will follow the Führer and will use all their strength to build the Reich."[73]

On November 29, 1933, the former head of Catholic Action in Munich, Dr. Muhler, was arrested for allegedly having spread reports of atrocities (*Greuelnachrichten*) in the concentration camp at Dachau near Munich. The Bavarian nobleman Von Aretin, then a prisoner in Dachau and witness to numerous acts of torture and murder, recalls in his memoirs published after the war that the inmates heard of the arrest of Muhler and hoped that now the pulpits would perhaps take notice of the horrendous deeds of barbarism taking place under their very noses.[74] Cardinal Faulhaber, in a series of three Advent sermons, indeed sounded a more critical note. He protested against the threatening relapse into the paganism of the ancient Germanic tribes, defended the Old Testament and warned that "the individual must not be deprived of his own dignity . . . or treated as a slave without rights of his own."[75] But at the same time, the chancery of Passau forbade Catholic organizations to criticize the government or its measures and asked them to stress and cultivate love of fatherland and national solidarity.[76] In the other corner of Germany, at Bremen, Bishop Berning declared before a mass meeting of Catholics that the Führer had told him personally of his intention to build the state upon Christian foundations and the Bishop exhorted his audience to serve the new Germany with love.[77] At that moment this certainly was the more typical word to be heard from a Catholic bishop.

The situation at year's end was summed up in an article in the Jesuit monthly *Stimmen der Zeit*. The swastika had proven its creative potential, "the person of Hitler has become the symbol of the faith of the German nation in its existence and future." The speedy conclusion of the Concordat has demonstrated that hostility need not prevail between the swastika and the Christian cross. "On the contrary: the symbol of nature only finds its fulfillment and consummation in the symbol of grace."[78]

Vicar General Mayer of Mainz, a vocal opponent of Nazism before 1933, now offered to hold a Church burial for Peter Gemeinder, the Nazi *Gauleiter* of Hessen who had died in 1931 and, according to prevailing regulations, had been refused a Christian funeral. Information had been received, the Vicar General stated, that Gemeinder shortly before his death had asked for a priest. Mayer proposed that the grave be belatedly blessed and a special funeral service be held for the soul of the deceased to which the local branch of the NSDAP should be invited.[79] The Gemeinder case at the time had created a considerable sensation; the Church now apparently wanted to make amends. But the Nazis rejected the offer of peace. Gemeinder's widow replied that *Reichsstatthalter* Sprenger had ordered her to withhold her consent to the planned ceremony.[80] This little episode better than anything else characterizes the position in which the Church found herself at the close of the first year of Nazi rule.

Modus Vivendi II

Tribulations of 5
the Catholic Organizations and Press

One of the basic characteristics of totalitarian regimes is an insistence on the monolithic unity of their people. Only thus can the necessary enthusiasm be generated and the mobilization of all forces for the attainment of the regime's future goals be achieved. Not only rival political organizations, but public associations, whatever their nature—occupational, social, youth, cultural or religious—must either be dissolved or incorporated into the movement controlling the state. Their continued independent existence would threaten the unanimity which the totalitarian regime pursues passionately and relentlessly. Failure to destroy them would leave intact rival objects of allegiance and would provide a haven for dissent. Similarly, all media of mass communications—newspapers, periodicals, radio —must be deprived of their independence. Public opinion cannot be left unregulated, and the concept of a free marketplace of ideas must yield to the regimentation of the printed and spoken word.

Soon after the destruction of all existing non-Nazi political parties and trade unions, therefore, the National Socialists began to move against the extensive network of associations controlled by the Catholic Church, and against the press directly or indirectly under her sponsorship. The spiritual and lay leaders of the Church were as unprepared for this assault as they were for most other hostile measures of the Nazi regime and remained at a loss to understand why the Nazi state so obstinately refused to conform to the expected, traditional authoritarian mold. Catholic leaders were shocked to discover that the National Socialist regime insisted on liquidating not only the organizations of the Church's liberal, Socialist and Communist enemies, but also those of the Church herself. Amid continuing protestations of loyalty the Church fell back upon the Concordat with the Holy Sea. This line of defense at best was able merely to delay the inevitable.

1. The Demise of the Catholic Organizations

The Concordat had been signed and ratified with the future of the Church's non-religious organizations left unresolved. The disposition of this issue was urgent. Leading National Socialists kept insisting that the Catholic organizations were surreptitiously continuing to propagate the "political Catholicism" of the now-defunct Catholic parties and interfered with their public appearances. Several Catholic associations, on the other hand, upon the ascendancy of Catholic Nazi majorities, were disbanding "voluntarily." At the beginning of August 1933 the *Katholischer Lehrerverband* (Catholic Teachers' Association) declared itself dissolved and led its members into the National Socialist Teachers' League. Similarly, many of the Catholic fraternities were being taken over from within. On August 1 Cardinal Bertram once again alerted the episcopate to this danger and asked them to insist on the maintenance and independence of the Catholic organizations.[1]

The German government's violations of the Concordat, Ambassador Bergen reported in October, had greatly upset Pius XI. Several members of the German episcopate had recently been in Rome on their *ad limina* visits. "The bishops," Bergen wrote, "have now lodged more or less numerous and agitated complaints with the Pope and have asked for energetic redress of grievances; at the same time, however, they have suggested a temperate procedure. This is especially true of Cardinal Bertram and, contrary to expectations, also of the Bavarian bishops, despite their especially strong complaints." While Pope Pius XI was visibly disturbed by these reports,

Bergen added, his Secretary of State, Pacelli, was taking "a realistic attitude" and was trying to discourage the Pope from issuing a public protest.[2] Behind Pacelli stood his trusted advisor, Monsignor Kaas, who, in his own words, did his best "to counteract the opposition trying to block the path of the new Germany."[3]

On the evening of October 22 *Ministerialdirektor* Buttmann arrived in Rome to conduct the negotiations over the implementation of the Concordat, especially Article 31 and the list of the protected organizations. Prior to the opening of the talks, he was handed a *pro memoria* of the Vatican, enumerating the violations of the Concordat. The curbs imposed upon the Catholic associations here occupied a prominent place. The note expressed the hope that the German government would order a prompt and effective halt to these encroachments upon the rights of the Church. "The self-restraint which the Holy See has heretofore observed in public has caused the Catholic conscience both in Germany and in the rest of the world to reach, in part, conclusions and judgments which, while lacking objective foundations, cannot leave the Holy See indifferent in the interest of its dignity and the high moral authority of its world-encompassing mission." If these conditions were not corrected soon, the Holy See would have no choice but to make its censure public.[4]

The negotiations, attended also by Archbishop Gröber, lasted from October 23 to 28 without leading to any resolution of outstanding difficulties. It was agreed, however, that a prohibition of simultaneous (dual) membership in state and Catholic organizations was inadmissible. This question was of considerable importance in view of the rumored establishment of the Hitler Youth as an official organization, sponsored by the state, which all German youth would be required to join. Shortly after his appointment as Reich Youth Leader on June 17, 1933, Baldur von Schirach had issued an order prohibiting simultaneous membership in the Hitler Youth (H.J.) and the Catholic youth organizations.[5] In the event of the H.J. becoming a state organization, this ban on dual membership would clearly mean the end of the Catholic youth associations. In this connection Pacelli stressed that the Holy See could not agree to the legitimacy of changes in any provisions of the Concordat by unilateral legislation, albeit in the form of "laws applicable to all"

(Concordat, Article 1). Such an interpretation, Pacelli insisted, would make the entire Concordat meaningless.[6]

Vice-Chancellor Papen and his AKD, meanwhile, were trying to enlist suport for a plan to bring the Catholic youth organizations collectively into the Hitler Youth, where they would receive religious care by Catholic clergymen, specifically appointed for this purpose. Such an arrangement had been worked out in Italy in connection with the fascist boys' organization, the *Balilla*. Papen was able to obtain the consent of several bishops to this proposal, including Cardinal Schulte of Cologne and Archbishop Gröber of Freiburg.[7] Cardinal Faulhaber, too, was agreeable if the individuality of the Catholic youth organizations could be protected.[8] But other bishops considered this to be surrender. Cardinal Bertram, on November 22, informed the episcopate that the Bishop of Hildesheim had lodged strong objections to Papen's plan: "Is this not treason against our youth, which until now has held out bravely?" he had asked.[9]

The Fulda Bishops' Conference of May 1933 had decided to oppose the establishment of an officially sponsored, interdenominational youth organization that would encompass all young people and educate them according to its own *Weltanschauung*.[10] But much had changed since May. Several bishops apparently now thought that by accepting Papen's plan they could secure at least the right to pastoral care within the Hitler Youth. When Gröber submitted the idea to Rome, Pope Pius XI promptly and firmly rejected it. "At first," Bergen reported, "the Pope wanted to have Archbishop Gröber's letter on this subject returned unanswered."[11] As Bertram informed the episcopate a few days later, Gröber had been told by telephone that the Holy See regarded this question as governed by the Concordat; the Pope therefore could not allow direct negotiations of the bishops with the German government.[12] The episode shows how far some members of the episcopate were prepared to go in accommodating Catholicism to the Nazi movement. Later a modified version of Papen's plan was to be presented to the Holy See through official channels.

The implementation of the Concordat remained dormant until Buttmann returned to Rome in the second half of December. The German emissary informed Pacelli that he was not empowered to continue formal negotiations since the government of the Reich was about to abolish the self-government of the German states, the *Länder*. After this constitutional reform a new concordat would be necessary. The Papal Secretary of State, surprised and worried over this new turn of events, asked for assurances that the Reich would continue to honor the obligations assumed in the Concordat just concluded. This request, on the basis of telephoned instructions from Hitler, Buttmann answered evasively. In particular, no commitment could be given that a new concordat would ultimately be concluded. Concerning the Catholic organizations, Buttmann explained to Pacelli that many of them were led by men who for years had been hostile to National Socialism, and this caused friction. "In the interest of the Catholic Church itself," Buttmann declared, "I consider it preferable for you here to bring about a new leadership and to carry through the consolidation of Catholic organizations in four or five large groups, which, as I knew, Archbishop Gröber favored." Pacelli reserved judgment on this suggestion.[13]

The idea of declaring the Concordat obsolete, adumbrated here just a few months after its conclusion, was to be taken up by Hitler several times later. For various political reasons this step was never taken. If Hitler could have his way without explicitly renouncing a much-publicized treaty, there obviously was no reason for him to repudiate the Concordat and thus cast doubt upon the trustworthiness of his commitments. In a lengthy memorandum handed Pacelli on January 15 Foreign Minister Neurath assured the Holy See that the Reich was anxious to implement the Concordat. The government had no intention of starting a Kulturkampf, he said, but it had the right to expect more support from the Church in the fight against Communism than had so far been forthcoming. Episcopal pronouncements were encumbered with reservations and many of the younger clergy, especially in southern Germany, made no secret of their dislike of the regime. Some of the current difficulties were caused by the extensive concessions made by the government in the Concordat. "Thus, without the broad reach of Article 31 the attempt would not have been made to list and revive a number of Catholic organizations; it goes beyond all expectations . . . and cannot be brought into harmony with the basic idea of Article 31."[14] These words boded no good.

At the suggestion of Papen and Bergen, Hitler on February 7

received Cardinal Schulte, known as one of the most irenical figures of the German episcopate. The government probably thought to capitalize on the existing differences of opinion among the German bishops. The two-hour talk, in addition to purely local matters affecting the archdiocese of Cologne or touching the question of Rosenberg's agitation for a German Church, revolved mainly around the future of the Catholic organizations. Schulte suggested keeping Catholic Action decentralized and based on the dioceses instead of organizing it on an all-German plane. Hitler seemed agreeable. The absorption and eventual destruction of the Catholic organizations obviously would be much easier on the local level, where the Nazis' tactics of capturing associations from within had proved highly successful. Schulte told Counselor Menshausen the next day that nothing definite had been concluded but that the talk with Hitler constituted "a good beginning."[15]

The most pressing issue was the status of the Catholic youth organizations, for friction between them and the Hitler Youth was strong. In several provinces the Catholic youth had been forbidden to wear uniforms, undertake outings and engage in para-military physical training. These restrictions further weakened their appeal and caused many of their members to join the Hitler Youth. In several other instances Hitler Youth units had been formed in Church-administered institutions or seminaries with members of the regular clergy in positions of leadership. Vicar General Riemer of Passau stated, with reference to such a group in the Benedictine monastery Schweikelberg in Bavaria, that as long as fathers of the monastery stayed in control, the Church might be able to reconcile herself to this development.[16]

The German Youth leader, Baldur von Schirach, would have preferred undertaking a frontal assault or leaving the ban on double membership which he had imposed earlier. But after some prodding by Papen he agreed in principle to the inclusion of the Catholic youth organizations in the Hitler Youth. The Catholic members would be given the opportunity to fulfill their religious duties by attending Sunday services and would also be released one afternoon a week for religious education. The denominational organizations could continue to exist but would be restricted "to the purely religious area."[17] In effect, this plan provided for the possibility of dual membership in the Hitler Youth and the Catholic organizations. It received Hitler's approval in a conference attended by Bergen and Buttmann held on March 29. Hitler stressed that "he did not want any other concessions to be made regarding the other Catholic organizations."[18]

Buttmann submitted the new plan to Pacelli in Rome a few days later. The Holy See was wary of trusting Schirach, known as an ardent follower of Rosenberg. On April 20 Pacelli wrote Bertram of his failure to make any headway in his talks with Buttmann; in view of this the Holy See had no objection if the German episcopate now wanted to undertake direct negotiations with the government. The bishops should beware, however, of making undue concessions.[19]

Meanwhile, the pressure on the Catholic organizations was increased steadily. In March the Hitler Youth started a wide membership campaign that appealed to the members of the Catholic youth organizations to abandon their old leaders, opposed to true German unity, and to join the ranks of the National Socialist movement. On April 27 Robert Ley, head of the *Deutsche Arbeitsfront* (German Labor Front), followed the example of Von Schirach and imposed a ban on double membership. Henceforth, it was to be impossible to to be a member of both the Nazi labor organization (DAF) and the Catholic workers' or journeymen's associations. Since membership in the DAF was fast becoming a condition of employment, Ley's ruling in effect spelled the death of the affected Catholic organizations.

Several bishops promptly appealed Ley's edict to the Reich Chancellor. Bishop Galen wired Hitler on May 1 requesting him to withdraw the order "so as not to permit the exclusion from the German community of so many loyal German men dedicated to the task of reconstruction."[20] Here again the bishops chose to follow a self-contradictory policy. Essentially, they wanted the Catholics to be part of the Nazi state and movement while at the same time they wished to maintain the Church's organizations in order to perpetuate religious values and to counteract the Nazis' teaching of "positive Christianity." What the bishops had a hard time learning was that the Nazis would not admit them to their ranks except on terms that ruled out the perpetuation of denominational characteristics and organizational loyalties, and that demanded the acceptance of the Nazis' monopoly of indoctrination.

On May 3 Minister of the Interior Frick asked Bertram to designate a delegation in order to undertake direct negotiations over the implementation of Article 31 of the Concordat. The German episcopate, at their plenary conference at Fulda from June 5-7, thereupon elected Bishops Berning and Bares and Archbishop Gröber, perhaps thinking that negotiations undertaken by men like Berning and Gröber, friendly to and in the good graces of the Nazi regime, would promise good results. The Conference also decided upon the customary joint pastoral letter. Its content and tone indicate that the bishops were becoming worried over the stepped-up assaults of the Nazis. The pastoral letter protested against the spread of neo-pagan errors and against the attacks upon the Church and its organizations. "In the face of such dangers we bishops may not remain silent."[21] The episcopate reaffirmed their desire to participate in the work of rebuilding the life of the people on the basis of Christianity, but warned against the attempt to substitute a "positive Christianity," without belief in Jesus Christ, for the Christianity of Holy Scripture. The Catholic associations, it said, were not disguised political organizations and desired nothing but to be reliable members of Church and State.[22]

The negotiations of the three bishops in the Ministry of the Interior began on June 25. The government's side consisted of representatives from the Ministry of the Interior, the Ministry of Ecclesiastical Affairs, leaders of the S.A., the Labor Front and the Hitler Youth, the last being represented by Baldur von Schirach; and Buttmann was chairman. According to a memo of Counselor Menshausen, they "were harmonious throughout and both sides showed themselves sincerely desirous of reaching agreement."[23] On June 27 the delegates of the episcopate were received by Hitler. Bishop Berning thanked the Chancellor for granting them an audience and pointed out "that the bishops had fully accepted the new state and had directed the people to do likewise. But they were very much worried whether the Concordat would be implemented in all its provisions." Hitler answered that he expected the Church to refrain from any criticism of State and Party and from entering the political arena.[24] At the request of Bishop Berning, Hitler promised to issue a public statement to the effect that "both Government and Party were favorable and helpfully disposed towards the activities of the Catholic Church, in her own sphere, and that neither would have anything to do with the so-called 'third religion,' the German National Church, and similar movements opposed to Christianity."[25]

While the negotiations were continuing, Bishop Bares suggested to Cardinal Bertram that the reading and publication of the joint pastoral letter adopted on June 7 be postponed. Despite the fact that the letter limited itself to purely religious questions, it would probably be misunderstood and therefore could hamper the talks. Bishop Berning supported Bares' position, and on June 27 Bertram consequently cabled all members of the episcopate to defer reading, explaining the reasons in a letter that followed the same day.[26]

On June 29 the negotiations in Berlin reached agreement on the implementation of Article 31 of the Concordat. The concessions made by the Church were far-reaching. The Catholic sports and labor associations were to be incorporated into Catholic Action. As soon as possible, but definitely within a year, these organizations were to be disbanded and their members absorbed by the Church's lay apostolate. Leaders with a record of past political activity would be replaced. The Catholic youth organizations could continue to exist insofar as they confined themselves to the religious and moral education of their members. In order to eliminate incidents, the bishops would forbid camping and the wearing of uniforms for the summer of 1934. Associations having a purely religious, cultural or charitable purpose, operating in conjunction with Catholic Action, were to be protected, but their activity on a greater than diocesan scale required the permission of the government. After these provisions had been fully implemented, the Hitler Youth and the German Labor Front would lift their ban on dual membership. Hitler, in his capacity of Chancellor and supreme leader of the NSDAP, would issue a public declaration forbidding State and Party authorities to deprecate the Church or its teaching, and affirming their neutrality in matters of religion.[27]

Bishop Berning carried this draft agreement to Cardinal Bertram in order to obtain his formal approval. The government had regarded the three representatives of the hierarchy as fully empowered to conclude an agreement, and no objections were expected from Bertram's side.[28] But the senior of the German episco-

pate, probably aghast at the concessions made by the three negotiators, sent a copy of Bishop Berning's report on the talks not only
to the other German bishops, but also to the Holy See. The agreement that had finally been reached after months of unsuccessful
negotiations, thus once again hung suspended.

The Vatican took a grim view of the situation. Not only had
the delegates of the episcopate in effect surrendered the Catholic
occupational and sports organizations, and given up much of the
mode of operation of the others, thereby going far beyond the concessions already made in the Concordat. But one day after this
humiliating document had been negotiated, the bloody events of
June 30 had taken place. This massacre had claimed several prominent Catholic figures, such as Dr. Erich Klausener, the head of
Catholic Action in Berlin, and Adalbert Probst, the leader of the
Catholic sports organization. In violation of Catholic doctrine, their
bodies had been cremated and the ashes sent to their families.
Finally, on July 25, the Austrian Catholic Chancellor, Engelbert
Dollfuss, was murdered by Hitler's henchmen as part of an abortive
Nazi putsch. Ambassador Bergen reported a few days later from the
Vatican that the Pope was greatly upset over the killing of Klausener
and Probst, the execution of so many others without the benefit of
prior spiritual assistance and the murder of Dollfuss. Pope Pius,
Bergen wrote, therefore "at the moment is supposed to be little
inclined to enter into negotiations with the Reich government, and
he has resolutely refused to give his unconditional consent to [the
results of] the talks between the government of the Reich and the
episcopate, against which several German bishops already have
raised objections."[29]

Bishop Berning's report had been distributed to the episcopate
and their comment solicited. Most of them, it appears, opposed
ratification of the agreement. The events of June 30 undoubtedly
did not contribute to a friendly reception of the terms worked out
in Berlin. The government, moreover, had just forbidden the publication of the joint pastoral letter of June 7, and the Gestapo had
confiscated all copies of the still-unread pronouncement. This repressive measure contributed to the feeling of disenchantment on
the part of the bishops. In particular, many expressed the fear that
the accord would be worthless unless the Nazi party and its organs

were made more explicitly responsible for observing the agreement.[30] Bishop Galen suggested that if Hitler did not issue the promised order of pacification to State and Party authorities, the Church should condemn, as it had done in the case of the *Action Française,* the neopagan teachings that were jeopardizing the morals and faith of the German Catholics. Orders should then also be issued prohibiting participation and membership in organizations and meetings that involved danger of contact with these heresies. "Not all, but very many, German Catholics are today fully prepared to listen to the word of the Church and to obey it even at the cost of sacrifices."[31] This is the first instance on record when any member of the German episcopate contemplated a step that amounted to re-instituting the ban on membership in the Nazi party. Bishop Galen continued to belong to that group of bishops prepared to resort to more forthright measures, but this point of view, up to the very end of the Nazi regime, remained in the minority.

In Berlin, meanwhile, where the rejection of the accord by the Vatican and the episcopate was not yet known, snags had developed over the contemplated declaration that Hitler was supposed to make after the formal approval of the agreement. The Führer had disagreed with the wording proposed by Frick on July 7, and he had asked for changes. A new draft submitted on August 4 met Hitler's approval. The contemplated declaration forbade all disparaging remarks about the Church's institutions or doctrines. "The National Socialist State and the NSDAP are opposed to any interference in religious controversies. All State and Party administrative offices shall, in particular, refrain from proselytizing on behalf of any kind of religious movement."[32] But this statement was never made public. Early in September the Holy See communicated its rejection of the draft agreement worked out in the June negotiations.

Pacelli, in a note dated September 2, indicated that "the concessions so far made by the representatives of the German Reich Government in various essential matters are below the degree of religious freedom guaranteed by the text of the Concordat." The Holy See could not agree to the dissolution of the Catholic occupational organizations; the decision whether to retain or create a supra-diocesan, or national, organization for the constituent societies incorporated in Catholic Action was one to be made by the Church alone. Moreover, the government, and not the Hitler Youth or the Labor Front, should commit itself to lift the ban on dual membership. Opinions voiced by the representatives of the NSDAP in the course of the June negotiations anyway cast doubt upon the willingness of the Party to consider itself bound by agreements entered into by the government. Therefore more specific arrangements would have to be made to guarantee that the NSDAP would adhere to the Concordat and its accompanying agreements, and would cease to propagate anti-Christian neopaganism, as Rosenberg was continually advocating. The necessary modifications in the draft agreement, Pacelli proposed, should be worked out in new negotiations with members of the German hierarchy.[33]

Talks between the same negotiating teams as in the June discussions were resumed on September 14 and continued until September 20. The three bishops proposed that the Catholic youth organizations be allowed recreational activities such as gymnastics, swimming and hiking. They also argued that the occupational organizations be converted into sections of Catholic Action but should be allowed to maintain their identity. Both of these demands were turned down by Buttmann, who consulted Hitler on these revisions. "The Reich Chancellor had, however, expressly stated," the Embassy to the Holy See was informed, "that the Concordat and the provisions for its application were binding upon the Party too." Hitler still stood ready to issue the public declaration promised the representatives of the hierarchy in June.[34] The Embassy at the Vatican was instructed to tell Pacelli that the responsibility for the delay in reaching an early and final agreement lay with the Church, which had insisted on first consulting all members of the German hierarchy.[35]

Soon thereafter the Papal Secretary of State left for Buenos Aires to attend the Eucharistic Congress held there from October 10-15. During his absence from Rome, Ambassador Bergen was received by the Pope, who again expressed his concern about events in Germany. Bergen, in his report on the audience, suggested that no final agreement be concluded before Pacelli's return; "without his moderating influence the danger that, under certain circumstances, the Pope will take disastrous decisions is considerably increased."[36] But the negotiations, in any event, were deadlocked. New talks held in early November 1934 again failed to break the impasse, and the same fate befell informal consultations between Buttmann and Nuncio Orsenigo that started in December.

The situation in the final months of 1934 was somewhat less tense. The government wished to secure the votes of the predominantly Catholic population of the Saar for return to Germany, and therefore had relaxed the pressures. But few had illusions that this lull would last long. In a letter to Bishop Buchberger of Regensburg, Cardinal Faulhaber expressed the fear that after the plebiscite on January 15, 1935, the struggle would begin anew. In the absence of an agreement on Article 31 of the Concordat, Faulhaber held, the Catholic organizations were doomed to die a slow death.[37]

The negotiations on the status of the Catholic organizations collapsed formally at the end of January 1935. The Papal Nuncio was told on January 28 that "in accordance with the decision which the Führer and Chancellor had reached in the meantime, the Reich government was abiding by the outcome of the negotiations with the representatives of the German hierarchy, which were completed on June 29, 1934, and could make no further concessions on important points."[38] With the return of the Saar safely achieved the regime now could relinquish its conciliatory posture. The *Leipziger Neueste Nachrichten* on April 9 published a speech of Baldur von Schirach in which he threatened the Catholic youth organizations: "It will be decided in the coming weeks whether the Catholics will possess enough sense to give up on their own accord this cliquish and disloyal system of theirs or whether it will be necessary to use force."[39]

Pressure on the remaining members of the Catholic occupational associations was also renewed. On June 1 the archbishops of Munich and Bamberg directed a joint pastoral letter to the Catholic Workers' Associations in which they affirmed the willingness of the Catholic workers to support the great aim of the Führer to provide work for all, and demanded an end to the ban on dual membership. The German Labor Front (DAF), the two archbishops insisted, had no right to subject Catholic workers to economic disadvantages just because they wished to remain faithful to their Church and to their own organizations. These organizations were necessary to uphold Catholic social and religious teachings, especially since the DAF insisted on giving its members ideological indoctrination that was not free from neopaganism.[40]

In a widely publicized speech at the beginning of July Minister of Interior Frick leveled new and strong attacks upon the Catholic organizations. National Socialism, Frick declared on July 7, demanded that Germany's public life be liberated from the divisive denominational influences. "What is the sense in still having Catholic associations of civil servants? We do not want Catholic or Protestant civil servants, we want German civil servants." Similarly, the Catholic occupational and youth organizations were active in areas where the National Socialist state alone should have jurisdiction. These organizations no longer were compatible with the new times; they were threats to the *Volksgemeinschaft*.[41] On July 16 Göring, Minister President of Prussia, issued an edict against "political Catholicism" in which he announced that the Catholic youth organizations engaged in other than strictly religious activity would be suppressed.[42] A few days later police regulations issued first in Prussia and Bavaria, but soon extended to the entire Reich, put into official decrees what Schirach had long demanded. The Catholic youth organizations were forbidden to engage in any activity not of a purely religious nature and were enjoined from wearing uniforms or insignia.[43] These ordinances were accompanied by a vigorous press campaign that accused the Catholic youth organizations of being in league with seditious Communist elements.

On August 20 the German episcopate met in plenary conference at Fulda. The serious situation of the Catholic organizations held the center of the discussions. A long and detailed memorandum had been submitted to the Bishops' Conference by representatives of all the Catholic associations, who described their tribulations and demanded more forceful support from the hierarchy. The Catholic organizations, the memo declared, refrained from any political or subversive activity, and they were fully prepared to serve the German fatherland and the National Socialist state. The bishops should indicate publicly that they stood behind the organizations and regarded their suffering as the suffering of the Church. All too frequently, the memo complained, highly placed churchmen minimized the importance of the Catholic associations. It had even happened that the Church disowned a suppressed society or an arrested leader with the argument: He has been too daring, he should have given in; the organizations are not synonymous with the Church. More forthright support would probably not be able to change the course of the regime, but that was not the main issue. Unless the leaders knew that the Church wanted them to go on existing and struggling, they could not carry on with their difficult task. What is intolerable, the memo stressed emphatically, is "the martyrdom without mandate."[44]

The Bishops' Conference thereupon issued a special pastoral letter addressed to the Catholic organizations, reaffirming the support of the episcopate. "We have gladly received the solemn declaration of the leaders of the Catholic associations that as always they serve the German people and fatherland with self-sacrificing courage and fidelity," the bishops stated. We are pleased "that they reject all subversive attitudes and conduct, refrain from any political activity and especially will resolutely repel all attempted approaches of Communism." Given these conditions, the provisions of the Concordat were fulfilled and the Catholic organizations entitled to the protection of the state. The bishops expressed the hope that the leaders, lay or clerical, would continue their important work "in full loyalty to Church and State."[45] In the joint pastoral letter adopted by the Conference the faithful were exhorted to continue to support the Catholic associations. The bishops again stressed that the organizations of the Church were sincerely patriotic and willing to do their civic duties. "Catholics do not stage revolts and do not offer violent resistance."[46]

On June 7 Cardinal Schulte of Cologne had suggested to Bertram that the three German cardinals turn directly to Hitler and submit to him a detailed memorandum that would set forth their grievances and ask for redress. A draft composed by Bishop Galen of Münster was enclosed.[47] Bishop Berning, after a meeting with Frick, also favored this step. The Minister of the Interior had told him that only the direct intervention of the Führer could bring about a change in the situation.[48] Such a memorandum was approved by the Fulda Bishops' Conference in August and, signed by all the participants, sent to Hitler on August 23 by Cardinal Faulhaber. Here, again, the episcopate pleaded for the Catholic organizations that were faced with annihilation in clear violation of the Concordat. "We bishops, under whose supervision the Catholic organizations operate, guarantee that these organizations do not cultivate political tendencies, or yet, which would be madness, tendencies hostile to the present regime." With the State ruled by an authoritarian government rather than by political parties, the bishops conceded, political education was no longer necessary. More than 95 per cent of the members of the Catholic workers' associations already belonged to the German Labor Front. But the co-operation of Catholics seemed of no avail. Could the state not silence those elements in the movement hostile to the Church, the bishops asked? The continuation of the ban on dual membership and the recurring attacks could only mean the death of the Catholic organizations even before the negotiations on Article 31 of the Concordat were resumed.[49]

The newly appointed Minister of Ecclesiastical Affairs, Hanns Kerrl, on September 9, 1935, proposed to the German bishops that they submit a new list of organizations desiring protection under the Concordat.[50] Such a list was prepared by Bishop Berning and, after approval by the other bishops, sent to Berlin. In a letter to Kerrl, Bertram expressed the hope that new negotiations would finally solve the thorny problem. "The state has every reason," he declared, "to consider these organizations as valuable assistants in the task of providing culture and education for the people and as helpers in the defense against Bolshevism and Communism by developing the resources of religious character education."[51] These negotiations were undertaken by Kerrl and several of his officials and Bishops Berning and Preysing (the new Bishop of Berlin). At a later stage a representative of the Ministry of the Interior and Archbishop Hauck of Bamberg also attended. But the results were as fruitless as those of the earlier negotiations.

A special conference of the German episcopate was called for January 1936, amid increasing pressure on Catholics to join the Nazi organizations and stepped-up anti-Catholic propaganda, especially in the Hitler Youth. The Bishops decided to inform the Ministry of Ecclesiastical Affairs that in view of the present attitude of the H.J. leadership and because of the anti-Christian propaganda conducted in the meetings of the H.J., the episcopate could not recommend to the faithful to send their children to the Hitler Youth.[52] But it soon became clear that the Church could not hold this line. The pressures brought to bear upon children and parents were too great. The episcopate, therefore, confined itself to warning

the parents not to entrust their children to those leaders of the
H.J. who were actively hostile to the Church.[53] A special pastoral
letter of the German bishops issued in May and directed to Catholic
youth asked them to leave organizations in which their faith was
being threatened.[54] The conflict reached a climax in the decree of
December 1, 1936, providing for the organization of the entire youth
of Germany in the Hitler Youth—from now on an official organization sponsored by the State.

The end of the Catholic organizations was near. Early in 1937
new talks were held in Berlin with representatives of the Hitler
Youth in order to obtain a lifting of the ban on dual membership,
but these were unsuccessful. Pope Pius XI, in his encyclical *Mit
brennender Sorge* of March 14, to which we will return in more
detail later, demanded that the national youth association organized
by the state "be cleansed from all activities hostile in spirit to
Christian faith and to the Church." Only then could Catholic
parents "give the state what is demanded from them in the name
of the state without taking from God what belongs to God. No
one," Pope Pius went on, "has any idea of putting stumbling blocks
[in the way of] leading German Youth to the realization of true
national unity, to the fostering of a noble love of liberty and steadfast loyalty to their country." The Church could not reconcile herself to the "systematically inspired opposition set up between these
educational aims and the aims of religion."[55] But the Nazis had no
intention of allowing the Catholics to support National Socialist
"educational aims" *qua* Catholics. On June 18 the Reich Youth
leader reaffirmed the ban on dual membership; since by this time
membership in the Hitler Youth was in fact, if not yet legally,
compulsory, this order spelled the death of the Catholic youth
associations.

All through the year 1937, meanwhile, Catholic organizations
were being dissolved locally and regionally. The Catholic Young
Men's Association was suppressed in the dioceses of Breslau, Paderborn, Trier and Münster. Bishop Galen, in the course of a sermon
delivered in November, protested against this dissolution and against
the fact that "a decree of February 28, 1933, of the late President
Hindenburg, designed to meet Communist activities, is invoked in
order to destroy Catholic associations. It is a perverse and wanton

insult to German Catholics and their priests and bishops. It is a flagrant injustice to the leaders and members of our Youth Associations, who with untiring selflessness have successfully aimed at one thing only: to lead the youth of Germany to fidelity to Christ and to love of their Fatherland. . . ."[56] When in January 1938 the Gestapo in Bavaria suppressed the Catholic Young Men's Association, the secondary school fraternity *Neudeutschland,* and the young ladies' sodalities, Cardinal Faulhaber protested against these repressive acts, the confiscations of property and the violation of the Concordat. "We reserve the right," Faulhaber declared in the name of the Bavarian bishops, "to submit specific instances, provable legally, that point up the, in part, rather strange methods by which, in a state based on the rule of law, this order was put into effect."[57] A joint pastoral letter of the Bavarian episcopate, read on February 6, insisted that Catholics were not Communists, but Christians, and had always promoted the well-being of their country. "We do not harm the state but support it." As far as the sodalities of the Blessed Virgin Mary are concerned, the pastoral letter stated, they continue in their existence ecclesiastically and with all ecclesiastical rights, favors and indulgences.[58]

The year 1938 saw the dissolution of the Catholic students' associations throughout Germany. On October 4 Minister of the Interior Frick forbade teachers and civil servants to belong to "confessional organizations." Practically all of the Catholic journeymen's associations at that point had already lost their houses and property. On February 6, 1939, the Young Men's Association was dissolved nationally. By the time the war broke out in September the Nazi State had succeeded in fully destroying the once so powerful network of Catholic organizations.

An uneven contest had come to an end. The Nazis had gone about their work gradually but methodically. They had utilized defamation, intimidation, economic reprisals and outright force as soon as they deemed public opinion sufficiently prepared. It is clear that the Church could not prevail in this fight; the existence of the Concordat perhaps delayed matters but in the long run it could not protect the Catholic organizations against the assaults of a powerful state. But if the Church thus stood little chance of winning, no matter what her tactics, it certainly doomed all likelihood of successful resistance by her constant affirmation of loyalty to the regime. The rank and file of the Catholic organizations were ill-prepared for battle with the Nazi state and movement, which the Church hierarchy, apart from certain un-Christian ideological aberrations, regarded as perfectly acceptable partners.

Time and again the bishops indicated that they would permit organized Catholicism to become a closely related part of the Nazi movement if only the regime would halt its anti-Catholic agitation. They supported or acquiesced in the destruction of all anti-Nazi organizations and they had no objections in principle to the monopoly of the Nazi movement in state and society. A National Socialist state maintaining the same attitude to the Church as Mussolini's Fascist Italy—live-and-let-live—would have suited them. Their actions and attitudes demonstrate, again, that the bishops failed to grasp the basic fact that it was of the essence of Nazi totalitarianism to eliminate from public life entirely the influence of the churches. Many of the declarations of loyalty that abound in the appeals of the Church to the government were clearly rhetoric in the language of the Third Reich, inserted for tactical reasons. But for every one in this category is another in which the ultra-nationalistic sentiment was sincerely felt. Equipped, or better perhaps, burdened with such a mental arsenal the Church indeed was no match for the Nazi State.

2. The Gleichschaltung of the Catholic Press

German Catholicism entered the Third Reich supported by a strong array of daily newspapers, weeklies and periodicals of all kinds. The number of dailies alone exceeded 400, as against 120 for the National Socialists. But with the help of the "Decree for the Protection of People and State" of February 28, 1933, the Nazis soon began to redress the balance. During the electoral campaign in February and following the elections in March, many Catholic dailies were forbidden publication for several days at a time, and pressure was soon brought to bear upon the others to conform to the political line of the new regime. With the use of threats the Nazis also prevailed upon many Catholics to cancel their subscriptions to a Catholic daily and to buy the Nazi paper instead.

This tactic further weakened the Catholic press. The plenary conference of the German bishops at Fulda in late August 1933 concluded: "If the persecution and suppression of the Catholic press continues unhindered as in the last few weeks, the German Catholic press will soon have ceased to exist."[59]

But the danger to the continued existence of a Catholic press— that is, a press dedicated to the defence of the prerogatives of the Church—did not stem from Nazi pressure alone. Influential Catholic newspapers like the *Augsburger Postzeitung, Badischer Beobachter* and others shared in the new groundswell of optimism and opportunism, and soon began to pursue a strictly pro-Nazi course. The *Germania* in Berlin, since 1871 the chief organ of the Center party, under the new editorship of Emil Ritter turned about-face from being a mainstay of the Church to supporting the AKD of Vice-Chancellor Papen. On June 27 the *Katholischer Pressverein für Bayern* (Catholic Newspapers' Association of Bavaria) adopted a new set of guidelines that called for the support of "the policy of national liberation by the present government, the strengthening of the authority of the state, . . . the struggle against Liberalism, Marxism and above all Bolshevism and for a peaceful understanding between Church and State."[60] A press under the shadow of such a pledge to the new masters of the state would avail the Church but little in an hour of crisis.

The process of enforced *Gleichschaltung* picked up momentum during the summer of 1933. Pressure on the publishers led to the discharge from the editorial and news staff of all Jews, Marxists or others deemed politically unreliable, and to the appointment of Nazis to positions of influence and control. The legal ratification of this purge came on October 4 with the promulgation of the *Schriftleitergesetz* (Law Concerning Editors). Journalism now became a "public vocation" regulated by law. Editors had to meet a number of qualifications, including Aryan descent and the ability to influence public opinion. The decision on whether an editor met all the requirements was to be made by the *Reichspressekammer* (National Chamber of the Press) in Goebbels' Propaganda Ministry. Editors were obligated to keep out of the newspapers anything liable to weaken the German Reich or to serve selfish interests.[61] The new law covered newspapers and political periodicals exclusive of those published under official auspices.

With the appointment and continuation of all editors subject to Goebbels' veto, the independence of the Catholic daily press was effectively destroyed. Like the other German dailies, they were already operating under censorship and were required to print articles and editorials prepared by the Propaganda Ministry. When the *Augsburger Postzeitung*, following instructions, published articles defending the compulsory sterilization law but was forbidden to print the warnings of the episcopate against this legislation, the Vatican protested. Pacelli insisted that he was not concerned with measures aiming at the political uniformity of the press in matters exclusively within the jurisdiction of the state, but with "that lack of freedom that hinders the deployment of the Church's religious mission."[62] Accompanied by such tacit acceptance of the regime's totalitarian aspirations, Pacelli's memorandum failed to impress the Nazis.

A new ordinance issued on April 24, 1935, doomed those Catholic daily newspapers still in existence: no paper from now on was allowed to print articles with a religious content. Support and promotion of a newspaper by a religious group was of itself proof of "lack of independence" and punishable by suppression. A statement issued by Max Amann, president of the *Reichspressekammer*, pointed out that the Catholic Church no longer needed a "Catholic press," since the government of the Reich now protected the Church.[63]

Cardinal Bertram promptly protested in the name of the episcopate. The new Reich, he argued—if indeed it was to be based on a "viable positive Christianity" and continue to be helped by the Catholic Church, "an important agent for the building of the new state and for the preservation of the German nationality"— needed a Catholic daily press. The implementation of the new order would make it impossible for the Catholic papers to ward off the recurring attacks of anti-Christian circles, would make them lose their Catholic subscribers and soon lead to their bankruptcy. Unless the ordinance was revoked or changed, Bertram threatened, the episcopate would have to inform the faithful of this grave threat to the freedom of the Church to propagate her teachings.[64] When this intervention proved futile, the bishops in their joint pastoral letter of August 22 made their grievance public: "The freedom of the press, as we note with regret, is restricted to such an extent that the formerly Catholic newspapers may no longer publish religious articles and at times are forced to print articles which hurt the Catholic reader."[65]

From 1935 there no longer existed a Catholic daily press. Deprived of their religious character, these newspapers could not successfully compete with the other dailies. Many ceased publication entirely; others continued, but were no longer distinguishable from the rest of the press that in unison sang the praise of the Third Reich. But the Church still had her diocesan papers, and the struggle over these lasted longer. The more direct control of the episcopate over the Sunday weeklies proved of value and made possible greater unity of hierarchical action.

The *Schriftleitergesetz* of October 1933 had provided for the screening of the editors of all newspapers and political periodicals by the *Reichspressekammer*. The question whether the Catholic Sunday papers and the Catholic periodical journals were to be regarded as political in character, and thus subject to the new press law, was the topic of negotiations with representatives of the Propaganda Ministry in the fall of 1933. These talks were conducted by Bishop Bares of Hildesheim (later Berlin) and Walter Adolph, editor-in-chief of the diocesan paper of Berlin, and ended with the exemption of the diocesan weeklies published under the auspices of the bishops. At the same time, the president of the Press Chamber ordered the establishment of a special division within the *Reichspressekammer* to be called *Fachschaft der katholisch-kirchlichen Presse*. On December 16 Vicar Capitular Steinmann of Berlin informed the publishers and editors of the Catholic weeklies and periodicals of the creation of the division and asked them to register.[66] Joining the *Fachschaft* meant automatic membership in the Chamber of Culture, which in turn was the precondition of any journalistic activity in the Third Reich. As head of the *Fachschaft* Amann confirmed Walter Adolph. This appointment brought about the unique situation of a Catholic clergyman heading a division of Goebbels' *Reichspressekammer*.

After the Propaganda Ministry had agreed to waive the requirements of the *Schriftleitergesetz* for the diocesan Sunday papers, Cardinal Bertram asked that the same privilege be extended to the Catholic theological journals and the press of the Catholic organizations. These periodicals, he argued, were also official and subject to the Church authorities. "We strive to obtain for these ecclesiastical journals not the individualistic-liberal freedom of the press; the episcopate has always regarded them as bearers of public, religious tasks fulfilled in the name of the Church."[67] The Ministry agreed to consider the waiving of some of the technical requirements of the press law for the editors of these papers, but refused to exempt them from registration and screening.[68] For a while, nevertheless, these journals continued to function relatively undisturbed.

The Catholic weeklies and the rest of the periodical press benefited from the suppression of the Catholic dailies and were able to expand their circulation. In May 1936 there were 416 such journals; their combined circulation had increased from 9,651,868 in the first quarter of 1933 to 11,437,925 in the second quarter of 1935. The 84 diocesan Sunday papers alone had around 3,000,000 subscribers.[69] An editorial in one of the largest of these, the *Münchener Katholische Kirchenzeitung,* noted in April 1935 that the situation of the diocesan weeklies in the new state was quite advantageous. It goes without saying, the paper stressed, that this position is made use of only with "the staunchest—typically Catholic —fulfilment of duties not only toward the Church but also toward the fatherland."[70] The price was met. Like the episcopate, under whose direct supervision the diocesan papers were published, most of the editors saw no reason to take issue with the policies of the Third Reich except for religious questions involving Rosenberg and the neo-pagan movement. But soon even this criticism was to be curtailed. An order of Amann issued in July 1935 forbade the Catholic periodical press to touch upon political issues or local news.[71] The head of the *Fachschaft,* Walter Adolph, interpreted this order as not ruling out the discussion of religious topics,[72] but the local Gestapo authorities took an increasingly dim view of these polemics. In August 1935 the *Kirchenblatt* of Münster, for example, was put under prior censorship and the same fate befell the *Münchener Katholische Kirchenzeitung* in November. This meant that the text of each issue had to be submitted and cleared by the Gestapo before printing or distribution. The head of the Munich police recorded two months later that the order had had a salutary effect.[73]

In other instances individual issues of Catholic periodicals were confiscated. In January 1936 the organ of the Catholic youth movement, *Michael,* was suppressed completely for lack of sufficient National Socialist conviction. In vain did Walter Adolph argue that while the Catholic press did assume a positive attitude to the National Socialist state, it could not adopt the same position with regard to all aspects of the National Socialist *Weltanschauung.*[74] When these various measures failed to force the Catholic papers into line, Goebbels directed the president of the *Reichspressekammer* to revoke exemption from the *Schriftleitergesetz* in all instances where the weeklies intruded upon the "political arena."[75] In a lengthy set of directives Amann thereupon asked the *Fachschaft* to enforce, effective April 1, 1936, the non-political character of the Catholic periodical press. The papers, in text and advertisements, should limit themselves very strictly to the religious area without, however, engaging in polemics on controversial questions. The continuation of such polemics threatened national unity and created a hostile mood against Party and State.[76]

The net was being tightened. On February 20 Adolph was told that all of the existing papers would have to register and comply with the provisions of the *Schriftleitergesetz.* Cardinal Bertram and Bishop Preysing protested this ruling and tried to obtain a stay of Amann's order.[77] On March 23 Bertram informed the episcopate of the serious situation that had arisen. Compliance with the order would mean the increasing subordination of the Catholic papers to outside direction. Bertram then posed the question, soon to become the crucial dilemma facing the Church, whether the bishops wanted to forego the continued appearance of these papers or comply with the law in order to preserve the papers' help in pastoral care. In the latter case, Bertram pointed out, they would have to accept all results following from this act of submission.[78]

Walter Adolph, the Catholic head of the *Fachschaft,* was caught in the very middle of this dispute. But before the ambiguity of his position could create a serious problem for him personally or for the Church he was dismissed. On July 1 Amann informed Adolph that he had decided to replace him with a person more in tune with the aims of the *Reichspressekammer.*[79] Amann's choice was Anton Willi, a trusted Nazi and S.S. leader. Bishop Preysing promptly protested Adolph's dismissal to Goebbels but the latter brushed it aside. The change had become necessary, Goebbels pointed out, on account of the conflict of duties necessarily encountered by a cleric in an official position of this nature.[80] The Church now faced Goebbels' machine for regimentation without a shield.

One of Willi's first orders provided that each diocese could now have only one diocesan paper. The bishops were asked to inform the *Fachschaft* which paper had been designated as the official *Bistumsblatt*.[81] Most of them complied, though some did so under protest. The Fulda Bishops' Conference in August discussed the new situation. Willi's order meant that more than two-thirds of the existing weeklies would go out of existence. The remaining ones were now subject to the *Schriftleitergesetz,* and their editors would probably have to be replaced by laymen acceptable to Goebbels. It was therefore decided not to recognize the binding character of the press law for the Catholic periodical press and to forbid the clerical editors (about two-thirds of the editors belonged to the clergy) to register under it.[82]

Cardinal Bertram once more petitioned Goebbels to revoke the restrictive orders concerning content, number and editorship of the periodical press. The demand to relate all contributions to the purely religious sphere, Bertram argued, meant an unnatural separation between religion and life, and denied an essential contact with the reader. Subjection of the Church's teaching through the printed word to an outside agency was a violation of one of the Church's most important liberties.[83]

The Nazis in turn not only failed to heed these appeals, but decreed further restrictive measures. On October 1 the Minister of Ecclesiastical Affairs forbade publication of pastoral letters in the diocesan weeklies or in any other form but the official gazettes distributed to the clergy. Many of these pastoral letters, Kerrl stated, had expressed criticism of measures of State and Party and this could not be tolerated.[84] The bishops again protested. Cardinal Bertram insisted that no pastoral letter of the episcopate had criticized the State, the movement or the Führer. The bishops had merely attempted to protect the integrity of the Church and her teachings.[85] Meanwhile the *Fachschaft* was putting pressure on the Catholic press to comply with the provisions of the press law.

The German episcopate meeting at Fulda on January 12, 1937, decided upon one last gamble. The Conference reaffirmed the decision of the previous year not to comply with the *Schriftleitergesetz.* Should the Catholic periodical press be forced under the law, the bishops would order the Catholic press to cease, and inform the faithful of the reasons for this step.[86] The decision was communicated to Goebbels in the hope that the threat of closing down more than 400 Catholic weeklies and periodicals would lead to the revocation of the order in question. This strategy failed. On March 30 Bertram informed the episcopate that Goebbels had refused to reconsider. The decision to quit rather than publish under outside control had been meant as a threat. Now that the bluff had been called, Bertram counseled retreat and compliance with the law. Before carrying out the January decision, he wrote, one would have to see whether in concrete cases the authorities would indeed "pose intolerable demands for the journals or their editors."[87]

Some of the bishops were willing to face the possibility of a shutdown. When in February 1937 the *Katholische Kirchenblatt für die Stadt Münster* was ordered by the regional office of the Propaganda Ministry to print an article describing a Catholic secondary schoolboy accused of serious sexual offenses as a leader of Catholic youth, Bishop Galen refused to comply. The Gestapo, thereupon, forbade the diocesan weekly to appear until such time as it obeyed the order of the Propaganda Ministry. Galen did not yield. He explained to the clergy that since these compulsory texts had to be printed without the possibilty of indicating their true authorship, the readers of the paper might falsely assume that this article carried the approval of the Church authorities. "Such a deception of the Catholics I cannot permit."[88] After waiting three months the Gestapo countered by suppressing the paper for good.

Not all the bishops were willing to pay this price for adherence to principle. The case of the *Martinus-Blatt,* the official weekly for the diocese of Mainz, was one of many where Church authorities opted for continued publication even if it meant submitting to conditions set by Goebbels' Propaganda Ministry. During the summer of 1937 the clerical editor of the *Martinus-Blatt,* Father Mertens, in accordance with the requirements of the press law, had applied for confirmation as editor. While his application was pending the paper was being edited by the publisher and by another Catholic layman. Father Mertens was supposed to serve, pending his approval as editor, as theological consultant and representative of the diocesan chancery, but the two temporary editors ignored him completely. Mertens complained to the Vicar General of Mainz about the opportunistic line of the publisher and his helper, and he argued that the paper should speak up on matters that simply cried for comment.[89] In November Mertens was informed that his application for confirmation as editor had been turned down, and he was forbidden to work on the paper. After the publisher had appointed a lay Catholic acceptable to the Nazis as editor, Mertens pointed out to the Vicar General that the new editor was not a theologian and therefore could not guarantee the orthodoxy of the paper, published as the official organ of the diocese. He suggested that the publisher be deprived of the right to use the subtitle "Diocesan Paper for the Bishopric of Mainz." This was necessary, he urged, "in order to prevent the deception of the Catholic people."[90] But the Church authorities did not follow his advice, the Chancery appointing a less strong-minded theological consultant.

Martinus-Blatt had a readership of nearly half a million readers. There can be little doubt that many of them were confirmed in their support of the Hitler regime by receiving guidance from a paper published under official Church auspices but actually edited by Catholics complying with the directives of the Propaganda Ministry. To give just one example: On the occasion of Hitler's fiftieth birthday in 1939 the *Martinus-Blatt* thanked and congratulated the "beloved Führer and Reich Chancellor, the powerful inspirer, preserver and protector of the Greater German fatherland created by him." On the same page there was printed a proclamation of special prayers for the Führer and fatherland by the Bishop of Mainz for the same occasion.[91] How in such circumstances could even those readers who knew of the new editorship distinguish between ordered rhetoric and conduct expected of them by their bishop? Certainly the simple man in the street would have to deduce that the Führer, praised by Church and State alike, was indeed a blessing for Germany.

The deceptive results of the tactics used to keep a Catholic paper alive were compounded in those instances where priests remained responsible editors of the diocesan papers. The faithful readers then could see even less reason to doubt the authoritative character of the pronouncements. Clerical editors continued to function, for example, in the case of the weeklies published by the archdioceses of Breslau and Cologne, confirmed as editors under the press law. The *Passauer Bistumsblatt,* owned and published by the Bishopric of Passau and carrying the designation "Journal of Information of the Episcopal See," was another diocesan paper edited by a priest from the first to the last day. The *Passauer Bistumsblatt* fully complied with all directives of the authorities and, especially after the outbreak of the war, became in effect, "a captive auxiliary of the Goebbels propaganda ministry," as Gordon Zahn has aptly characterized the function of these papers.[92] The assurances given to this author by Dr. Emil Janik, the former and present editor of the *Passauer Bistumsblatt,* that he printed articles of patriotic content but no National Socialist propaganda[93] are not supported by fact unless one chooses to regard exhortations to pray for the Führer and to give him unflinching support in war and peace as signs of mere patriotism.

The assertion of Altmeyer, a Catholic expert in this subject, that from July 1, 1936, on the Catholic periodical press cannot be considered to have had official ecclesiastical status, is plainly incorrect in cases like the *Passauer Bistumsblatt.* At best it represents a half-truth in all those other instances where, as in the case of the *Martinus-Blatt,* the bishops continued to let these weeklies appear under the designation "Diocesan Paper."[94] The Catholic readers continued to regard these papers as representing the voice of their Church. Even those who suspected or knew that some of the articles were printed on orders of the Nazis had to conclude that since the bishops allowed these materials to be published in papers called "diocesan," the Church did not regard this propaganda as offensive to or in violation of Catholic doctrine. If the Church wanted to be rid of responsibility for content of these papers it had only to deprive them of the right to use the masthead "Diocesan Paper." The impression of full identity between Catholic press and hierarchy was further strengthened by the fact that the difference between the pronouncements of the bishops and the content of the diocesan papers was one of degree, not substance.

When Bishop Preysing reported on the condition of the Catholic press to the Fulda Bishops' Conference of August 1938, he observed that many publishers and editors were giving in to the pressures exerted by the authorities, who wanted the Catholic papers to strengthen the National Socialist state and ideology from the religious side. Other editors, he went on, fearful of their livelihood, put their papers at the service of the Nazis to a far greater extent than that actually demanded. Such papers, Preysing warned, were increasingly likely to confuse and deceive the Catholics. Therefore, he contended, it would soon become necessary to explain to the faithful the true state of affairs.[95] This suggestion was never implemented. Apart from general statements to the effect that the Catholic press was hindered in its free functioning, most Catholics never were enlightened concretely.

Catholic papers that did not display sufficient co-operation were suppressed. Bishop Preysing's own diocesan weekly, for example, was proscribed in September 1938, and the same fate met many others during the course of the years 1938 and 1939. Other papers had to cease publication, since the restrictions imposed on their advertising and content had made them no longer economically viable, or because of insufficient allocation of paper. From January 1, 1934, to October 19, 1939, the number of Catholic weeklies and other periodicals decreased from 435 to 124, or by more than 71 per cent. Seventy-four of these papers were suppressed, 61 ceased for various other reasons and 176 died because of lack of newsprint.[96]

Those papers that stayed alive paid a high price in conformity. When the *Passauer Bistumsblatt* in April 1939 was reprimanded by the *Fachschaft* for showing insufficient patriotic zeal, Vicar General Riemer enumerated the articles which the paper had published on occasions like Hitler's birthday, the annexations of Memel and Bohemia or the day of the National Socialist accession to power. These articles, Riemer wrote Amann in a letter signed with "Heil Hitler," "better than words should convince the *Reichspressekammer* of our positive attitude to the State."[97] Father Muckermann, in his weekly *Der Deutsche Weg* appearing in Holland, as early as April 1936, had called the Catholic press in the Third Reich a "disgusting instrumentality of the lie."[98]

With the outbreak of the war, the pressure to serve the needs of the National Socialist propaganda machine increased manifoldly and the Catholic press, now even more than before, became one of the forces sustaining the Nazi regime. A directive issued in September 1939 by Willi, the head of the *Fachschaft,* reminded the publishers and editors of the Catholic press that from then on all items published had to have one purpose and one aim only: "to increase the power of resistance and the readiness to make sacrifices of our people to the highest possible degree." Every article should strengthen "the belief in the ultimate victory of Germany."[99]

The Catholic press remaining in existence complied fully and, as this author concludes, willingly. What was demanded here by the state authorities did not differ materially from what the bishops in their pastoral pronouncements were exhorting the faithful to do; that is, to muster all forces in defense and service of the fatherland. The Catholic press, like the rest of the German press, now stood under prior censorship, and the regional offices of the Propaganda Ministry even more frequently than in earlier years were telling them what to stress and what to omit. But apart from these general directives the papers were left free to choose the appropriate way in which to comply. The Nazis knew that prescribed texts would reveal all too clearly the hand of the censor and they preferred to let the papers say what they wanted them to say in the editors' own words.

As far as the Catholic press was concerned this method worked well, and the Catholic papers, as we shall see again in a later chapter, displayed patriotic enthusiasm and wholehearted support of the war effort. Only occasional reminders to use the appropriate tone and language were necessary. The propaganda office for the district of Cologne in Aachen, for example, in November 1939 issued an order to the confessional press to cease treating the war as a matter of fate and providence and to emphasize more strongly a confidence in victory.[100] Similarly, before Christmas the papers were admonished not to describe Christmas as a feast of peace and to stress the certainty of final victory, which alone could guarantee peace.[101] All these instructions were obeyed faithfully.

One example of the close interplay between Goebbels' propaganda machine and the Catholic press will have to suffice here. In March 1940, in preparation for the strike against the West, the confessional press was asked in the coming weeks to dwell on the topic of plutocracy: "Taking as a point of departure the words of

Jesus: 'You cannot simultaneously serve God and Mammon . . .' it should not be difficult to find a transition from the condemnations of Mammon by Christ to the subject 'Plutocracy'."[102] The Catholic press responded promptly. The *St. Konradsblatt,* the archdiocesan weekly of Freiburg, called the war a struggle against capitalism and plutocracy, both of which had been condemned by the encyclicals of Popes Leo XIII and Pius XI. "This international plutocracy today, through the war started by it [sic!], has been called into court."[103] The *Passauer Bistumsblatt* declared that the present war was a fight of the German people for *Lebensraum* and "against the English plutocracy."[104] The monthly journal for the theory and practice of preaching, *Haec Loquere et Exhortare,* insisted that Germany, in battling the plutocratic nations, was acting in conformity with natural law and Papal teaching, and expressed the hope that justice and love would win out over plutocracy and capitalism.[105] Clearly, there was no need for the Propaganda Ministry to force the Catholic press to print prepared copy.

But the Nazis were masters hard to please. In September 1940 the Propaganda Ministry charged the *Passauer Bistumsblatt,* of all papers, with insufficient support of the war effort. Dr. Emil Janik, the clerical editor, replied that this reproach was unjust and attached a list of articles of contemporary appeal.

> During the course of the preceding year the editor has regarded it as an obvious duty to write a word of positive appreciation, without special request, for the victorious conclusion of the Polish campaign, the [attempted] assassination in Munich, the birthday of the Führer, the national holiday of the German people, the great victory in the West, in short for all important events of our national life. . . . The aim of the *Passauer Bistumsblatt* has always been and will continue to be in the future to make with its religious publications an important contribution for the greatness of the German nation and for the victorious outcome of the world historical struggle.   Heil Hitler![106]

Bishop Wienken, the head of the secretariat of the German episcopate in Berlin, intervened for the diocesan weekly of Passau with the Propaganda Ministry, but he also was told that the paper showed insufficient patriotic zeal. When he communicated this information to the chancery of Passau, Vicar General Riemer replied that the finding was unfair. The editorial board of the paper, he wrote

Wienken, as well as the Bishop himself and his chancery, were sincerely convinced that they had done their best to strengthen the resolution of the readers to carry on until victory had been achieved. Many readers, in fact, had criticized the editor for printing too many patriotic articles, had regarded these as dictated and had rejected them on that account. "This means," Riemer went on, "that such articles have to be composed and printed with a certain discretion so that they will have the effect intended by the state and desired by the editorial board."[107]

Other papers, it appears, were having similar difficulties. Bishop Berning, newly in charge of the Catholic press and its problems, convened a conference on December 12 in Berlin to which he invited a number of editors, publishers and Church dignitaries. The delegates discussed the question of the content of the Catholic periodicals. It was agreed that "if the diocesan papers on their own encourage the soldiers faithfully to do their duty and to be ready to make sacrifices as well as call upon the home front to adopt an attitude anchored in Christian courage and confidence in God, any influence exerted upon the diocesan papers by other authorities will become superfluous."[108] In order to provide the guidance necessary for the implementation of this general policy, the delegates decided to establish a newsletter that would go to the editors of the Catholic weeklies. At the end of January the Propaganda Ministry gave its consent to this enterprise, and confirmed as editor the lay Catholic Dr. Eduard Hemmerle.

The first issue of *Mitteilungen und Ratschläge für die Kath-olisch-Kirchliche Presse* (Notices and Suggestions for the Catholic-Ecclesiastical Press), labeled "Confidential," appeared on February 5, 1941. It contained a preface by Bishop Berning that explained the aims of the newsletter. "The decisive struggle," the Bishop of Osnabrück wrote, "in which our people are engaged, touches every-one of us, and the Catholic newspapers, therefore, cannot pass it up unnoticed." Their task is to explain and appreciate these events in the light of the Catholic faith, and the *Mitteilungen* will help them fulfil this role.[109]

During the following months the *Mitteilungen* told the diocesan press how better to support the German war effort. Excessive zeal was to be avoided, Dr. Hemmerle emphasized in the second issue, for exaggerations cast doubt upon the sincerity of author and paper. Instead the weeklies should stress in a dignified manner the ties between Catholic and German thinking, and strengthen the readers' willingness to fight and endure hardships. On the occasion of Hitler's fifty-second birthday on April 20, 1941, the papers were to call for prayers for the Führer's well-being, and to draw attention to the great victories which the German armies had achieved under his leadership. The pursuit of such a patriotic line, it was hoped, would make the directives of the Propaganda Ministry "superfluous" and impress the regime with the important contribution which the Catholic press was prepared to make on its own volition. But that strategy, too, failed to save the life of the diocesan press. On April 25 the *Reichspressekammer* informed the Catholic weeklies that they would receive no further allocations of paper and would have to cease publication not later than June 1, 1941.[110]

The suppression of the diocesan weeklies was explained as necessitated by scarcity of paper, and this shortage was indeed quite real. Along with 190 Catholic papers the directive halted the publication of about 1,200 periodicals of various types, and shut down all of the Protestant press as well. But many other papers continued to appear, and the decision on which to close down and which to continue clearly had been based on criteria of utility as well as on ideological considerations. Previously, on March 1, Bormann, the head of the Party Chancellery, had suggested to Goebbels that in view of the scarcity of material, labor and machinery all publications that were not absolutely essential, especially the confessional press, be severely curtailed.[111] The Ministry of Ecclesiastical Affairs and the *Reichspressekammer* tried to argue the importance of the confessional papers for the war effort, but leading figures in the Propaganda Ministry and the Party Chancellery were adamant and insisted on suppression.[112] Field Marshal Walter von Brauchitsch asked that at least *Der Neue Wille,* a paper published with the endorsement of the Catholic Army Bishop and widely distributed among the armed forces, be exempted, but this intervention proved similarly fruitless.[113] Clearly, Goebbels and the strongly anti-Christian Bormann used this opportunity, when some curtailment of the press had become necessary, to get rid of most remnants of the confessional press. As in other instances involving the struggle against the churches, ideological compulsiveness won out over considerations of military morale.

The way in which the diocesan weeklies disappeared from the scene was in keeping with their earlier conduct. The *Reichspressekammer* sent out a notice explaining the closing down as a requirement of the war economy and asking the editors to include this formulation in any announcement of suspension of publication made by them. All of the papers complied. Bishop Buchberger of Regensburg noted that "for the sake of the dear fatherland" he was prepared to make this sacrifice.[114]

On January 1, 1934, the Catholic Church in Germany had had 435 periodicals. In July 1941 a mere 27 were still being published, most of them professional journals. Two years later the number was down to 7.[115] The official diocesan gazettes, published by the bishops for the information of the clergy, were the only publications of the Church that appeared relatively unhindered until the end of the war. Several times these gazettes were threatened with prior censorship as well as with being subjected to the requirements of the *Schriftleitergesetz*, but the Church was able to ward off these restrictive measures. Occasionally the gazettes were forbidden to print a certain pastoral letter; in October 1935 they were asked no longer to publish translations of articles from *L'Osservatore Romano*.[116] After the suppression of the diocesan weeklies in 1941 Bishops Berning and Wienken were able to obtain the consent of the Propaganda Ministry to a monthly four-page supplement to the diocesan gazettes that would convey news about other dioceses and the Church in the world at large.[117] The information was collected and distributed to the dioceses by Dr. Hemmerle. In this way it proved possible to inform the clergy, for example, about tribulations of the Church in the *Warthegau,* the part of Poland annexed to Germany, and the confiscations of monasteries. These supplements came out at irregular intervals until the end of the Nazi regime in 1945.[118]

What Gordon Zahn has called the wartime function of the Catholic press as "a captive auxiliary of the Goebbels Propaganda Ministry" has been defended by others as a necessary compromise in order to save the very existence of these papers. Altmeyer, for example, argues, that it remained possible at least to continue to propagate Catholic truths, whereas a voluntary suspension of publication, as tentatively decided by the episcopate in January 1937, would have meant "the radical capitulation before National Socialism."[119] There can be no doubt that the diocesan weeklies in particular were an important medium for the Church through which she continued to reach a wide audience. A decision to stop publishing rather than submit to outside pressures would have involved giving up this valuable channel of communication. But any benefits that accrued to the Church's pastoral role were paid for dearly. The assertion of Altmeyer that none of the contents violated Church doctrine is hardly the whole story. Catholic teaching, moreover, knows of sins of omission as well as of commission.

As related, the Church never carried out its threat, made in 1937, to liquidate the remaining Catholic press on its own, because the bishops wanted to preserve the papers' help for pastoral guidance. But very clearly one important additional reason was the inadequate understanding of the real nature of the Nazi regime. If the episcopate at that time had seen in Hitler the personification of blatant immorality which is common knowledge today, it is doubtful that the hierarchy would have allowed the Catholic press to continue to support and praise him and his rule. The same holds true, *a fortiori*, for the help extended in the war effort. For reasons to be analyzed in detail in a later chapter, it occurred to few churchmen to question the justice of Germany's cause; most of them, therefore, willingly adopted a positive attitude to Hitler's wars. It is no accident that the question of whether to cease publication was never seriously debated after the outbreak of the war in 1939. The patriotic line demanded by the regime was accepted by the Catholic press and their spiritual superiors as a matter of course.

In the last number of the *Passauer Bistumsblatt* Bishop Landersdorfer praised the important services the paper had rendered during its five years of existence. It had provided an important link between Bishop and flock, and it had been for almost every Catholic home a source of valuable "instruction and stimulation." There is no hint here that the diocesan paper was regarded no longer by either the Bishop or the readers as the authentic voice of the Church, as some have attempted to argue. Quite the contrary. "I have ac-

The Ideological Contest 6

1. The Collision With Neopaganism

The optimism in wide circles of German Catholicism engendered by the conclusion of the Concordat soon gave way to more sober second thoughts. The expected acceptance of organized Catholicism as a partner in the Third Reich did not materialize. To the contrary, the regime now unleashed new charges of political unreliability and spread anew the bogy of "political Catholicism." On January 24, 1934, came the greatest shock of all—the appointment of Alfred Rosenberg as deputy of the Führer for the supervision of the spiritual and ideological training of the National Socialist party. The man who more than anyone else had caused the earlier negative attitude of the Church to the Nazi movement now had become Hitler's plenipotentiary for all questions involving the movement's philosophy. Instead of purging the Party of anti-Catholic elements, as the Church had hoped, Hitler now had demonstrated his confidence in the Church's archenemy.

Some solace was derived by the Church from Hitler's alleged opposition to Rosenberg's religious teachings. On April 26, 1933, Hitler had told Bishop Berning and Monsignor Steinmann that Rosenberg's *Mythus* was no more than a private publication, and he affirmed the same view in his talk with Cardinal Schulte on

February 7, 1934. According to Schulte's notes of this meeting, Hitler stated emphatically that he did not like Rosenberg's book. He supported Rosenberg, the theoretician of the National Socialist party, but did not identify himself with Rosenberg, the author of the *Mythus*.[1] Two days later, on February 9, the Sacred Congregation of the Holy Office in Rome announced that it had placed Rosenberg's *Mythus des 20. Jahrhunderts* on the Index of Forbidden Books.*

The Fulda Bishops' Conference of June 1934 noted with surprise and anxiety that "contrary to earlier declarations of the Führer, the National Socialist movement itself now wanted to constitute a *Weltanschauung*."[2] The joint pastoral letter, nevertheless, did not attack the Nazi party and its teachings but directed its criticism at the proponents and concepts of neopaganism. "One book" that undermined the belief in the Christian religion was mentioned, but any more precise identification was omitted. Positive Christianity, the bishops declared in this pronouncement (which was later withdrawn in order not to disturb the negotiations over the implementation of the Concordat), was to be found only where Christ was recognized as the son of God. Not that which was useful to the people was moral, they stated, but that which coincided with the commands of God. Religion could not be based on blood and race or other dogmas of human creation, but only on divine revelation taught by the Church and its visible head, the Vicar of Christ in Rome.[3]

It is doubtful that many of the bishops in June 1934 still believed in the distinction between what they euphemistically called "neopaganism" and National Socialism. They did know that Rosenberg's teaching of a new faith, anchored in the myth of the Nordic blood, was widely praised in Party circles, and that it was increasingly recommended as the official doctrine of the Nazi party. But the only way in which the Church could go on supporting the new regime while at the same time fighting the offensive religious beliefs of leading party figures like Rosenberg was to distinguish

---

* It is tempting to speculate whether the Vatican would have taken this step in the absence of Hitler's repeated statements dissociating himself from Rosenberg's book. Rome never put Hitler's writings on the Index; the Führer until the end of his reign was allowed to remain a member of the Church, i.e. he was not excommunicated.

between the Nazi movement itself and the aberrations of certain echelons. Also, perhaps some of the bishops in 1934 still hoped for a break between Hitler and Rosenberg. Whatever their private views, the bishops for a long time in their public pronouncements continued to insist that they criticized not state and movement, but the neopaganism of some party leaders.

The advantages expected from this tactic largely failed to materialize. The joint pastoral letter of June 1934, for example, even though not read from the pulpits, had been printed and distributed widely. The Gestapo promptly confiscated all unsold copies and forbade the publication of the pastoral letter by the press and even by the diocesan gazettes on the grounds that the letter was likely to jeopardize public order and deprecate the authority of state and movement.[4] In vain did Cardinal Bertram plead that the episcopate had had no intention of attacking state or movement.[5] The Nazi regime was unwilling to tolerate criticism.

A more forthright critique of Rosenberg's *Mythus* was undertaken by a number of Catholic scholars in the fall of 1934. In order to protect the publication against confiscation by the Gestapo, Cardinal Schulte of Cologne was prevailed upon to let the pamphlet be printed and published as a supplement to the official diocesan gazette. When Schulte at the last moment lost courage and withdrew his consent, Bishop Galen of Münster was approached and readily agreed to sponsor publication.[6] The October issue of the diocesan gazette of Münster thus appeared with a supplement entitled *Studien zum Mythus des XX. Jahrhunderts*. In a preface Galen recommended the work to the clergy as one written "in a spirit of love for the German fatherland, for the Holy Church and for the truth."[7] Additional installments appeared in December and an epilogue was published in early 1935. The authors, who remained anonymous, subjected Rosenberg's work to a scholarly but severe criticism. The many misstatements and outright errors in facts contained in the book were noted, and the insults to Pope and Church protested. Excerpts from the *Studien* were also published by Cardinal Schulte's diocesan gazette, and reprints of the pamphlet exceeded 100,000 copies. Though the Gestapo confiscated the pamphlet in several places, it nevertheless reached a wide audience. The battle between the Church and Rosenberg was joined.

When Rosenberg answered his critics in a new short book, *An die Dunkelmänner unserer Zeit,* Rome promptly put this, too, on the Index.[8] The next move was for the German bishops, in a lengthy memorandum to Hitler decided upon at their August 1935 Conference at Fulda, to point out that Rosenberg's books were given maximum support and publicity by various party organs; the public therefore could but conclude that neopaganism and National Socialism were identical. The enemies of the Church, the bishops complained, were allowed to carry on their agitation completely unhindered, while "the dictatorship of the Gestapo" suppressed any attempts of the Church to defend herself and her teachings.[9]

At the same Conference a joint pastoral letter of the episcopate noted with regret that lectures on religious topics could no longer be delivered outside the churches and asked the faithful to pay special attention to the sermons of their bishops. The number of the enemies of the Church had now become legion, the pastoral letter said. These foes of Christianity were divided into numerous groups but they were all agreed upon their hatred of the Roman Catholic Church. As always in her history, the Church would insist on obedience to the authorities, but if a law of the state violated natural law and the commands of God, the word of the Apostles had to be invoked "to obey God rather than men."[10] The regime countered by forbidding the publication of the bishops' pronouncement in any other medium but the diocesan gazettes to the clergy.

The religious struggle now had reached dimensions that began to worry the Nazis. The Gestapo of Aachen at the end of 1934 reported that many clerics who earlier had been sympathetic to the movement, or even supporters, were adopting a hostile attitude because of the "*Mythus* problem." "Given the mentality of the Catholic population, who in large measure stand almost completely behind the clergy, this means a serious threat to the state."[11] In July 1935 the same office concluded that wide segments of the Catholic population were fully prepared to go along with the state if this could be achieved without doing violence to their religious beliefs.[12]

As a means of minimizing religious conflict, the different segments of the neopagan movement which earlier had operated with the tacit encouragement of the Nazi party were now subjected to various restrictions. In December 1935 the Bavarian Gestapo forbade all public meetings and lectures of Ludendorff's heathen movement,[13] and the edict was later extended to cover Professor Hauer's German Faith movement as well. An order of Himmler, issued in September 1935, forbade members of the S.S. to take any leading role in religious organizations, including the German Faith movement, and strictly forbade all manifestations of religious intolerance or scorn of religious symbols.[14] The fact that such orders continued to be issued at rather frequent intervals seems to indicate that the implementation of this directive met with difficulties. But there can be no doubt that the regime now began to regard the neopagans as somewhat more of a liability than an asset. These groups not only aggravated relations with the Christian churches, but also created a fervor that might rival the enthusiasm the Nazis were trying to enlist for their own movement. Religious faith was to be identified with a sect as little as with a church; instead it was to be focused upon the National Socialist cause exclusively. The Nazis wanted the whole man, and they were unwilling to share the allegiance of their members with anybody, no matter how anti-Christian his bearing.

The teachings of Rosenberg alone continued to be propagated on the broadest scale. His espousal of a religion based on unswerving loyalty to race, blood and soil served the interests of the Nazi movement far better than the highbrow sectarianism of a Ludendorff, Hauer or Reventlow. Rosenberg's ideas were of the essence of the Nazi *Weltanschauung*, and Hitler supported them fully. In the fall of 1935 Abbot Schachleiter, the veteran Catholic National Socialist, pleaded with the Minister for Ecclesiastical Affairs to ask Rosenberg to revise his *Mythus* so that Catholics could support the National Social movement without qualms of conscience. This request drew a politely worded rebuff.[15] The Führer's reservations over the *Mythus* were of a tactical nature and did not stem from any love for Christianity. As he had told Rauschning several years earlier, Hitler preferred a campaign of vilification to doctrinal disputes. Early in 1935, therefore, the regime began a series of trials of members of the religious orders accused of violating the foreign currency laws. Supported by a noisy and hostile publicity in the press, these proceedings aimed at discrediting the orders and the Church in the eyes of the German public. At the same time, the first campaign against the confessional schools was begun in Bavaria.

The Church continued to defend herself as best she could without risking a rupture of working relations with the regime. For their troubles the bishops still blamed not Hitler and his government or party, but those who allegedly misunderstood the Nazi party's teaching of positive Christianity. A joint pastoral letter issued in January 1936 emphasized that if the Church forbade the faithful to read certain books, periodicals and newspapers, it did so without wanting to encroach upon the prerogatives of State or Party.[16]

The regime stepped up its drive against the religious orders in May by instituting trials for sexual perversity. These proceedings were given detailed and lurid coverage by the press; the Catholic monasteries were described as breeding places of filth and vice. In another area extensive pressure brought to bear upon Catholic parents led to the liquidation of most confessional schools. Still the Church responded defensively. A pastoral letter issued in November by the bishops of the church provinces of Cologne and Paderborn protested the ever-stronger attacks upon Church and faith, and asked in a tone of desperation whether these developments could go on much longer.[17] As it turned out, worse was yet to come.

The Vatican had been following events in Germany with growing anxiety. In numerous notes the Holy See had protested the systematic violations of the Concordat by the Hitler government. Pope Pius XI had threatened several times to bring his complaints into the open, and it had taken the moderating influence of his Secretary of State, Pacelli, to prevent a rupture of relations.[18] In the spring of 1937 Pius XI finally made public his grievances in an encyclical letter that was smuggled into Germany, secretely printed and within a few days distributed by messenger to the clergy all over the country. On March 21, Palm Sunday, the Papal encyclical, *Mit brennender Sorge,* was read from the pulpits of all Catholic churches in Germany.[19]

"With deep anxiety and with ever-growing dismay," Pius XI said, he had watched the tribulations of the Catholic Church in Germany. The Concordat of 1933 was now being violated openly and the conscience of the faithful oppressed as never before. In these circumstances "a word of truth and spiritual encouragement" was essential. After such introductory remarks (Sections 1-8) the Pontiff proceeded to restate those articles of faith obscured by Nazi ideology. True belief in God, he declared, was irreconcilable with the deification of earthly values such as race, people or the state. Important as these were in the natural order, they could never be the ultimate norm of all things. Belief in a national God or a national religion, similarly, was a grave error. The God of Christianity could not be imprisoned "within the frontiers of a single people, within the pedigree of one single race" (Sections 9-13).

After speaking about the obligation of true belief in Christ, the definitive character of divine revelation and the primacy of the Bishop of Rome (Sections 14-24) Pope Pius went on to take issue with the Nazi principle that "Right is what is advantageous to the people." What was morally illicit, he insisted, could never be to the true advantage of the people.

> This fundamental principle, cut off from the moral law, would mean in relations between states a perpetual state of war amongst the various nations; in the life of the state it confuses advantage and right, and refuses to recognize the fundamental fact that man possesses rights given to him by God which must be preserved from every attempt by the community to deny, suppress, or hinder their exercise.

Human laws contrary to natural law, Pope Pius declared, are not "obligatory in conscience." Regulations concerning schools that took no account of the rights of parents which are theirs by natural law were therefore not lawful; and the enrollments of Catholic pupils in interdenominational schools, "which have just taken place in circumstances of notorious coercion are the effects of violence and void of all legality" (Sections 33-37).

Pope Pius ended the encyclical with the admonition to the priests and religious of the Church in Germany to continue to serve truth and to unmask and confute error whatever its form or disguise. He urged the faithful among the laity to remain true to Christ and to keep defending the rights which a solemn agreement had guaranteed them and the Church.

The reading of the Papal encyclical took the government of

the Reich by surprise. The Gestapo belatedly confiscated all copies it could lay its hands on, twelve print shops were closed and dispossessed without compensation for having printed the letter and strong protests were lodged with the bishops and the Holy See. The Foreign Ministry called the document a summons to battle against the leadership of the German state and a grave violation of the contractual obligations arising from the Concordat.[20] On April 6 the furious Hitler ordered the resumption of the foreign exchange and immorality trials against Catholic clergymen which had been halted since shortly before the Olympic Games in Berlin in the summer of 1936.[21] The idea of renouncing the Concordat, a step contemplated by Hitler for some time, was given new currency. During his state visit to Rome in May 1938 Hitler demonstratively omitted the customary courtesy call on the Pope.[22]

Many writers, influenced in part by the violent reaction of the Nazi government to the papal pronouncement, have hailed the encyclical letter *Mit brennender Sorge* as a decisive repudiation of the National Socialist state and *Weltanschauung*.[23] More judicious observers have noted that the encyclical was moderate in tone and merely intimated that the condemned neopagan doctrines were favored by the German authorities. It is indeed a document in which, as one Catholic writer has put it, "with considerable skill, the extravagances of German Nazi doctrine are picked out for condemnation in a way that would not involve the condemnation of political and social Totalitarianism."[24] A confirmation of this evaluation can be found in Pacelli's reply to the note of protest of the German government. "The Holy See," the Papal Secretary of State declared, "which has friendly, correct, or at least tolerable relations with states of one or another constitutional form and orientation, will never interfere in the question of what concrete form of government a certain people chooses to regard as best suited to its nature and requirements. With respect to Germany also, it has remained true to this principle and intends so to continue."[25]

If the government of the Reich was prepared to abandon the policies hostile to the Church, Pacelli was saying in effect, the door to friendly relations was still open. While some of Pius' language is sweeping and can be given a wider construction, basically the

Pope had condemned neopaganism and the denial of religious freedom—no less and no more.

One reason for the conciliatory tone of the encyclical is suggested in the document itself. "We have weighed every word of the Encyclical in the balance of truth and also love," the Pope declared. "Neither did we wish by inopportune silence to be guilty of not having made the situation clear, nor by excessive severity to harden the hearts of those who since they are placed under Our pastoral responsibility are no less the objects of Our pastoral charity because they are now wandering in the paths of error and estrangement" (Section 49). "Many," the Pontiff noted with "pastoral anxiety" at the beginning of the encyclical, "forsake the way of truth" (Section 2). These remarks were to the point. Under the impact of the relentlessly pursued anti-Catholic propaganda of the Nazis, large numbers of Catholics were leaving the Church; this state of affairs dictated prudence and moderation. In 1934 about 26,000 had given notice of withdrawal from the Church; by 1936 the number had gone well over 46,000; and in 1937 the figure was to reach the all-time high of 108,000.[26] In such adverse circumstances the Church felt it necessary to tread cautiously.

The year 1937 was not a good one for the Vatican. The Spanish Civil War had strengthened the fear of Bolshevism. Just five days after issuing *Mit brennender Sorge* Pope Pius published the encyclical, *Divini Redemptoris,* against atheistic Communism. As Ambassador Bergen reported from Rome, the condemnation of Communism, which was regarded as a most urgent necessity, was seen to have "necessitated a like action against the similar phenomena which, intentionally or unintentionally, were resulting from [certain features of National Socialism]. . . ."[27] But a cautious path was followed most of all, perhaps, because the Holy See was no more opposed to the central political doctrines of Nazism than the German bishops themselves. Any full assessment of the ideological warfare between the Church and the Nazi regime must take into account the evidence that the Church's struggle against neopaganism was accompanied by an unchecked and often congenial absorption of certain other elements of National Socialist ideology. This was the other side of the coin, as it were.

2. Tactics of Adaptation

The attempt of Catholic spokesmen in 1933 to find common ground with Nazism has been described in an earlier chapter. These endeavors continued in 1934. The misgivings voiced by some Catholics, declared Archbishop Gröber, do not involve the state, but are directed against those in the movement who seek to block "the peaceful integration of the Catholics into the new type of government." Frenchmen can be Catholics and ardent Frenchman, Italians may be fascists as well as good Catholics. The same privilege, Gröber insisted, must be granted the German Catholics.[28] Bishop Berning published a book that stressed the link between Catholic thinking and national consciousness. The age of individualism, he declared, had now yielded to a new era that justifiably sought a return to the ties of blood.[29] Berning sent a copy of this book to Hitler—"as a token of my devotion"—and asked the Führer to take notice of the services which the Church in the course of her history had rendered "the German nationality as a community of blood, language and culture."[30] Monsignor Hartz of the free prelature of Schneidemühl in his pastoral letter issued for Lent 1934 praised Hitler as one who had saved Germany from "the poison of Liberalism . . . [and] the pest of Communism. . . ."[31] The Church, declared Bishop Hilfrich of Limburg on the same occasion, has always supported the principle of authority and she will now "gladly do her share so that the idea of [secular] authoritarian leadership will also be accepted with conviction in the hearts of men."[32]

These pronouncements by members of the German hierarchy were matched by those of lesser dignitaries and prominent laymen. Canon Algermissen saw the German people's natural values, given by God, symbolized in the swastika. He called for a close link between natural and supernatural values, between swastika and cross. It was the task of Catholic pastoral care, the noted theologian observed, to investigate the possibility of a "synthesis of Teutonism and Christianity."[33] Dr. Anton Stonner, an expert on religious instruction, saw parallels between the Christian institutions of mission and monastery, the leadership principle and the idea of following [*Gefolgschaft*] as practiced in the S.A. and S.S. The totalitarian character of the new state, according to Stonner, did not have to lead to difficulties in the relations between Church and State. The Church was also totalitarian, but her claims were in a different plane. The importance attributed by the new regime to the values of *Volk* should be supported, for Christian revelation made the identification with one's own people a duty.[34] Dr. Jakob Hommes called the National Socialist movement a healthy force that would prevent the suicide of Western civilization threatened by individualism, rationalism and humanitarianism bequeathed by the Enlightenment.[35] Franz Taeschner, a Catholic publicist, praised "the Führer, gifted with genius," who had been sent by providence in order to achieve the fulfilment of Catholic social ideas. He called upon his readers to be staunch National Socialists as well as staunch Catholics.[36]

The bloody events of June 30, 1934, did not halt the professions of ideological agreement from within the Catholic camp. Desiderius Breitenstein, a Franciscan father, in the late summer of 1934 noted certain differences between National Socialism and Catholicism but stressed that these by no means foreclosed the possibilities of ideological rapprochement.[37] The displacement of the democratic creed by the leadership principle, a Catholic writer suggested, suited the Catholic Church well. "For in the Roman Catholic Church, from the beginning until the present day, the authoritarian leadership principle has determined the character and activity of the Church." The leaders of the Church were now no longer in conflict, but in step with the spirit of the time.[38]

After his dismissal as Vice-Chancellor, in July 1934, Papen dissolved the *Arbeitsgemeinschaft Katholischer Deutscher* (AKD). In a public statement announcing the dissolution Papen thanked his collaborators for their help in cementing the spiritual unity of the German people and called on them to continue to work for the reconciliation of Catholicism and National Socialism.[39] Most of them stayed with this cause. For example, Kuno Brombacher, the representative of the AKD in Baden, in a book that received an informal *nihil obstat* from Archbishop Gröber, again demanded the union of cross and swastika.[40] A year later Brombacher and Emil Ritter, the former editor-in-chief of the *Germania* in Berlin, jointly exhorted all Catholics to continue to participate in Hitler's grand design even if they were not wanted by some of the Führer's lieutenants. "The only authentic National Socialism is that of Adolf Hitler."[41] The publication of this book was made possible by the friendly intervention of Bishop Galen,[42] but Brombacher soon despaired of his fellow Catholics and joined the Old Catholic Church. His effectiveness as mediator between Church and State there was no greater. The Nazis were as distrustful of the Old Catholics, who wanted a German Catholic Church independent of Rome, as they were of all other religious groups, and gave them no encouragement. The Old Catholic Church, therefore, never became a significant force in Nazi Germany.[43]

Despite the evidence of the cases of Papen and Brombacher that the Nazis had no use for collaborators, the Roman Catholic bishops continued to pursue a collaborative line. They, too, made a concerted effort to find common ground between Catholic and National Socialist thinking. Addressing the synod of the archdiocese of Breslau in 1935, Cardinal Bertram reminded his clergy that many National Socialist ideas were already contained in Catholic teaching. The Church had always admitted the significance of race, soil and blood, which were valuable divine gifts and received special consecration through Christianity.[44] Vicar General Miltenberger of Würzburg in 1937 issued a very similar directive to the clergy of his diocese:

> If a priest should heap scorn on or ridicule the concepts of blood, soil, race, he would thereby not only risk political attacks and legal prosecution, but also offend theologically and against his Church. For what is expressed in these words belongs to the especially valuable natural possessions which God has given us and which even represent the natural foundation for the supernatural possession. For that we are Christians and Catholics we certainly owe primarily to the fact that through God's providence we were born into our family environment and our fatherland and our race. [The right rank order of these values is to be clarified] . . . and one must help the people to incorporate all these concepts, which are presented to them with such great enthusiasm, into their religious *Weltanschauung*.[45]

So widespread was this effort on the part of the Church to appropriate National Socialist concepts considered popular, that the Nazis saw a systematic plot of "Political Catholicism" to conquer National Socialism from within. In former times, a report emanating from Himmler's Gestapo found, the Church had stressed the values of "liberty, equality and fraternity; now they speak instead of nationality, authoritarian leadership, blood and soil."[46] Whether the Church, indeed, acted in accordance with a considered plan, as the Nazis surmised, is a question impossible to answer definitely. But the attempt at adapting Catholic ideas to the new climate of opinion was real indeed, sometimes embracing nearly all of National Socialist ideology minus Rosenberg's religious teaching. A few illustrations must suffice here.

Guidelines for religious instruction that were issued by the German episcopate in February 1936 stressed the importance of recognizing willingly all that was true in the current set of ideas. "Only in cases of real necessity" should teachers ward off attacks upon Catholic doctrine; otherwise a positive exposition should be adhered to. "Race, soil, blood and people are precious natural values which God the Lord has created and the care of which he has entrusted to us Germans."[47] A handbook on topical religious problems edited by Archbishop Gröber and published "with the recommendation of the German episcopate" defended the right of every people to maintain undisturbed their previous racial stock and to adopt morally admissible safeguards for this purpose. Race and Christianity are not contradictions, but orders of a different kind that supplement one another.[48] "Blood and race," declared Cardinal Faulhaber in a sermon in 1936, ". . . have participated in the shaping of German history."[49]

The acceptance of the struggle against the values of the Enlightenment was another favorite theme. The present age, noted Archbishop Gröber's *Handbuch,* seeks to overcome the children of the Enlightenment: liberalism and individualism. The values of community, tradition, custom, symbolism and mysticism are emphasized. "Christian thinking regards these endeavors of returning to the true and complete foundations of human nature as decisive attempts at overcoming the Enlightenment. [Christianity] by supporting these new cultural and educational goals, can make a substantial contribution from its own resources, the spirit of reverence for the eternal realities and values, toward the renewal that has begun."[50] The previous century had exaggerated the concern for the individual; the reforms introduced by National Socialism were "a necessary correction of the liberal *Weltanschauung.*"[51] Indeed, if the state today assumed a totalitarian character in the political realm, this was fully justified because of the threats posed by Bolshevism. The totalitarian claims of the state should halt merely before the innermost religious convictions of man. Hitler himself had condemned the intrusion of the state into the religious sphere.[52]

The readiness of the Catholics to serve the fatherland even at the cost of their lives was stressed as often as possible. "The Führer of the Third Reich," declared the *Handbuch* of Archbishop Gröber, "has freed the German man from his external humiliation and from the inner weakness caused by Marxism and has returned him to the ancestral Germanic values of honor, loyalty and courage. . . ."[53] But Christianity, too, it was emphasized, inculcated the willingness to make sacrifices and to perform heroic deeds. The services rendered by the Catholics on the field of battle in the war of 1914-1918 were frequently cited, and much was made of the Catholic religion of Albert Leo Schlageter, an insurgent against the French in the Ruhr who after his execution in 1923 had become a celebrated Nazi hero and martyr. "In the battles and hardships of the World War as well as in the bitter distress of the post-war years," declared Bishop Buchberger of Regensburg in 1935, "we German Catholics have not been surpassed by anyone in readiness to make sacrifices, love of our country and fidelity to the fatherland. . . . And in the struggle for the freedom of our fatherland after the war, a staunchly Catholic man, Leo Schlageter, became the shining example of love of the fatherland unto death."[54] The Christian *Weltanschauung,* Cardinal Faulhaber pointed out in a sermon delivered in November 1936, demanded willing suffering as well as heroic performances. This synthesis was exemplified by the Catholic officer Schlageter and the heroes of the Alcazar in the Spanish Civil War.[55]

The Catholic press, even before 1933, had occasionally participated in the cult of the Nazi martyr Schlageter. In the years after the National Socialist accession to power, the glorification of Schlageter—"a shining example of the possibility of being a good Catholic as well as a good German inspired by burning love for people and fatherland"[56]—became a recurring feature of the Catholic papers. The Nazi Propaganda Ministry finally put a stop to this practice of borrowing the heroes of the Nazi movement by forbidding any mention of Horst Wessel and Schlageter in the confessional press.[57]

Professor Otto Schilling, a prominent Catholic theologian, published an article in 1934 in which he defended the right of the German people to "enlarged *Lebensraum,*" and pleaded for the return of the colonies unjustly taken away from Germany after the World War. Invoking the concept of *sedium occupatio,* Schilling argued that such a redress of national grievances would be in conformity with natural law.[58] The same position was taken by many other Catholic figures. Gröber's *Handbuch* urged the peaceful resolution of conflicts between nations, but added that the love of peace must not lead to the abandonment of a "powerful assertion of national honor, freedom and *Lebensraum.*"[59] Also active in nourishing the idea of a strong Germany was the *Reichsverband für die katholischen Auslandsdeutschen* (National Association for German Catholics Abroad). Bishop Berning, the patron of this organization, demanded the return of the German colonies at a national congress held in 1936 at Frankfurt. Dr. Emil Clemens Scherer, the association's general secretary, declared on the same occasion that the *Reichsverband* had promised the Führer to support the national awakening by enlisting the resources of Catholic missionary activity.[60] For its pro-German and pro-Nazi activity among the German minorities of Poland, Rumania and Jugoslavia the organization received substantial subsidies from the German government.[61]

The Nazis on the whole placed no value on these attempts on the part of German Catholicism to ingratiate itself with the National Socialist regime. The books of Bishop Alois Hudal, head of the German Catholic community in Rome, were suppressed, even though the Austrian-born bishop dedicated himself to the task of "paving the way for an understanding of National Socialism from the Christian standpoint."[62] An internal report of the Gestapo about "Political Catholicism" in 1937 warned that the Church was appropriating National Socialist symbols and terminology. Increasingly now one could hear slogans like "Jesus is our Führer,"

"Heil Bishop," etc. In this manner, the Gestapo report charged, the Church hoped to conquer National Socialism as once she had overcome the German heathens.[63]

This appraisal by the Nazis of the Church's tactics was shared by some anti-Nazis outside Germany. A few months earlier the *Christliche Ständestaat*, a Catholic anti-Nazi weekly appearing in Vienna, had subjected the ideological tactics of German Catholicism to a searching investigation and had come to virtually the same conclusion. German Catholic apologetics, the writer suggested, could with justice display the sign, "We carry all items that are sold by the competition, only in better quality." The difference between National Socialist and Catholic outpourings on the subjects of race, the leadership principle, nation, defense of the fatherland, etc., the article complained, was minimal. Everywhere the Catholics try to outdo the Nazis in chauvinistic zeal.[64]

Justified in large measure as this complaint was, it would be wrong to conclude that even bishops like Berning and Gröber completely identified themselves with the National Socialist ideology. Many of their endorsements of specific points of the National Socialist program and practice were encumbered with qualifications and reservations, as the Nazis never ceased to complain. All bishops insisted repeatedly that race, no matter how important, could not determine morality and they objected to the idea of a master race. Though rejecting liberalism, many bishops nevertheless warned against extravagant claims of the *Volksgemeinschaft* that would leave the individual without rights of his own. The Church fought, albeit unsuccessfully, the monopoly of education demanded by the Nazi state. On the important issue of compulsory sterilization, a subject to be dealt with in a later chapter, the Church took a totally negative stand.

The most important position taken by the Church was its insistence on not being entombed in the sacristy. She refused to be limited to worship and ritual, and stressed that the Church's teaching encompassed all aspects of life, private as well as public. It was the Church's assertion of the superiority of divine law over the man-made dogmas of nation and race, coupled with the Church's claim to penetrate all areas of human existence, which more than anything else infuriated the Nazis and made them see in the Church a most dangerous enemy. No matter what the tactics of the Church, declared the Gestapo report of 1937, and irrespective of whether the bishops use legal or illegal means, "between the National Socialist state and the Catholic Church there can be no peace. The totalitarian claims of the Church challenge those of the state."[65]

After the initialing of the Concordat, Papen told a press conference held in Rome, "The clear definition of respective competences will in the future eliminate all conflict between Church and State."[66] In later years many Catholic bishops also kept repeating that despite the totalitarian ambitions of State and Church a mutually satisfactory delineation of jurisdiction was possible. As late as February 1938 Bishop Ehrenfried of Würzburg expressed the desire that "the totalitarianism of the State and the totalitarianism of the Church" should coexist "without conflicts and bitterness."[67] The Nazis, for their part, never had any illusions on this score. Göring's decree on "Political Catholicism" of July 1935 merely made explicit and official the distrustful attitude the Nazis had exhibited all along. The bishops used the pulpit, Göring charged, to criticize institutions and measures of State and Party. The religious function of worship was abused for political ends. The Church, he insisted, could not be allowed to invoke God against the state, "an enormity which we can witness in open or concealed form every Sunday."[68]

This limitation on her teaching function, the Church, in principle at least, did not accept. Göring's decree was vigorously criticized by *L'Osservatore Romano,* which reaffirmed the right of the Church to concern herself critically with those aspects of public life that raised moral questions.[69] The German bishops similarly maintained that they could not relinquish the Church's prerogative of confronting all aspects of life with the Christian faith. "As long as religion belongs unto the pulpits," declared Cardinal Faulhaber in 1935, "and that will be the case as long as there are pulpits, questions of *Weltanschauung* also belong unto the pulpit."[70] Christianity, insisted Archbishop Gröber's *Handbuch,* "has a total character that encompasses *all* of human life. Her nature demands that she permeate not only private and family life but public life as well" (Gröber's italics).[71] When the bishops tell the faithful that whatever is in opposition to divine law is not permitted, the Fulda Bishops' Conference of August 1935 reminded the clergy, they do this not out of a desire for political power, but in fulfilment of a duty of conscience.[72] Even Papen, on one of the rare occasions when he publicly voiced criticism of the Nazi regime, argued in his much-publicized speech in 1934 at Marburg, that the Church must be granted the right to oppose the state's totalitarian claims when those intruded into the realm of religion.[73]

The refusal of the Church to be pushed back into the sacristy had solid roots in Church doctrine, and was stated and restated repeatedly by the German bishops. But while the principle involved could not be surrendered by the Church, in practice the episcopate did not live up to the full implications of their theoretical all-embracing concern with the moral dimensions of human life. Anxious not to jeopardize their relations with the Nazi regime more than absolutely necessary, the episcopate adhered to certain self-imposed restrictions upon the scope of their moral teaching. The bishops frequently asserted their duty to speak up, to preach the word of God "in season, out of season" (II Tim. 4:2). We bishops, Cardinal Faulhaber insisted in 1934, must proclaim the moral law not only to the simple folks, but to the great ones on earth as well.[74] We would rather go to jail or face death, the Bavarian Bishops declared in 1936, than become unfaithful to our pastoral duty.[75] The pronouncement of the general principle, in retrospect, is more impressive than the practice of it in the reality of actual life situations.

3. In the Shadow of Murder

Some of the self-imposed limitations upon the practice of the Church's moral teachings were the result not so much of fear of adverse consequences, but of misunderstandings about the nature of the Nazi regime itself. Here once again we come upon the impossible-to-avoid conclusion that the Church for a long time regarded the National Socialist state as merely another authoritarian regime, and in line with her traditional political neutrality, the Church did not consider it her duty to evaluate the supposedly "purely political" aspects of Nazi rule. "It is not our job," Bishop

Galen told the deans of the diocese of Münster in 1935, "to pass judgments on political organization and form of government of the German people, on measures and proceedings of the state, to mourn after past forms of government, to criticize present state policies." The authoritarian state, recognized by the Holy See, he continued, relieves the individual almost completely of the duty and possibility of concerning himself with such political questions. Those ministering to the souls of man should therefore gladly leave politics to those who were called to make political decisions.[76] Purely political considerations, the Papal Secretary of State declared in a note to the German government in 1936, will never disturb good and peaceful relations between Church and State. The suspicions still held by the government on that score, Pacelli pleaded, were without foundation.[77] Other German bishops also repeatedly emphasized their lack of concern with the strictly political features of the Nazi dictatorship. Even Bishop Preysing of Berlin, who, more than any other member of the episcopate, courageously expressed concern over the repressive features of Nazi rule, spoke out against the dictatorship exercised over the conscience of men, and not against the total lack of political rights in the Third Reich.

One must conclude that the view of the Nazi regime as merely another conventional political system was based on an unsophisticated political perspective. But how is one to evaluate the silence of the episcopate over clearly immoral features of Nazi rule like the concentration camps or the Blood Purge of 1934—features that were the logical consequences of an ideology that glorified brute force? In such instances the professed duty of the bishops to proclaim the moral law, whether welcome or not, ran head-on into the overriding concern of the episcopate to maintain working relations with the regime in order to protect the pastoral function of the Church.

The massacre of June 30, 1934, claimed the lives of several hundred persons, including such prominent Catholics as Dr. Erich Klausener, head of Catholic Action in Berlin; the Catholic youth leader Adalbert Probst; Dr. Fritz Gerlich, former editor of *Der Gerade Weg;* and Dr. Fritz Beck, a leader of Catholic students. The world watched incredulously as these acts of murder were subsequently legalized by Hitler and his henchmen as measures taken "for the defense of the state." The barbarity of the Hitler regime now stood exposed for all to see. The German Catholics and the world at large waited anxiously for the reaction of the Church. But none was to be forthcoming.

On June 24, 1934, Dr. Klausener had admonished a big rally of Berlin Catholics to remain loyal to people and fatherland. In a telegram to Hitler, signed by Bishop Bares and Klausener, the participants had sent the Chancellor "respectful greetings" and had pledged their loyalty.[78] Six days later, on orders of Gestapo chief Heydrich, Klausener was shot dead in his office. His ashes were subsequently sent to his family with the standard Nazi notification that Klausener had committed suicide. Publicly the Church at first kept discreetly silent. Two weeks later the chancery of Berlin instructed the clergy "with regard to the events of the last few weeks to maintain the necessary restraint and not to lose sight of the welfare of the Church as a whole."[79] At the Church of St. Matthias, to which Klausener had belonged, and only there, an announcement was read that denied that Klausener had been involved in seditious activities or had committed suicide.

The case of Adalbert Probst was not much different. This leader of the Catholic sports organization *Deutsche Jugendkraft* (DJK), according to the Gestapo, had been "shot while trying to escape." Monsignor Wolker, the spiritual adviser of the Catholic youth organizations, notified the diocesan leaders of the DJK of the Gestapo's explanation, and ordered that the information be relayed to all local branches without any addition "in order to prevent the formation of wild and incorrect rumors."[80] This was the sum of the public response by the Church.

Bishop Bares of Berlin addressed a letter to Hitler in which he denied the possibility that Klausener could have been engaged in subversive activity. Klausener, according to Bares, had "repeatedly, both in private and in public, professed his support of the existing National Socialist state." In the interest of the disastrous results which this death could have, especially in the Saar, Bares called on Hitler to speak "a clarifying and liberating word."[81] Several months later, after no satisfactory reply had been received, Bares again turned to Hitler and expressed his conviction that

Klausener could not possibly have been a traitor or committed suicide. "I am moved to undertake this new step in the Klausener case," Bares wrote, "not out of criticism of the state's actions, but out of concern for the preservation of the authority of the state."[82] This was the non-public response of the Church to the Blood Purge.

The reaction of the outside world was one of revulsion. Voices were now also heard from within the Catholic camp calling on the German bishops to speak up in public protest against the killings and the regime that had perpetrated them. The *Christliche Ständestaat* called Hitler "the gravedigger of German civilization" and added, "Whoever today still hopes for a reform or conversion of National Socialism refuses to see and hear."[83] The well-known German Catholic author, Waldemar Gurian, in a pamphlet written in Switzerland and smuggled into Germany, argued that the silence of the German bishops following the Blood Purge threatened to create a serious crisis of confidence in the Church. "The silence of the German bishops," Gurian declared, "is perhaps more terrible than anything else that has happened on June 30. For the silence destroys the last moral authority in Germany, it introduces insecurity into the ranks of the faithful, it threatens to lead to an estrangement between bishops and people who can no longer understand this silence." St. Ambrose of Milan in the fourth century had imposed penance on the Emperor Theodosius the Great who was guilty of a massacre. The German bishops, Gurian argued, likewise should condemn Hitler's crimes and defend the moral order for which the Church considers herself responsible.[84] In a sermon delivered a year and a half later, in early 1936, Bishop Galen spoke of "fresh graves" that contained the ashes of men the German Catholics regarded as martyrs for their faith[85]—the only utterance of a German bishop that even approximated a public protest.

The other phenomenon that tested the moral quality of the bishops' unprotesting outlook on National Socialist political thinking and its concrete results was the concentration camp. Since 1933 the number of offenders taken into protective custody and put into concentration camps had been rising steadily. At first the victims were mostly Communists, Socialists and other political opponents of the Nazi regime. But the revival of Bismarck's "Pulpit

Paragraph," a decree against the abuse of the pulpit for political purposes, and the enforcement of the law of December 1934 forbidding "malicious slander of the State and Party," soon led to the imprisonment of many Catholic priests. Released inmates of a concentration camp were ordered to maintain strict secrecy about the goings-on in the camp; but word got out, nevertheless, and the bishops undoubtedly had ample information about the acts of brutality, torture and murder perpetrated in the camps. Provost Bernard Lichtenberg of Berlin is the only churchman known to have protested against the atrocities committed. In the spring of 1935 he submitted to Göring a written report on the hideous treatment meted out to the inmates of the concentration camp of Esterwege.[86] His courageous act stood alone.

There is no evidence in the relevant archives to indicate any action on the part of the Catholic episcopate that could be called appropriate in coming to grips with this monstrous practice. In fact, the bishops, in the interest of pastoral care, tried instead to come to terms with the institution of the concentration camp as best they could. At first the Gestapo had agreed to allow Catholic priests to hold weekly services and to hear confessions in the camps. After Heydrich in 1934 had forbidden auricular confession in prisons and camps, the bishops pleaded with Hitler to revoke the ban. The priests entrusted with hearing confession, the memorandum submitted to Hitler in 1935 promised, will of course "hold the prisoner to absolute truthfulness and recognition of the authority of the state and thus contribute to the inner reform and correction of the prisoners."[87] A little later, it appears, the privilege of holding divine services was also withdrawn. In 1938 Cardinal Bertram petitioned the Gestapo in Berlin again to allow such services in the concentration camps. The priests fulfilling this task, he promised, would strictly observe camp rules and would be told "specifically to maintain strictest silence."[88] This request, too, was denied.

In June 1936 Bishop Berning of Osnabrück, member of the Prussian State Council, visited a number of concentration camps in his diocese. The *Kölnische Volkszeitung* reported that the Bishop had commended the furnishings of the camps visited. Addressing the inmates in the camp Aschendorfer Moor, Berning reminded them of the duty of obedience and fidelity towards people and state that was demanded by their religious faith. In a talk to the guards the Bishop was reported to have praised their work in the camp, and to have ended with three *Sieg Heil* for Führer and father-land.[89] Father Friedrich Muckermann's weekly *Der Deutsche Weg* in Holland, which later verified the fact of the visits with the diocesan chancery of Osnabrück, commented in a tone of despera-tion, "We face the shocking truth that the only word which a German bishop until today has publicly said about the barbarities of the concentration camps is a word of glorification of Hitler and of a system that has brought about these barbarities."[90]

German Catholics in exile were following the tactics and ideological concessions of the German episcopate with growing dismay. In December 1934 Father Muckermann expressed the hope that Rome and the German episcopate would soon proclaim the identity of National Socialism and neopaganism. The differentia-tion between the well-meaning Hitler and his bad lieutenants was no longer feasible and merely confused the faithful. The time had come, Father Muckermann declared, openly to denounce National Socialism and its regime of infamy.

> A great moment has arrived for the Church. The rights of man are in danger. Nobody dares to speak up against those dictators who treat man like a slave. Nobody, in the face of the concentration camps, the murders, the assaults upon liberty, utters the divine word: "This you may not do!" Were the Church to speak it, she would fulfil her high calling and the answer would be an enthusiastic echo all over the world.[91]

But the word was not spoken. Waldemar Gurian in 1935 re-minded the German bishops that the mission of the Church con-sisted not only in administering the sacraments, but also in defend-ing morality "in a world which, as the Third Reich, has forgotten it."[92] A year later Gurian pointed out the harmful effects of the failure of the episcopate to raise their voice against Nazi terrorism.

> The effects of this silence is to bewilder Christians and to disillusion most bitterly non-Christians, who might have other-wise been converted but actually are losing all confidence in the Church as a result of her failing to show her disapproval of flagrant injustice. Needless to say, in this case silence does not mean consent, but it gives the impression that if only formulas

and methods could be found that guaranteed the Church her outward existence and a certain moral influence on individuals . . . the battle would be over.[93]

An underlying premise of these criticisms of the episcopate was the assumption that large numbers of German Catholics were eagerly awaiting their bishops' denunciation of the Nazi regime and were willing to support the Church in the event of an open clash with the state. There exists no way of certifying or disproving the accuracy of this assumption, though in the perspective of today it seems over-optimistic. We do know that the bishops themselves did not share it. In June 1935 Bishop Buchberger of Regensburg wrote Cardinal Bertram that in the event of a rupture of relations with the regime the fidelity of many Catholics toward their Church would fail the test. Prudence therefore dictated, Buchberger counseled, "to evade a formal break as long as possible."[94] A few months later Bishop Galen made the same pessimistic appraisal of the willingness of the German Catholics to side with their Church against the regime. Would the faithful, he asked at a conference of deans, be prepared "in case of need to 'obey God rather than man'? I cannot help fearing," Galen answered his own question, "that many will weaken in their faith and loyalty and that the strength of the Church will be impaired." Only a minority would retain their fidelity; most of the faithful were not prepared to withstand the demands of an all-out fight. There was therefore no alternative, Galen concluded, but to continue the little-glorious but no less promising trench warfare.[95]

Other observers on the scene saw the situation in a different light. They attributed the low spirits of the rank-and-file Catholics to the wavering tactics and evasive compromises of their bishops. After spending two years in Germany and Austria, the English Catholic writer William Teeling concluded in 1937 that the Pope and the bishops "fail to realize the strength they have behind them, if only they might have leadership and courage."[96] Teeling's observation, in the perspective of today, seems plausible. The bishops' failure to call a spade a spade, their attempts to trade on the popularity of certain Nazi ideas, their continued admonishments to clergy and faithful not to criticize state and Party certainly were little suited to instill anti-Nazi sentiment in their followers. The

Church, Father Muckermann concluded in March 1938, had never yet denounced the National Socialist system as such. She had limited herself to preserving certain aspects of her institutional existence. In failing to defend not only the liberty of the Church, but human liberty itself, Father Muckermann insisted, the bishops had inadvertently doomed the chances of winning the struggle against their oppressors.[97]

Whether the Church, after burning all bridges, would have emerged from the troubles and turmoil of the Nazi period stronger than it did by using vacillation and compromise none can tell. The answer may well be in the negative. But how is the strength of the Church to be measured? How much is sheer survival of the institution to count as against the preservation of moral integrity? There comes a time, a troubled German Jesuit inside Germany wrote in 1935, when all temporizing has to be abandoned. "There are moments when, without any tangible utility, something has to be said for no other reason but that it is true. If it is not said, the moral order of the world suffers a blow that is harder to overcome than its violation by brute force."[98] In the eyes of many observers the Church in Germany today still pays the price for not having listened to this voice of conscience.

7 The Church and Hitler's Foreign Policy

Hitler's imperialistic aims were clearly stated in *Mein Kampf*. All Germans were to be united in the resurrected German Reich; France, the mortal enemy of Germany, was to be deprived of its power in Europe; new *Lebensraum* was to be gained in the east. Aware of the military weakness of Germany and concerned about a preventive attack by the European powers, Hitler in his first years stressed Nazi Germany's peaceful intentions: the revision of the treaty of Versailles, for example, would have to be accomplished without the use of force. Under the cloak of this policy of peace, preparations could proceed for rearmament and, eventually, war. Many inside and outside of Germany were taken in by this maneuver, and their number included most German Catholics who followed their lay and clerical leaders.

1. Exit From the League of Nations

On October 14, 1933, Hitler announced that since Germany had been refused equality of rights, both moral and material, it was withdrawing from the Disarmament Conference and the League of Nations. The German people would be asked to approve this decision in a plebiscite on November 12, to be combined with the election of a new Reichstag. The propagandistic purpose of this "election" was openly acknowledged, for there was to be only one list of handpicked candidates. The mobilization of popular support, aimed at demonstrating the unity of the German people behind the Nazi regime, was undertaken on a grand scale.

The Catholic forces, it appears, did not need much convincing. A day after Hitler had announced the withdrawal of Germany from the League of Nations, Vicar Capitular Steinmann and Dr. Klausener, acting in the name of Berlin's Catholic Action, telegraphed Hitler: "In this hour of decision for the nation, the Catholics of the diocese of Berlin, possessed of unshakable love to people and fatherland, unanimously support the Führer and Chancellor in his struggle for equal rights, the honor of the nation and the restoration of a just peace between all peoples."[1] Similarly, the Catholic Students' Association sent word to Hitler, "After the historic decisions of October 14, students and old boys [alte Herren] organized in the Catholic Burschenschaft pledge anew unflinching loyalty to the Führer of the German people in his struggle for the honor and freedom of the fatherland."[2]

The episcopate faced the question of whether it, too, should take a public stand on elections and plebiscite. Negotiations in Rome over the recognition of the Catholic organizations and other issues connected with the implementation of the Concordat were making little progress, while in the meantime harassment and repressive measures continued unabated. In a lengthy note of protest, on October 19, Cardinal Pacelli enumerated "the difficulties and persecutions, carried to a virtually intolerable degree, which the Catholic Church in Germany is now enduring in open violation of the Concordat" and he warned that "the Catholic population, offended in its sentiments, disappointed in its expectations," looked with ever-growing impatience to its bishops from whom it expected "words of fearless remonstrance in behalf of those who are suffering and oppressed."[3] In these circumstances the question arose whether, in spite of these infringements of the Concordat by the government, the episcopate should now make a statement of support on election day. Archbishop Gröber, who participated in the talks in Rome, informed Cardinal Bertram on October 27 that churchmen in Rome, and he personally, favored the issuance of an episcopal declaration. The government would undoubtedly welcome such a statement as a patriotic act of the first magnitude. The problem lay in its formulation:

> A declaration without qualifications would never be understood by the Catholic population. On the other hand, the omission of a declaration in these portentous and fateful times for our fatherland would be interpreted as a sign of insufficient patriotism. The practical consequences of such an omission, too, can hardly be anticipated. It will therefore be necessary to combine dignity and love of fatherland, and to connect the sorrow over the incidents that have still occurred of late with confidence in early redress. The government, moreover, would not only have to speak words but follow up with deeds. In consequence of these, above all, the declaration of the bishops would be understood by the Catholic rank and file and receive a further justification.[4]

Cardinal Bertram sent copies of Gröber's letter to the rest of the episcopate and solicited their views. In an accompanying note Bertram stated that he personally would prefer not to issue a declaration for so purely political an occasion, "in order not to create a precedent for all other and probably still more difficult situations that might arise in the new Reich." But he would bow to the judgment of the majority. He also included a draft of a statement for use in case it be decided to take a public stand. Replies should be sent by special delivery to be received by November 5.[5]

In the meantime the Nazis were beginning to put pressure on individual bishops to support their cause on November 12. The mayor and Party leader of Passau, on October 28, invoking instructions from the Bavarian government, demanded that the clergy be ordered to turn out on election day and that they in turn exhort their parishioners to do likewise.[6] The Bishop of Speyer, when pressured by party leaders of his region, explained in a public statement that the Church was first awaiting assurances from Berlin regarding the fulfillment of the Concordat.[7] Meanwhile, Bishops Gröber and Berning attempted unsuccessfully to obtain an interview with Hitler or Göring in order to secure confirmation of the list of protected organizations and redress of their grievances. They suggested that the election manifesto be withheld until November 8.

If no satisfaction had been obtained by that date, "one should seriously consider whether a declaration should be issued."[8] Other bishops, too, it appears, were hesitant. Cardinal Bertram on November 5 informed the episcopate that the replies to his circular letter had revealed a complete lack of agreement on the basic question of whether the bishops should take a public stand, as well as on how to formulate such a statement. He enclosed the text of a declaration to be issued in his archdiocese, but indicated that his draft was by no means binding upon others.[9]

Despite the complete lack of response from the government with respect to the implementation of the Concordat, most bishops issued pronouncements on the elections. Archbishop Gröber called on the Catholics in his archdiocese to prove their solidarity with the German people by doing their patriotic duty on November 12. Germany had left the League of Nations in order to achieve equal rights. This demand was in consonance with "national honor as well as with the Christian law of morality and international law." Gröber expressed the hope that the Chancellor's word would be honored and the Concordat of peace be fulfilled.[10] This statement was also accepted by the dioceses of Berlin, Paderborn and Osnabrück. Cardinal Bertram's declaration differentiated between the plebiscite and the elections. Concerning the former, he asked for a response out of concern for equal rights for the fatherland in the family of nations and the protection of peace. How to vote in the poll for the Reichstag, a purely political act, was left to the determination of each voter.[11] This declaration was also adopted by the Bishop of Limburg. Bishop Sebastian of Speyer emphasized that a "yes" vote in the plebiscite was dictated by both patriotic and Christian principles. He had decided to comply with the repeated urgings of the *Gauleitung* to issue a statement for this important day after being assured that the leaders of the party in the Palatinate strongly disapproved of the maltreatment of Catholics that had occurred here and there. With regard to the Reichstag elections, the Bishop stated that in compliance with the provisions of the Concordat he would refrain from issuing instructions.[12]

The declaration published by the other bishops of Bavaria, composed by Cardinal Faulhaber, similarly asked for a positive vote in the plebiscite. "In this way the Catholics will profess anew their loyalty to people and fatherland and their agreement with the farsighted and forceful efforts of the Führer to spare the German people the terror of war and the horrors of Bolshevism, to secure public order and create work for the unemployed." The bishops stressed that such a vote did not signify approval of all the incidents of the last months, of the measures taken in Bavaria against the Catholic organizations and of all other matters burdening their conscience. They had confidence that the Concordat would be implemented and Catholics be afforded full equality in the state. The elections for the Reichstag were a partisan issue and therefore, in accordance with Article 32 of the Concordat, outside their competence. This declaration, a postscript added, was not meant to be read from the pulpit.[13]

There is no way of measuring the effect of these episcopal manifestos upon the outcome of the elections in any precise way. Even if we take into account the growing pressure to conform and the occasional outright coercion utilized by the regime during the vote, it is fairly clear that Hitler's act of defiance of the outside world was greeted by most Germans, still resentful of the lost war and the Versailles treaty, with genuine enthusiasm. Once again the Catholic bishops were merely reflecting public opinion. The number of those approving Germany's withdrawal from the League of Nations, 95 per cent of those voting, probably would not have been affected in any decisive degree by a different stand of the episcopate.

But the bishops' declaration did confirm the orthodoxy of the patriotic and nationalistic sentiments so widespread in the Catholic camp. The chauvinistic propaganda of the Nazis was thus helped to success by the Church's recognition and appreciation of Hitler's allegedly peaceful intentions. Moreover, even though most bishops maintained a formally neutral position with regard to the elections to the Reichstag, the exhortation to vote for Hitler's foreign policy could do nothing but help gain votes for the single slate of candidates which the Nazis had submitted to the electorate. Thus, even when we make allowance for the elimination of all political opposition and the absence of a positive alternative on the ballot, the fact that the Nazis now rolled up 92 per cent of all the votes cast and were able to double their electoral strength, was probably, at least in

some measure, because of the not unfriendly attitude of the episcopate to the regime. An analysis of the election returns confirms
that whereas the Catholic areas of Germany on March 5, 1933, had
still resisted the inroads of Nazism to some degree, the Catholic
vote on November 12 hardly revealed a picture different from the
rest of the population. Even in Catholic Bavaria the Nazi list now
obtained well over 90 per cent of the vote.[14] The bishops might ask
the faithful to approve of Hitler's foreign policy only and refrain
from urging a vote for the Nazi slate. But the rank-and-file Catholics
did not make these distinctions, especially after Goebbels had
threatened to invalidate all those "yes" ballots in the plebiscite
that were not matched by a "yes" vote for the Nazis' Reichstag
list.[15]

Despite the near certainty of a smashing victory, the Nazis did
not fail to take offense at the bishops' reservations. For example,
they reacted to the modest words of criticism contained in the
election manifesto of the Bavarian episcopate with the paranoia
typical of all dictatorial regimes. The bishops were enjoined from
having the declaration read from the pulpit, and the press was
forbidden to print it.[16] On the eve of the plebiscite the Bavarian
radio publicized the first paragraph of the manifesto only, which
gave the appearance that the bishops supported the government
without any qualifications whatsoever. The Bavarian Council of
Ministers, meeting two days after the plebiscite, called the declaration a stab in the back to the German people fighting for their
freedom, and a protest was lodged with the Papal Nuncio. It was
also decided to get in touch with the bishops and to warn them
against repeating such subversive tactics. Hitler, too, was informed.[17]
Talking with Pacelli on December 18, Buttmann praised the
declaration of Gröber, which had not differentiated between plebiscite and Reichstag elections, and added with regard to that of
Bertram and the Bavarian bishops, "No electoral manifesto at all
would have been better than this one."[18]

Cardinal Faulhaber protested to the Bavarian State Chancellery against the curbs imposed by the authorities. The declaration, he pointed out, had been solicited by the government, only
to be suppressed later in a most arbitrary manner and in clear
violation of Section 4 of the Concordat. He had agreed that the

Bavarian radio omit the second section containing some criticism, but had expressed the hope that at least the last paragraph be read where reference was made to the Concordat. The bishops, in any event, had not criticized the political measures of the government and were still prepared to yield the state its due and to support it in its difficult tasks. But they were duty bound to teach the moral law of the Church and they could not tolerate such interference with their rights as Germans and bishops. "We shall remember this prohibition when in the future, perhaps in connection with the Saar question or at other patriotic occasions, another proclamation should be demanded from us."[19]

By the time of the Saar plebiscite this resolve had been forgotten.

2. The Saar Plebiscite

An annex to the Versailles treaty had put the Saar territory under the rule of a commission representing the League of Nations. It had also provided that fifteen years after the treaty came into force the population of the Saar could express their desires for the future in a plebiscite. There were to be three alternatives: (a) maintenance of the status quo; (b) union with France; (c) union with Germany.

The population of the Saar was almost entirely German. Most of the population—72.6 per cent in 1927—was Catholic. Despite the territory's formally independent status, the ties to Germany remained strong.

The fact that the Saar Catholics remained under the jurisdiction of the Bishops of Trier and Speyer strengthened the emotional links with the Reich.[20] In order to eliminate the influence of the two German bishops, the French occupation authorities and the Commission of the League of Nations repeatedly had attempted to obtain the consent of the Holy See to the establishment of a separate bishopric for the Saar. The French paper *Le Matin* asserted in 1922 that for the Bishop of Speyer "the love of Germany was a hundred times more important than the love of God."[21] Exaggerated as this comment no doubt was, the Bishops of Trier and Speyer were ardent nationalists and actively propagated pro-German sentiments. But a bishopric for the Saar was never created by the Vatican, which declared itself prepared at the most to appoint an Apostolic Administrator for the territory, who would function under the tutelage of the Bishops of Trier and Speyer. This compromise was rejected; and the two bishops continued to take an active part in Saar affairs.[22]

As the plebiscite approached political agitation assumed new intensity. In July 1933 the National Socialists organized the *Deutsche Front,* which, using threats and strong-arm methods and generously financed by Germany, soon emerged as the dominant political force in the territory. In October of the same year, the Center party of the Saar, yielding to threats of what would happen after the day of reckoning in 1935, declared itself dissolved, and merged with the new pro-German front. Hitler was determined to score a propaganda triumph by securing a huge vote for the return of the Saar to the fatherland, and no effort was spared to bring about this result. That the people of the territory would opt for this choice had really never been in doubt until the Nazis' accession to power in 1933. Now, however, the number grew who desired retention of the status quo, and the harassment of the Catholic Church in the Reich provided good argument for them. The position that the Catholic hierarchy would assume in the Saar issue clearly could prove decisive.

In the fall of 1933 the French renewed their pressure for the appointment of a fully empowered Apostolic Administrator, and this time the Vatican promised redress.[23] On November 7 Ambassador Bergen reported that the Pope had appointed Monsignor Gustavo Testa to visit the Saar.[24] To counteract the French complaints about the pro-German activity of certain members of the clergy, Monsignor Kaas, after consultation with Bergen, got in touch with Bishop Bornewasser of Trier and suggested that he submit counter-charges. Bornewasser, thereupon, hurried to Rome. Whereas the year before, he told Bergen, no more than 2 per cent of the Saar people would have voted for the status quo, he now estimated that 25 per cent would do so.[25] On November 18 Bornewasser met with Pacelli and Kaas. He urged the Papal Secretary of State to avoid anything that might be interpreted by the Catholics of the Saar as a partisan measure. Pacelli replied that the appointment of an Apostolic Administrator and a concomitant suspension of the jurisdiction of the two German bishops was out of the question, but that the Pope had felt constrained to order the dispatch of a Visitor. The French had not only complained about the clergy, but had argued that the propaganda of the National Socialists seriously threatened a free vote. The Apostolic Visitor, thus, had the additional task of informing the Holy See about general conditions in the territory. Finally, the combined pleading of Bornewasser and Kaas could only obtain Pacelli's promise not to stress publicly the official character of Testa's mission.[26]

On November 27 Monsignor Testa arrived in Saarbrücken. Before his departure from Rome he had already declared himself willing to meet Vice-Chancellor Papen, the German government's plenipotentiary for Saar questions. This talk took place on December 7 in Trier with Bishop Bornewasser also in attendance. Testa told Papen that according to his impressions the Saar was thoroughly German; he acknowledged that his trip was mainly a courtesy gesture toward the French government. The Papal legate regretted that certain incidents in Germany had had a harmful effect upon the atmosphere in the Saar, and Papen replied that the government was anxious to conduct talks with the Curia in order to dispose of these troublesome matters as soon as possible. The Vice-Chancellor noted, "[Testa] doubtless has sympathies for Germany and the National Socialist regime."[27] The German press, too, stressed Testa's pro-German attitudes, which he was said to have shown as long ago as 1923 on a similar mission to the Ruhr.[28]

Bishop Bornewasser kept in touch with Papen. In the spring of 1934 he wrote the Vice-Chancellor that in the last few months he had become a pessimist. He had welcomed the formation of the *Deutsche Front* and only the preceding week had ordered all monasteries to join it *en bloc*. He also still felt confident that a majority of the Saar inhabitants would vote for return to the fatherland. But he was depressed on account of the [Nazis'] threats to the religious and moral well-being of the Reich. "It goes without saying, that apart from a small circle of confidants I never express this pessimism in front of the clergy (especially not the Saar clergy) or the people. In all my speeches and sermons I try to comfort the people and to encourage them with a view to the divine providence which is always at work, even in our time, and by pointing out that which is thoroughly good in the new Reich." He also was worried whether the League of Nations would consent to the return of the Saar to Germany. Much hate and discord could be avoided if Germany could find a way to achieve the return of the Saar without a plebiscite.[29] In view of the rumors circulating in the Saar about an impending *coup d'état* by the *Deutsche Front,* this was a rather ominous statement.

The bishop did not keep his partisanship a secret. After having received Franz Reichert, the head of the *Arbeitsgemeinschaft Katholischer Deutscher* (AKD) in the Saar, Bornewasser in early April of 1934 authorized Reichert to issue a news release according to which the Bishop had confirmed "that for the clergy of the diocese it went without saying that they would do their utmost for the return of the Saar to the German Reich."[30]

The situation changed sharply after Hitler's Blood Purge of June 30 which, as we have seen, along with several hundred other victims claimed the lives of a number of prominent Catholic leaders. While Catholics in the Reich learned of the extent of the massacre only gradually, the impact on the Catholics of the Saar, who still had access to an anti-Nazi press, was immediate and drastic. Requiem masses for Klausener and Probst held throughout the territory drew overflowing crowds, including many leaders of the *Deutsche Front.* The recently founded *Neue Saar Post,* a Catholic newspaper edited by Father Johannes Hoffmann and strongly opposed to the Saar's return to a Nazi-ruled Germany, now gained many new adherents. It was widely believed, a well-informed observer recalls, "that the odds were now even, that the Church held the balance, and that unless Hitler should succeed in rehabilitating himself and should placate the Church, or unless the Nazi regime should be overthrown before January [the plebiscite had been scheduled for January 13, 1935], the Territory might be indefinitely lost to the Reich."[31]

When on July 29 the Catholic youth organizations of the Saar met in Saarbrücken for their "Day of Confession of Faith," a mass meeting to be attended also by the Bishops of Trier and Speyer, attention was fixed on the position the Church would now assume. But for the two bishops nothing had changed. Bishop Bornewasser in his address attacked (without naming it) the *Neue Saar Post,* and

both he and Bishop Sebastian signed a telegram to President Hindenburg which read: "50,000 Catholic *Jungmänner* and *Jungmäd-
chen* of the Saar territory, assembled in Saarbrücken to demonstrate
their loyalty to their spiritual leaders, the Bishops of Trier and
Speyer, from the western border country of Germany send their
greetings and assurances of unwavering fidelity to the sovereign of
the German Reich."[32] The Plebiscite Commission appointed by the
League of Nations regarded this telegram as a violation of the
pledge made by Germany to prevent any of its nationals from ex-
erting direct or indirect pressure likely to affect the freedom of the
voting. Permission to hold this meeting, the Commission reported
to the League of Nations, had been granted because of its alleged
purely religious purpose; the bishops had abused the Commission's
indulgence.[33] But the League took no action.

After the attack by Bornewasser on the *Neue Saar Post* many
priests in the Saar canceled their subscription to it. Others complained to Rome about the political pressures exerted on them by
their bishops. Bishop Sebastian of Speyer recently had transferred
three curates under attack by the *Deutsche Front* because of their
anti-Nazi sermons from the Saar into the German part of his diocese.[34] On August 4 Ambassador Bergen at the Vatican sent word
that Monsignor Testa had returned to Rome; Testa's report to the
Pope and the Papal Secretary of State had also mentioned instances
of disciplinary measures being taken against clerics supporting the
status quo. The French ambassador was renewing his demand for
a Papal legate with greater powers.[35]

Bishop Bornewasser, it appears, was aware of these complaints,
for on August 22 he addressed a lengthy letter to Pacelli in which
he tried to justify his conduct. "During my almost thirteen years as
bishop," he wrote, "I have never interfered in the political affairs
of the Saar, though in private talks I have never made it a secret
that I regarded the return of the purely German Saar to its German
fatherland as a foregone conclusion." He had been forced publicly
to disown support of the *Neue Saar Post* and its espousal of the
status quo because of recurring rumors that he sympathized with its
views but was not allowed to express them. Any other reaction
would have cost him the trust of those hundreds of thousands of
Saar Catholics who longed to return to Germany. Also, he had to

counter the ever-more-widespread assertion that if the Saar were to be lost to Germany, the Catholic clergy would have to shoulder the blame, so for this reason he had written to the German Chancellor. He understood fully, Bornewasser continued, why some priests were embittered on account of the unfortunate events in Germany, but they should be more farsighted. He was convinced that his position was one best calculated to further the future interests of the Catholics in the Saar.[36]

Bornewasser had written his letter to Hitler after a long talk with the *Gauleiter* of the Palatinate, Josef Bürckel. On August 7 the latter had become Hitler's plenipotentiary for the Saar in the place of Papen, who had been relieved of his post and made German Minister to Vienna. On August 27 Bürckel personally delivered Bornewasser's letter to Hitler. In it the Bishop expressed his grave concern over the future of the Saar. "I do so in order that all possible hindrances can still be removed at this late hour that might impede the return of the people of the Saar to the fatherland." The conduct of the Nazis in the territory and the treatment of the Church in Germany caused serious misgivings among the Catholics of the Saar. He requested that Hitler take all appropriate measures that "for the immediate time ahead would prevent these dangerous and painful effects."[37] Bornewasser sent copies of this letter to the Foreign Ministry, the Bishop of Speyer, Cardinal Bertram and Monsignor Kaas in Rome. In a covering note addressed to the latter, Bornewasser pointed out that Cardinal Schulte of Cologne had been very glad about this letter to Hitler, "also in the interest of the bishops."[38]

On September 11 the Vatican sent a new Papal legate and observer to the Saar, Monsignor Giovanni Panico, a former chargé d'affaires of the Apostolic nunciature at Prague. Monsignor Testa had been appointed Apostolic Delegate for Palestine. Rumors had it that the French had pressed for the dispatch of a less pro-German Papal representative, but the new delegate was to prove no different in this respect. Counselor Braun von Stumm of the Foreign Ministry's press department characterized Panico's political outlook— after talking to him at a social function in Von Stumm's home— in these words: "Very much impressed by the good qualities of Italian Fascism, he openly acknowledged that he personally also wished success to National Socialism (Hitler)." Panico mentioned to Von Stumm that the Bishops of Trier and Speyer would probably issue orders forbidding their clergy to make political speeches in public. According to Panico, the main reason for this step was the bishops' aim to deprive clerical supporters of the status quo of chances for publicity. Priests friendly to Germany did not require the opportunity for public appearances, since the pro-German position of the two bishops had been repeatedly and clearly expressed. Special speeches to prove the Church's patriotic stand were no longer necessary.[39]

Bishop Bornewasser up to this point had merely counseled the clergy not to interfere in political matters, but this was not enough in the eyes of the Nazis. On October 17 Saar Plenipotentiary Bürckel attacked the Church's formal neutrality in a lengthy letter to Foreign Minister Neurath. He suggested that the Curia be warned of the dangerous consequences of such a policy for the interests of the Church and its privileged position under the Concordat. "The loyalty of man to his national community as part of the order of creation, in which man is integrated by his birth and kind, has been ordained by God, and the Church has therefore always acknowledged the duty of holding Christians to their loyalty in relation to this Divine order of Creation." As long as the Church demanded this loyalty, she did not violate the neutrality imposed by the rules of the plebiscite, which merely forbade the use of coercion. The German Reich, Bürckel wrote, did not insist that the Church canvass for National Socialism as such. But neither could the government tolerate the Church's surrender of any of her spiritual claims.

> The Saar question is for us no political question in the usual French liberal sense; it is a question of nationality. We have the right, therefore, to demand professions of allegiance by our *Volksgenossen* to their national community; we have also the right to demand this of the Catholic clergy who belong to our people. The Curia has no right to demand neutrality, that is to say, to oblige the clergy to refrain from openly and publicly professing allegiance to their own people.[40]

A copy of Bürckel's letter was sent by the Foreign Ministry to Ambassador Bergen at the Holy See with the suggestion to employ the arguments contained therein in oral communications with the

Curia. Bergen was told to emphasize that unless the line of neutrality was changed, the Church after the vote would be in real danger.[41] Bergen replied that even though he had made those points many times before, the Curia insisted on its strict neutrality. He had been told that if the Holy See took even the smallest measure which could be construed as being one-sidedly in Germany's favor, France would come forward with counter-claims and again ask for the establishment of an autonomous ecclesiastical jurisdiction for the Saar. The Curia agreed that the Saar was German land and belonged to Germany. It was therefore "not only natural and legitimate, but even obligatory for the outcome of the Plebiscite to be in favor of Germany." But as long as the present tensions and difficulties, which the Church encountered in the Reich, prevailed, it would have to be left to the conscience of every individual Catholic whether he should vote for Germany.[42]

Another attempt to dissuade the Vatican from its neutrality was undertaken a few days later when three Catholic members of the *Deutsche Front,* led by Max Müller, an assistant of Bürckel, called on Pacelli at the Vatican. The audience, which took place on November 7, was arranged by the German legation. Müller reported in detail his unsuccessful attempts to get the Bishops of Trier and Speyer to issue an order that would silence the clergy who defended the status quo. Pacelli replied that the German bishops and clergy had complete freedom of action.[43] Anxious to use this statement of the Papal Secretary of State, Müller, upon his return from Rome, asked to be received by the two bishops. Bornewasser, piqued by the idea of receiving instructions from the Vatican through an official of the German government, at first refused to see Müller. He finally consented when Müller informed him that in addition to news from the Vatican he also had to deliver a message from Hitler. This meeting took place in Trier on November 17.[44]

Perhaps to spare themselves the embarrassment of acting under orders, the Bishops of Trier and Speyer, before receiving Müller, issued the ruling which the Nazis had been waiting for. Dated November 12, the order forbade the clergy of the two dioceses to speak in public at political meetings held in the Saar. "The same restraint is to be exercised in the pulpit and in meetings of Catholic organizations." Priests should refrain from recommending news-papers, periodicals and books from the pulpit. Any work for a newspaper or periodical required permission of the chanceries. "We want to and must prevent by means of this order that politics be carried into the Church and introduced into pastoral care. Our order does not touch the moral duty to love the ancestral nationality and be faithful to the fatherland. According to Catholic teaching the fulfilment of these two duties is a moral virtue."[45]

The Nazi organ *Deutsche Front* made explicit what the bishops had implied: "Whoever on January 13 votes against Germany and for the status quo, violates, according to Catholic teaching, the moral virtues of love and fidelity to the ancestral nationality." The *Neue Saar Post,* making the best of a bad situation, reacted with a vague statement of acknowledgement.[46] Efforts to rally the Catholics against return to Nazi Germany continued. After a meeting on November 30 a new Catholic party for the status quo came into being that took the name *Deutscher Volksbund für Christlich-soziale Gemeinschaft* (German People's League for Christian-social Com-munity). It was said to include among its founders over seventy Catholic priests.[47]

The bishops now acted more forcefully. A new order dated December 3 reminded the clergy that the instructions of November 12 had admittedly spoken only of public appearances at political meetings. "But we regard it as political activity of far greater extent if clerics participate in a meeting which has the declared purpose of creating a new political organization."[48] The *Neue Saar Post,* in order not "to undermine the authority of the Church," refrained from comment. But the status quo paper *Generalanzeiger* showed less restraint and wrote under the headline "Bishops as Agents of Goebbels": "If the Bishops of Trier and Speyer do not want to become martyrs for the freedom of the Catholic Church, and instead wish to live as civil servants of the Third Reich, they will have to bear responsibility for this before their conscience."[49]

In order not to leave any ambiguity, on December 5 Bishop Bornewasser sent a confidential follow-up communication to all deans (senior priests) in the Saar territory. The names of the priests associated with the newly founded *Volksbund* would soon become public knowledge, Bornewasser wrote. How will these priests, then, and especially after January 13, be able to continue to minister to their parishes, where a big majority will surely vote for return to Germany? The support given by seventy priests to the highly questionable and false aims of the new Party was a serious blow, not only to the well-being of the Catholics of the Saar, but to that of German Catholicism as a whole. "In agreement with the Bishop of Speyer, I must say that the 30th of November was one of the bitterest days of our episcopate."[50]

Max Müller, the assistant to Saar Plenipotentiary Bürckel, had in November relayed Hitler's invitation to Bishops Bornewasser and Sebastian to meet with him to discuss their complaints regarding the treatment of the Church. Both had declined. Bornewasser had told Müller that he had nothing to add to his letter of August 27, which had never been answered. Moreover, such a visit could not be kept secret, and might be exploited by those opposed to a return of the Saar.[51] Thereupon Minister of the Interior Frick, in the name of Hitler, finally replied to Bornewasser. He thanked him for his patriotic stand on the Saar question and added: "If the German episcopate were to succeed, as your Excellency has succeeded in the Saar territory, to win so many brave and courageous clergymen, convinced of their duty to Germany, for the support of the Third Reich and for participation in the work of rebuilding, then soon even the last possibilities of friction would be eliminated. . . ."[52]

Tension between Church and State, indeed, had recently abated. On account of the great importance attributed by the Nazis to an overwhelming vote of the Saar population for return, the Church in Germany had been treated somewhat more gently during the last months of 1934. Now the Nazis could pressure the bishops for additional help. On December 14 Müller asked Bornewasser to choose a Catholic priest to broadcast a Christmas celebration over the German radio during which Saar Plenipotentiary Bürckel would make an address. The Bishop of Trier declined on the grounds that a priest in such a role would be inconsistent with his November order to the clergy.[53] A few days later Müller proposed that the entire German episcopate issue a declaration, perhaps in the form of a New Year's message to the people of the Saar, in which it be made clear that their criticism of neopaganism was not aimed at National Socialism. This suggestion, repeated on December 27, was turned down by Bornewasser, who argued that this might jeopardize the League of Nations' confirmation of the results of the plebiscite.[54]

But some of the German bishops were, apparently, of a different opinion as to any possible endangering of the outcome through episcopal pronouncements. At the all-German Fulda Bishops' Conference in June 1934 it had been decided not to issue a joint declaration for the Saar plebiscite and to leave it to the discretion of the Bishops of Trier and Speyer whether they wanted to take a public stand. Cardinal Schulte of Cologne now decided to reopen this question, and did so by putting a *fait accompli* before the German episcopate: on December 26 the six bishops of the Cologne church province (Schulte, Berning, Bornewasser, Hilfrich, Vogt, Galen) issued a proclamation that was to be read from all the pulpits of their dioceses on January 6, 1935, one week before the plebiscite.

The idea of issuing such a declaration was suggested to Cardinal Schulte by Bishop Galen of Münster.[55] In a letter to Bürckel, Bornewasser went out of his way to point out that the proclamation was in no way connected with Müller's requests,[56] and there is no reason to doubt his word. The declaration is in keeping with the patriotic sentiments which both Galen and Schulte expressed on other occasions, and might have been published even if the Nazis had not requested it. It read:

> On Sunday, January 13, a plebiscite will be held in the Saar Territory on the question whether this German land and its people shall remain under the separation from the German Reich forced upon them by the dictated peace of Versailles [*Versailler Gewaltfrieden*]. This decision, to be made in a few days at the Saar and fraught with fateful consequences for the future of our fatherland, no true German can face with indifference. As German Catholics we are duty bound to stand up for the greatness, welfare, and peace of our fatherland. Our most effective help is prayer. We, therefore, order that on said Sunday in all churches three Lord's Prayers and Ave Marias be recited with the faithful after the general prayer in order to implore for a result of the Saar plebiscite that will bring blessings for our German people.[57]

Cardinal Schulte sent a copy of this proclamation to the other German bishops and asked them to concur. All of them agreed and published the declaration, though we do not know how enthusiastic they were about Schulte's tactics. Cardinal Faulhaber was somewhat annoyed. Faulhaber reminded Cardinal Schulte in a letter that it was Faulhaber who at the Fulda Conference in June had raised the question of issuing such a statement. Following the negative decision he had practiced strict restraint in this political question. He had also assured himself that this course of conduct had the approval of the Bishop of Trier and the Apostolic Delegate. "Since the Holy Father has expressed himself on the Saar Plebiscite in the only general form possible by stating that the Catholics of the Saar could not be prevented by qualms of conscience from voting for return to Germany, I felt even more reason to adhere to the decision of the Fulda Conference." In any event, if this decision was to be reversed, it had to be done by a joint declaration of the entire episcopate. "Otherwise, the schism among the German bishops would be revealed of which so much is spoken in Germany as well as abroad. And what a spectacle would it be if now the French episcopate, too, would order prayers for their congregations!" But since the Cologne statement was a fact, he would inquire from the Bavarian bishops whether they wished to follow suit and publish the declaration.[58]

Seven of the eight bishops of Bavaria voted for going along with the Cologne statement. The identity of the lone dissenter is not known. Faulhaber, as he informed the bishops two days later, had also approved, on condition that the entire German episcopate publish the declaration. One bishop, he reported, had voiced misgivings and asked whether the bishops could oblige the state as long as their pastoral letter (of June 1934) was forbidden publication. Would people not consider such a proclamation work done to order? Why should the bishops use the provocative phrase "dictated peace" if even the German government in recent months spoke only of peace and reconciliation? But for the sake of preserving unanimity, Faulhaber concluded in his letter, the Bavarian bishops would accept the Cologne draft.[59] In fact, the declaration of the Bavarian episcopate, as finally published, revealed two minor changes. The reference to the "dictated peace of Versailles" was omitted, and the entire pronouncement was introduced by a short preamble in which it was mentioned that the province of Cologne had originated this call for prayer.[60]

In the Saar territory, meanwhile, a heated electoral campaign was reaching a climax. The Nazis, now sure of victory, were threatening retribution to all those who on January 13 might dare to vote against return to the fatherland. A special effort was made to neutralize Catholic fears of the Nazis' anti-Catholicism by describing in glowing colors the condition of the Catholic Church in the Reich. For this purpose, beginning on October 1, the AKD distributed a new weekly newspaper, *Der Deutsche Katholik an der Saar*. The paper dwelt on the ideological similarities between Catholicism and National Socialism, while an illustrated supplement, *Der Kampfruf wider den Antichrist*, printed horror pictures of atrocities from Bolshevik-ruled Russia that were contrasted with the peace and prosperity of Hitler's Germany. After the AKD had unsuccessfully tried to obtain Bornewasser's endorsement for this paper, the Bishop informed the deans of the Saar that "he wanted nothing to do with this enterprise since *in the interest of Germany and of the Church* he had the duty to practice the utmost restraint" (Bornewasser's italics).[61] This paper's propaganda was in such bad taste that Bornewasser on December 1 felt constrained to draw Bürckel's attention to the damage being caused by it.[62]

From the other side the Catholics of the Saar were being wooed by the *Volksbund*. Meetings were held every Sunday, with banners proclaiming "For return to Germany, but not to Hitler Germany" and, "Christ is our leader, not Hitler." From the extremely bitter attacks of the *Deutsche Front* press on the *Volksbund* it was clear that the Nazis considered this organization a menace to an overwhelming vote for the Third Reich.[63]

Pro-German Catholic circles also began to worry over the *Volksbund*'s agitation. On January 3 the twelve deans of the territory issued a public statement aimed at refuting the claims of the *Volksbund* that a great majority of the Saar clergy supported the status quo. In actual fact, the deans maintained, quite the contrary was true. "In conformity with the order of the right reverend Bishops of Trier and Speyer of November 12, we priests regard love and fidelity to our German people and fatherland as a moral virtue imposed upon us and our faithful, and we shall act according to our duty." The deans expressed the hope and wish that after the return of the Saar the last difficulties in the relations between

Church and State would be eliminated. "This wish is based on the repeated declarations of the Führer and Chancellor and of other ministers that the German Reich will stand and be built on the foundation of positive Christianity."[64]

The *Neue Saar Post*, which until this time had exhibited remarkable restraint, now went over to the offensive. The following day it gave a report on how, according to trustworthy information, the declaration of the deans had come about. Monsignor Schlich of Saarbrücken, who had drawn up the statement in accordance with "instructions of higher authority," had telephoned each dean individually and told each that he already had the signatures of all the others. Reminded of their obligation to be obedient, all had eventually signed. The *Neue Saar Post* asserted again that most of the clergy supported the program of the *Volksbund*; the Party had four priests in its executive committee, including one dean. Mentioning the murder of Klausener, Probst and Gerlich, the newspaper predicted that after "the removal of the last difficulties" in the relations between the Church and the Third Reich there would emerge, not a peace with the Church, but the peace of the graveyard. Concerning the pastoral letter of the Cologne church province that had just been released, the paper insisted that by voting for the status quo Catholics would do just what the bishops had exhorted them to do; that is, "stand up for the greatness, welfare and peace of our fatherland." The best and only true way to serve Germany was to block the return of the Saar to the "un-German National Socialist dictatorship."[65]

But behind this optimism displayed for the benefit of the public lay deep concern over the effects of the pressures exerted by the hierarchy. Would the Catholics of the Saar dare flout the instructions of their superiors, who so clearly asked them to vote for a return to Germany? On January 9 the *Neue Saar Post* reported that the *Volksbund* had sent a telegram to the Papal Secretary of State. This urgent message drew the attention of Pacelli to the use made by the Nazis of the prayer declaration of the German bishops, and pleaded with him to take immediate steps that would remove the moral constraint now threatening a free vote.[66] At the same time Ambassador Bergen at the Vatican sent word that he had just heard of a French protest to the Holy See against the pronouncement of the German bishops and that Pacelli was concerned.[67] On January 5 the Plebiscite Commission lodged their objections with the Bishops of Trier and Speyer against the statement of the deans and the prayer proclamation. As far as these concerned the churches in the territory, the Commission contended, both statements had to be regarded as partisan acts in favor of the Saar's return to Germany and thus were likely to endanger the freedom of voting. This protest was handed to the Saar press for publication simultaneously with its delivery to the two bishops.[68]

The Bishops of Trier and Speyer were not to be deflected from their course. The protest of the Plebiscite Commission was ignored[69] and the prayer proclamation was read from the pulpits on January 6 as orginally ordered. The bishops were heartened in their stand by the absence of any action on the part of the Vatican. An editorial in the semi-official *L'Osservatore Romano* on January 7-8 again emphasized the neutrality and impartiality of the Holy See in the Saar Plebiscite. "The Holy See . . . wishes only that every faithful son of the Church should conduct himself in accordance with the dictates of an upright Catholic conscience."[70] During an audience granted to French Foreign Minister Pierre Laval on January 7 Pope Pius XI was said to have expressed the view that the prayer proclamation of the German bishops had prejudiced the outcome of the plebiscite and that the Holy See would reprimand them for their mistake. This report was made by the special correspondent of the *Petit Journal* in Rome, but it was quickly declared a fabrication by Ambassador Bergen. The latter suggested that the Bishops of Trier and Speyer publicly declare the falsity of any rumors about the Holy See's criticism of their conduct in the Saar question. Bishop Bornewasser complied promptly with this request[71] and his denial of a reprimand drew no comment from the Vatican.

On January 9 *L'Osservatore Romano* criticized a particularly clumsy article in the Nazi paper *Der Deutsche Katholik an der Saar* written by a Catholic priest. When the jubilant *Neue Saar Post* featured the Vatican paper's comment under the headline "The Holy See condemns Nazi Catholicism," *L'Osservatore Romano* hurried to deny that its editorial had had any political implications and stressed again the absolute neutrality of the Holy See.[72] This neutrality played straight into the hands of Bishops Bornewasser and Sebastian. The duty, proclaimed by the Holy See, to follow the "dictates of an upright Catholic conscience" to most Catholics implied the duty to follow the leadership of their bishops. For, as one priest protesting against the letter of the Plebiscite Commission to the bishops wrote to the *Saarbrücker Zeitung*, "The Pope and the bishops united with him have the power, as the teaching Church, called by God, to form and lead our Catholic conscience."[73]

The day of the plebiscite arrived amid solemn exhortations to the Saar population from all sides to remain calm. Across the German border an organ of the Catholic youth organization, *Junge Front*, printed a last-minute reminder to the Catholics of the Saar to heed their duty as Germans and Catholics. Signed by the spiritual leaders of the Catholic youth organizations, Monsignor Ludwig Wolker and Father Ludwig Esch, the appeal asked the Catholics to rejoin their brothers as "the unity of blood and language, law and history" demanded.[74] But the extent to which the Saar people followed the combined counsel of the German Church and state came as a complete surprise to all parties. When by the early morning hours of January 15 all the ballots had been counted, the results showed that virtually all registered voters had voted and that over 90 per cent of them had chosen union with Germany. The vote for Germany did not fall below 83 per cent in any single voting district.[75] Within four days of the plebiscite the Council of the League of Nations accepted the union of the Saar territory and Germany, the official transfer of sovereignty to take place on March 1, 1935.

On January 15, as soon as the Plebiscite Commission had announced the outcome of the vote, Hitler went on the air and hailed the great victory for Germany. The Bishops of Trier and Speyer, too, relieved of the need to equivocate, gave vent to expressions of joy. Bornewasser sent a telegram of congratulations to Bürckel in which he expressed his "great pleasure at the splendid victory" that the fatherland had achieved.[76] On the same day Bishop Sebastian issued a special pastoral letter to his diocesans in the Saar. He thanked them for the fidelity they had kept to the German fatherland over fifteen years and he praised God for having bestowed upon them such a marvelous disposition. "Your loyalty on January 13 is the newest and most shining proof that the Catholic Church and German nationality are not opposites, as today it is often maintained. No—Catholicism inspires its followers with love and fidelity also to the earthly fatherland that manifests itself in joyful readiness to make sacrifices at all times."[77] Special services of thanks were held in the entire dioceses of Trier and Speyer on the Sunday following the plebiscite, and on January 26 Sebastian declared in a sermon at St. Ingbert (Saar) that the results of the plebiscite could not be explained by natural factors alone. God himself had spoken and had dealt a devastating reply to those who considered the Catholics patriotically unreliable.[78]

The other German bishops were relieved and happy too. A large vote for the status quo, even if it had not resulted in the loss of the territory to Germany, undoubtedly would have caused new charges that the Church was untrustworthy and, being an international organization, lacking in sympathy for the special problems of the German people. Cardinal Schulte telegraphed Bornewasser "Congratulations and expressions of happiness at the happy conclusion of a difficult time."[79] The Archbishop of Paderborn, Kaspar Klein, gave orders on January 14 that on the following day, after the announcement of a favorable outcome of the plebiscite, the bells be rung in all the churches of the archdiocese.[80] The same instruction was handed down by the Vicar General of the diocese of Passau,[81] and there is reason to assume that the remaining dioceses acted in like manner. On March 1, the day of the official return of the Saar to Germany, the churches again participated in the celebrations. The bells rang out, flags were displayed and special prayers of thanks said.[82]

How decisive was the intervention of the Catholic hierarchy in the plebiscite? According to the often-repeated claims of the bishops themselves, the role of the Catholic episcopate in the attainment of this overwhelming victory was crucial. A solid majority for the return to Germany, Bishop Bornewasser declared on January 27, had always existed.

> But the fact that this majority became so strong that it surprised the whole world is due, next to the loyal attitude of the people of the Saar themselves, to the strong words of the German episcopate. As the bishop most involved, I do not state this in

order to reap appreciation and thanks. The German episcopate, in a serious hour, did its patriotic duty and whoever does his duty does not need thanks or appreciation. His fulfilled duty represents his compensation. I have mentioned it only in order that the historical truth will attain its due.[83]

In later years it was especially Bornewasser, who, in order to strengthen his standing with the authorities, often invoked the services he had rendered the German cause.[84]

The Nazis, for their part, tried to minimize the role of the Catholic bishops in order to prevent the Church from gaining prestige. But they had to acknowledge the help of the episcopate, even if grudgingly. A week before the plebiscite Goebbels declared at the opening of the Saar exhibition in Berlin that the Church had taken "a positive German position" on the Saar question. It was due in part to the efforts of the Bishop of Trier, he went on to say, that the Saar had not been made into an independent bishopric, separate from Germany.[85] Goebbels was quite right. The fact that the Saar remained part of the German Church and thus under the influence of a German clergy was an important reason for the prevalence of a strong pro-German sentiment. There was a time in 1934, moreover, when the fate of the Saar hung in the balance. After the Blood Purge of June 30 sentiment for deferring a return to Germany was strong and an anti-Nazi Church might well have made the difference. Had the Bishops of Trier and Speyer not curbed the status quo movement with their disciplinary measures, it is possible that the outcome on January 13 might have been different indeed.

The reasons for the German bishops' stand lay primarily in their strong personal patriotism. Historically the Saar was German territory and they saw no reason to give it up, even temporarily, just because Germany was now ruled by the National Socialists. The episcopate had always assailed the "dictated peace of Versailles" and had supported those calling for its revision. Moreover, feeling for Germany in the Saar had always run high, and the bishops thus thought to be on the winning side. When sentiments for postponing a return to the fatherland began to grow, they moved to suppress it because they were afraid of the harmful consequences for the Church in Germany of a big status-quo vote.

Finally, they probably hoped that their patriotic stand would strengthen the episcopate in the eyes of the Nazis and would pave the way for a settlement of all outstanding difficulties. The Catholics of the Saar had remained loyal to the fatherland for fifteen difficult years, a Catholic paper wrote after the plebiscite. On voting day they had known how to distinguish between history and ephemeral politics. "Such loyalty produces its compensation—it will not be disappointed and discouraged. All of German Catholicism from now on will be able to invoke with happiness and gratitude the results of the plebiscite brought about by the Catholics of the Saar."[86] But this expectation of reward, probably shared by many of the bishops, was to be thoroughly disappointed.

To the Nazis the return of the Saar meant the abandonment of the temporary soft line with the Church and the setting-about to destroy its influence in public life. In the Saar itself the co-operation established during the plebiscite campaign soon gave way to harassment and outright repression of the Catholic organizations. If anything, the situation here was worse than in the Reich, since the government did not recognize the validity of the *Reichskonkordat* for the Saar. Lengthy negotiations between Bürckel and the Bishops of Trier and Speyer about a new *modus vivendi* ended in failure. Monsignor Schlich of Saarbrücken, an enthusiastic supporter of the return to the fatherland, eventually had to flee abroad in order to escape arrest.

When the Bishop of Speyer in the spring of 1935 complained to Rome about the difficulties the Church was encountering in the Saar, the Papal Secretary of State replied that he had not expected anything else.

> The Holy See made it its business to show as much understanding as possible for the position taken by the right reverend bishops. Endeavoring to prevent any shadow being cast upon its neutrality in a political question, the Holy See, beyond some instructions and counsel, refrained from impeding the freedom of action and the sincerely held estimates of the right reverend ordinaries. Of course, the Holy See has not been free of serious misgivings about certain particulars of the episcopal pronouncements, especially as these concerned the early creation of safeguards for the time after the plebiscite.[87]

This was a politely phrased rebuke. Had it been administered more forcefully and before the plebiscite, such an action might have had an important bearing on the results. Unfortunately, what irked the Vatican most, it appears, was not the decision of the bishops to make common cause with the Nazis, but the failure to make their support conditional upon definite promises, and the tactical blunder of not deriving benefits for the Church from their services to the Reich.

3. The Occupation of the Demilitarized Rhineland.

On March 16, 1935, Hitler established universal military training. Germany was to have a peacetime army of thirty-six divisions, about half a million men. This public repudiation of the Versailles treaty's military restrictions drew French and British protests but no action. On May 21 Hitler delivered another of his speeches proclaiming Germany's peaceful intentions. He promised to respect the non-military clauses of the Versailles treaty, including its territorial provisions. Germany would honor its obligations arising out of the Locarno treaty and observe the demilitarization of the Rhineland.

No one outside a small circle of military men knew at this moment that Minister of Defense Blomberg had already been ordered by Hitler to prepare plans for the reoccupation of the left bank of the Rhine. The general mood in Germany was one of pride and rejoicing that the nation had succeeded in breaking the shackles of Versailles.[88] In his New Year's Eve sermon in the cathedral of Freiburg, Archbishop Gröber gave thanks for the blessings that God had bestowed upon Germany in the year 1935. "The strength of the German people has blossomed forth manifold and unemployment has decreased to a surprising degree. Newly rearmed, the Reich again now takes its place in the family of nations and in place of the dishonor that since the Versailles treaty has besmirched the German name the world is faced by a united, upward-striving and power-conscious state."[89]

In the early morning hours of March 7, 1936, German troops crossed the Rhine bridges and entered the demilitarized zone. Notes handed to the Ambassadors of Britain, France and Italy renounced Germany's adherence to the Locarno treaty that had just been violated. The bishops of the Rhineland hurried to express their joy. The same day Cardinal Schulte of Cologne sent a telegram of welcome to General Blomberg, commander-in-chief of the armed forces, in which he greeted the *Wehrmacht,* "guardians of peace and order."[90] On March 8 Bishop Galen of Münster cabled Freiherr von Fritsch, supreme commander of the army, "In the name of the staunchly German Catholics of the diocese of Münster and especially of the lower Rhine, I welcome the German armed forces, which from today on will again shield the German Rhine, as protection and symbol of German honor and German justice."[91] In an interview with the *Frankfurter Zeitung* Bishop Sebastian of Speyer thanked God for "bestowing upon the homeland the happiness and honor of renewed military preparedness" and welcomed the entry of "our valiant armed forces into our border country."[92] Similar words of greeting were issued by the Bishops of Mainz and Trier, but theirs were at the solicitation of the government.[93]

As in his withdrawal from the League of Nations, Hitler again dissolved the Reichstag and scheduled new "elections" and a plebiscite for March 29 to endorse the occupation of the Rhineland. So once again the bishops faced the question of whether or not they should take a public stand. Whereas in October 1933 there had been two ballots—one for the plebiscite and the other for electing the new Reichstag—the voters now had only one ballot, with the choice of voting "yes" or "no." The proposal to issue a proclamation this time came from Cardinals Schulte and Faulhaber. Thereupon Cardinal Bertram, on March 16, circulated a draft of such a statement to the German episcopate.[94] Faulhaber told the Bavarian bishops that he originally had had doubts about this step. Pastoral letters were still being confiscated; the negotiations concerning the implementation of the Concordat were deadlocked; agitation against the Pope, the bishops and Catholic dogmas continued unabatedly. But since individual priests probably would issue statements on their own, perhaps without any qualifications, it was preferable to have a joint declaration.[95]

On the other hand, Konrad von Preysing, the new Bishop of Berlin, was skeptical. In a letter distributed to all the German bishops he raised several questions about the proposed manifestation: could the bishops come to a decision at a time when the precise question to be voted upon was not even known? "Do we bishops have the task and the mandate to take an authoritative stand on a matter of foreign policy? Can the episcopate issue binding directions to the Catholic citizens in a political question?" In view of these uncertainties, Preysing proposed either to defer a decision or to decide in the negative right now.[96] These arguments found the consent of other bishops. The Bishop of Mainz informed Preysing that he fully agreed with Preysing's misgivings and that he, too, was opposed to any proclamation.[97] The Bishops of Würzburg and Bamberg, likewise, registered their disapproval. Cardinals Bertram and Faulhaber, thereupon, sent out word that there would be no joint declaration of the German episcopate and that each bishop should act as he saw fit.[98]

Most of the manifestos actually published were read from the pulpits on March 22, the Sunday preceding the plebiscite. Cardinal Schulte told his diocesans that he was aware of their ardent wish "to manifest their patriotism in this hour of national decisions." But since many were hesitant to do so lest their affirmative vote be interpreted as approving the measures taken against the Church and Christianity, he felt called upon to make a declaration that should "pave the way to a decisive 'yes': we give our vote to the fatherland, but this does not signify agreement with things for which our conscience could not assume responsibility. In view of this public and solemn declaration, all Catholics now can in good conscience vote 'yes', knowing thus to stand up before the whole world for the honor, freedom and security of our German fatherland." This declaration, Schulte concluded, did not limit the free decision of every voter and was not meant to exert influence in purely political matters.[99] The same statement, save for an unimportant concluding sentence, was also issued by Cardinal Faulhaber and Bishop Sigismund von Ow of Passau.[100] Bishop Galen of Münster, Archbishop Gröber of Freiburg and Bishop Buchberger of Regensburg published differently worded manifestos of identical content.[101] Even Bishop Preysing of Berlin, who earlier had voiced serious reservations, now told his flock that they could vote for the honor and freedom of the fatherland and do so with the intention of promoting "the vital necessities of the German people, the peace of the world, internal peace. . . ."[102] How many other members of the episcopate issued such manifestos we do not know.

Most probably the Nazis did not specifically solicit these declarations, though the frenzy of the campaign was such that the bishops perhaps felt constrained to participate and to do their share. Many of them, undoubtedly, felt genuinely enthusiastic about Hitler's bold stroke. When Bishop Galen thanked the Führer for all he had done for the honor of the German people and asked the blessing of the Almighty God for the Führer's further endeavors,[103] this clearly was more than ordered rhetoric. Archbishop Gröber, whose manifesto, because of its qualifications, was barred by the Gestapo from being printed in the diocesan papers, wrote the *Reichsstatthalter* that he would gladly have made an enthusiastic and unqualified appeal for support of the Führer in his struggle with the outside world. Unfortunately, however, the plebiscite was coupled with the election of delegates to the Reichstag, many of whom were sworn enemies of the Church.[104] Quite obviously, the bishops were prepared to support Hitler's tough line in foreign policy with fervor if the regime made it possible for them to do so.

On March 29, according to the official count, 45,453,691 Germans, or 99 per cent of those entitled to vote, went to the polls. Of these, 44,461,278, or 98.8 per cent of those voting, voiced their approval of Hitler's leadership. Shirer recalls some irregularities and the fear on the part of some Germans that a "no" vote would be discovered by the Gestapo. But the general mood was indeed one of ardent support. "The junking of Versailles and the appearance of German soldiers marching again into what was, after all, German territory were things that almost all Germans naturally approved."[105] The Gestapo of Aachen was able to report that the church authorities had been most co-operative and that the Catholic population had shown full patriotic zeal.[106] In Munich the secret police noted that the clergy, apart from a few cases of opposition, had conducted itself "patriotically and loyal to the Führer."[107] The government, it appears, was pleased with the Church. As early as March 11 the Gestapo had received orders to cease all hostile measures against the clergy and Catholic organizations.[108] On April 9 the Minister of Ecclesiastical Affairs, Hanns Kerrl, issued the following order:

> Under the impression of the overwhelming showing of confidence by the German people on March 29, 1936, I request that

all police measures against Protestant and Catholic priests, inasmuch as those involve prohibitions of residence and lecturing imposed before March 29, 1936, be annulled without exception and effective immediately. Insofar as priests still remain in protective custody I request immediate report on whether here too annulment is not appropriate. . . .[109]

In the view of the regime, the bishops and their flocks had done their patriotic duty and their loyalty should be rewarded. As soon as a month later, however, the government started the notorious morality trials against members of the religious orders, aimed at discrediting the reputation of the Church in the eyes of the German people. Clearly, the Nazis had no permanent use for their Catholic would-be friends.

4. The Struggle Against Bolshevism.

"Germany is the bulwark of the West against Bolshevism," Hitler stated in an interview with the foreign press in November 1935.[110] Inside and outside Germany he thus justified his program of rearmament. In late July 1936 Germany began to provide military assistance to the rebellion of General Franco against the Spanish Republic. The intervention in the Spanish Civil War not only provided valuable experience for Germany's young *Luftwaffe*, but it also helped build up close relations with Mussolini's Italy. In October 1936 the so-called "Rome–Berlin Axis" came into being; a month later Hitler signed the Anti-Comintern pact with Japan, to which Italy acceded soon thereafter. These diplomatic maneuvers were accompanied by Hitler's repeated claims to be the defender of Western civilization. In a private conversation, before coming to power, he had outlined the basic underlying strategy: "I have got . . . to keep the Versailles Power in line by holding aloft the bogy of Bolshevism—make them believe that a Nazi Germany is the last bulwark against the Red flood. That's the only way to come through the danger period, to get rid of Versailles and rearm. I can talk peace and mean war."[111] The trick worked—abroad and at home.

The German bishops had always praised Hitler's anti-Communist posture and now they responded eagerly to the new call for a united stand against Bolshevism. They were encouraged in this line by the Vatican's policy of indulgence toward Germany. The Vatican was worried about the Popular Front governments in Spain and France and, following the outbreak of the Spanish Civil War, by the anti-religious persecutions in the republican camp. The joint pastoral letter of the German episcopate issued at Fulda on August 19, 1936, contained extensive praise of Hitler's foreign policy. Spurred by the atrocity stories headlined by the German press, the bishops adopted the Nazis' analysis of the Spanish Civil War as a struggle between good and evil. Germany, they declared, had to build up its strength "so that in later times not only a Europe cleansed from Bolshevism, but the entire rescued civilized world will be able to be thankful to us." If Spain were to succumb to Bolshevism, the future of Europe would be in serious danger. "The task which this imposes upon our people and fatherland follows as a matter of course. May our Führer, with God's help, succeed in completing this terribly difficult undertaking with un-shakeable determination and faithful participation of all *Volks-genossen!*" The bishops went on to state their lack of understand-ing for the hostility shown the Church's organizations, the Catholic press and the confessional schools. "We Catholics, after all, want nothing else but to share in promoting the German people's well-being according to the fundamentals of our faith and to pre-serve for its blessing those forces which in the past have made Germany glorious and great."[112]

According to a report of the American Ambassador in Berlin, William E. Dodd, the passages in the pastoral letter dealing with Bolshevism "were drafted in concert with an official from the Church Ministry whose hand may perhaps be seen in the effusive compliments paid the *Führer* for his fight against Bolshevism." Dodd noted that the Church seemed to be in a position of weakness as a result of the successful campaign of discredit carried out by the government during the preceding months. The much-publicized trials against members of the Catholic orders on charges of cur-rency smuggling and immorality had lost the Church support.[113] But if the Church thought in this manner to recoup some of the losses and to regain the good will of the government, the plan failed. As on previous occasions the government did not allow the press to publish the text of the bishops' pastoral letter, and if the pressure was released a bit, this was mainly because of the Olympic Games during which Hitler sought to impress the foreign visitors with only the best aspects of the new Germany.

On September 9, 1936, at the annual party rally at Nuremberg, Hitler again lashed out against the Bolshevik danger, while the same theme was struck, also that day, by Pope Pius XI at the Vatican before a group of Spanish refugees.[114] "The coincidence that these two great speeches were delivered on the same day and the congruence of their main ideas," remarked the chancery of Trier in a pamphlet, "appear to us as convincing demonstration of what the hour demands; to wit, a sympathetic co-operation of State and Church in Germany for the combined fight against the common enemy."[115] Almost identical words were used by the new Bishop of Passau at his inauguration on October 21. Bolshevism, Bishop Landersdorfer declared, today was the fiercest enemy of the Catholic Church, as events in Soviet Russia, Mexico and Spain sufficiently proved. If nothing else, the need to repel this mutual foe dictated "the harmonious collaboration of Church and State."[116]

A few days later, on November 4, Cardinal Faulhaber was received by Hitler in his mountain retreat on the Obersalzberg near Berchtesgaden. This meeting had been arranged by Nuncio Orsenigo and State Secretary Lammers, and lasted three hours. The atmosphere, Faulhaber wrote in his report to the German episcopate, at first was extremely tense but gradually became more and more friendly and the talk ended on a fully harmonious note. Hitler even asked the Cardinal to dine with him.[117] The Chancellor dwelt at length on the disastrous results of a Bolshevik victory in Spain. "The Catholic Church should not deceive herself: if National Socialism does not succeed in defeating Bolshevism, then Church and Christianity in Europe too are finished. Bolshevism is the mortal enemy of the Church as much as of Fascism." Faulhaber replied that the Church had always been aware of this threat. The German bishops had stated their views on Bolshevism in their joint pastoral letter of 1936 and in earlier years. He had been present personally when Pius XI in 1933 called the Chancellor of the German Reich the first statesman who, together with the Pope, had clearly recognized the Bolshevik danger. He, Faulhaber, over the years, had continuously warned against the Red menace.

The talk also covered the tensions existing between Church and Party: Hitler again disclaimed any intention of being a religious reformer. Toward the end the Chancellor told Faulhaber: "Think about all this, Cardinal, and consult with the other leaders of the Church how you can support the great undertaking of National Socialism to prevent the victory of Bolshevism and how you can achieve a peaceful relationship to the state. Either National Socialism and the Church are both victorious or they perish together. Rest assured, I shall do away with all those small things that stand in the way of a harmonious co-operation, . . . I do not wish to engage in horse trading. You know that I am opposed to compromises, but let this be a last attempt." The Cardinal in his report to the German episcopate remarked in this connection, "the bishops now will have to make definite proposals either in the form of a new memorandum or in a new pastoral letter."

Faulhaber returned from the Obersalzberg much impressed by Hitler's statesmanlike qualities. The Führer, he wrote in his report, "is in better command of diplomatic and social etiquette than a born sovereign." In front of others, too, he spoke of the Führer's simplicity of manner.[118] The fact that Faulhaber had visited Hitler became known, but the content of the conversation remained a closely guarded secret.[119] At the conference of the Bavarian bishops held at Regensburg at the end of November Faulhaber gave an oral report about his talk with Hitler. The conference thereupon decided "jointly with the other German bishops, anew to condemn Bolshevism which represents the greatest danger for the peace of Europe and the Christian civilization of our country. In addition, the pastoral letter to be issued by this Conference will once again affirm our loyal and positive attitude, demanded by the fourth commandment, toward today's form of government and the Führer."[120] This pastoral letter was read from the pulpits on December 13. The pronouncement listed the Church's difficulties and complaints, but assured the Führer that the bishops "support with all available moral resources his world-historical struggle aimed at repelling Bolshevism."[121] It is a measure of the astuteness of the Nazis that they suppressed the text of this pastoral letter because of its "unfounded criticism of the views and measures of State and Party."[122] They had no intention of being deflected from their goal of silencing and destroying all rival objects of loyalty by the Church's offer to make common cause against Bolshevism.

About a week later Cardinal Faulhaber submitted to the German bishops the draft of a new episcopal proclamation against Bolshevism. In his covering letter he mentioned that the text had been approved by the eight Bavarian bishops and by seven others whom he had visited personally. It had not yet been possible, Faulhaber went on to say, to send everyone his report about the talk with the Chancellor. "This report would make it clear that the proposed pastoral letter is necessary." Some bishops had little hope that Hitler would keep his promises but saw no possibility of rejecting the Chancellor's offer. "The aim of the new pastoral letter is, therefore, to preserve the basis for new negotiations. More I cannot tell. This pastoral letter has been expected by the highest Church and State authorities for some time already and some even accused me of tactics of delay. But it could and should not have come out any earlier because the opinion of every single bishop had to be obtained [beforehand] and because the impression of work done to order had to be avoided. This would harm the reputation of both parties." The proposed formulation, Faulhaber concluded, would not be regarded as "Byzantinism." Our people will not be upset, since we maintain our complaints and "we do not care a rap about whether this pastoral letter will please the emigrants."[123]

Faulhaber's draft was approved by the other bishops, and the joint pastoral letter, dated December 24, 1936, was read from the pulpits on the first Sunday of the new year, January 3, 1937. A fateful hour has arrived, the bishops warned: Russian Bolshevism has started its march toward Europe. "The Führer and Chancellor of the Reich, Adolf Hitler, has sighted the advance of Bolshevism from afar and his thoughts and aspirations aim at averting the horrible danger from our German people and the entire occident. The German bishops consider it their duty to support the head of the German Reich by all those means which the Church has at its disposal." Co-operation in repelling this threat is a religious task. We do not intend to intrude into the political realm or yet to call for a new war. But we must mobilize all the spiritual and moral forces of the Church in order "to strengthen confidence in the Führer."

The Church's role in supporting the struggle of the Third Reich against Bolshevism, the bishops went on, could be far more forceful and effective if the constant attacks against Christianity would cease and if the Church were to enjoy those freedoms guaranteed it by divine law and by the Concordat. But the Catholics would follow the Führer despite the lack of confidence in their reliability. "Even where we repulse inroads upon the rights of the Church, we want to respect the rights of the state in its proper jurisdiction and to see also the good and great elements in the work of the Führer. We, your bishops, therefore conclude with this admonition: Do not allow yourself to be talked into discontent and sulkiness by dissatisfied people. Such a mood has always provided a fertile soil for Bolshevik sentiments!"[124]

The bishops thus had fulfilled their share of the bargain. They had once again declared their support of Hitler's foreign policy and they had admonished the faithful to have full confidence in the Führer's leadership. But the *quid pro quo* never materialized. As long as the Church insisted on defending the confessional schools, the Catholic organizations and other rights guaranteed by the Concordat, the Nazis were unwilling to halt their war of attrition. Cardinal Faulhaber might insist that the bishops had not criticized the State or the Party or the Nazi's political system,[125] but these affirmations of loyalty were of no avail. The regime would settle for nothing less than a Church restricted to the sacristy and available upon command for unqualified assistance in moments of national importance.

Could the bishops have arrived at a different appraisal of Hitler's claim to be the savior of Western civilization and of his intervention in the Spanish Civil War? Could they have known that the republican regime attacked by General Franco in 1936 was not Communist? One is inclined to answer these questions in the affirmative. Faulhaber's bitter comment about "the emigrants," whose opinion the bishops could safely disregard, indicates that at least occasionally the episcopate had access to some of the anti-Nazi publications published by Catholic refugees abroad. He knew to whom he was referring and so did his associates.

Every week in Lucerne, Waldemar Gurian was publishing the *Deutsche Briefe*; the Jesuit Father Friedrich Muckermann in Holland brought out the weekly *Der Deutsche Weg;* in Paris three times a month unknown hands put out a bulletin of information entitled *Kulturkampf*; and German Catholics in Kattowitz published *Der Deutsche in Polen.* Copies of all these papers were being smuggled into Germany. Also, it was still possible and involved little risk to listen to foreign radio broadcasts. Hence, if the German bishops persisted in their nationalistic line the reasons therefore will have to be sought elsewhere than in lack of correct information.

After the joint pastoral letter against Bolshevism had been read in January 1937, Father Muckermann in *Der Deutsche Weg* expressed his amazement and consternation at the tactics of the German bishops. We find it hard to understand, he wrote, "that despite the events of June 30, despite the inhuman brutalities perpetrated in the concentration camps, despite the currency and defamation trials, despite the personal insults against individual princes of the Church, against the Holy Father and the entire Church, and in spite of all hostile measures amounting to another Kulturkampf, . . . the bishops find words of appreciation for what (next to Bolshevism) is their worst enemy. . . ."[126] The Catholic anti-Nazi organ *Kulturkampf* concluded: if the Nazis would only stop their attacks against the Church, National Socialism and the German Catholics could again become allies.[127]

This is the way it looked to the emigrants. Inside Germany the episcopate saw no reason why it should not be happy with a National Socialist regime shorn of certain unfortunate anti-Catholic side effects.

5. The Annexation of Austria

Having bluffed and blustered his way for four years, toward the end of 1937 Hitler felt strong enough to start his program of outright expansion. The Western powers were staring, hypnotized, as Germany's program of rearmament progressed steadily. Hitler was ready for his first aggressive move—the annexation of Austria. In his speech before the Reichstag on May 21, 1935, Hitler had assured the world, "Germany neither intends nor wishes to interfere in the internal affairs of Austria, to annex Austria, or to conclude an *Anschluss*."[128] But by March 1938 things were different. An ultimatum brought about the appointment of the Austrian Nazi Seyss-Inquart as Chancellor, who, on orders of Göring, asked for German troops "to prevent threatening bloodshed." In the early morning hours of March 12, 1938, Hitler's army crossed the Austrian frontier and on the next day Austria was declared a province of the German Reich. On the heels of the troops came Himmler's terror squads. In Vienna alone more than 70,000 people were arrested and the Jews of the city were subjected by the Nazis to orgies of humiliation and sadism. The independence of Austria had come to an end. Its more than 6,000,000 people now could begin to enjoy the dubious blessings of life in the Third Reich.

On March 18 Hitler announced that the German people, as those of the new *Ostmark*, would be asked to vote on the *Anschluss* in a plebiscite on April 10. Also, again, there were to be new "elections" to the Reichstag. Hitler this time was determined to achieve unanimity of support: a propaganda campaign of unheard-of dimensions was generated in order to deliver the vote; and the churches, too, were again to take part.

On March 15 Cardinal Innitzer, Archbishop of Vienna, visited Hitler. Three days later the Catholic episcopate of Austria issued a widely publicized statement, in large part drafted by the Nazis, praising the accomplishments of German National Socialism in the areas of internal and foreign policy, and asking the faithful on April 10 to approve the union with Germany.[129] In earlier years the opposition of the Austrian bishops to National Socialism had been expressed many times; as late as February 1938 Innitzer had called for the continued independence of Austria. Widespread astonishment at this swift about-face was compounded when, in addition to the joint statement, two letters from Innitzer to *Gauleiter* Bürckel were made public, ending with the greeting, "Heil Hitler."[130] Several of the German bishops had been using this salutation for years,[131] but word of this had never reached the public.

On April 1 Innitzer sent a telegram to Cardinal Bertram in which he expressed the hope that the German bishops would concur in the declaration of the Austrian episcopate on the plebiscite, and added that this declaration should not be "burdened by clauses and conditions." The head of the German hierarchy merely acknowledged the message.[132] A manifestation of such blunt opportunism was too much even for a veteran diplomat like Bertram.

But the German bishops, of course, knew that they would also have to comment on the *Anschluss.* The electoral campaign was to reach its climax on April 9, named *"Tag des Grossdeutschen Reiches"* (The Day of the Greater German Reich). An elaborate program was laid out, to be concluded by an evening mass meeting in Vienna that would be addressed by Hitler. At the end of this rally, according to an order of the Minister for Ecclesiastical Affairs Kerrl, the bells of all the churches in Germany and Austria were to ring out as part of this "overwhelming expression of confidence of the entire nation in the Führer and his work."[133]

On several previous occasions the bishops had pointed out to the authorities that, at the very least, they should be consulted and informed before an order to ring the church bells was to be issued. Cardinal Bertram in 1935 had summarized the prevailing view in this manner: "Only the church authorities may order the peal of the bells. This is so because of the purely ecclesiastical character of the consecrated bells, because of the provisions of canon 1169 [of the Canon Law], and last but not least because of the religious sentiments of the people. These sentiments are especially profound and pious with regard to the peal of bells and should be preserved."[134] The bishops had agreed to ring the bells on patriotic occasions like the return of the Saar, but they had tried to resist doing so on political occasions. Shortly after the Saar plebiscite Cardinal Faulhaber informed the Vicar General of Freiburg that he would not have a peal of bells on January 30, the day of the National Socialist accession to power. "I fear that the all-too-frequent ringing of bells on political occasions, that almost recalls the victory celebrations of the first year of the War [1914-1918], will damage the esteem in which the people hold the Church authorities. A later generation will altogether be at a loss to understand how the bishops, at a time when a joint pastoral letter is suppressed by the state. . . ."[135] Faulhaber did not complete the sentence, but it is clear that he alluded to the humiliating position in which the Church found herself in this connection. He did refuse to order a peal of church bells on the eve of the plebiscite of March 29, 1936, arguing that it "violates canon law to let the bells, which are consecrated for divine services and religious hours of commemoration, ring on purely political occasions."[136] But how was the *Anschluss* of Austria to be classified? Was the plebiscite ratifying this annexation, combined with the election of a new Reichstag, an event of political or patriotic significance?

It appears that the bishops did not question the patriotic character of the day and were willing to let the bells ring, though, as in the case of the re-entry of German troops into the Rhineland, an election was again involved and even though they had not first been consulted. Cardinal Bertram on April 3 issued an order to comply with the request of Kerrl. "The significance of this ringing of bells," his directions to the clergy stated, "follows from the greatness of the event, which provides the occasion for this proclamation, and from the intention which the Catholic Church always combines with the peal of bells. We take a most earnest and warm interest in all decisive events affecting people and fatherland, and our prayers for state and authorities (I Tim. 2:2), calling for God's blessing for Church and people, ascend unceasingly to the sky. In the same spirit the reverend clergy will urge the faithful to regard the ringing of the bells on this special occasion as an exhortation for such prayer."[137]

The archdiocesan chancery of Munich had, on April 1, already indicated its willingness to comply with Kerrl's order, but Faulhaber was not yet sure in what form the declaration should be issued. In a letter to the Bavarian bishops he suggested three possible ways: (1) a simple announcement; (2) a statement taking note of this joint ringing of the church bells of Germany and Austria; (3) a declaration ordering a ringing of the bells and stating that this was done to exhort the Catholics on April 10, "in this hour of world historical significance, to pledge their fidelity to the Führer and Chancellor of the Reich, Adolf Hitler, and to pray for the peaceful co-operation of Church and State in the Greater German Reich." Faulhaber added that he personally favored the third formula.[138] At least one bishop had misgivings about the phrase asking for a confession of loyalty to the Führer.[139] Faulhaber, thereupon, redrafted the statement, but even after the revision the Bavarian bishops did not come out with an identical declaration.

The directions issued to the clergy of the archdiocese of Munich spoke of an hour of world historical importance in which the Catholics, by ringing their church bells, wanted to bear witness to their sympathy and interest.[140] Bishop Buchberger of Regensburg ordered that the bells be rung "as expression of joy over the return of our Austrian brothers to the Greater German Reich."[141] The Bishop of Passau called for "a unanimous pledge of fidelity to the great German fatherland."[142] All of them exhorted the faithful to pray for the harmonious co-operation of Church and State in the new Greater German Reich.

The Vatican had been unhappy over Cardinal Innitzer's servile conduct. A broadcast from the Vatican radio on April 1 severely criticized the manifesto of the Austrian episcopate as an abuse of the Church's teaching function. Innitzer was summoned to Rome and was made to sign a statement, published by *L'Osservatore Romano* on April 7, to the effect that the earlier declaration of the Austrian bishops should not be understood as approval of what was incompatible with the laws of God or be seen as binding in conscience upon the faithful. Perhaps it was due to this rebuke by the Holy See that this time most of the German bishops did not issue electoral proclamations.

The episcopate was urged to make a public statement for April 10 by Franz Xaver Eberle, the Auxiliary Bishop of Augsburg, who had recently called on Hitler in order to propose peace between Church and State. This act of unauthorized diplomacy had drawn the rebuke of the German cardinals and of the Papal Secretary of State, to whom he had reported the talk with Hitler,[143] but Eberle was not giving up yet. On April 3 he addressed a letter to Cardinal Faulhaber: "When could the bishops find it easier and more pleasurable to invite [the faithful] to vote yes than where a patriotic deed of the greatest significance, the enlargement of our fatherland, is involved?"[144] But this time Faulhaber had decided otherwise. He asked the clergy "to exercise their civic right to vote and to participate without exception in the elections,"[145] but this order was merely an internal directive. Similarly, a statement of the Coadjutor-Bishop of Fulda, Dr. Johannes Dietz, exhorting the faithful to vote "yes" on April 10, appeared under not fully clarified circumstances in the *Fuldaer Zeitung* of April 2; but Dietz explained to his fellow bishops that he had not ordered this proclamation to be read from the pulpits of the diocese.[146]

Yet the Nazis, in any event, had the declaration of the Austrian bishops of March 18, and they made extensive use of it. The daily press featured the manifesto on the front pages, and an order of the *Reichspressekammer* required the diocesan Sunday papers to print the declaration together with pictures and statistics highlighting Germany's social and economic achievements since Hitler's accession to power in 1933. The editors at the same time were asked to celebrate the great event in additional articles of their own choice.[147] Some of the diocesan papers now were no longer under the full control of the local bishops, and these papers, of course, complied willingly. But even diocesan weeklies still edited by clergymen and published under the direct auspices of the bishops not only printed the compulsory text and pictures, but featured stories welcoming the returned brethren and calling upon the faithful to approve the *Anschluss*. The *Passauer Bistumsblatt,* for example, declared that "it corresponds to the natural order set by God if . . . men speaking the same language and of common blood and ancestry are joined in a great Reich of the Germans."[148]

Only one instance is known where a bishop forbade the paper under his supervision to oblige Goebbels' propaganda machine. Bishop Preysing of Berlin gave orders not to print any propaganda for the plebiscite on the grounds that the vote represented an expression of confidence in measures hostile to the Church and meant the election to the Reichstag of archenemies of the Church like Rosenberg and Ley.[149] When the publisher overruled the editor and inserted the compulsory text anyway, Preysing sent word to the clergy that this had been done against his express instructions and asked them to make use of this information when appropriate. His message should not, however, be read from the pulpit.[150] The same instruction was sent out by Vicar General Riemer of Passau regarding the declaration of the Austrian bishops but *not* as concerned the rest of the propaganda.[151] The information available makes it appear that most of the German churchmen resented the servile manner of Cardinal Innitzer, but this did not mean that they opposed the *Anschluss*.

On April 10, 1938, the German people at the polls were handed a ballot that read, "Do you pledge yourself to our Führer Adolf Hitler and therewith to the reunification of Austria with the German Reich carried out on March 13?" To this question 99.08 per cent of the voters were said to have replied in the affirmative. The Führer had come as close to a full 100 per cent as he could hope, and thereafter no further plebiscites were held. The administrative head of Lower Bavaria reported that most of the "no" votes had been cast, apart from past strongholds of Communism, in those areas where the Catholic parties had formerly been strong.[152] But if this was so, and perhaps not only in Lower Bavaria, the bishops could hardly take credit for those courageous few who were so far-sighted. Quite the contrary. Several instances are known where Church authorities rebuked individual priests who had stayed away from the polls and thereby had run into hostile demonstrations. In a case involving two curates in the diocese of Passau, the priests in question were made to issue a public apology and had to sign a statement drawn up by their Vicar General that read, "We affirm explicitly that our conduct did by no means aim at opposing the state existing today or the Führer."[153] In another instance, a priest in the diocese of Augsburg, who had capped his consistent refusal to use the "Heil Hitler" greeting with absence from the polls on April 10, was disciplined by being transferred to another parish. His conduct, the diocesan chancery wrote to him, revealed "lack of understanding for the total situation."[154]

One bishop, Dr. Johannes Baptista Sproll of Rottenburg, also refrained from voting on April 10, but not because of objections to Hitler's annexation of Austria. As he later explained to Cardinal Bertram, "I gladly welcomed the *Anschluss* of Austria and celebrated it with a general ringing of bells. Besides other general considerations, I was led to this attitude by my emotional sympathies."[155] But since a "yes" vote meant electing men he considered hostile to Christianity and Church, and since he did not want to negate his approval of the *Anschluss* by voting "no," Sproll stayed away from the polls. This led to hostile demonstrations and the bishop had to leave town. A request of the government to the Vatican to have Sproll recalled from his diocese was turned down by Pacelli. Ambassador Bergen reported that Pacelli, nevertheless, "according to all indications did not approve of the Bishop's actions" and that in clerical circles Sproll's conduct was called "very inept."[156] When Sproll, allegedly in accordance with express instructions from the Holy See, returned to Rottenburg on July 16, his palace was broken into and ransacked by a mob. The Bishop refused to leave again but he was eventually forcefully removed by the Gestapo and banished from his diocese.[157] It appears that Sproll was the only higher Church dignitary who failed to vote "yes" on April 10.

6. The Destruction of Czechoslovakia

Czechoslovakia's turn was next. On May 30, 1938, Hitler informed the supreme command of the armed forces that he had decided to smash Czechoslovakia by military action as soon as the political preparations made it possible. For this purpose Konrad Henlein, the leader of the Nazi party among the German minority in Czechoslovakia (the Sudeten Germans), was told to make demands which the Czech government would not be able to meet. At the same time Germany and the outside world were saturated with reports about the cruel suppression of the Sudeten Germans. Hitler's plans to stage a triumphant entry into Prague were temporarily frustrated by the attempts of Chamberlain and later Mussolini to mediate, but at the Munich conference of September 29 the Führer obtained most of his immediate demands without resort to war. The Western Allies' appeasement of Hitler also broke the back of the first military conspiracy against Hitler, whose plans called for the arrest of Hitler at the moment he issued his order to attack Czechoslovakia. On October 1, 1938, German troops marched into Czechoslovakia and occupied the Sudentenland.

The threat of war now seemed arrested, and all Europe experienced a profound feeling of relief. At the suggestion of Cardinal Faulhaber, the head of the German Bishops' Conference sent a telegram of appreciation to Hitler:

> The great deed of safeguarding international peace moves the German episcopate, acting in the name of the Catholics of all the German dioceses, respectfully to tender congratulations and thanks and to order a festive peal of bells on Sunday.
>
> In the name of the Cardinals of Germany
> Archbishop Cardinal Bertram.[158]

This telegram was widely publicized and undoubtedly strengthened the plausibility of Hitler's claim that it was he who had saved the peace.

On the following day, a Sunday, the church bells rung out and special services of thanksgiving were held. In the diocese of Berlin the following announcement was read from the pulpits:

> God has heard the prayer of all Christendom for peace. By His grace and the tireless efforts of the responsible statesmen the terrible affliction of a war has been averted from our fatherland and from Europe. In deepest thankfulness we desire now with a prayer and a *Te Deum* to praise God for His goodness in that He has preserved peace for us, a peace which has at the same time assured the return [*Anschluss*] of our Sudeten kinsmen to the German Reich.[159]

Cardinal Bertram issued a special pastoral letter to greet the Sudeten Germans, more than 90 per cent of whom were Catholics. The percentage of Catholics in the Greater German Reich now was about 10 per cent higher than in 1933, and this fact was not lost upon the bishops. The Catholic Church, Bertram declared, is a true people's church, and it therefore could not pass silently over the recent great events affecting Germany. The thanks to God for the preservation of peace were linked with the joy over the Sudeten Germans' reunion with Germany. It goes without saying, Bertram added, that you will render willing obedience and respect to the new authorities.[160]

Archbishop Hauck of Bamberg, whose archdiocese was also enriched by many new diocesans, similarly gave thanks for the safeguarding of peace which had brought in its wake the peaceful *Anschluss* of the Sudeten German *Volksgenossen*.[161] The diocesan Sunday paper of Munich declared that while thanking God "we did not forget to thank the man who has preserved the peace for us and yet at the same time has achieved the freedom of our German brothers in Bohemia. Together with the German cardinals, the entire Catholic community in the Greater German Reich thanks the Führer for the act of peace. . . ."[162]

The year 1938 had brought Hitler his greatest triumph. Austria had ben annexed; Czechoslovakia, deprived of her powerful frontier fortifications, lay practically defenseless at his feet. The *Passauer Bistumsblatt,* in an editorial for the sixth anniversary of the National Socialist assumption of power, hailed the new strong Germany that had freed herself of dishonorable and dictated treaties and in the preceding year had been able to "bring home 10-million German brothers and sisters."[163] On March 15, 1939, Hitler's armies occupied the rest of Czechoslovakia and the next day, from Hradschin Castle in Prague, Hitler proclaimed the Protectorate of Bohemia and Moravia. The newly formed Slovak state, too, came under German "protection." The Greater German Reich now for the first time subjected to its rule a non-German population. The conquest of *Lebensraum* had begun. The outbreak of open war was not far away.

Great Britain and France protested Hitler's newest violation of solemn promises and obligations, but the Führer could afford to disregard their objections. Ambassador Bergen reported from the Vatican that he had heard of urgent attempts "especially on the French side, to prevail upon the Pope to associate himself with the protests of the democratic states against the annexation of Bohemia and Moravia to the Reich. The Pope has declined these requests very firmly. He has given those around him to understand that he sees no reason to interfere in historic processes in which, from the political point of view, the Church is not interested."[164]

The occupant of the Holy See since March 3, 1939, was Pius XII, the former Secretary of State Pacelli, and the new Pope was anxious to placate Hitler in order to achieve an improvement of the situation of the Church in Germany. At the suggestion of the German cardinals, who were in Rome for the election of a successor to Pius XI, the new Pontiff had addressed the first of the customary notifications of election to Hitler. He had broken with protocol by signing the translation and had expressed his warm hope for friendly relations.[165] The death of the temperamental, and toward the end of his reign increasingly anti-German, Pius XI, had relaxed tensions and there was widespread hope for an early removal of differences between the Church and Hitler.

In early February 1939 a new Catholic weekly had begun to appear in Frankfurt-am-Main. Entitled *Der Neue Wille,* the paper supported a closer and friendlier relationship between German Catholicism and the National Socialist regime and movement. On March 19 this weekly praised Hitler as the builder of a great

German nation and Reich and called upon the Catholic bishops, too engulfed in memories of the medieval Reich, to recognize the Führer's plan for a new European order. "Now is the moment to make up for earlier neglect."[166] The opportunity for just such a gesture of good will presented itself in connection with the celebration of Hitler's fiftieth birthday on April 20. There is no evidence to link the bishops' elaborate participation in this festive event with the suggestion of *Der Neue Wille,* but the episcopate's bearing was as much in keeping with the ideas of this new Catholic pro-Nazi paper as it was with the milder wind blowing from the Holy See.

The birthday festivities were centered around the recent overwhelming success of the Führer's daring foreign policy. On the eve of the birthday Goebbels, in a radio broadcast, celebrated Hitler's achievement of a new order in Europe that, uniquely, had been attained without the shedding of blood. The Führer had only one goal—peace.[167] Also that evening the church bells rang in the great day. Cardinal Bertram had left it to the discretion of each bishop whether he wanted to have a peal of bells,[168] and all of them, it appears, had ordered it.[169] On April 20, the day of the birthday, Cardinal Bertram, in the name of the episcopate, sent a telegram of congratulations to Hitler.[170] Special votive masses in honor of the Archangel St. Michael, the patron saint of Germany, were celebrated in all the churches "to implore God's blessing upon Führer and people."[171] The Bishop of Mainz called for prayer for "the Führer and Chancellor, the inspirer, enlarger and protector of the Reich."[172] In Mainz, and in some other dioceses, the bells tolled again at noontime for half an hour. In all dioceses the churches displayed the national flag.[173]

The question of whether to show the swastika flag on the churches had caused considerable discussion earlier among the episcopate. The swastika flag was declared the national flag on September 15, 1935, but as early as on February 8, 1934, Archbishop Gröber had given orders to display it on patriotic occasions alongside the church flags.[174] The Bishop of Osnabrück had acted likewise.[175] Bishop Galen, on the other hand, even after the swastika flag had become official, forbade hoisting it on the churches, maintaining that the house of God was dedicated to Christ and therefore removed from secular use.[176] On October 5, 1935, the bishops were ordered by the government to show the swastika flag alone on national holidays. In vain did Cardinal Faulhaber argue that this order violated an old tradition and that the churches should remain above all politics.[177] Bertram was willing to give in, and wrote the Minister of the Interior that the Church authorities were agreeable to hoist the national colors on national holidays. But since the display of flags represented a public proclamation and even a glorification of a given fact, the Church had to reserve the right to refuse compliance when the celebration involved something irreconcilable with the Catholic faith and its moral law. As an example he gave the anniversary of the adoption of the sterilization law.[178] This stand was approved by the Fulda Bishops' Conference in August 1936,[179] and when General Ludendorff died in December 1937 the bishops refused to display flags on the grounds that, since Ludendorff had been a blasphemous agitator against Christianity, the display of flags at his funeral would constitute a dishonorable act.[180] On the other hand, the Church saw nothing wrong with honoring Hitler's birthday. The Führer was the supreme legal authority, to whom full respect had to be rendered.

On April 20 Nuncio Orsenigo personally delivered the congratulations of Pope Pius XII and, as dean of the diplomatic corps, those of the other ambassadors in Berlin.[181] The Catholic papers joined with the rest of the press in praising the Führer. The *Passauer Bistumsblatt,* alongside a large picture of Hitler, congratulated "the enlarger of the Reich" and expressed its thanks "that in these critical times the Führer carried the great responsibility for the great Reich of the Germans."[182] The organ of the Bavarian Association of Diocesan Priests, *Klerusblatt,* celebrated the momentous changes in the history of Germany achieved by Hitler: "The frontiers imposed upon us by the 'hate-peace' of Versailles are broken, the *Lebensraum* of the German people has been widened," multitudes of unemployed again have work. "God's holy providence has provided that in a decisive hour he [Hitler] be entrusted with the leadership of the German people."[183]

In 1935 Archbishop Gröber had published a book on the Catholics' duty to love the fatherland. "We Catholics," he wrote there, "do not need to seek a new line in the new state, but we simply continue on our path which we have walked with honor throughout German history until the present. We are patriotic because we are German *and Catholic*" (Gröber's italics).[184] The Church's support of the Führer's design for a new order in Europe was in the same tradition. It not only strengthened Hitler's position at home, but it effectively blocked all chances that the Church might pursue an independent line once Hitler's gamble failed and war did indeed break out. For too long, then, the bishops had been committed to the praise of Greater Germany and the acquisition of *Lebensraum*. When Hitler went to war on September 1, 1939, the Church was again behind him and called the faithful to do their duty to the fatherland. There was an inner logic that linked the seemingly innocuous hoisting of the swastika on the churches, and the aid and comfort given Hitler when he set out on his greatest adventure of all. The Church had had no eyes for Hitler's Blood Purge of 1934 and the barbarities of the concentration camps; with varying degrees of enthusiasm she had supported all of his earlier aggressive moves. She was in no position, politically or intellectually, to oppose him now when he plunged the world into a war that was to cause unimaginable misery and the death of many millions of human beings.

8 1939-1945:
The Church Goes to War

Catholic moral theology distinguishes between just and unjust wars and considers as sinful the participation of the faithful in conflicts deemed unjust. To be considered just a war must be declared by the legitimate authority and there must be a just cause. Also, recourse to war is permitted only as a last resort; hostilities must be conducted in accordance with natural and international law. These are the traditional four criteria of the just war developed by Catholic jurists and theologians many centuries ago.

In practice, however, few bishops have ever failed to support the wars waged by their own governments, and the German episcopate is no exception to this rule. Still somewhat suspected of being subservient to Rome, the German Catholics in the First World War tried their utmost to prove their patriotism; their bishops expressed no doubt about the justice of the German cause. The Bishop of Speyer, the later Cardinal Faulhaber, concluded in 1915 that the war waged by Germany to avenge the murder at Sarajevo would enter the annals of the ethics of war as "the prototype of a just war."[1]

During the following years, and especially after Hitler's accession to power, Catholicism never failed to point with pride to the great number of Catholics who had given their lives for the German fatherland in the war of 1914-1918. And the bishops repeatedly affirmed the readiness of the Catholics once again to make all necessary sacrifices demanded by their country. The Church, Archbishop Gröber declared in 1935, despite all endeavors to serve the cause of peace, is not opposed to all wars and rejects doctrinaire pacifism. "By thus stressing the link between the Catholic and his fatherland and people," he went on, "the Church, as her history shows, has become a force that protects and promotes the state."[2]

As the attacks of the Nazis upon the Church intensified, the bishops stepped up the fervor of their affirmations of national loyalty. The Fulda Bishops' Conference of 1937 praised those clerics who invoked their patriotic deeds and their medals earned in 1914-1918 in order "to ward off the attacks upon the rights of the Church and especially upon the honor and national sentiments of the clergy."[3] A number of books appeared at this time celebrating the glorious record of Catholic priests in the First World War. The time to remember those heroes was now, declared the editor of one such work published under the auspices of the archdiocesan chancery of Munich and Freising, "when the German people, through their leaders, have again become a nation. . . ."[4] The editor of a similar work asserted that God had rewarded the sacrifices of the theologians by letting Germany find "a Führer with a vision for great deeds."[5]

In line with their endorsement of Hitler's foreign policy, the German bishops seem not to have raised the queston whether a war waged for the Führer's expansionist aims would be just or unjust. They taught the faithful to be prepared to serve the fatherland, and Archbishop Gröber added that Catholic theologians had "never left it to the judgment of the individual [Catholic], with all his shortsightedness and emotionalism, in the event of war to decide its permissibility or lack of permissibility. Instead, this final decision has always been in the province of the lawful authority."[6] Any doubts that individual Catholics may have had about the justice of Hitler's cause were thus effectively discouraged. The Church apparently took for granted the right of once again blessing German arms. Instructions issued in the diocese of Passau at the height of the Munich crisis of 1938 asked the clergy, in the event of mobilization or war, to hold special services, to pray for an early successful termination of the war and to stress the duty of loyal service to the fatherland.[7] There is no evidence of any prior discussion whether the war in question would be deserving of divine support.

1. The Voice of the Episcopate

At the break of dawn on September 1, 1939, the German armies crossed the Polish frontier. Within a week's time the uneven contest brought German tanks into the outskirts of Warsaw. On September 3 France and England, realizing the futility of further appeasing Hitler, declared war upon Germany.

The decision to go to war against Poland had been taken by Hitler in May; by June 15 the Führer had in his hands the military plans for what was referred to as "Case White"; and at the end of June the Reich Defense Council had laid detailed plans for total mobilization. On August 15 advance mobilization orders had been given to the railways.[8] The bishops, too, by that time had received instructions marked "Top Secret" informing them where priests should report for military pastoral care.[9] When the Fulda Bishops' Conference of 1939, which for the first time included the bishops of Austria and the Sudetenland, met on August 22-24, the episcopate knew that war was imminent. It may have been for this reason that they decided to postpone the publication of their customary pastoral letter.[10]

A few days after the start of the war the bishops issued a joint pastoral letter, asking the Catholic soldiers to do their duty:

> In this decisive hour we encourage and admonish our Catholic soldiers, in obedience to the Führer, to do their duty and to be ready to sacrifice their whole person. We appeal to the faithful to join in ardent prayers that God's providence may lead this war to blessed success and peace for fatherland and people.[11]

In addition, most bishops also issued special messages for their own dioceses. Bishop Sproll of Rottenburg implored God's blessing on all those who had followed the call of the Führer and he asked the Lord to give them "courage and strength victoriously to fight for the dear fatherland or courageously to die for it."[12] Archbishop Gröber stressed that the Church now more than ever needed free play, "so that, as a result of this freedom and justice, the freedom and just cause of our people will receive the blessing of the Almighty."[13] Only Bishop Preysing of Berlin struck a different note, merely expressing his feeling of paternal concern for those called to arms.[14]

By September 17 practically all Polish forces had been defeated or surrounded and the siege of Warsaw had begun. On September 30 the Minister of Ecclesiastical Affairs, Kerrl, sent word that after the entry of the German troops into Warsaw, expected momentarily, the bells of all the churches should ring during the noon hour for seven days "out of grateful commemoration of the victory and of the dead."[15] Cardinal Bertram suggested compliance,[16] and the church bells in all dioceses rang out to celebrate Hitler's first victory.

Meanwhile the S.S. was beginning to execute the Führer's order to solve the Polish problem by murdering the country's intelligentsia. The clergy was one of the first victims. During the months of October and November 214 Polish priests were executed, among them the entire cathedral chapter of the bishopric of Pelplin. By the end of the year 1939 approximately 1,000 members of the Polish secular and regular clergy had been imprisoned, many in newly constructed concentration camps.[17]

On September 21 Cardinal Hlond, the Primate of Poland, had arrived in Rome and had personally reported the German atrocities to the Pope. The Vatican radio and L'Osservatore Romano told the story to the world. But in spite of these reports the German bishops continued to support the war effort. Let us pray for our courageous soldiers, declared Cardinal Schulte in a pastoral letter issued in November 1939, "so that, after an honorable victory and peace, they can soon celebrate a happy return to their homes."[18]

The Catholic press expressed the same sentiments. On April 11, 1939, the Reichspressekammer had admonished the editors and publishers that from now on all articles had to strengthen faith in a German victory, and the entrapped Catholic papers, as already discussed, co-operated fully. The clerical editor of the Passauer Bistumsblatt celebrated the quick victory over Poland and protested the attempt of the Western Allies to drive a wedge between government and people.[19] The Klerusblatt, organ of the Bavarian Priests' Association, exhorted everyone, out of religious conviction, to serve his country and to support the German armies that had gone to war "to defend the homeland."[20] This war, declared the weekly of the diocese of Hildesheim, is being conducted by the enemy as "a war against a holy natural law, against the right of the German people for their liberty. . . ."[21] And the diocesan paper of Breslau, the see of Cardinal Bertram, termed the conflict a struggle of the German people "for their self-preservation" and "for a just distribution of necessary *Lebensraum*." Germany was engaged in "a holy struggle not for the mere reconquest and repossession of stolen territories, but for the highest on earth: life in accordance with God's commands."[22] Any Catholic momentarily doubting the justice of the German cause would indeed conclude that Hitler's aims, blessed by the bishops and their papers, were noble and just.

On May 10, 1940, Hitler's armies invaded Belgium, Holland and Luxemburg. The same day, Pope Pius XII sent telegrams of sympathy to the sovereign rulers of the three countries whose neutrality had been violated, in which he deplored the fact that the people of the Low Countries, "against their will and their rights," had been exposed to the cruelties of war.[23] On May 12 *L'Osservatore Romano* printed the full text of these telegrams. The German press ignored them; but at least two Catholic, pro-Nazi papers attacked the Pope because of this anti-German stand.[24] The German bishops undoubtedly knew of Pius' action, yet their full support of the German war effort remained unchanged.

The swift defeat of France led to new outbursts of patriotic zeal and pride. Archbishop Schulte of Cologne issued a special proclamation in which he gave thanks for the tremendous victory achieved by the German armies.[25] Bishop Bornewasser of Trier praised the armed forces that had fought "a struggle unparalled in world history" and ordered a special mass of thanks.[26] The church bells again tolled at noontime for a week, and flags were displayed for ten days. From now on, the diocesan chanceries instructed the clergy, the bells on patriotic occasions could be rung without waiting for specific authorization from the church authorities.[27] At the end of the first year of war the diocesan paper of Freiburg hailed the great successes of the courageous German soldiers as proof that God guided history and called for a final and resolute struggle against "that old bastion of ruthless capitalism—England."[28]

But in the eyes of the regime the Church was not yet doing

enough. The Fulda Bishops' Conference had met in August and, deeply divided on what tactics to adopt,[29] had failed to issue the customary joint pastoral letter; this annoyed the Nazis, who had expected a forceful victory message.[30] At a meeting with a high official of the Propaganda Ministry held in September, Bishop Wienken, the permanent negotiator of the episcopate in Berlin, was told that the state expected more enthusiastic backing of the war effort. All writings not fully devoted to this end would have to be eliminated. Upon hearing this Bertram ordered Wienken to seek a new meeting. This second talk took place on September 21 and Bishop Wienken, in Bertram's name, delivered a statement clarifying the Church's position. He pointed out "that the Church assents to the just war, especially one conducted for the safeguarding of state and people, that she prays for a victorious termination of the present war in a peace beneficial for Germany and Europe, [and] rouses the faithful to fulfill the civic and military virtues." All Church authorities, Wienken stressed, were doing their share "with the greatest readiness" as the pastoral letters issued at the beginning of the war showed.[31]

Bishop Wienken had suggested that Catholic authors and priests be instructed to treat the Church's teaching on war with great care and to avoid anything detrimental to the state or the war effort. These instructions were issued a short time later. The archdiocesan chancery of Breslau in November gave orders "carefully to avoid everything that could have an injurious effect upon Germany's war situation and impair the brave and joyous confidence of soldiers and people, or be understood in this way." Instead one should stress those supernatural resources that were suitable "for strengthening the traits and virtues of Catholics important for the war, such as confidence in God, courage, bravery, love of the fatherland, readiness to make sacrifices, moderation at home and at the front.[32] The same orders were issued by the dioceses of Osnabrück and Trier[33] and probably in all the others as well.

During the following months the bishops made a special effort not to incur new charges of insufficient patriotic concern. Many members of the episcopate now no longer besought merely a peace beneficial to Germany, the customary phrase hitherto used, but prayed explicitly for a German victory. Bishop Berning of Osnabrück, in a pastoral letter of November 1940, asked the faithful to "pray that God grant us victory";[34] Archbishop Gröber in February 1941 expressed his hope for an honorable peace that would guarantee Germany "the necessary *Lebensraum* and the influence in the world to which she was entitled." Gröber stated that, despite much anti-Christian agitation, he had confidence in those "who with God's help are leading Germany to her victorious greatness."[35] The pastoral letter of Bishop Kaller of Ermland, issued in January 1941, was probably the most enthusiastic and drew the praise even of police Chief Heydrich.[36]

> We joyously profess our allegiance to the German *Volksgemeinschaft* and feel ourselves linked to it in good as well as in bad times . . . In this staunchly Christian spirit we also now participate wholeheartedly in the great struggle of our people for the protection of their life and importance in the world. With admiration we look upon our army, which in courageous fighting under extraordinary leadership has achieved and continues to achieve unparalleled success. We thank God for his support. Especially as Christians we are determined to rally all our strength so that the final victory will be secured for our fatherland. Especially as believing Christians, inspired by God's love, we faithfully stand behind our Führer who with firm hands guides the fortunes of our people.[37]

Hitler's attack upon the Soviet Union on June 22, 1941, further solidified the episcopate's backing. The bishops had always welcomed Hitler's struggle against Bolshevism and had assured the Führer of their support. "If ever the German people were to face the task of assuming the leadership in the defense against Bolshevism," Cardinal Faulhaber had declared in a sermon in December 1936, "then they cannot and may not forego their strongest ally in this struggle, Christianity."[38] Now that this fight had indeed erupted, the episcopate followed through with their promise.

The joint pastoral letter of the Fulda Bishops' Conference of June 1941, adopted four days after the invasion of Russia, did not make any special reference to Hitler's latest military venture and merely repeated the standard exhortations to the faithful to fulfil their duty to the fatherland, which service not only helped their country, "but at the same time follows God's holy will."[39] Kerrl, in a letter to Bertram, expressed the regime's dismay at the fact that the start of the struggle against Bolshevism had gone without special mention.[40] But soon individual bishops made up for this neglect. Bishop Rackl of Eichstätt, in a pastoral letter issued in September, termed the campaign in the east "a crusade, a holy war for homeland and people, for faith and church, for Christ and His most holy cross."[41] Lorenz Jäger, the new Archbishop of Paderborn, spoke of a struggle "for the protection of Christianity in our fatherland, for the rescue of the Church from the threat of anti-Christian Bolshevism."[42] Bishop Kumpfmüller of Augsburg compared the Bolshevik danger to that posed by the Turks in earlier centuries and asked for an "early, final victory over the enemies of our faith."[43] Cardinal Faulhaber accompanied the confiscation of the church bells with the remark that "for the dear fatherland we will make also this sacrifice if now it has become necessary for a successful end of the war and for the defeat of Bolshevism."[44] Bishop Galen of Münster, known as a courageous critic of the regime, nevertheless repeatedly expressed his hope for a German victory;[45] the Nazis used patriotic passages from his pastoral letters in their campaign to enlist volunteers for the S.S. units recruited in Holland and other occupied countries.[46]

As long as the German armies continued their advance into Russia the German bishops maintained their calls for a German victory. A pastoral letter of Archbishop Gröber, issued for People's Memorial Day, March 15, 1942, and adopted also by Bishop Galen, praised the victorious German soldiers who were fighting a crusade against Bolshevism and were protecting Europe against the Red tide.[47] A new prayer issued in May 1942 by the archdiocesan chancery of Breslau asked for God's blessing for the German soldiers so that "their weapons would be victorious in the struggle against godless Bolshevism.[48] Archbishop Jäger even showed sympathy for the Nazis' campaign of vilification against the Slavic *Untermenschen* (subhumans) and characterized Russia as a country whose people, "because of their hostility to God and their hatred of Christ, had almost degenerated into animals."[49] But when Hitler's military star began to show signs of waning, the enthusiasm of the bishops weakened considerably and the clamor for a German victory was increasingly replaced by expressions of hope for an honorable and beneficial peace. From 1943 on numerous reports by Party and State officials took note of this cooling of spirit and complained that the Church no longer prayed for victory, but only for an early peace.[50]

But this tactical change did not mean that the episcopate now hoped for a German defeat. Cardinal Faulhaber, in a communication to the Ministry of Ecclesiastical Affairs of October 1943, defended the Church against this accusation. "Nobody in his heart," he wrote, "can possibly wish an unsuccessful outcome of the war. Every reasonable person knows that in such a case the State and the Church, and organized society altogether, would be overturned by the Russian chaos."[51] Fearful of a Russian victory, the bishops continued to exhort the faithful to fulfil their duty to the fatherland; as late as January 1945 Archbishop Jäger admonished the Catholics to do their share in the struggle against Germany's two great enemies —"liberalism and individualism on one side, collectivism on the other."[52] In April 1945, after Allied troops had entered the town of Sendenhorst near Münster, where Bishop Galen had taken refuge from the bombing attacks, British and American newsmen sought to interview the Bishop. But Galen refused to talk to them on the grounds that as a German bishop he felt and suffered with his German people. In a statement released for Easter, his first pronouncement after the start of the Allied occupation, he said that his heart had bled at "the sight of the passing troops of our enemy."[53]

Bishop Galen's sorrowful reaction to the Allied victory over Germany perhaps was a somewhat extreme case; born of a noble family, Galen had been known as a great patriot and nationalist. But we cannot conclude that the other members of the episcopate felt very different. With the exception of Bishop Preysing of Berlin, who carefully refrained from any support of Hitler's wars, all German bishops until the very last days of the conflict called on the faithful to do their patriotic duty. This position, we may assume, represented sincerely felt loyalty to their country. The fact that Germany was ruled by the Nazis, who harassed and persecuted the Church and were guilty of untold other crimes, made no difference. The conclusion reached by Gordon Zahn is his analysis of this problem is indeed inescapable: Deeply involved in the nationalistic myths of *Volk* and *Vaterland* and determined to prove that Catholics were good and loyal Germans, "in World War II, the leading spokesmen of the Catholic Church in Germany did become channels of

Nazi control over their followers, whether by their general exhortations to loyal obedience to legitimate authority or by their even more direct efforts to rally these followers to the defense of *Volk, Vaterland* and *Heimat* as a Christian duty."[54]

Speaking of Hitler's war, Heinrich Lübke, the President of the West German government, stated in 1960, "No one who was not completely blinded or wholly naive could be completely free of the pressing awareness that this was not a just war."[55] Should we assume that the German bishops were free of such blindness and naïveté, that they did realize the injustice of Hitler's cause and that they committed the theological enormity of sending their followers to serve and die in an unjust war? Or should we assume just such blindness and accept at face value the bishops' often-asserted beliefs that Germany was fighting a just war for the attainment of *Lebensraum* and for the defense against plutocracy and Bolshevism? All the evidence at our command makes us conclude that the episcopate, at least during the first three years of the war and probably later as well, did not doubt the justice of the German cause.

The preservation of this conviction probably was not always easy. Pope Pius XII, indirectly, yet unequivocally, had condemned the German aggression against the Low Countries. Gradually the bishops received detailed information about the brutal treatment of the Polish Catholics, about the systematic starvation of Russian prisoners of war and about mass shootings of hostages in all of Nazi-occupied Europe. A report circulating among the diocesan chanceries on conditions in Poland showed that as of October 1, 1941, in the archdiocese of Posen alone, 74 priests had been shot or had died in concentration camps and 451 were being held in prisons or camps. Of the 441 churches of the archdiocese only 30 still were open for the Poles.[56] Catholic military chaplains in the east, meanwhile, were witnessing tens of thousands of Russian prisoners being killed by hunger. One priest recorded in his diary on February 19, 1942, that several hundred corpses were being brought to a mass grave near his station in Russia every day, the total number being already 19,000.[57] All this clearly violated traditional Catholic teaching on the prerequisites of a just war.

The episcopate tried to lighten its burden of conscience by several times protesting the treatment of the Polish Church to the government in Berlin.[58] The joint pastoral letter of August 1943 declared that it was wrong to kill "innocent hostages and unarmed prisoners of war,"[59] and in the same year both Bishop Galen and the new Archbishop of Cologne, Josef Frings, warned against hatred of the enemy.[60] But such criticism of the way Hitler and his generals conducted the war did not affect the bishops' unwavering support of the German war effort. These atrocities, in their eyes, were unfortunate side effects. The basic injustice of Hitler's expansionist plans seems never to have penetrated their consciousness.

There were, of course, some German Catholics who were troubled about supporting Hitler's wars. A theologian of great repute, who, at the time of his sudden death, was slated to become a bishop, concluded in 1940 that the war on Germany's side was unjust.[61] Many Catholics, we may assume, served in the armed forces without enthusiasm and with misgivings. But only seven Catholics in the entire Greater German Reich, according to Gordon Zahn's researches, decided openly to refuse military service. Six of these men were executed, the seventh survived by being declared insane. In almost all these cases the Church brought pressure to bear upon these conscientious objectors in an effort to get them to conform to the official line. After his arrest the Pallotine priest Franz Reinisch was denied Holy Communion by the Catholic prison chaplain on the grounds that he had violated his Christian duty by refusing to take the military oath of allegiance to Hitler.[62] Josef Fleischer, a layman, recalls that he was visited in prison by a high Church dignitary who tried to persuade him to abandon his refusal to serve, and who finally left in a fit of anger declaring that people like Fleischer deserved to be "shortened by a head."[63] Even the relatively innocuous statement of a parish priest made in 1939 that he waited for the end of "this awfully stupid war" and that those fed up should be allowed to go home, drew a reprimand from his diocesan chancery; the priest in question was made to send his apology to the officer to whose soldiers he had made the comment.[64]

But by and large the Catholics willingly followed the exhortations of their bishops to do their Christian duty and fight for the fatherland. Given the episcopate's years of support of Hitler's aggressive foreign policy, probably few could have understood had the bishops suddenly objected to the acquisition of *Lebensraum*. Roman

Catholic soldiers, a study has shown, did not desert in disproportionate numbers; "practically no case was noted of a desertion because of moral repugnance against Nazi atrocities."[65] Most German Catholics followed the call of the state to go to war without worrying about the justice or injustice of the German cause, and in this attitude they were confirmed by the teachings of their Church. The statement of Archbishop Gröber made in 1935, that not the individual, but the lawful authorities must decide the justice of a given war, has been quoted earlier. After the war had broken out the same idea was expressed by other churchmen. To the question posed in the title of his pamphlet, "What is to be done?", a prominent theologian early in 1940 gave this answer:

> Now there is no point in raising the question of the just war and introducing all sorts of "ifs," "ands" or "buts." A scientific judgment concerning the causes and origins of the war is absolutely impossible today because the prerequisites for such a judgment are not available to us. This must wait until a later time when the documents of both sides are available. Now the individual has but one course open to him; to do his best with faith in the cause of his people. For this, one cannot demand mathematical proof. This would no longer be faith, but, instead, a reckoning; and service to the people is based on faith and trust, not on calculation. Today that is self-evident to all patriots.[66]

One may sympathize with the predicament of a simple German soldier who had no way of ascertaining whether Poland had indeed mistreated the German minority and fired the first shots in 1939. Nor could he find out on his own whether Holland and Belgium had really violated their neutrality, as alleged by the Nazi propagandists, and had thus provoked the German attack. It is understandable if the man in the street took his government's word in these matters. But the bishops did have additional sources of information. Theirs was the task of teaching the flock, of illuminating moral questions and dilemmas, of providing moral leadership. When war broke out they did indeed teach the faithful how to conduct themselves in this new situation: they placed them under the moral obligation to support the national war effort.

The Catholic episcopate therefore must bear some share of the responsibility for the immeasurable suffering which Hitler's armies inflicted upon Europe. Had the bishops been in doubt concerning the justice of the German cause, they should have remained silent. Instead, until the very end of the war they exhorted their followers to shed their blood in the service of God and country. If, as some have argued, the episcopate acted thus out of unwillingness to require martyrdom of their followers by directing them to refuse military service in an unjust war, this tactic also ended in failure. For, as Zahn puts it, "the bishops did call for martyrdom on the part of the German Catholics—but it was a 'martyrdom' for *Volk* and *Vaterland* and not for the religious values represented by the traditional Catholic morality of war."[67]

2. The Army Bishop

In his talk with Cardinal Faulhaber in November 1936 Hitler once again had affirmed the importance of religion for state and society and especially the soldier in combat. "Man cannot exist without belief in God. The soldier who for three and four days lies under intense bombardment needs a religious prop."[68] It was for this strictly utilitarian reason that Hitler continued the policy of his predecessors to establish a system of pastoral care for the armed forces. After the outbreak of the war, the Catholic military chaplaincy comprised about 560 priests. With the exception of the air force, where Göring had forbidden the appointment of military chaplains, most of the military commanders supported the institution. The appointment of an army bishop to head this program had been provided by the Concordat with the Holy See in 1933. Finally, on February 20, 1938, after a five-year delay, Franz Josef Rarkowski had been consecrated as *episcopus castrensis*. The reasons for this delay are of interest and significance.

The prolonged controversy resulting from the government's demand for the establishment of an exempt military chaplaincy (discussed in Chapter III, section 1) had found its solution in Article 27 of the Concordat. The Holy See and the German government, by mutual agreement, were to select the army bishop. After consultation, and in agreement with the government, an Apostolic Brief was to be issued that would regulate the system of military pastoral care in points of detail. The first draft of this brief was handed to the government on June 26, 1934.[69] The German bishops, who for many years had fought the appointment of an army bishop and who had finally swallowed the bitter pill in order to obtain the Concordat, had made the Holy See insert a provision that excluded the army bishop from the deliberations of the Fulda Bishops' Conference except when matters affecting the military chaplaincy were to be discussed. He also was to be held responsible for carrying out all decisions of the German episcopate. The government at first objected, arguing that the army bishop thus would have an inferior status, but it finally retreated and consented to let the German bishops themselves handle this matter. On September 19, 1935, the Apostolic Brief containing the statutes of the military chaplaincy was issued essentially as demanded by the German episcopate and the Holy See.[70]

The question of whether the army bishop should or should not be allowed to participate in the deliberations of the Fulda Bishops' Conference was not unrelated to the identity of the candidate for this office. The government was known to favor the appointment of Rarkowski, the acting head of the military chaplaincy since 1929, a man close to the late President Hindenburg. As the Foreign Ministry informed Ambassador Bergen at the Vatican in July 1935, Rarkowski also enjoyed the confidence of the Nazi party.[71] Most of the German bishops, on the other hand, were strongly opposed to the candidacy of Rarkowski. It was known that Rarkowski had managed to be admitted to the study of theology without graduation from high school, that he had studied for the priesthood in Switzerland rather than in Germany, had left a religious order and was generally considered by the bishops to be an upstart without the requisite educational background.[72] All these were strikes against him as a member of the episcopate. In recent years some Catholic writers, embarrassed by Rarkowski's extreme nationalistic and pro-Nazi views, have pointed up the fact that a majority of the German bishops from the beginning opposed Rarkowski. The reason, it now seems, stemmed from the episcopate's feeling that he was their inferior and a threat to their status rather than from the unacceptability of his political ideas.

Nuncio Orsenigo, charged by the Vatican with handling the negotiations with the German government over the appointment, argued that Rarkowski was too old for the post (he was then sixty-two) and denied that any other factors were involved.[73] He proposed instead that the appointment go to Karl Büchler, a priest from Düsseldorf with experience in pastoral care for the police forces in the Rhineland. Meanwhile Kerrl, the Minister of Ecclesiastical Affairs, was supporting the candidacy of Bishop Eberle of Augsburg.[74] But Büchler was vetoed by Hess, the deputy of the Führer, who branded Büchler as a particularly dangerous character. "His craftiness," he informed Blomberg, the Minister of War, "goes so far that when dealing with Party and State authorities he pretends to be a National Socialist, while in reality he is their sworn enemy."[75] The reasons why Eberle, a great admirer of Hitler, failed to get the post are not known, just as the full record about the subsequent negotiations is still missing. In August 1936 the original candidate of the government, Rarkowski, was appointed acting army bishop, and on February 20, 1938, he was finally consecrated in a lavish ceremony conducted by Nuncio Orsenigo, assisted by Bishops Preysing and Galen.[76]

According to one report Rarkowski promised Monsignor Kaas in Rome to retire from the office of army bishop at an early date.[77] If this was ever his intention, he must have changed his mind, for Rarkowski continued in his post until the end of World War II. His pastoral letters are ultra-nationalistic and militaristic in the extreme; no word of explicit or even implicit criticism of the Nazi regime ever crossed his lips. Since Rarkowski was in far closer contact with the millions of Catholics in Hitler's armies than his fellow bishops, his importance for the German war effort was considerable.

The outbreak of the war in September 1939 brought the following statement from the Army Bishop:

> In this serious hour when our German people must undergo the trials of a test of fire in a struggle for its natural and God-given right to live . . . I turn to you soldiers who stand ready at the front and who bear the great and honorable responsibility of guarding and defending with the sword the life of the German nation. . . . Each of you knows what is at stake for our people in these stormy days; and, in whatever is asked of you, each sees before him the shining example of a true warrior, our Führer and Supreme Commander, the first and most valiant soldier of the Greater German Reich, who is even now with you at the battlefront.[78]

Rarkowski always did his best to bring out the justice of the German cause. In October 1939, at the end of the first victorious campaign, he noted that "the Almighty God had visibly blessed the struggle against Poland that had been forced upon us."[79] At the first anniversary of the outbreak of hostilities, Rarkowski assured his soldiers:

> The German people, who for one year now have been fighting against their detractors, have an untroubled conscience and know which nations before God and history are burdened with the responsibility for this gigantic struggle that is raging now. They also know who has wickedly provoked this war. They know that they themselves are fighting a just war, born of the necessity of national self-defense, out of the impossibility of solving peacefully a heavy and burdensome question of justice involving the very existence of the state and of correcting by other means a burning injustice inflicted upon us. They begrudged us our place in the sun and sought to destroy us forever. They sought to make us into helots, and therefore there is no question in our minds on which side right and, with it, God's help is to be found. . . . Other people, arrayed against us, also pray to God and implore victory. God is indeed in the same manner the father of all people, but he is not, at one and the same time, the advocate of justice and injustice, of honesty and falsehood.[80]

After Hitler's attack upon the Soviet Union Rarkowski called Germany "the savior and champion of Europe." We know, he added, that this war against Russia is waged by us as "a European crusade," a task similar to that fulfilled in earlier times by the Teutonic knights. The Army Bishop ended this pastoral letter, like almost all others, with the exhortation to Catholics to fight for a German victory, "a victory that will allow Europe to breathe freely again and will promise all nations a new future."[81]

Another theme running through Rarkowski's pastoral pronouncements was the admonition to perfect obedience. Every soldier, upon entering military service, had to take the following oath of allegiance: "I swear by God this holy oath that I shall render unconditional obedience to the Führer of the German Reich and people, Adolf Hitler, the Supreme Commander of the Armed Forces, and that as a brave soldier I shall be prepared at all times to risk my life for this oath."[82] Recruits were told by their superiors that the soldier in taking this oath "pledged himself to the person of the

Führer and at the same time to the Third Reich and the National Socialist *Weltanschauung.*" The oath, it was stressed, "excluded all reservations."[83]

Catholic theologians have always taught that an oath cannot make lawful what otherwise is morally illicit. The German bishops, when this and similar oaths for civil servants were first introduced by Hitler, went a step further and told the faithful that since no oath could obligate a Christian to do that which violated God's commands and laws, they might take these oaths and, as required by the Nazis, swear full obedience to Hitler without reservations and restrictions. "Such reservations and restrictions are not necessary for the Catholic Christian," they added, since an oath by definition cannot contain anything in conflict with the duty owed to God.[84]

This declaration of the episcopate may have been good moral theology and it certainly served a useful purpose. The waiver issued by the bishops made it possible for Catholics to take these oaths of allegiance to Hitler without pangs of conscience, thereby eliminating a possible conflict of loyalties. Notwithstanding, this declaration also paved the way to that spirit of blind obedience which accounts for so many of the crimes committed by Nazi Germany, especially during World War II. The overwhelming majority of the Catholic soldiers took their military oath to Hitler to mean what it said, and served him and his subordinates with "unconditional obedience" and "without reservations and restrictions." The Army Bishop did his part in preventing any doubts from arising on this score.

The official Catholic songbook, handed to Catholic conscripts, had this to say on the subject: "The Armed Forces are the armorbearers of the German people. They protect the German people and fatherland, the people united in National Socialism, and their *Lebensraum.* . . . The honor of the soldiers lies in unconditional risking of their person for people and fatherland that includes the sacrifice of life."[85] And to this the Army Bishop never tired of adding in his pastoral letters that the Catholic soldier was obligated by his oath always to do his duty toward Führer and people. "Whatever the times demand in efforts, blood and tears," Rarkowski insisted in August 1942, "whatever the Führer and Supreme Commander commands you soldiers to do and whatever your country expects from you: behind all this stands God himself with his will and command." The Christian soldier "remains staunchly loyal to his military oath, to his country, his people and to his Führer, not out of expectation of reward, not out of fear of punishment, but out of holiest conviction of conscience."[86] In the same pastoral letter Rarkowski admitted that the struggle against "the Bolshevik *Untermenschentum*" (subhumanity) subjected the soul of the German soldier to a severe test. Without going into any details, he asked them to preserve their souls from all perversion and degradation. But how could the Catholic soldier maintain his moral integrity if at the same time he was exhorted to remain faithful to his military oath; that is, asked to render unconditional obedience to Hitler's criminal orders?

The mental reservations which the Catholic bishops, including perhaps the Army Bishop, made in this matter were absent from the practice of their followers. At divine services in the field the Catholic soldiers prayed to God for their Führer and Supreme Commander and asked, "Let us all, under his leadership, see in the devotion to people and fatherland a holy task, so that, through faith, obedience and fidelity we will obtain the eternal resting place in Your light and Your peace."[87] These constant admonitions to obey the Führer proved stronger than the scriptural injunction in times of bad leaders to obey God rather than men, which the bishops at home referred to occasionally, but not the Army Bishop, Rarkowski. In military pastoral care morality, for the most part, was identified with sexual morality. As one former Catholic recruit recalls, there was plenty of talk of the Bolshevik threat and just defense, of how to avoid sexual adventures, "but no word about Hitler, no word about anti-Semitism, about possible conflicts between command and conscience."[88]

Some of the German bishops, as Zahn notes, may have rationalized their support of the German war effort by distinguishing between the war fought for the defense of people and fatherland (a goal they approved) and the war for domination over other people and for the defense of the Nazi regime as such (disapproved). But no such mental construct, it is evident, dominated the thinking of Bishop Rarkowski. An article of Rarkowski published in a newspaper for Catholic soldiers on the first wartime anniversary of Hitler's birthday is typical of the Army Bishop's mentality:

> Today it is an already incontestable fact that Adolf Hitler has taken on a fateful meaning for our people and for the entire world. No other German statesman before him brought about such mighty changes in the most widely different areas of the people's existence as he has. . . . He has brought the big change; through his contributions we have learned to see new values in words like *Heimat* and *Volk,* in national honor and national history. He has awakened us to a recognition of our task as Germans. In the light of our national heritage, he has discovered the life principle of the German people and by his acts he has made it effective. . . . May our thanksgiving and our readiness to repay loyalty with loyalty find expression in the prayer that means more to us in these days than it did in the quiet days of peace: "Bless, Oh God, our Führer and Supreme Commander in all the tasks placed upon him. . . ."[89]

Hitler's drive to impose Nazi rule upon all of Europe was finally checked and defeated by the combined efforts of Russia and the Western Allies. The Catholic Army Bishop thereupon relinquished his post and retired, having done what he had conceived to be his duty. Before history some share in the responsibility for the havoc and suffering Hitler's armies caused humanity will be his.

3. Pope Pius XII: Dilemmas of Neutrality

Article 24 of the concordat of 1929 between Italy and the Holy See had obligated the Papacy to remain neutral in temporal disputes between nations. At the same time the Pope had retained the right to mediate in such conflicts and to exercise his "moral and spiritual influence." The neutrality accepted by the Vatican in this treaty with Mussolini did not represent a concession. In modern times, the Pope, being the head of a world-wide Church, had usually found it necessary to steer a neutral course. An armed conflict, especially one between Catholic citizens of different nations, undoubtedly created a serious evil of a spiritual nature in which the Pontiff, as supreme moral teacher, was entitled to intervene and to pass judgment on the rights of the warring parties. But such an intervention would have incurred a serious risk of undermining the status of local Church hierarchies who, out of patriotism or tactical considerations, usually sided with their own country's war effort. To denounce as unjust a war of an aggressor nation containing a large Catholic population would have subjected the Catholics of that country to a conflict of loyalties in which the victory of nationalistic sentiments over a universal morality of peace and justice would probably have been a foregone conclusion. The ability of the Papacy to provide moral leadership being limited by what the faithful can accept, the Holy See had, therefore, traditionally refrained from declaring a particular war as just or unjust. Instead the Vatican had allowed the ecclesiastical authorities of each belligerent country to support their own government and had merely counseled the Catholics of the countries at war to fight humanely and with charity toward their enemies.

The difficult situation in which the Holy See finds itself in each new war between Christian nations has always given an additional impetus to the Vatican's striving for peace in the world. Prior to the outbreak of World War II Pope Pius XII similarly attempted to mediate between the Western Allies and the Axis powers, and his appeals for peace continued up to the German attack upon Poland.[90] But once the war had actually started the Holy See assumed the traditional posture of neutrality. When the British Ambassador at the Vatican suggested to the Papal Secretary of State on September 1, 1939, that the publication of the last-minute unsuccessful peace appeal of Pope Pius be accompanied by an expression of regret that the German government, despite the Papal appeal, had plunged the world into war, Maglione turned down this request as too specific an intervention in international politics.[91] In an address to the Polish colony in Rome, which included the recently arrived Polish primate, Cardinal Hlond, Pius XII on September 30 expressed carefully worded sentiments of sympathy and appreciation for the Polish people, but any reference to the German act of aggression against Poland was conspicuously absent. On October 14 an article in *L'Osservatore Romano* explained that the sorrow of Pope Pius over the suffering of Poland could not express itself in forms that were irreconcilable with his position as common father of all the faithful.[92]

After England and France had declared war on Germany the Catholic bishops of these two countries added their voice to that of the Polish bishops and called for a crusade against Nazi Germany for freedom and human brotherhood. The Archbishop of Cambrai called France's fight a "war in defense of civilization, of the law of nations, human morality, liberty, in short, of humanity."[93] The British episcopate declared similarly that Britain was defending a just cause and fighting for truth and Christianity.[94] The German bishops for their part, as we have seen, also were convinced that they were fighting a just war. Of course, by definition, and as all Catholic theologians are agreed, no war can be objectively just on both sides. If one side defends rights, the other is necessarily violating rights.[95] But Pius XII remained aloof: he told all Catholics that they should fight with valor and charity on whatever side they found themselves.

As Zahn concludes, this kind of advice reduces "the whole structure of the 'just war–unjust war' theology to the status of a patently useless and socially meaningless intellectual exercise."[96] Yet, what was the Pope to do? In the final analysis his stand reflected not so much a personal failure to be courageous and uphold the cause of justice, but the demands of an institution which, for close to 2,000 years, has put its survival as a channel in the salvation of individual souls before the moral demands of its own gospel.

On November 8 Pope Pius XII replied to a message of the French episcopate in which the bishops had explained why they sided with their own government. The Pope told the French bishops that he fully understood their position, and that it was their right as loyal citizens of the French nation to support all measures aimed at defending the security and future of their fatherland.[97] A few weeks before Italy declared war upon England and France Pope Pius sent a message to the metropolitans of Italy in which he told them in the event of war to fulfill all duties imposed by justified patriotic sentiments, but at the same time not to desert the supernatural values of mildness and love.[98] And in December 1939 the Supreme Pontiff issued a pastoral letter to the clergy serving as military chaplains in the armed forces of the warring nations in which he asked them to have full confidence in their respective military bishops. The present war, Pius declared, should be seen as a manifestation of God's providence, as the will of a Heavenly Father who always turned evil into good. The Pope asked them "as fighters under the flags of their country to fight also for the Church. . . ."[99] The army bishops of each camp meanwhile were praying to that same God asking him to bless the armies of their country, and their country only, with victory. To whose prayer was the Almighty to listen?

On October 20, 1939, Pope Pius issued his first encyclical to the bishops of the world. Once again the Supreme Pontiff called for the peaceful resolution of international conflicts and expressed his sympathy for all his children, especially for those persecuted and oppressed. "The blood of countless human beings, even noncombatants, raises a piteous dirge over a nation such as our dear Poland, which . . . has a right to the generous and brotherly sympathy of the whole world, while it awaits, relying on powerful intercession of Mary, help of Christians, the hour of resurrection in harmony with the principles of justice and true peace."[100] The Western Allies broadcast the text of the encyclical and dropped leaflets over Germany containing a German translation of the Papal letter. But the Gestapo considered the Pope's pronouncement innocuous and ambiguous enough to allow the encyclical to be read from the pulpits.[101] After the unsuccessful assassination attempt upon Hitler in Munich on November 8 the Papal Nuncio in Berlin on November 10, in addition to the felicitations of the diplomatic corps, delivered the special personal congratulations of Pope Pius on the Führer's miraculous escape. Four days later the Nuncio called on State Secretary Weizsäcker to express congratulations in this manner also to the government of the Reich.[102]

On November 30 Russia attacked Finland. To this act of aggression the Pope could respond in a more forthright manner: the interests of no sizable Catholic population would be jeopardized. In his Christmas address to the College of Cardinals Pope Pius condemned as a violation of international law the "calculated act of aggression against a small, industrious and peaceful nation, on the pretext of a threat which was neither real nor intended, nor even possible."[103] Officials in Rosenberg's office for propaganda and indoctrination considered this passage as directed against Germany's attack on Poland.[104] But the Pope, a few days later, went out of his way to assure the German official, Menshausen, that he was not opposed to the totalitarian nations. To Menshausen's remark that

Papal declarations were being interpreted by the Western Allies as directed against the Axis powers, Pope Pius replied that Germany was also construing them in her favor. The Pope indicated that he took special care to phrase his declarations in such a way that they could not be misunderstood and seem to point against Germany.[105]

The Vatican paper, *L'Osservatore Romano,* meanwhile had repeatedly published reports on the persecution of the Polish Church, and the Vatican Radio on September 28 had allowed Cardinal Hlond to broadcast a message to the Poles of the world. The Pope was not too happy about the Polish Primate's presence in Rome and wanted him to go back to Poland, but the German government refused to allow the return of the anti-German Cardinal.[106] On January 6, 1940, Cardinal Hlond submitted a new and detailed report to Pius XII on the deportations and arrests of Polish priests, the closing of churches and the brutal treatment meted out to the Polish population. The Vatican radio on January 23 broadcast excerpts from this report.[107] The Germans now submitted a sharply worded protest, and on January 29 Ambassador Bergen was able to report that the Papal Secretary of State had ordered the immediate cessation of all such broadcasts.[108]

When on May 10 Hitler invaded the Low Countries, Pius XII for one short moment forsook the strict neutrality he had hitherto maintained and to which he thereafter returned for the remainder of the war. The telegrams of sympathy sent to the sovereign rulers of the three countries whose neutrality had been violated did not name the guilty party, but the reference to people exposed to the cruelties of war "against their will and rights" was unmistakably aimed against the aggressor, Germany. When the Duce expressed his concern over these telegrams, the Pope defended the action as one of pastoral concern and stressed that he had taken care to avoid a political word like "invasion."[109] Ambassador Bergen, too, was told that the Pontiff had not wanted to condemn the German attack.[110] But these explanations clearly were diplomatic gestures, and the Pope's action drew angry comments from the German government as well as from certain pro-Nazi Catholics.

In a message addressed to the Fulda Bishops' Conference of August 1940 Pope Pius defended the dispatch of the three telegrams. A German statesman in 1914, he wrote, had been able to call the

German invasion of Belgium an act outside of international law without having his patriotism questioned. Why, then, could the father of Christendom not express his sympathy to nations in diplomatic relations with the Holy See at the shocking repetition of this action? His declaration, Pius said, had been prompted by humane and moral considerations only and was not an unfriendly political act directed against the German people. Only those who doubted the often-repeated assurances of the German government to be guided after the conclusion of the war by considerations of justice could regard his hope for the restoration of independence to the three nations as an anti-German act. The Supreme Pontiff reaffirmed his absolute neutrality but added that this impartiality might not be identified with silence in the face of injustice. He expressed his surprise over the weekly *Der Neue Wille* and over a "teacher of theology" who had misinterpreted his moral concern.[111]

The Pope's chiding remarks on *Der Neue Wille,* a Catholic pro-Nazi paper appearing with the endorsement of Bishop Rarkowski, were soon followed by a broadcast in German over the Vatican radio that criticized the Army Bishop directly. Commenting upon Rarkowski's pastoral letter issued at the first anniversary of the outbreak of the war in which he had asserted that Germany was fighting a just war, the Vatican radio said:

> The German episcopate has so far avoided taking a position on this war that would transcend their pastoral duty toward the faithful. If the Army Bishop has read or heard what the Head of his Church has repeatedly and unequivocally said about the injustice done to Poland, he must be aware of the discrepancy between his assertion and the position of the Holy See. Many Catholics do not at all share the political and historical viewpoint of the Army Bishop, but are convinced that Hitler's war unfortunately is not a just war and that God's blessing therefore cannot be upon it. . . . It almost looks as if the Army Bishop sometimes finds it easier to get into line with the Nazis than with his Church.[112]

The Foreign Ministry ordered a vigorous protest against this broadcast, but Bishop Rarkowski probably never heard of the broadcast or any other criticism of his pastoral pronouncements by the Holy See; otherwise—so thinks his Vicar General—he would have submitted and changed his line.[113] This is quite credible. On the other hand, the broadcast had singled out for criticism ideas of Bishop Rarkowski frequently voiced by other members of the episcopate as well; and the Army Bishop, therefore, might have felt entitled to disregard the rebuke even if he had heard of it. The Vatican radio's broadcasts, finally, did not have official status, and Rarkowski could have dismissed the attack as the unauthorized opinion of an anti-German member of the Curia, which indeed it may have been. When, beginning in late 1940 and lasting well into 1942, most of the German bishops more and more frequently called for a German victory and vigorously defended the justice of the German cause, Pope Pius, to the best of our present knowledge, did not attempt to restrain them.

Italian opposition to the editorial policies of *L'Osservatore Romano* increased after the publication of the three telegrams of Pope Pius to the sovereign rulers of the Low Countries. After the entry of Italy into the war on the side of Nazi Germany the paper was asked to publish the military communiqués of the Axis powers only. Otherwise the government threatened to forbid its sale in Italy. *L'Osservatore Romano* thereupon resolved to publish no military reports at all, and the readers of the paper were informed of this decision on June 14.[114] From that time on the Vatican's semi-official newspaper adhered to a strictly neutral line.

Criticism of the Pope's neutrality grew, especially in the English-speaking world, as more and more information was received about the brutal treatment of the Polish Church and the harsh occupation policies of the Nazis. An English broadcast over the Vatican radio in September 1940 defended the "silence of the Pope." The Supreme Pontiff was the father of 400-million Catholics and "the less he commits himself one-sidedly, the greater will be the respect and adoration tended to him." In moral questions, the broadcast admitted, no neutrality was possible, but in many instances it was not yet feasible to determine where justice and injustice lay.[115] The Vatican radio strongly implied that the war was not clearly just on either side.

The Holy See's uneasy course of neutrality continued to draw criticism in Germany as well. Rosenberg's propaganda never ceased accusing the Pope of being in league with the Western Allies.[116] In February 1941 Cardinal Bertram advised the German bishops that this charge was false and that the Holy Father was strictly impartial.[117] In the same month Pius XII assured Bishop Galen that his love went out to all children of the Church without distinction of country and people and on both sides of the opposing fronts.[118]

The Holy See maintained its neutrality when Germany attacked the Soviet Union in June 1941, even when the German bishops called for a crusade against Bolshevism. But the Vatican may not have been too unhappy about Germany's new act of aggression. Ambassador Bergen was told by a Vatican spokesman, shortly after the German invasion of Russia, that the alignment of atheistic Russia on the side of the Western democracies had robbed the latter of all justification to speak of a crusade for Christianity. For this reason, and also on account of the weakening of Russian power that was to be expected from Russia's involvement in the war, Bergen wrote, the Vatican welcomed the new turn of events.[119]

As Hitler's drive in Russia bogged down the Vatican became increasingly fearful of the spread of Bolshevism into Central and Western Europe. Shortly before the outbreak of World War II Waldemar Gurian had observed:

> It may safely be said that the Vatican wishes to avoid anything that might seem like participation in an anti-Fascist front. A similar factor—and not the least—is the resolve not to give indirect support to atheistic Bolshevism by taking active measures against Hitler.[120]

When the Russian armies began to advance in a westward direction the old fears quickened and the Holy See therefore carefully refrained from any action or pronouncement that might weaken the German war effort. In January 1943 Pope Pius addressed a letter of encouragement to the German Catholics in which he reaffirmed his striving for "a true and lasting peace that would safeguard the vital interests of all people."[121] In a covering letter to Cardinal Bertram the Papal Secretary of State left it to the discretion of the German episcopate to decide whether and when the Pope's letter should be published. Everything had to be avoided, Maglione stressed, that might create the impression that the Supreme Pontiff wanted to harm Germany.[122] In September 1943 the new Ambassador at the Vatican, Ernst von Weizsäcker, reported that Maglione regarded the fate of Europe as dependent upon "the victorious resistance of Germany at the Russian front." In case the German armies collapsed there the only possible bulwark against Bolshevism would fall and European civilization be lost.[123] Similar views were said to be held by other members of the Curia and by the German colony in Rome, including Monsignor Kaas.[124]

The desire of the Holy See not to weaken the German power of resistance against Russia was one of the most important reasons why all efforts on the part of the Allies failed to persuade the Vatican publicly to denounce German atrocities, including the extermination of the Jews in Europe. For another, Pope Pius wanted to avoid being blamed later for a German defeat as had happened to Pope Benedict XV (1914-1922). After the war had ended Pius XII declared that he had always condemned acts of injustice and moral outrages and had merely avoided expressions that could have done more harm than good.[125]

The available record shows that the Pope was more circumspect than his own words would indicate. On several occasions Pope Pius voiced regret over the treatment of noncombatants, and he always mentioned his concern for a more humane conduct of the war. But in line with his policy of strict neutrality the Pope never named the guilty party; his statements always expressed sympathy for the victims but never condemned those responsible for the atrocities. When in October 1941 Harold H. Tittmann, the assistant of Roosevelt's special emissary to the Vatican, tried to get the Pope to issue a public protest against the Germans' mass shooting of hostages, he was told that this could not be done since it would jeopardize the situation of the German Catholics.[126]

In numerous diplomatic notes the Holy See pleaded for the persecuted Polish Church,[127] and the Papal Nuncio in Berlin frequently intervened in favor of Polish and French priests, and occasionally also for prisoners of war who, for various offenses, had been condemned to death.[128] In May 1940 the Papal Secretary of State asked for an Italian intervention with the German government to prevent the bombing of Paris and the strafing of refugees on the crowded highways of France.[129] It may well be that quiet diplomacy in many of these situations was more effective than a public protest. Undoubtedly, the carefully worded statements of Pius XII helped to preserve the neutrality of the Vatican. But, on the other hand, as two

Italian historians have put it, "one cannot help thinking that it is not by generalizations and reticence that the moral leadership of the world, which is, after all, the function of the Papacy, can be rendered effective."[130]

The Papacy in World War II found itself in a particularly difficult situation. Far more than in earlier conflicts the war between the Axis powers and the Western Allies was fought also on the ideological plane. The German bishops spoke of a fight against liberalism and of a crusade against Bolshevism; the episcopate of France, England and, later, the United States of America called for a struggle against Hitlerian barbarism. The Holy See made the best of this predicament. The Pope exhorted all Catholics to do their patriotic duty and praised those who served and died for their fatherland. In his letter to the German bishops of August 1940 Pius XII expressed his admiration for the German Catholics who "loyal unto death give proof of their willingness to share the sacrifices and sufferings of the other *Volksgenossen*."[131] A Papal communication with a similar content addressed in 1939 to the French bishops, seeking God's blessing for the fight against these same *Volksgenossen*, has already been mentioned. Leaving nothing undone the Holy See also sent words of appreciation to the Pallotine Fathers in Germany after one member of their society, Franz Reinisch, had been executed as a conscientious objector. "The Holy Father," the Papal Secretary of State wrote, "is in doubt whether he should tender his sympathy to you on account of the loss of a member of such noble bearing, or whether he should congratulate you on the glory which that man has gained."[132] The praise of the Supreme Pontiff thus could be earned by fighting and dying for Hitler, by giving one's life to the anti-Fascist struggle, as well as by refusing military service on grounds of conscience.

4. The Uneasy Truce

After the outbreak of war in September 1939 the bishops issued pastoral instructions to the clergy admonishing them to strengthen the war effort and to exercise maximum restraint in discussing political and military questions. Those of Bishop Rackl of Eichstätt, for example, stated:

During the difficult time of war we priests will fulfill our patriotic duty with the greatest conscientiousness, will carry and help the people to bear the burden of this time of emergency. It is the task of pastoral care to make good in the religion of Jesus Christ the preparedness to bring sacrifices and love to people and homeland. . . . In the interest of the fatherland and our official position as well as our personal safety we shall exercise the greatest restraint in all conversations involving political, military and economic matters.[133]

Similar instructions not to jeopardize the unity of the inner front were repeated from time to time. In February 1940 the Bishop of Hildesheim told his clergy:

It is the holy duty of the Church and her servants to preach the gospel of Christ in pure and uncurtailed form. This principle is valid also today. But this preaching and teaching surely can be reconciled with tactful consideration of the demands of wartime. *All that could be considered as disturbing and weakening the unity of our national strength . . . is therefore, as until now, to be avoided.* Some things also, which at another time perhaps would not have given offense, must now in changed circumstances remain unsaid. I take this opportunity expressly to point this out (Bishop Machens's italics).[134]

The Church thus had done her share in declaring a truce in the ideological dispute between Church and State. Hitler also decided to refrain from any polemics or hostile measures against the Church that might weaken the war effort. An edict of the Minister of Ecclesiastical Affairs of January 6, 1940, based on the Führer's amnesty of September 9, 1939, restored the salaries to a large number of priests who had had their state subsidy cut off because of minor infractions of the law.[135] During his visit to Rome in March 1940 Ribbentrop told Pius XII that the Führer wanted "to maintain the existing truce and, if possible, to expand it. In this respect Germany had made very considerable preliminary concessions. The Führer had quashed no less than seven thousand indictments of Catholic clergymen."[136] In July 1940 Hitler once again let it be known that he wished to avoid all measures not absolutely necessary that could worsen the relationship of State and Party to the Church.[137] And in the monologues at his military headquarters recorded by Bormann, Hitler never tired of emphasizing that the showdown with the Church unfortunately would have to be postponed until the end of the war. "Once the war is over we will put a swift end to the Concordat," he declared in July 1942. The financial subsidies would be eliminated at once and all old accounts be settled. Until then all provocative steps had to be avoided.[138] When, in the desperate days of defeat and manpower shortage of October 1944, Rosenberg proposed to draft the entire clergy for labor services, Hitler rejected the idea.[139] As a shrewd tactician he sensed that such a measure would do more harm than good.

Not all of Hitler's henchmen were willing to accept this truce. The system of pastoral care in the armed forces was opposed by many leaders of the Party who did their best to undermine its effectiveness. From the beginning of the war religious literature sent to soldiers had to pass the censorship of the Propaganda Ministry, and by 1942 most of the religious tracts distributed by the chaplains had been suppressed.[140] In August 1940 Goebbels issued orders to the *Gauleiters* to organize memorial ceremonies for fallen soldiers in order to overcome the influence and activities of the churches in this sphere. The Party, he argued, was the custodian of all realms of life. Until now, certain restraints had had to be observed. Now, after the victorious conclusion of the war against France, Goebbels continued, the offensive could again be taken.[141] On October 29, 1940, it was decreed that following an air raid alarm during the preceding night church services might not be held before 10 A.M.[142] From September 1940 till July 1941 the property of over 100 monasteries was confiscated and the monks and nuns expelled from their houses.[143] In April 1941 the Bavarian Minister of Education and Religious Affairs, Adolf Wagner, ordered the gradual removal of crucifixes from the schools.[144] Bormann, the head of the Party Chancellery and increasingly one of the most powerful men in the Nazi state, in June 1941 informed the *Gauleiters* that the influence of the churches would have to be curtailed as much as possible, for National Socialism and Christianity were irreconcilable.[145] The closing down of the diocesan weeklies, mentioned earlier, also took place at this time.

The removal of the crucifixes in Bavaria and the wave of confiscations of Church property in all parts of the Reich were vigorously protested by the bishops and caused considerable unrest among the population.[146] On July 30, 1941, Hitler ordered Bormann to stop all

seizures of monasteries or other Church property without first obtaining his personal permission, and Bormann passed the order
along to the *Gauleiters*.[147] Papen, who talked to the Führer in September 1941, recalls that Hitler was upset about these actions
against the Church, and blamed the hotheads of the Party for "this
nonsense."[148] But even after the Führer had forbidden such confiscations they continued sporadically. On August 23 Kerrl complained
to the head of the Reich Chancellery that on account of such occurrences, which were taking place without his being consulted
or even informed beforehand, his continuation as Minister of Ecclesiastical Affairs was becoming "increasingly unbearable."[149] Bormann, when queried about these new confiscations, excused them as
decided before the *Führerbefehl* of July 30.

For the most part, however, and despite occasional new seizures
of Church property, the uneasy truce was now being observed. A
conference of Gestapo church specialists, convened in Berlin in
September 1941, agreed that all sweeping actions against the Church
would have to stop.[150] A month later an order of Heydrich laid down
that all measures which in any way could weaken the power of resistance of the German people had definitely to be avoided.[151] A
thirty-point program for a neo-pagan "National Reich Church,"
circulated as a leaflet in Germany and attributed by the Allied
propaganda to Rosenberg, was disowned by the government; and
Heydrich, in a report to the Foreign Ministry, atributed the reap-
pearance of this leaflet to Catholic elements out to defame the
regime. The author of this program, he reported, was an eccentric
in Stettin who had composed it in 1937 and had later been arrested
for disrupting divine services.[152] In January 1942 Rosenberg, with the
concurrence of Bormann, forbade any further discussion of religious questions in the Party's work of ideological indoctrination.[153]
And in April 1943 Bormann once again issued a strict order against
"any policy of petty annoyance" of the Church.[154] The official line
now was to ignore the Church as much as possible.

During the first year of the war the regime's policy had been
to encourage the Church to show patriotic concern and to support
the German war effort. For this purpose the Gestapo had even organized the mailing of letters to clergymen, allegedly originating in
a *Katholischer Pfarrer-Notbund* (Emergency League of Catholic

Priests), that accused the episcopate of not doing enough for a German victory, and asked priests to put pressure on the bishops to adopt a more patriotic attitude.[155] But when the Church did indeed exert herself in support of the war, the Nazis began to fear that such a patriotic stand would unduly enhance the reputation of the Church and they tried to hush up all information about it.

Already in December 1939 Rosenberg had written Göring that the Church was out to regain her lost positions by delivering martial sermons,[156] and in May 1941 Bormann warned all *Gauleiters* not to be misled by the clever tactics of the Church, which was propagandistically exploiting the fact that many clerics at the front had received medals for bravery and was bragging about the number of priests killed in action, all in order to improve her bargaining position at the day of reckoning after the war.[157] In talks between officials of the Propaganda Ministry and the Party Chancellery held in December 1941, it was argued that German propaganda abroad should ignore the declarations of the bishops in support of the German war effort in order not to strengthen their position at home.[158] A Gestapo bulletin of June 1942 decried the fact that many Party members were still attending divine services and attributed this state of affairs to the growth of religious sentiment caused by the tribulations of war. The Church, the report went on, systematically used National Socialist concepts and expanded her influence by pointing to the large number of priests in the armed forces as proof that being a Catholic not only did not detract from heroism, but actually facilitated it.[159]

In early 1942 a letter was circulated widely in Germany, allegedly written by the recently killed number one ace of the *Luftwaffe*, the Catholic Werner Mölders. In this letter Mölders had reported with pride that the Catholics, on account of their dedication, were now finally being accepted as full-fledged Germans and were enjoying the respect of those who earlier had taunted them as meek and other-worldly. The regime became so upset over this testimony to the patriotism of the Catholics that they declared the letter a forgery and offered a reward of 100,000 marks for information leading to the apprehension of the real author.[160]

Once again, then, the good will of the Catholics was being misinterpreted. The Church was acting out of sincere patriotic sentiment, but the Nazis did not believe her professions of loyalty. In February 1940 Archbishop Gröber directed a lengthy letter to the Reich Defense Council in which he protested against these aspersions and reaffirmed the dedication of the Catholics to the national cause. The Church, he wrote, at the beginning of the war had taken steps to effect a truce, but certain elements on the other side were unwilling to honor it.[161] Two months later, on the occasion of Hitler's birthday, April 20, 1940, in the name of the episcopate Cardinal Bertram congratulated the Reich Chancellor and Führer. The "most cordial felicitations" of the bishops, Bertram wrote, go to the Führer, together with the "fervent prayers which on April 20 the Catholics of Germany send to heaven from the altars for people, army, fatherland, for state and Führer." The German Catholics, Bertram insisted, contrary to the thinking of certain circles, were fully loyal and merely wanted to maintain Germany in the Christian faith. Only thus could the necessary strength be mustered successfully to conclude the war. Bertram ended his letter with the request that Hitler not take offense at this pleading for the rights of the Church, but regard it as "inseparable from the sincere wishes which the supreme pastors of millions of your subjects cherish for people and fatherland, for state and Führer."[162]

During the following years, and until Germany's military collapse in 1945, the bishops periodically protested the regime's nonobservance of the truce that was supposed to prevail between Church and State. Whenever members of the episcopate criticized specific measures of the state, they hastened to add that these criticisms should not give comfort to the enemy or weaken the inner front. The joint pastoral letter of the Cologne and Paderborn church provinces of March 1942, which reaffirmed the natural rights of life, liberty and property, and decried the arbitrary detention and killing of innocents, ended with the following typical admonishment to the faithful:

> That which we bishops had to tell you today with grievously moved soul may not however serve anyone as an excuse to neglect his national duties. On the contrary! With the full authority of our holy office we urge you again today: In this time of war fulfil your patriotic duties most conscientiously! Don't let anyone surpass you in willingness to make sacrifices and readiness to do your share! Be faithful to our people![163]

The Church, declared Bishop Landersdorfer in December 1941, supported the struggle against Bolshevism and hoped that it would be possible "once and for all to render this pest harmless." Even though, as the Bishop observed, it was difficult to avoid the impression that the help of the Church in this war was not at all welcomed by the government, the Catholics, despite all harassment of the Church, had to continue serving their people.[164]

The Nazis were biding their time, impatiently waiting for the day on which they could afford to settle final accounts with the Church. Reacting to a memorandum of Cardinal Bertram, Goebbels wrote in his diary on May 16, 1943: "I could just burst with rage when I think that we cannot possibly call the guilty ones to account now. We shall have to save our vengeance until later."[165] The Church, for her part, honored the truce, and in the event of a German victory would undoubtedly have invoked with pride her services to the war effort. When Germany lost the war, the Church could point to her many protests against specific acts of wrongdoing and to the fact that she had been persecuted by the Nazi state. Unhappily this persecution had nothing to do with the Church's attitude to Hitler's wars, which the Church supported wholeheartedly. In fact, much of the regime's hostility was due to the desire to get rid of an unwanted ally whom the Nazis intended to destroy as a force in Germany as soon as the war was over.

9 The Conflict Over Nazi Eugenic Policies

The eugenic policies of the Nazi regime should not have come as a surprise to anyone. Nazi writings and propaganda had always stressed the importance of achieving a pure and a healthy race; at the annual Party gathering at Nuremberg in 1929 Hitler had held up ancient Sparta's policy of selective infanticide as a model. "If Germany every year would have one million children and eliminate 700-800,000 of the weakest, the end result would probably be an increase in [national] strength."[1] The ideal moment to implement all of these ideas, fortunately, never appeared, but Hitler's intentions, when he assumed power in Germany, were a matter of public record.

1. Compulsory Sterilization

The Fulda Bishops' Conference of May 1933 had before it the draft of a law providing for voluntary sterilization, and the episcopate, as was to be expected, recorded their opposition to this proposed legislation on the grounds that it violated traditional Catholic teaching as reaffirmed most recently in the encyclical *Casti Connubii* (On Christian Marriage) issued in 1930 by Pope Pius XI.[2] But Hitler's mind on the issue was made up. On July 14, 1933, in the same cabinet session that approved the Concordat with the Holy See,

258

the new government approved a "Law for the Prevention of Hereditarily Diseased Offspring." In order not to jeopardize the successful conclusion of the Concordat, publication of this decree was put off until July 25. The statute, which provided for compulsory sterilization of all persons afflicted with certain diseases or disabilities, was to take effect on January 1, 1934.[3]

The slap in the face administered to the Church at the very time when Hitler was promising to respect Catholic faith and morality was discussed by the Fulda Bishops' Conference in August. After hearing several expert opinions on the new law, the bishops decided to submit a memorandum to the Ministry of the Interior that would explain the Catholic position. The government was to be asked to frame the implementing ordinances in such a way that Catholic physicians, judges, nurses and other employees would not be subjected to conflicts of conscience. Catholics, especially parents and directors of asylums, were to be told at a later time how to conduct themselves.[4]

On September 12 Cardinal Bertram submitted the protest of the bishops to Minister of the Interior Frick. He expressed the hope that representatives of the episcopate would be consulted concerning the implementation of the law and added: "Much as the Church regrets the conflict between Church and State legislation, she cannot pass silently over this violation of the Catholic moral law."[5] About one month later Bertram informed the other bishops that the episcopate's protest had been submitted to the government, and that Archbishop Gröber and Bishop Berning had started negotiations. These steps, Bertram went on, seemed necessary before the conflict could be made public. He did not think it wise at this point to inform the Catholics in detail of what had been done so far.[6] The clergy was advised to base their attitude to the sterilization law on the Papal encyclical *Casti Connubii*.[7]

In early November Gröber and Berning were able to report that the government was willing to exempt directors of Catholic institutions from the duty of applying for the sterilization of patients under their care. The Catholic directors would merely have to report the names of all patients afflicted with diseases requiring sterilization. In the case of Catholic physicians employed in state institutions the situation looked less hopeful, the bishops thought, though

the government was willing to consider the objections of the episcopate. The officials of the Ministry of the Interior, with whom the two
bishops had been negotiating, had granted the Church the right
to inform the faithful of the Catholic position on sterilization.[8]

Cardinal Bertram thereupon ordered the drafting of a pastoral
letter on marriage in which the illicit practice of sterilization was to
be explained. But Vice-Chancellor Papen, who had heard of this
contemplated statement, warned Bertram that in view of the concessions already made to the Catholic viewpoint, and because
negotiations were still in progress, such a public pronouncement
would be very unwise. Bertram agreed. He suggested to the episcopate that they read, in place of the planned pastoral letter, a brief
addition to the pulpit instructions on marriage that were handed
down every year on the second Sunday after Epiphany (January 6).[9]
Without explicit reference to the sterilization law, the faithful consequently were told in January 1934 that according to Catholic
doctrine it was forbidden to volunteer for sterilization or apply for
the sterilization of another. "We appreciate every consideration for
this basic principle."[10] Bishop Galen was a bit more outspoken: in
his pastoral letter of January 29, 1934, he expressed regret that the
innocent inheritors of certain genetic traits, "in violation of the
inalienable right to the integrity of their body," were being subjected to violence.[11]

The Nazis were enraged over these criticisms and accused the
Church of incitement to disobedience. Cardinal Faulhaber, writing
to Frick, rejected these attacks as unwarranted. "The bishops repeatedly and in no uncertain terms have declared their willingness
to promote the peaceful co-operation of Church and State. However,
in those questions where a law of the state conflicts with an eternal
command of God, the bishops cannot through silence betray their
holy office." The argument that Article 1 of the Concordat gave the
government the right to restrict the Church's teachings of the gospel
through "laws applicable to all" Faulhaber termed unacceptable.[12]

Regulations for the enforcement of the sterilization law had
been issued on December 5, 1933. They contained two main concessions to the Catholic position: persons suffering from hereditary
diseases could be exempt from sterilization if they committed themselves or were already confined to an institution, and physicians ob-

jecting on grounds of conscience would not be obligated to conduct or assist in these operations.[13] But no special provision had been made for state-employed Catholic doctors and judges who, under the law, had the duty to apply for and to enforce sterilization orders.

After the government had made it clear that it was not prepared to make further compromises, Bertram inquired from the episcopate what the Church should do in this difficult situation. Some Catholic civil servants were in serious conflicts of conscience; priests hearing confession were waiting for guidance on whether they should advise these men to resign from their offices rather than comply with the law. A prominent theologian, whose opinion was forwarded by Bertram, had regarded it as illicit co-operation in a sinful act for Catholic officials to file applications for sterilization. But, he had suggested, priests need not deny the sacraments to officials who were not aware of the sinful character of such applications, or who acted in good faith when they complied with the law and kept their positions rather than risk dismissal and subject their families to economic ruin. Bertram himself agreed with the expert's opinion on the illicitness of filing applications for sterilization but expressed strong doubts on the issue of confessions. Once it became known that confessors did not object to these applications, he argued, the Church would be accused of teaching something in theory but reconciling herself with the same sinful act in practice. The spread of such views "would lead to the loss of all respect for the moral law and for the authority of the Church." It would cause a scandal and thus make it mandatory that the well-being of the official yield to the common good, that is, to "the preservation of morality among the people."[14]

But Bertram's opinion did not convince all members of the episcopate. Two Catholic theologians at the University of Braunsberg (East Prussia), Hans Barion and Carl Eschweiler, had made it known that they did not regard the sterilization law as being in conflict with Catholic doctrine. Even though the two professors had been suspended by the Church,[15] many rank-and-file Catholics, encouraged by their views, complied with the demands of the sterilization law—the course least likely to lead to adverse consequences. Bertram himself had admitted in his letter that only very few Catholic officials were even bothered by the conflict of conscience that had arisen, and, with this mood of uncertainty prevailing, several bish-ops decided to adopt a more conciliatory position. In particular, it proved impossible to obtain unanimity of opinion on how con-fessors should treat Catholic officials who filed applications for sterilization. A pamphlet published at the monastery of Beuron ad-vised priests hearing confession not to pose troubling questions to persons known to be involved with the machinery of the steriliza-tion law.[16] The conference of the bishops of the Cologne church province in March 1935, on the other hand, suggested that as long as no uniform stand could be found, no instructions at all be issued to confessors "so as not to cause confusion."[17] In practice, it would seem, the Church had reconciled herself to the fact that most Catho-lic officials helped enforce the sterilization law.

During the first year of the law's operation 32,268 sterilizations were carried out; in 1935, 73,174 persons were sterilized and 63,547 in 1936.[18] Each of these last figures was higher than the number sterilized in over fifty years in the United States, where from the time of the enactment of the first sterilization law in 1907 until 1958, 60,166 sterilizations took place; furthermore, some of these were voluntary.[19] Individual priests protesting against the sterilization law drew penalties, including the loss of the right to give religious instruction in the public schools; and in July 1935 Frick, in a widely publicized speech, gave notice that the regime would not tolerate any further sabotage of the law. *L'Osservatore Romano* defended the duty of the German Catholics to disregard a law they thought immoral, and the Papal Secretary of State, Pacelli, in several notes to the government argued similarly that the Holy See could not grant the state the power to determine the morality of legislation, and therefore reserved the right of the Church to criticize ordinances in conflict with divine law.[20] But in practice the episcopate was on a path of retreat.

With the help of an elaborate casuistry the bishops had decided that Catholic physicians and social workers might report to the authorities those inflicted with ills calling for sterilization.[21] *Report-ing* was "material co-operation" which was lawful, since the act of reporting in itself was morally indifferent, and since the official in question would otherwise suffer harm, that is, lose his job. To sub-mit an *application* for the sterilization of a person, on the other hand, was "formal co-operation" which, being an essential part of an evil action, was sinful; but this position, as we have seen, the Church did not attempt to enforce.

When the question arose whether Catholic nurses might assist in sterilization operations, the Church at first pronounced a resolute "no."[22] But in 1940 the Sacred Congregation of the Holy Office in Rome ruled that Catholic nurses in state-run hospitals could assist at such operations if a sufficiently important reason was present. "A very weighty reason is given, for example, when in case of refusal the nurses would be dismissed from the hospital and their places would be taken by others who not only would render such co-operation but also, perhaps out of hostility to religion, become the cause of patients, even those in danger of death, having to forgo the sacraments."[23] The German bishops initially ruled that since the main purpose of marriage was procreation, sterilized persons might not partake of the sacrament of matrimony. "The Church has great sympathy for such persons," declared Archbishop Gröber in January 1935, "but she cannot change her basic position, based on the natural law."[24] But soon this decision was reversed,[25] perhaps out of fear of alienating the growing number of Catholics who had actually been sterilized.

2. Euthanasia

On September 1, 1939, Hitler issued an order to kill all persons with incurable diseases. The idea of compulsory euthanasia had been in Hitler's mind for some time, but he had postponed acting because of expected objections from Church circles. The start of the war seemed the propitious moment for inaugurating this still more radical eugenic program, which at the same time promised to yield much needed hospital space and to eliminate "useless eaters."

In the first euthanasia installation opened in December 1939 the victims were shot. As the program expanded, gassing in rooms disguised as showers was introduced. There were several such establishments in Germany, the largest being Grafeneck in Württemberg and Hadamar in Hesse. Questionnaires were sent to all mental hospitals; on the basis of replies to a number of questions on the patients' health a committee of doctors made the selection for euthanasia. The next of kin were notified that the patients had died of some ordinary disease and that their bodies had been cremated. Until August 1941, when the program was stopped, about 70,000 patients had been gassed. Most of these were mentally deficient or incurably insane. A good many cases are also recorded of persons with nervous breakdowns being done away with.[26]

Though the euthanasia program was classified top secret, word gradually leaked out. Patients were said to have died of appendicitis who had had their appendix removed years earlier; mentally retarded or slightly unbalanced patients, who had been visited regularly by their families, suddenly died of cerebral edema. Furthermore, the operation involved large numbers of male and female nurses, drivers, guards and crematorium stokers; people living in the vicinity of these establishments could see being admitted an unending stream of patients that far outran the capacity of the buildings. A cloud of smoke hung above the crematories; children would shout as the trucks with new patients passed, "Here come some more to be gassed."[27] The euthanasia program had become an open secret, officials reported. The population, including Party members, the report added, reacted with revulsion and horror. Soon rumors began to circulate that gravely wounded soldiers also would be killed.

On August 11, 1940, Cardinal Bertram, in the name of the episcopate, lodged a protest with the head of the Reich Chancellery, Lammers. He pointed out that already in 1934 the Church had gone on record as opposing euthanasia, and he drew attention to the indignation aroused by the killing of patients arbitrarily declared unworthy of life. Such destruction of the innocent not only violated the Christian moral law, but offended against the moral sense of the German people and threatened to jeopardize the reputation of Germany in the world.[28] A few months later Cardinal Faulhaber submitted another protest to Minister of Justice Gürtner. Despite all attempts at secrecy, Faulhaber pointed out, everyone now knew that large numbers of patients were being killed in the course of a compulsory euthanasia program. The Catholics, he said, were ardently waiting for a word from their bishops. These actions were in conflict with divine and natural law and, moreover, would seriously undermine the confidence of the people in the word of state authorities. The killing of these innocent people, Faulhaber ended his letter, raised a moral issue which could not be ignored. "I have deemed it my duty of conscience to speak out in this ethico-legal, non-political question, for as a Catholic bishop I may not remain silent when the preservation of the moral foundations of all public order is at stake. . . ."[29]

These and additional protests by other bishops and Protestant churchmen were ignored, and the killings continued. Bishop Galen of Münster thereupon decided to denounce these acts of murder publicly. In a sermon delivered on August 3, 1941, in the St. Lamberti Church at Münster, Galen told in detail how the innocent sick were being killed while their families were misled by false death notices. In eloquent language Galen branded these deeds as criminal; he demanded the prosecution for murder of those per-petrating them. The sanctity of human life, he insisted, could be infringed upon only in cases of self-defense or in a just war. Once humans were treated like machines or animals that were no longer useful, there was no way of being sure where the killing would stop. Even invalids, cripples and wounded soldiers could no longer feel sure of their lives. Who could have confidence in a physician once doctors sanctioned and participated in the slaying of those deemed unproductive? Woe unto the German people, Galen de-clared, when innocents not only could be killed, but their slayers remain unpunished.[30]

The impact of this act of public protest was far-reaching. The accusing words of Bishop Galen, especially his references to the threat of death hanging over invalids and seriously wounded soldiers, spread like wildfire. Copies of the sermon were distributed in all corners of Germany and among the soldiers at the front. The Bish-op's protest struck such a responsive chord and increased his popularity so enormously that the government found it impossible to proceed against him. Several officials proposed that Galen be hanged, and Bormann agreed that the death sentence would be ap-propriate punishment for this act of treason. But Goebbels feared "that the population of Münster could be regarded as lost during the war, if anything were done against the Bishop, and in that fear one safely could include the whole of Westphalia."[31] This calmer counsel prevailed, for the Führer, too, was afraid to make a martyr of Galen and, though furious, was forced to defer his desired vengeance.[32]

Shortly after Galen's sermon of August 3, 1941, the euthanasia program was officially halted by a *Führerbefehl* of which no written record has been found. What has been called "wild euthanasia" continued despite Hitler's order, claiming the lives of many Germans as well as foreign slave laborers, but the large-scale program remained suspended. The stop order came at the time when the inmates of Catholic asylums were to have been removed to the killing centers. From time to time in their sermons and pastoral letters the bishops reaffirmed their opposition to the destruction of "unproductive life," and these pronouncements probably helped stave off a renewal of the program. Early in 1943 new questionnaires were sent to the Catholic asylums requesting information on the health of the inmates. Bertram informed Frick that since the forms were identical with those used in 1940 during the preparation of the euthanasia program, the Church could not allow the directors of Church-controlled hospitals to co-operate in this census.[33] Fortunately, the fears of the episcopate were groundless and the program was not revived.

The forceful reaction of the Catholic Church, especially the sermon of Bishop Galen against the killing of the mentally infirm, was probably the most important reason why Hitler was forced to abandon the euthanasia program. These public protests helped form and solidify public opinion and contributed to the general feeling of outrage which eventually led the Führer to order the suspension of the euthanasia program. Here was an example of the strength, power and influence of public opinion in Hitler's state ruled by brute force, and that at a time when the Führer stood at the zenith of his military successes. Had German public opinion shown a similar response against other crimes of the Nazi regime committed on an even greater scale, such as the extermination of the Jews of Europe, the results might well have been similarly telling.

But the large majority of the very people who had been outraged when their sons and daughters, brothers and sisters had been put to death, failed to react in the same manner when their Jewish neighbors were deported and eventually killed in the very gas chambers designed for and first tried out in the euthanasia program.

As Poliakov has observed, "the extermination of the so-called 'useless mouths' concerned German lives that were flesh of their flesh";[34] the disaster befalling the Jews, the culmination of years of vicious anti-Semitic propaganda, did not give rise to similar humane feelings.

There is little doubt that the vigor of the popular outcry against the euthanasia program encouraged the Catholic Church to take a strong stand. The bishops knew that here they had the public behind them. When Hitler proceeded to "The Final Solution of the Jewish Question," no such sentiments showed themselves, and the episcopate therefore hesitated to risk a clash with the regime. That German public opinion and the Church were a force to be reckoned with in principle and could have played a role in the Jewish disaster as well—that is the lesson to be derived from the fate of Hitler's euthanasia program.

10 The Jewish Question

Rolf Hochhuth's controversial play *Der Stellvertreter* (The Deputy), dealing with the failure of Pope Pius XII publicly to protest the Nazis' destruction of the Jews of Europe, has dramatized a problem as old as Christianity itself. What is more, Hochhuth has personalized a problem which cannot adequately be understood in terms of personalties. The attitude of the Roman Catholic Church toward National Socialist anti-Semitism must be seen in the context of the still partially unresolved 2,000-year-old conflict between Church and Synagogue.

1. The Setting

Despite similarities between many anti-Jewish measures of the medieval Church and those enacted by the Nazi regime, the differences between Hitler's racial anti-Semitism and Christian anti-Judaism were many. Nazi anti-Semitism was rooted in a perverted social Darwinism, a view of the world that differentiated between superior and inferior people according to their racial stock, and demanded the elimination of those considered an impediment to racial purity and national greatness. Christian hostility to the Jews was built on certain theological conceptions developed in the first three centuries of Christianity. Except for a limited period in Spain, when "pure"—that is Christian—blood (*limpieza de sangre*) was demanded as a condition of belonging to the community of the redeemed in Christ, the Christian churches have always accepted Jewish converts and disregarded racial ancestry and national origin. All those baptized could be Christians.

And yet, significant as these distinctions between modern anti-Semitism and Christian anti-Judaism are, it is also true that the Nazis' ferocious assault upon European Jewry took place in a climate of opinion conditioned for such an outrage by centuries of Christian hostility to the Jewish religion and people. Numerous Christian theologians throughout the history of Christianity had painted the Jews as a people who had betrayed God and had called upon themselves a permanent curse by crucifying Jesus the Christ. The historical accuracy of the cry, "His blood be upon us and upon our children," and the orthodoxy of a theological interpretation that saw in these words an acknowledgment of the guilt of all Jews for the death of Jesus have been successfully challenged by recent scholarship.[1] But for many centuries Christian preaching and religious instruction derived their intensely anti-Jewish character from just such conceptions.[2] In medieval times the recital of the Passion of Christ in Good Friday sermons was frequently followed by acts of violence against the Jews, for whom this holy day became a day of dread. Hitler's racial anti-Semitism and its logical outgrowth, Auschwitz, a French Jewish scholar has concluded, appeared on ground which previous centuries had prepared. "Without centuries of Christian catechism, preaching and vituperation, the Hitlerian teachings, propaganda and vituperation would not have been possible."[3]

By the nineteenth century the Jews of western and central Europe had largely been emancipated. Most of the restrictive measures imposed by the Church and secular rulers had been eliminated; superstitious beliefs, like those in Jewish ritual murder, had been condemned by both Pope and philosopher. But the Enlightenment and the growth of secular thinking had not eliminated the antagonism between Christian and Jew; the old hatreds reappeared clothed in a different garb. The new anti-Semitism found political, economic and social arguments to buttress its hostility toward the Jews. Yet the old notions of the Jews as killers of Christ and murderers of innocent Christian children continued to fester in the popular mind and provided nourishment for the more recent brand of anti-Jewish sentiment.[4]

Some elements of German Catholicism during the nineteenth century, as Catholic Nazis later proudly noted, shared in the growth of this new anti-Semitism. Publicists like Karl von Vogelsang (1818-1890) and Joseph Edmund Jörg (1819-1901) argued for breaking the yoke of economic exploitation under which the Christian nations were suffering. "The people," warned Jörg in the *Historisch-Politische Blätter* of 1860, "have their irrepressible instinct and woe unto the Jewish outrages when once it flares up."[5]

Two Catholic bishops were also to be found preaching this gospel. Bishop Martin of Paderborn (1812-1879) exposed Jewish wickedness in the Talmud and concluded that the stories of Jewish ritual murder of Christian children at Eastertime were true.[6] Bishop Keppler of Rottenburg (1852-1926) returned from a visit to the Holy Land amazed at the poverty of the Jews of Jerusalem. "It is hard to believe," he wrote, "that these are tribal brothers of that perverted part of the Jewish people which outside of Palestine constitutes a thorn in the side of Christian peoples, reduces them to servitude with the golden chains of millions and with pens saturated with poison, contaminates the public wells of education and morality by throwing into them sickening and purulent substances."[7]

Goaded by the fact that many prominent Jews participated in the anti-Catholic drive of the 1870s, the press of the Catholic Center party in the summer of 1875 began a vigorous anti-Semitic campaign. The Party expected political benefit from its onslaught against "Jews and Liberals," but, as one well-informed student of the period correctly notes, the sheer vehemence of the attack revealed the existence of deeper roots.[8] The campaign soon ended as abruptly as it had started, but Catholic hostility toward "Jewish liberalism" remained strong for many years and was to experience a full revival in the Third Reich. Even a progressive Catholic like Matthias Erzberger was not entirely free of anti-Semitic sentiment. The charge of the Socialists that the Christian trade unions included Catholic priests, an alien element in the working-class movement, Erzberger met by describing the excessive Jewish influence in the Social Democratic party, using the pejorative phrase *stark verjudet*.[9]

Beginnings of racial anti-Semitism, too, were to be found. Christianity, observed one writer later to attain prominence as a Center party politician, forbids the hatred of other races. "But Christianity does not prohibit defense against the harmful influences caused by the peculiarities of a certain race."[10] German Catholicism, unlike its Austrian counterpart, never brought forth a prominent anti-Semite such as Karl Lueger in Vienna. But the undercurrents were there just the same.

During the Weimar republic organized German Catholicism came into repeated conflicts with the growing National Socialist movement, but anti-Semitism was not one of the primary bones of contention. On the contrary, many Catholic publicists—like the Franciscan father, Erhard Schlund—agreed with the Nazis on the importance of fighting the Jews' "hegemony in finance, the destructive influence of the Jews in religion, morality, literature and art, and political and social life." The nationalist movement, the same author observed, had a healthy core, "the endeavor to maintain the purity of the German blood and German race." Around this good core there lay merely a bad shell of extremism.[11]

This plea for a moderate anti-Semitism was a fairly typical and perfectly respectable view inside the Church. The Jesuit Gustav Gundlach, for example, writing in a reference work edited by Bishop Buchberger of Regensburg, argued that a political anti-Semitism, fighting the Jews' "exaggerated and harmful influence," was permitted as long as it utilized morally admissible means.[12] Bishop Buchberger himself concluded in 1931 that it was "justified self-defense" to ward off the rule of "an overly powerful Jewish capital." It was unjust and un-Christian merely to blame all Jews for these failings or to convert this economic struggle into one of race or religion.[13] Vicar General Mayer of Mainz found that Hitler in *Mein Kampf* had "appropriately described" the bad influence of the Jews in press, theater and literature. Still, it was un-Christian to hate other races and to subject the Jews and foreigners to disabilities through discriminatory legislation that would merely bring about reprisals from other countries.[14]

The charge of excessive Jewish influence in German public life was factually false and morally indefensible. In the press of the Left, for example, which was attacked as totally *verjudet,* less than 20 of 400 editors were Jews.[15] But even if the figures had yielded a different picture, such a disproportionate respresentation should not have given rise to concern unless the critics had already been convinced beforehand that Jews were dangerous and harmful. A finding that 90 per cent of all editors were blondes, for example, would not have provoked an anti-blonde movement. But reasoned argument was, of course, notably absent from the anti-Semitic agitation, especially in that emanating from the more extreme camp. There, also, one could find a number of Catholic clergymen. In the eyes of Curate Roth, an early supporter of the Hitler movement, the Jews were a morally inferior race who would have to be eliminated from public life. "If in the course of proceeding against the Jews as a race some good and harmless Jews, with whom immorality because of inheritance is latent, will have to suffer together with the guilty ones, this is not a violation of Christian love of one's neighbor as long as the Church recognizes also the moral justification of war, for example, where many more 'innocents' than 'guilty' have to suffer."[16] Roth, who later became an official in the Nazi Ministry of Ecclesiastical Affairs, was allowed to wield his poisonous pen without ever being formally disciplined by the Church.

Similar views were propounded by Dr. Haeuser, whose book appeared in 1923 with the *Imprimatur* of the diocese of Regensburg. Haeuser called the Jews Germany's cross, a people disowned by God and under their own curse. They carried much of the blame for Germany having lost the war and they had taken a dominant role in the revolution of 1918. The time had come to put them in their place, though Haeuser stressed that the Jews should be allowed to live as guests in Germany.[17] Father Senn called even German Catholicism *verjudet* and termed the Hitler movement, despite certain exaggerations, "the last big opportunity to throw off the Jewish yoke."[18]

Catholic anti-Semitism manifested itself in still another form. The people of Deggendorf in Bavaria for many years had been commemorating the miraculous emergence of "a lovely little child" from a consecrated wafer which allegedly had been stolen and "tortured" by the Jews of the town on September 30, 1337. On the same day, the chroniclers reported, the pious citizens of Deggendorf, acting "out of legitimate zeal pleasing to God," killed off all the Jews. "God grant," the inscription under a picture depicting the massacre and exhibited in one of the town's churches said, "that our fatherland be forever free from this hellish scum." In a play composed by a Benedictine monk and performed every year during the week-long celebrations, the Jews were called names such as "brood of Judas," "hordes of the devil," "poison mixers," etc. The historical accuracy of this tale of blasphemy and miraculous recovery had never been certified, but in view of the 10,000 guests that every year attended the commemoration exercises and the wholesome religious atmosphere created by them, the Church authorities saw little reason to be sticklers for historical truth. The effects of this perpetuation of the worst medieval anti-Jewish prejudices upon contemporary attitudes toward the Jews are not difficult to guess.[19]

Concentrating her fire upon liberals and freethinkers, many of whom were of Jewish descent, the Church during the Weimar republic did practically nothing to stem the inroads anti-Semitism was making on German life. The number of individual Catholics, both clerics and laymen, who fought the hostility to their Jewish fellow citizens was also very small. The *Verein für die Abwehr des Antisemitismus,* an organization of Christians and Jews struggling against the rising anti-Semitic agitation, had two Catholic priests on its board of sponsors—the curate Franz Rödel being the only active priest–participant in the work of the group. Only a few Catholic voices were raised against the anti-Semitic tirades of the Nazis and their allies. Franz Steffen, a Catholic journalist, rejected the slanderous attack upon the Jews as false, and called anti-Semitism un-Christian and in conflict with Catholic doctrine. After disposing of the Jews, Steffen prophesied, the Nazis would next turn against the Catholics. "No believing Catholic may join the ranks of these people, no Catholic may support them in any way or help them into power through his vote, for he would thereby forge chains for our religious freedom."[20] A Catholic editor objected to the publication of one of the more notoriously inflammatory anti-Semitic books by a Catholic publisher in Paderborn and asked the Catholics to remember that anti-Semitism and anti-Catholicism usually grew on the same soil.[21] Father Muckermann, in January 1932, protested the immoral and criminal designs of the Nazis, who were marching through the streets calling for death to the Jews. Muckermann mentioned the recently committed 109 defacements of Jewish cemeteries and synagogues and added that to expose these outrages is "our Christian, human and German duty."[22]

The German bishops during these years spoke up against the Nazis' glorification of race and blood, but they had practically nothing to say specifically about the widespread anti-Semitic propaganda and acts of violence. Cardinal Faulhaber in a sermon delivered in 1923 declared that every human life was precious, including that of a Jew.[23] In 1932 Cardinal Schulte, in reply to a letter from a Jewish organization seeking help, expressed his sympathies in the face of the numerous acts of vandalism, especially the desecration of Jewish graves, that had occurred in Cologne.[24] But a Church that justified moderate anti-Semitism and merely objected to extreme and immoral acts was ill-prepared to provide an effective antidote to the Nazis' gospel of hate. The roots of the Church's failure to protest or act against the later National Socialist policy of extermination lie right here, in the highly ambivalent attitude of the Church toward the Jews which we can trace from the early days of Christianity up to Hitler's accession to power and beyond.

2. Rehearsal for Destruction

Hitler, upon engaging in his first measures against the Jews, was well aware of the Church's long anti-Jewish record. In his talk with Bishop Berning and Monsignor Steinmann on April 26, 1933, he reminded his visitors that the Church for 1,500 years had regarded the Jews as parasites, had banished them into ghettos, and had forbidden Christians to work for them. "He saw in the Jews nothing but pernicious enemies of the State and Church, and therefore he wanted to drive the Jews out more and more, especially from academic life and the public professions."[25] He, Hitler said, merely intended to do more effectively what the Church had attempted to accomplish for so long. This service to a common cause, and not the elevation of race above religion, motivated his hostility toward the Jews.[26]

The reaction of the two Church dignitaries to Hitler's attempt to identify his brand of anti-Semitism with the age-old anti-Judaism of the Church is not known. What we do know, however, is that from the time Hitler came to power all the German bishops began declaring their appreciation of the important natural values of race and racial purity, and they limited their dissent to insisting that this goal be achieved without resort to immoral means. The article on "Race" in the authoritative handbook on topical religious problems, edited by Archbishop Gröber, expressed this position in the following words:

> Every people bears itself the responsibility for its successful existence, and the intake of entirely foreign blood will always represent a risk for a nationality that has proven its historical worth. Hence, no people may be denied the right to maintain undisturbed their previous racial stock and to enact safeguards for this purpose. The Christian religion merely demands that the means used do not offend against the moral law and natural justice.[27]

In his celebrated Advent sermons of 1933 Cardinal Faulhaber observed that the Church did not have "any objection to the endeavor to keep the national characteristics of a people as far as possible pure and unadulterated, and to foster their national spirit by emphasis upon the common ties of blood which unite them." The defense and love of one's own race should not lead, however, to the hatred of other nations, and the loyalty to one's race did not supersede the obligations to the Church.[28] For these qualifications Faulhaber was severely criticized by the Nazis and his palace was fired on—needlessly so, as it turned out, for few German Catholics paid attention to Faulhaber's reservations. When Hitler started to pursue the purity of the German blood in his own ruthless way, the overwhelming majority of the German Catholics, as we shall see later, dutifully obeyed his orders and promptly forgot the warnings against using extreme and immoral means in the defense of one's race given out by their bishops.

The Church's reluctance to antagonize the Nazis unnecessarily can be seen in the way she defended the Old Testament. Rosenberg's attacks upon the "Jewish Bible," an alleged affront to every true German, hit the Church in a cardinal point of doctrine, where no yielding was possible. All members of the episcopate, therefore, resolutely and repeatedly reaffirmed their fidelity to the Old Testament. In several instances, Catholic teachers of religion who refused to teach the Old Testament were deprived of the *missio canonica* (ecclesiastical teaching license). Cardinal Faulhaber's Advent sermons in 1933, in particular, are remembered for their eloquent vindication of the sacred character of the scriptures of the Old Testament. But Faulhaber went out of his way to make clear that he was not concerned with defending his Jewish contemporaries. We must distinguish, he told the faithful, between the people of Israel before the death of Christ, who were vehicles of divine revelation, and the Jews after the death of Christ, who have become restless wanderers over the earth. But even the Jewish people of ancient times could not justly claim credit for the wisdom of the Old Testament. So unique were these laws that one was bound to say: "People of Israel, this did not grow in your own garden of your own planting. This condemnation of usurious land-grabbing, this war against the oppression of the farmer by debt, this prohibition of usury, is not the product of your spirit."[29] It, therefore, is little short of falsification of history when Faulhaber's sermons in 1933 are hailed by one recent Catholic writer as a "condemnation of the persecution of the Jews."[30]

Whatever ambiguity may still have attached to his position after these pronouncements, Faulhaber soon acted to dispel. In the summer of 1934 a Social Democratic paper in Prague published a sermon against race hatred which Faulhaber had allegedly preached. The Basel *National-Zeitung* in Switzerland reprinted excerpts from this sermon, and the World Jewish Congress at a meeting in Geneva praised the Cardinal's courageous stand. But the sermon turned out to be a fabrication, and Faulhaber had his secretary write a widely publicized letter to the Jewish organization protesting against "the use of his name by a conference that demands the commercial boycott of Germany, that is, economic war." The Cardinal, the letter continued, "in his Advent sermons of the previous year has defended the Old Testament of the Children of Israel but not taken a position with regard to the Jewish question of today."[31]

Lesser Church dignitaries quite naturally took the cue from their Archbishop. An article written by a canon of the cathedral chapter of Regensburg, and published in *Klerusblatt*, the organ of the Bavarian Priests' Association, advised Catholic teachers to point out to pupils that the sacred books of the Old Testament were not only beyond the Jewish mentality, but in direct conflict with it. "The greatest miracle of the Bible is that the true religion could hold its own and maintain itself against the voice of the Semitic blood."[32]

The embarrassing fact that Jesus had been a Jew was handled in a similar manner. In a pastoral letter of 1939 Archbishop Gröber conceded that Jesus Christ could not be made into an Aryan, but the Son of God had been fundamentally different from the Jews of his time—so much so that they had hated him and demanded his crucifixion, and "their murderous hatred has continued in later centuries."[33] Jesus had been a Jew, admitted Bishop Hilfrich of Limburg in his pastoral letter for Lent 1939, but "the Christian religion has not grown out of the nature of this people, that is, is not influenced by their racial characteristics. Rather it has had to make its way against this people." The Jewish people, the Bishop added, were guilty of the murder of God and had been under a curse since the day of the crucifixion. Christianity, the Bishop of Limburg concluded, was therefore not to be regarded as a product of the Jews; it was not a foreign doctrine or un-German. "Once accepted by our ancestors, it finds itself in the most intimate union with the Germanic spirit."[34]

The attempt to swim with the anti-Semitic tide was even more pronounced in the previously cited *Handbuch* of Archbishop Gröber. Marxism here was defined as "the materialistic socialism founded primarily by the Jew Karl Marx,"[35] and Bolshevism was characterized as "an Asiatic state despotism, in point of fact in the service of a group of terrorists led by Jews."[36] The Führer, the same article found, had correctly described the struggle against this evil force as a defense of European civilization against Asiatic barbarism. "No people can avoid this clash between its national tradition and Marxism, which is opposed to national ties and led mostly by Jewish agitators and revolutionaries."[37] The article on "Art" pointed out that most of the unhealthy and un-German manifestations in art since the nineteenth century had been the work of Jews or those under Jewish influence. The politicizing of art was also in good part due to "the uprooted and atheistically perverted Jew."[38]

When convenient and useful, the Church used the concept "Jew" after the manner of the Nazis, that is, as a term of racial classification. Early in their rule, the Nazis had begun to make extensive propagandistic use of a nineteenth century rabble-rousing anti-clerical book, *Der Pfaffenspiegel*. Soon the sorry spectacle developed of the Church trying to undermine the effectiveness of this piece by arguing that the Protestant author, Otto von Corvin, had been a half-Jew, while the Nazis retorted that he was fully "Aryan."

In pronouncements read from the pulpit, pastoral letters and articles in church newspapers the Church supported this charge by invoking the authority of the notorious anti-Semitic *Handbuch der Judenfrage* by Theodor Fritsch—a work which, according to Waldemar Gurian, should never be quoted by respectable writers and scholars[39]—where Corvin had been listed as the son of a Jewess. Even Provost Lichtenberg, a man who later paid with his life for trying to help the Jews, found it necessary in 1935 to address a personal letter to Hitler in which he protested the use of the book and pointed out that Corvin, "according to the latest research, was not of Aryan descent."[40] A few days later the Catholic press all over Germany reported newly revealed evidence according to which Corvin "had been not only a Jew, but also a convict."[41]

When the Nazis challenged the non-Aryan ancestry of Corvin, one of their favorite church-baiting authors, the Catholic polemicists fell back upon the fact that Corvin's book had originally been published by a Jewish firm, that he had been a friend of Jews and that Corvin had exhibited traits such as lack of compassion, cold sarcasm, a presumptuous self-confidence, "in short, all that which today again we regard as especially opposed to the Aryan mentality." In view of these characteristics, one Catholic writer concluded, Corvin could well have been of Jewish descent, even if, as now shown, he in fact was not.[42] Corvin, another author wrote, had all his life been under the pronounced influence of "liberal–freethinking–Freemason Judaism." No wonder his contemporaries regarded this un-German personality as a Jew.[43]

Some bishops, despite all evidence to the contrary, were unwilling to forego the disparaging argument of Corvin's Jewish ancestry. Bishop Buchberger in a pastoral letter in February 1937, called Corvin a "half-Jew and Freemason," and as late as January

1942 Archbishop Gröber spoke of the author of the *Pfaffenspiegel* as a "half-Jewish writer."[44]

If such language could be endorsed and used by members of the episcopate, it is no wonder that lower-ranking figures in the Church felt free to express their anti-Semitic sentiments still more openly. Thus the theologian Karl Adam defended the preservation of the German people's pure blood as a justified act of self-defense, for blood was the physiological basis of all thinking and feeling, and "the myth of the German, his culture and his history are decisively shaped by blood." The repulsion of the Jewish mentality in press, literature, science and art now undertaken by the state was a necessary measure, though "the Christian conscience must insist that these legal ordinances be implemented in a spirit of justice and love."[45] Thus also an article on the revolution of 1918 in the paper of the Bavarian priests exposed the role of the Jews in this stab in the back of the undefeated German army. "While the front made superhuman sacrifices and fought with admirable bravery against a world of enemies, the Jew Emil Barth equipped his *Untermenschen* [subhumans] with hand grenades and automatic pistols in order to attack the national defense from the rear. . . ." These acts of treason, the article suggested, actually began in 1914, when the Jew Karl Liebknecht refused to vote for the war appropriations.[46]

And so it went. The Jews had had a "demoralizing influence on religiosity and national character."[47] The Jews, as a spiritual community, had brought the German people "more damage than benefit."[48] The Jews had displayed a mortal hatred for Jesus, while the Aryan Pontius Pilate would gladly have let him go free. The Jews had been "the first and most cruel persecutors of the young Church."[49] The Jews had killed Jesus and in their boundless hatred of Christianity were still in the forefront of those seeking to destroy the Church.[50] These are some relevant examples of Catholic writing during the years 1933-1939, all published in journals edited by priests or in books bearing the *Imprimatur*. From this ruthless intellectual onslaught upon the Jews it was but a small step to the position of the veteran National Socialist priest, Father Senn, who in 1934 hailed Hitler as "the tool of God, called upon to overcome Judaism. . . ."[51]

If we take into account this climate of opinion within the

Church, we will find it easier to understand why the Church retreated in the face of the Nazis' anti-Semitic legislation, even where these ordinances touched upon vital domains of ecclesiastical jurisdiction such as the sacrament of matrimony. According to canon law, the Church has exclusive jurisdiction over the marriage of Catholics. In practice, however, the Church in many countries had recognized the right of the state to impose certain conditions on marriage, so long as these did not conflict with natural law. For example, the state could insist on fulfillment of certain medical prerequisites, require the consent of parents to the marriage of minors, etc; in Germany the Church had agreed that normally a civil marriage ceremony had to precede the ceremony conducted by the priest, though Article 26 of the Concordat of 1933 had somewhat broadened the kinds of instances in which a priest could disregard this legal requirement.[52] How should the Church respond, however, if the state imposed requirements such as the prohibition of marriage between baptized persons belonging to different races?

As early as 1934 the Church had made clear to the Nazi government that the enactment of a law forbidding racially mixed marriages would create a very difficult situation. In the eyes of the Church, the German bishops pointed out in a memorandum, every Catholic, whether born to a pure German or to a racially mixed marriage, whether baptized as a child or as an adult, was equally entitled to the sacraments. Hence, if two baptized persons of racially mixed stock insisted on being married by a priest, the latter would have to comply, even if the state were to have prohibited such a union.[53]

This, however, is precisely what the state soon did, for one of the practical results of the so-called Nuremberg laws of September 15, 1935, was to make it illegal for two Catholics to marry when one was considered racially "non-Aryan" under the standards set up by the law. (Since the persecution of the Jews had led to many new conversions to the Catholic religion, the number of such marriages was undoubtedly rising at the time.) The central office of information of the German episcopate in Berlin reported in September 1935 that earlier Catholic couples of racially mixed descent had been traveling to England to get married there, but now even those marriages had become illegal, and the Church had a very serious problem on its hands.[54] What did she do? In some instances priests circumvented the law by using a provision of the Concordat of 1933 which, in cases of "great moral emergency," permitted a church marriage without a preceding civil ceremony;[55] but by and large the Church conformed to the law, bowing to what earlier she had termed an inadmissible infringement of her spiritual jurisdiction.

For some elements in the Church, to be sure, bowing was unnecessary, for they actually welcomed the Nuremberg laws. While a distinguished German Catholic in exile, Waldemar Gurian, was denouncing the Nuremberg ordinances as violations of natural law and of the moral teachings of the Church, and declaring that they were "only a stage on the way toward the complete physical destruction of the Jews,"[56] an article in the *Klerusblatt* of January 1936 was justifying the new anti-Jewish statutes as indispensable safeguards for the qualitative makeup of the German people.[57] So, too, Bishop Hudal, the head of the German Church in Rome, said that the Nuremberg laws were a necessary measure of self-defense against the influx of foreign elements. The Church in her own legislation, the Bishop contended, had held a radical position on the Jewish question "until the walls of the Ghetto had been torn down in the nineteenth century by the liberal state first and not by the Church." Consequently, from the point of view of the Church, there could be no objection to laws containing discriminatory provisions for Jews. "The principles of the modern state [based on the rule of equal treatment before the law] have been created by the French Revolution and are not the best from the standpoint of Christianity and nationality."[58]

The Church surrendered in a similar fashion when the so-called Aryan clause was applied to clerical teachers of religion. This ordinance, enacted in 1938, meant that priests teaching religion in the public schools had to submit proof of their Aryan descent before they could continue in their posts. However, the policy in question affected very few clerics and had no further ramifications. Such was not the case when the Church agreed to supply data from her own records on the religious origin of those under her care. A decree of April 7, 1933, which resulted in the discharge of numerous Catholic civil servants, had also provided for the dismissal of all Jews (except front-line veterans of the first World War, those in government service since 1914, and close relatives of fallen soldiers) from the civil service. Henceforth, anyone applying for government employment—and soon for various other positions as well—had to submit proof that he was not a Jew. Since prior to 1874-1876 births had been registered only by the churches, the latter were asked to help in determining who was or was not fully Aryan, for under Nazi law this depended on the racial (i.e., religious) status of parents and grandparents. The Church co-operated as a matter of course, complaining only that priests already overburdened with work were not receiving compensation for this special service to the state.[59] The very question of whether the Church should lend its help to the Nazi state in sorting out people of Jewish descent was never debated. On the contrary. "We have always unselfishly worked for the people without regard to gratitude or ingratitude," a priest wrote in the *Klerusblatt* in September of 1934. "We shall also do our best to help in this service to the people."[60] And the co-operation of the Church in this matter continued right through the war years, when the price of being Jewish was no longer dismissal from a government job and loss of livelihood, but deportation and outright physical destruction.[61]

The bishops sometimes sought to protect the non-Aryan Catholics, for whom the Church felt a special responsibility. The Ministry of Ecclesiastical Affairs in 1936 asked for statistics about the number of Jews converted to the Catholic Church in the years 1900-1935. Cardinal Bertram suggested that this request be complied with.[62] But when the Ministry later sought permission to consult the diocesan files on conversions and mixed marriages, the Church withheld her consent "on grounds of pastoral secrecy."[63] For the same reason Cardinal Bertram in 1938 refused to open the diocesan archives to researchers working for a new state institute for the study of the Jewish question.[64]

The Church's concern for Catholic non-Aryans expressed itself in other ways as well. In September 1933 Archbishop Bertram had inquired from the Papal Secretary of State whether the Holy See could not put in a good word with the German government for the Jewish converts to the Catholic religion who were being made destitute on account of their "non-Aryan descent."[65] Soon the *St.*

Raphaelsverein, a Catholic organization founded in 1871 for the protection of German émigrés and presided over by Bishop Berning, began to take care of these Catholics. In a notice published in all the diocesan gazettes in November 1933 the *St. Raphaelsverein* acknowledged that these non-Aryans were not fully German and gave them the advice "for the time being to feel themselves as guests [*Gastvolk*]."[66] But despite this concession to Nazi ways of thinking, the organization tried its best to retrain or otherwise facilitate the emigration of Catholic non-Aryans. This help was extended to practicing Catholics provided they were not in trouble with the Nazi state on political grounds.[67] Similarly, an organization of "Christian-German Citizens of Non-Aryan or not Pure Aryan Descent," established in 1933 with the encouragement of the Church and later renamed *Paulus Bund*, insisted in its bylaws that membership was open only to Christians "who take their stand alongside the new Germany."[68] In the years 1936-1937 the *St. Raphaelsverein* helped 516 Catholic non-Aryans; in 1938 it facilitated the emigration of 1,850 such persons.[69] Occasionally Jews married to Catholics were also aided. But the recent claim of a German Catholic paper[70] that the *St. Raphaelsverein* helped 1,950 Jews to emigrate and supported 25,000 Jews has no foundation in fact unless one still wants to use the concept, Jew, as a term of racial classification.

During these years prior to the adoption of the "Final Solution of the Jewish Question," the Church extended neither aid nor sympathy to other than Catholic non-Aryans. A few instances are on record where individual churchmen spoke up in defense of the Jews. In March 1933 a priest in the Rhineland in a sermon characterized the vilification of the Jews as unjust and was fined 500 marks for abuse of the pulpit.[71] Another priest, in Bavaria in 1936, declared that the stories being told in Germany about the Jews were a pack of lies.[72] There probably were other such occurrences, and here and there acts of Good Samaritanism may have taken place that have remained unrecorded. But the Church as such, speaking through the voice of her bishops, remained silent.

In 1934 a German Catholic priest, who for reasons of safety chose to remain anonymous, took his Church to task for this quiescence in the face of injustice. The Church, he argued, had a special duty to oppose the growing hatred of the Jews that was spreading even among believing Christians, and her failure to preach brotherly love toward the Jews jeopardized not only the Christian religion, but civilization itself. The Nazis' treatment of the Jews, the priest argued, violated justice, truth and love—yet the Church did not feel called upon to respond. She was, he said, too preoccupied with her own confessional interests. "What a good opportunity would the Jewish question have afforded for a truly 'Catholic Action'!"[73]

The hands-off policy of the Church stood out especially in the fateful days of November 1938. The Nazis, in the wake of the assassination of a German embassy official in Paris by a seventeen-year-old Jewish boy, unloosed a pogrom that has entered history under the name *"Kristallnacht"* (the night of glass). During the night of November 9-10 the display windows of Jewish shops all over Germany were shattered, about 20,000 male Jews were arrested and herded into concentration camps, 191 synagogues were set on fire and 76 others completely destroyed.[74] Thirty-six Jews were killed during this well-organized action; a much larger number succumbed to the sadistic treatment meted out to them in Buchenwald and other concentration camps where they were imprisoned. Cardinal Faulhaber is said to have provided a truck for the Chief Rabbi of Munich so that he could save some of the religious objects from his synagogue before it was completely demolished.[75] Provost Lichtenberg in Berlin, on the morning after the pogrom, prayed for the persecuted non-Aryan Christians and Jews, and added, "What took place yesterday, we know; what will be tomorrow, we do not know; but what happens today that we have witnessed; outside [this church] the synagogue is burning, and that also is a house of God."[76] Lichtenberg's protest remained a solitary act of witness. His bishops remained silent in the face of the burning temples and the first round-up of the Jews.

3. The Final Solution

In a speech delivered on January 30, 1939, the Führer served public notice of his intentions: "If international Jewry should succeed, in Europe or elsewhere, in precipitating nations into a world war, the result will not be the Bolshevization of Europe and a victory for Judaism, but the extermination of the Jewish race."[77] A few months later Hitler attacked Poland and World War II began. On July 31, 1941, Heydrich was charged "with making all necessary preparation . . . for bringing about a complete solution of the Jewish question in the German sphere of influence in Europe."[78] The machinery of destruction went into action.

It began with a decree, dated September 1, 1941, which provided that all Jews six years of age or over could appear in public only when marked with a Jewish star; they were not to leave their place of domicile without special permission. The marking of the Jews had first been applied in Poland, and now the system of identification was extended to the entire Reich. The decree covered so-called Mosaic Jews as well as baptized Jews; only those who had converted before September 15, 1935, the date of the Nuremberg laws, and non-Aryans married to an Aryan partner were exempt from this order.

The wearing of the Jewish star had a paralyzing effect upon those who were forced to do so. Even more than before, the Jews now felt themselves a separate group marked for a fate about which some were beginning to have forebodings. Many were afraid to leave their houses, and this fear created a special problem for the affected Catholics. In a number of towns these Catholic non-Aryans applied to the police for permission not to have to wear the Jewish star when going to and attending church services, and they asked their bishops to support their applications.[79] The bishops were sympathetic to this request, as they were upset over the prospect of "Jews" attending services, which could only aggravate the hostility of the Nazis toward the Church. Also they were not sure how their parishioners would react to these Jewish Catholics.

On September 17 Cardinal Bertram addressed a letter to the episcopate in which he took up this new problem. His counsel was to avoid "rash measures that could hurt the feelings of the Jewish Catholics, as the introduction of special Jewish benches, separation when administering the sacraments, introduction of special services in specific churches or private houses." The segregation of the Catholic non-Aryans would violate Christian principles and, therefore, should be avoided as long as possible. The priests, Bertram suggested, might however advise the Jewish Catholics to attend the early mass whenever possible. An admonishment to the faithful to exercise brotherly love toward the non-Aryans similarly should be postponed until disturbances resulted. "Only when substantial difficulties result from attendance at church by the non-Aryan Catholics," the Archbishop of Breslau continued, "(like staying away of officials, Party members and others, demonstrative leaving of divine services), should the Catholic non-Aryans be consulted about the holding of special services." In case a reminder to the faithful to treat the Jewish Catholics with love should become necessary, Bertram suggested a statement that included St. Paul's admonishments to the Romans and Galatians not to forget that among those believing in Christ there is neither Jew nor Greek, for all are one in Jesus Christ (Romans 10:12, Galatians 3:28).[80]

In Berlin, meanwhile, Bishops Wienken and Berning were trying to obtain permission from the Gestapo for the Jewish Catholics not to wear the Star of David while in Church, but their efforts failed. On October 27 Berning wrote Bertram that the Gestapo had refused any concessions in this matter. On the other hand, Berning reported, almost nowhere had difficulties resulted from the attendance of the non-Aryan Catholics at divine services. A certain number had merely refrained from coming to church.[81] The Catholic Church thus had been spared the adoption of racial segregation.

Mass deportations of German Jews toward the east began on October 15, 1941. Bishop Berning, in the letter just referred to, informed Bertram that while discussing the question of the Jewish star with the Gestapo he had also pointed out the harshness accompanying "the evacuation of the non-Aryans" and had requested some ameliorations. He had been told that Christian non-Aryans would be evacuated only in exceptional cases, such as when earlier conflicts with the Gestapo had occurred. For the time being non-Aryans in mixed marriages would not be affected by these measures. The Church authorities, Berning continued, could obtain from the local Gestapo offices the dates scheduled for the deportations from their town, they could find out whether Christian non-Aryans were among those to be deported and in such cases exercise pastoral care before deportation. Those deported, he had been told, would go into the eastern territories, where they could participate in the divine services of the Poles.[82]

The promises made by the Gestapo to Bishop Berning were not honored. On October 27 the Bishop of Limburg informed Bishop Wienken, the episcopate's troubleshooter in Berlin, that the transport of Jews from Frankfurt earlier in the month had included Catholic non-Aryans to whom no preferred treatment had been granted. Their fate was especially sad since they were being regarded by their *Rassengenossen* (racial partners) as apostates. Hilfrich inquired whether for this reason it might not be possible to achieve their exemption. If that were impossible they should at least be put into special settlements, where they could be given religious care more easily.[83] Wienken replied a few days later that negotiations about the deportation of Catholic non-Aryans had been started at the highest level.[84] The bishops of the Cologne and Paderborn church provinces, meeting in November 1941, also suggested that the government be petitioned in matters of the deportations. They furthermore recommended that non-Aryan or half-Aryan priests and nuns volunteer to accompany the deportees in order to hold services for them and provide religious instruction for the children.[85]

While the bishops were preoccupied with the Catholic non-Aryans' pastoral care before deportation and during their resettlement, rumors were spreading about the fate of the Jews in the east. These rumors had been making the rounds ever since the attack upon Russia on June 22, 1941, which had brought in its wake the employment of special detachments (*Einsatzgruppen*) assigned to the job of murdering Jews. Soldiers returning from the Eastern Front were telling horrible stories, how in occupied Russia Jewish civilians—men, women and children—were being lined up and machine-gunned by the thousands. Their military superiors had issued orders forbidding such talebearing, as well as the taking of snapshots at mass executions, but the gruesome reports persisted. By the end of 1941 the first news had also trickled back about the fate of the deported German Jews who had been shot by mobile killing detachments near Riga and Minsk.[86] In the spring of 1942 the leaflets of the "White Rose," composed by a group of students and a professor of philosophy at the University of Munich, told of the murder of 300,000 Jews in Poland and asked why the German people remained so apathetic in the face of these revolting crimes.[87]

In December 1941 the first death camp began operations near Lodz. Sobibor, Treblinka and Auschwitz went into operation in the course of the year 1942. By the end of 1942 more than 100,000 German Jews had been sent to their death in the east, and the vague rumors about their fate had been replaced now by hard and persistent reports that included details of the mass gassings. In August 1942 Colonel Kurt Gerstein, who had joined the S.S. to investigate the stories of extermination for himself, tried to tell the Papal Nuncio in Berlin about a gassing he had witnessed near Lublin. When Monsignor Orsenigo refused to receive him, he told his story to Dr. Winter, the legal advisor of Bishop Preysing of Berlin, and to numbers of other persons. He also requested that the report be forwarded to the Holy See.[88] During the same period other reports about the extermination of the Jews reached the bishops through Catholic officers serving in Poland and Russia.[89] For a long time Dr. Joseph Müller, an officer in Canaris's Military Intelligence Service and also a confidant of Cardinal Faulhaber, had kept the episcopate well-informed about the systematic atrocities committed in Poland.[90] Another source of information was Dr. Hans Globke, a Catholic and a high official in the Ministry of the Interior entrusted with handling racial matters. It is, then, clear that by the end of the year 1942 at the latest, the German episcopate was possessed of quite accurate knowledge of the horrible events unfolding in the east.

Until 1942 half-Jews and quarter-Jews, the so-called *Mischlinge,* as well as non-Aryans married to Aryans, had been exempt both from wearing the yellow star and from deportation. The number of such persons in the Reich-Protektorat area was estimated at above 150,000.[91] Though the Nuremberg laws had forbidden marriages between Jews and Aryans, they had not annulled existing mixed marriages. With the progress of the Final Solution, however, this loophole was now to be closed. A conference of experts in March 1942 decided upon the compulsory dissolution of racially mixed marriages, to be followed by the deportation of the Jewish partner. If the Aryan partner failed to apply for a divorce within a certain period of time, the public prosecutor was to file a petition for divorce, which the courts would have to grant.

The bishops heard of the contemplated measure through Dr. Globke in the Ministry of the Interior, and they reacted promptly. On November 11, 1942, Archbishop Bertram, in the name of the episcopate, addressed a letter of protest againt the planned compulsory divorce legislation to the Ministers of Justice, Interior and Ecclesiastical Affairs. The intervention of the bishops, he insisted, was not due "to lack of love for the German nationality, lack of a feeling of national dignity, and also not to underestimation of the harmful Jewish influences upon German culture and national interests." The bishops merely felt called upon to emphasize that the duty of humane treatment also existed toward the members of other races. Among the persons affected by the contemplated measure, Bertram went on, were many thousands of Catholics whose marriages, according to Catholic doctrine, were indissoluble. Respect for the religious rights of the Catholic Christians was an indispensable condition for the peaceful co-operation of Church and State, which had never been as necessary as in the present situation. The bishops therefore hoped, the letter ended, that the government would withdraw the planned divorce ordinance.[92]

Despite the fact that the ordinance was still tied up in bureaucratic difficulties, the Gestapo in February 1943, in the course of deporting the last German Jews, seized several thousand Christian non-Aryans in mixed marriages. In Berlin alone about 6,000 such men were arrested on February 27. But then something unexpected and unparalleled happened: their Aryan wives followed them to the place of temporary dentention and there they stood for several hours screaming and howling for their men. With the secrecy of the whole machinery of destruction threatened, the Gestapo yielded and the non-Aryan husbands were released.[93] Here was an example of what an outraged conscience could achieve, even against Hitler's terror apparatus.

The German episcopate, after the downfall of the Nazi regime, has taken credit for preventing the compulsory divorce of mixed marriages.[94] There is strong reason to assume that the lion's share of the credit belongs to the courageous women of Berlin who, in the last days of February 1943, dared to defy the seemingly all-powerful Gestapo and caused the Nazis to fear similar outbursts in the future if they moved to break up these marriages by divorce or deportation.

A few days after this unique event Bertram composed another letter. This time he also sent copies to the chief of the Reich Chancellery, Lammers, and to the *Reichssicherheitshauptamt* (RSHA),

Himmler's headquarters. About 8,000 Christian non-Aryans, Bertram complained, had been seized and deported. The episcopate could not silently accept these measures. He then repeated what in November 1942 he had said about the illegitimacy of compulsory divorce.[95] On April 16 Bishop Preysing informed his fellow bishops that the contemplated divorce decree was soon to be made public. He urged, for the time being, that the matter be treated as strictly confidential, but in the event that the order should be issued, a statement drawn up by Bertram was to be read from the pulpits. This statement, in a manner similar to the earlier letters of protest, reaffirmed the indissolubility of Christian marriage and the validity of this principle even in the case of racially mixed marriages. It asked for prayer for the unfortunates affected by the decree.[96]

About two months later Preysing sent word to his colleagues through a messenger that the threatened decree had been postponed. The bishops were asked to write letters to all the ministries; they should inquire in strong language as to the whereabouts of the deportees, demanding pastoral care for the Christians and threatening a public protest. The point of departure should be concern for the Christian Jews, "but beyond this one should speak clearly about the outrages inflicted upon the Jews generally."[97] We do not know how many bishops acted upon Preysing's request.

In November 1943 Bertram sent out another appeal in the name of the entire episcopate to the Minister of the Interior and the RSHA. The episcopate, he wrote, had received information according to which the non-Aryans evacuated from Germany were living in camps under conditions that would have to be called inhuman. A large number of the sufferers had already succumbed. "In view of the reputation of the German name at home and abroad," and in view of the commands of the Christian moral law concerning the duties owed fellow men even of foreign races, the bishops considered it necessary to plead for an amelioration of conditions in these camps. In particular, Bertram continued, the bishops wished to demand the benefit of pastoral care for the imprisoned Catholics. The episcopate would gladly designate priests for divine services and the administration of the sacraments in the camps.[98]

Bertram's letter neither employed strong language nor did it say anything very definite about the outrages against the Jews, as

Bishop Preysing had suggested. This conciliatory tone, his failure to call a spade a spade, was not owing to the lack of information about the extermination machinery, now operating at peak capacity. Additional proof, if such were indeed needed, can be found in Bertram's next and last letter to the government in this matter, dispatched in January 1944. Reports had been received, the Cardinal wrote, that the ordinances enacted for the Jews were now to be applied also to the *Mischlinge*. These Christians had already been declared unworthy of military service, could not attend institutions of higher learning, etc. Now one heard that they were to be conscripted into special formations for labor service. "All these measures," Bertram continued, "aim clearly at segregation at the end of which threatens extermination." In the name of the episcopate he felt obligated to point out that any change in the meaning of the term "Jew" now—that is, after the Nuremberg laws had been accepted as the final word in this matter for almost ten years—would seriously undermine confidence in the law. The legislation of 1935 had not regarded the *Mischlinge* as a danger to people and Reich. Since 1935 only the Jews had been involved in "certain special regulations." The *Mischlinge* were Germans and Christians, and had always been rejected by the Jews. "The German Catholics, indeed numerous Christians in Germany," Bertram warned, "would be deeply hurt if these fellow Christians now would have to meet a fate similar to that of the Jews." Ordinances segregating the *Mischlinge* would seriously threaten the unity of the inner front, a danger to be avoided at all cost. The bishops would not be able to reconcile it with their conscience to remain silent in the face of such measures.[99]

The bishops did make a few public pronouncements that criticized unjust treatment of foreign races, but these were couched in very general language, did not mention the Jews by name and might be considered equally directed at the Nazis' harsh policy toward the Slavic *Untermenschen* (subhumans). A pastoral letter of the new Archbishop of Cologne, Dr. Joseph Frings, read in his archdiocese on December 20, 1942, insisted that all men had the right to life, liberty, property and marriage, and that these rights might not be denied even to those "who are not of our blood or do not speak our language."[100] The joint pastoral letter of the German episcopate of August 1943 reminded the faithful that the killing of innocents was wrong even if done by the authorities and allegedly for the common good, as in the case of "men of foreign races and descent." The bishops called for love of "those innocent humans who are not of our people and blood" and of "the resettled." The pastoral letter stressed that the holiness of the bond of matrimony included so-called racially mixed marriages.[101] In his Christmas sermon of 1943 and in March 1944 Archbishop Frings again emphasized that it was wrong to kill innocents just because they belonged to another race.[102]

Ever since the defeat of the Third Reich these pronouncements have been cited as proof that the bishops did publicly protest the extermination of the Jews. Possibly some Catholics did indeed think of the Jews when their spiritual leaders castigated the murder of those not of German blood. But neither the word "Jew" nor "non-Aryan" ever crossed the lips of the bishops. The provincial administrator of the Regensburg area in Bavaria reported in October 1943 that the joint pastoral letter castigating the killing of innocents had not had any lasting effect: "The population pays scant attention to such involved pronouncements burdened with stipulations."[103]

Unlike the case of the extermination of Germans in the euthanasia program, where the episcopate did not mince words and succeeded in putting a stop to the killings, the bishops here played it safe. The effect of their public protests on the Final Solution consequently was nil. These very general statements neither changed the policies of the government nor inspired any change in the behavior of German Catholics. The trains shipping Jews to their doom continued to roll; the factories where Jewish slave laborers were worked to death kept on consuming their victims; the guards maintained their stations and saw to it that none escaped. Close to half the population of the Greater German Reich (43.1 per cent in 1939) was Catholic, and even among the S.S., despite all pressures to leave the Church, almost a fourth (22.7 per cent on December 31, 1938)[104] belonged to the Catholic faith. Yet their bishops might just as well not have said a word on the killing of innocents. The machinery of extermination continued to function smoothly, with everyone conscientiously doing his assigned job. The episcopate had repeatedly issued orders to exclude from the sacraments Catholics who engaged in dueling or who agreed to have their bodies cremated. The word that would have forbidden the faithful, on pain of excommunication, to go on participating in the massacre of the Jews was never spoken. And so Catholics went on participating conscientiously, along with other Germans.

There was, however, at least one Catholic churchman in Germany for whom the Christian duty to love one's neighbor amounted to more than a pious formula—the sixty-six-year-old Provost Lichtenberg of Berlin, who, right through the stepped-up anti-Semitic agitation, continued to say a daily prayer for the Jews. He was finally arrested on October 23, 1941, a week after the first of the mass deportation of Jews had begun. During questioning by Himmler's henchmen, the Provost asserted that the deportation of the Jews was irreconcilable with the Christian moral law, and asked to be allowed to accompany the deportees as their spiritual adviser. Sentenced to two years imprisonment for abuse of the pulpit, Lichtenberg was seized by the Gestapo upon his release in October 1943 and shipped off to the concentration camp at Dachau. He died during the transport on November 5, 1943.[105]

The passivity of the German episcopate in the face of the Jewish tragedy stands in marked contrast to the conduct of the French, Belgian and Dutch bishops. In Holland, where the Church as early as 1934 had prohibited the participation of Catholics in the Dutch Nazi movement, the bishops in 1942 immediately and publicly protested the first deportations of Dutch Jews,[106] and in May 1943 they forbade the collaboration of Catholic policemen in the hunting down of Jews, even at the cost of losing their jobs.[107] In Belgium members of the episcopate actively supported the rescue efforts of their clergy, who hid many hundreds of Jewish children.[108] And in France the highest dignitaries of the Church repeatedly used their pulpits to denounce the deportations and to condemn the barbarous treatment of the Jews.[109]

Throughout western Europe untold numbers of priests and members of the monastic clergy organized the rescue of Jews, hid them in monasteries, parish houses and private homes. Many lay Catholics in France, Holland and Belgium acted in a similar fashion, thus saving thousands of Jewish lives. The concern of the Gentile populations of these countries for their Jewish fellow citizens was undoubtedly one of the key factors behind the bold public protests of the French, Dutch and Belgian bishops—just as the absence of such solicitude in Germany goes a long way toward explaining the apathy of their German counterparts.

To be sure, the episcopate of the occupied countries was acting against a foreign oppressor, whereas the German bishops would have had to oppose their own government, which they regarded as the legitimate authority. But the German episcopate had demonstrated their willingness to risk such a clash and exhibited their power to mold public opinion and achieve results in the euthanasia program. If they failed to speak up for the Jews facing the same gas chambers, one of the main reasons was the widespread indifference of the German population. In France, Belgium and Holland declarations of solidarity and help for the Jews were almost universally regarded as signs of patriotism. In Germany, on the other hand, the bishops in so acting would have incurred new charges of being un-German and in league with Germany's mortal enemies. Their own followers would probably have failed to understand and approve such sympathy for the Jews, whom the Church for many long years had branded as a harmful factor in German life.

As late as March 1941 Archbishop Gröber, in a pastoral letter abounding in anti-Jewish utterances, had blamed the Jews for the death of Christ and added that "the self-imposed curse of the Jews, 'His blood be upon us and upon our children,' has come true terribly until the present time, until today."[110] Now, when the bishops perhaps might have wanted to protest the inhuman treatment of the Jews, they found themselves prisoners of their own anti-Semitic teachings. As in Poland, where the clergy similarly conformed to the indifference of their surroundings, an important reason why the German episcopate did not act against the "Final Solution of the Jewish Question" was their fear that in such an endeavor they could not count on the support of their faithful. That the Church had done her share in inculcating the very sentiments which now stood in the way of a more Christian conduct adds a tragic element to this sad story.

Once again, then, the failure of the episcopate mirrored the failures of the Catholic *milieu*. In sharp contrast to the countries of western Europe, in Germany only a handful of Jews were hidden by the clergy or otherwise helped by them in their hour of distress.[111] A few cases are recorded where individual Catholics hid and saved Jews,[112] but only in Berlin did a significant number of Jews find refuge with friends and neighbors; according to Provost Grüber, most of these courageous men and women were workers, often not connected with any church.[113] In Freiburg, Dr. Gertrud Luckner, an official of the *Caritas* (the large Catholic philanthropic organization) helped Jews to get across the Swiss border, sent packages to deportees and distributed money from a special fund established by the episcopate for non-Aryans. She was arrested in November 1943 while trying to bring a sum of money to the few remaining Jews in Berlin, and spent the rest of the war in a concentration camp.[114]

There were, then, exceptions but the over-all picture was one of indifference and apathy. "Among the Christians," a group of German Protestant and Catholic theologians concluded in 1950, "a few courageously helped the persecuted, but the large majority failed disgracefully in the face of this unheard-of provocation of the merciful God."[115] Well over 100,000 German Jews were sent to an unknown fate in the east about which few Germans initially had any precise knowledge, but about which few, on the other hand, could have had any great illusions. Yet, these deportations went off without causing a ripple. The reports of the *Regierungspräsidenten* (provincial administrators), generally known for their candidness, noted that the deportation of the Jews had caused no adverse public reactions. The report from Ansbach in Bavaria was one of the shortest: "Except for some suicides and attempted suicides no trouble whatsoever was encountered."[116] The Church, custodian of Christian love and charity, stood by silently.

4. The Role of the Papacy

In April 1933 a communication reached Pope Pius XI from Germany expressing grave concern about the Nazis' anti-Semitic aims and requesting the Supreme Pontiff to issue an encyclical on the Jewish question. The letter was written by the philosopher, Dr. Edith Stein, a Jewish convert to Catholicism and later known as Sister Teresia Benedicta a Cruce of the Order of the Carmelites.[117] Edith Stein's request was not granted. Nine years later, in August

1942, the Gestapo removed her from a Dutch monastery, where she had sought refuge, and sent her to Auschwitz to be gassed. The debate whether or not the Papacy could have prevented or should at least have vigorously protested the massacre of the Jews of Europe, of which Edith Stein was one of the victims, has been going on ever since and has acquired new vigor as a result of Hochhuth's play *Der Stellvertreter.*

In 1928 Pius XI had accompanied the dissolution of the missionary society, "The Friends of Israel," with a condemnation of anti-Semitism.[118] But once the Nazis were established in power, the Pontiff, like the German episcopate, seems to have limited his concern to Catholic non-Aryans. At the request of Cardinal Bertram the Papal Secretary of State in September 1933 put in "a word on behalf of those German Catholics" who were of Jewish descent and for this reason suffering "social and economic difficulties."[119] In the following years the Holy See repeatedly took issue with the Nazis' glorification of race, but the Jewish question specifically was never discussed. In 1934 the influential Jesuit magazine *Civiltà Cattolica,* published in Rome and traditionally close to Vatican thinking, noted with regret that the anti-Semitism of the Nazis "did not stem from the religious convictions nor the Christian conscience . . . but from their desire to upset the order of religion and society." The *Civiltà Cattolica* added that "we could understand them, or even praise them, if their policy were restricted within acceptable bounds of defense against the Jewish organizations and institutions. . . ."[120] In 1936 the same journal published another article on the subject, emphasizing that opposition to Nazi racialism should not be interpreted as a rejection of anti-Semitism, and arguing—as the magazine had done since 1890—that the Christian world (though without un-Christian hatred) must defend itself against the Jewish threat by suspending the civic rights of Jews and returning them to the ghettos.[121]

Pius XI's encyclical *Mit brennender Sorge* of March 1937 rejected the myths of race and blood as contrary to revealed Christian truth, but it neither mentioned nor criticized anti-Semitism *per se.* Nor was anti-Semitism mentioned in the statement of the Roman Congregation of Seminaries and Universities, issued on April 13, 1938, and attacking as erroneous eight theses taken from the arsenal of Nazi doctrine.[122] On September 7, 1938, during a reception for Catholic pilgrims from Belgium, Pius XI is said to have condemned the participation of Catholics in anti-Semitic movements and to have added that Christians, the spiritual descendants of the Patriarch Abraham, were "spiritually Semites." But this statement was omitted by all the Italian papers, including *L'Osservatore Romano,* from their account of the Pope's address.[123]

The Vatican's criticisms of the new Italian racial legislation introduced in 1938 centered upon those parts which conflicted with the canon law's provisions concerning marriage. When Italian theaters and other public facilities in December 1938 began to exclude Jews, *L'Osservatore Romano* complained that these measures no longer merely aimed at the segregation of the Jews, but smacked of un-Christian persecution.[124] The *Civiltà Cattolica* similarly objected to being claimed as an ally by the Fascist press extolling racial anti-Semitism. "As always," writes a well-informed recent student of the period, "the views of *Civiltà Cattolica* were in accord with those of the Pontiff, though it was clear that the Jesuit fathers had nothing against a moderate anti-Jewish policy in Italy."[125]

The elevation of Cardinal Pacelli to the Papacy in the spring of 1939 brought to the chair of St. Peter a man noted for his pro-German sentiments and diplomatic skill. Hochhuth's Pope possessed of "aristocratic coldness" and eyes having an "icy glow" is perhaps a bit stylized, but all biographers agree that Pius XII, in contrast to his predecessor, was unemotional and dispassionate, as well as a master in the language of diplomatic ambiguity. "Pius XII," recalls Cardinal Tardini, "was by nature meek and almost timid. He was not born with the temperament of a fighter. In this he was different from his great predecessor."[126] Whether Pius XI would have reacted to the massacre of the Jews during World War II differently from Pacelli is a question on which it is tempting to speculate, but to which no definite answer is possible.

That the Holy See had no intrinsic objection to a policy of subjecting the Jews to discriminatory legislation became again clear when in June 1941 Marshal Pétain's Vichy government introduced a series of "Jewish statutes." The cardinals and archbishops of France made known their strong disapproval of these measures. But Léon Bérard, the Vichy Ambassador at the Holy See, was able to report to

Pétain, after lengthy consultations with high Church officials, that the Vatican did not consider such laws in conflict with Catholic teaching. The Holy See merely counseled that no provisions on marriage be added to the statutes and "that the precepts of justice and charity be considered in the application of the law."[127] In August 1941 the consequences of this discriminatory policy could not yet be clearly seen, but the episode illustrates anew the Vatican's willingness to go along with anti-Semitic measures, administered with "justice and charity." When mass deportations from France got under way in 1942 the Papal Nuncio, without invoking the authority of the Holy See, requested Laval to mitigate the severity of the measures taken against the Jews of Vichy France,[128] but such pleas by that time could no longer halt the machinery of destruction.

Meanwhile, there was growing criticism of the Pope's failure to protest publicly against Nazi atrocities and especially against the murder of the Jews in the Polish death factories. Harold H. Tittmann, the assistant to Roosevelt's personal representative at the Holy See, Myron C. Taylor, in July 1942 pointed out to the Vatican that its silence was "endangering its moral prestige and is undermining faith both in the Church and in the Holy Father himself."[129] After authorization by Secretary of State Hull, Tittmann and several other diplomatic representatives at the Vatican in September 1942 formally requested that the Pope condemn the "incredible horrors" perpetrated by the Nazis. A few days later Taylor forwarded to the Papal Secretary of State, Luigi Maglione, a memorandum of the Jewish Agency for Palestine that reported mass executions of Jews in Poland and occupied Russia, and told of deportations to death camps from Germany, Belgium, Holland, France, Slovakia, etc. Taylor inquired whether the Vatican could confirm these reports, and, if so, "whether the Holy Father has any suggestions as to any practical manner in which the forces of civilized public opinion could be utilized in order to prevent a continuation of these barbarities."[130]

On October 10 the Holy See replied to Taylor's note that up to the present time it had not been possible to verify the accuracy of the severe measures reportedly taken against the Jews. The statement added, "It is well known that the Holy See is taking advantage of every opportunity offered in order to mitigate the suffering of non-

Aryans."[131] In conversation with high-placed officials of the Curia, Tittmann was told that the Pope's silence was due to the following reasons: the desire of the Holy See to maintain its absolute neutrality in the world-wide conflict, the importance of Papal pronouncements standing the test of time (which quality was difficult to achieve in the heat of the passions of war and the errors resulting therefrom) and the fear that any clearly pointed protest would worsen the situation of Catholics in the Nazi-occupied countries. The Pope hesitated to condemn German atrocities, Tittmann also learned, because he did not want to incur later the reproach of the German people that the Catholic Church had contributed to their defeat.[132] After the Western Allies in December 1942 had vigorously denounced the cold-blooded extermination of the Jews, Tittmann again inquired from the Papal Secretary of State whether the Holy See could not issue a similar pronouncement. Maglione answered that the Holy See, in line with its policy of neutrality, could not protest particular atrocities and had to limit itself to condemning immoral actions in general. He assured Tittmann that everything possible was being done behind the scenes to help the Jews.[133]

Two days later, in the course of a lengthy Christmas message broadcast over the Vatican radio, Pope Pius made another of his many calls for a more humane conduct of hostilities. All men of good will, the Pope demanded, should bring the life of the nations again into conformity with the divine law. Humanity owed the resolution to build a better world to "the hundreds of thousands who, without personal guilt, sometimes for no other reason but on account of their nationality or descent, were doomed to death or exposed to a progressive deterioration of their condition."[134] Addressing the Sacred College of Cardinals in June 1943 the Pontiff spoke of his twofold duty to be impartial and to point up moral errors. He had given special attention, he recalled, to the plight of those who were still being harassed because of their nationality or descent, and who, without personal guilt, were subjected to measures that spelled destruction. Much had been done for the unfortunates that could not be described yet. Every public statement had had to be carefully weighed "in the interest of those suffering so that their situation would not inadvertently be made still more difficult and unbearable." Unfortunately, Pius XII added, the

Church's pleas for compassion and the observance of the elementary norms of humanity had encountered doors "which no key was able to open."[135]

The precise nature of these interventions prior to June 1943 has not been revealed to this day. We do know that Nuncio Orsenigo in Berlin made inquiries several times about mass shootings and the fate of deported Jews. Ernst Woermann, the director of the political department of the German Foreign Ministry, on October 15, 1942, recorded that the Nuncio had made his representation with "some embarrassment and without emphasis."[136] State Secretary Weizsäcker told Monsignor Orsenigo on another such occasion that the Vatican had so far conducted itself "very cleverly" in these matters and that he would hope for a continuation of this policy. The Nuncio took the hint and "pointed out that he had not really touched this topic and that he had no desire to touch it."[137] Himmler, when received by Count Ciano on his visit to Rome in October 1942, praised the "discretion" of the Vatican.[138]

There were other diplomatic representations. That of the Nuncio in Vichy France has already been mentioned. In Slovakia, where 52,000 Jews had been deported in the spring of 1942, the Vatican in the summer of that year pointed out to the Quisling government, at whose head stood a Catholic priest, Dr. Josef Tiso, that the deported Jews had been sent away not for labor service, but for annihilation. The deportations ground to a halt, for Eichmann's emissary had instructions to avoid "political complications." Thereafter, the Slovakian Jews lived in relative security until September 1944.[139] However, the case of Catholic Slovakia was a special one, and in the over-all balance one has to agree with the Pope's own finding that the Holy See was unsuccessful in opening the doors that barred relief for the hapless victims. But did the Holy See try all the keys in its possession?

The Pope's policy of neutrality encountered its most crucial test when the Nazis began rounding up the 8,000 Jews of Rome in the fall of 1943. Prior to the start of the arrests, the Jewish community was told by the Nazis that unless it raised 50 kilograms of gold (the equivalent of $56,000) within thirty-six hours, 300 hostages would be taken. When it turned out that the Jews themselves could only raise 35 kilograms, the Chief Rabbi, Israel Zolli, asked for and received a loan from the Vatican treasury to cover the balance. The Pope approved of this transaction.[140] But the big question in everyone's mind was how the Supreme Pontiff would react when the deportation of the Jews from the Eternal City began.

The test came on the night of October 15-16. While the roundup was still going on a letter was delivered to General Stahel, the German military commander of Rome. Bearing the signature of Bishop Hudal, the head of the German Church in Rome, it said:

> I have just been informed by a high Vatican office in the immediate circle of the Holy Father that the arrests of Jews of Italian nationality have begun this morning. In the interest of the good relations which have existed until now between the Vatican and the high German military command . . . I would be very grateful if you would give an order to stop these arrests in Rome and its vicinity right away; I fear that otherwise the Pope will have to make an open stand which will serve the anti-German propaganda as a weapon against us.[141]

A day later, Ernst von Weizsäcker, the new German Ambassador at the Holy See, reported to Berlin that the Vatican was upset, especially since the deportations had taken place, as it were, right under the Pope's window:

> The people hostile to us in Rome are taking advantage of this affair to force the Vatican from its reserve. People say that the bishops of French cities, where similar incidents occurred, have taken a firm stand. The Pope, as supreme head of the Church and Bishop of Rome, cannot be more reticent than they. They are also drawing a parallel between the stronger character of Pius XI and that of the present Pope.[142]

Contrary to Hudal's and Weizsäcker's apprehensions, however, the man in the Vatican palace remained silent. On October 18, over 1,000 Roman Jews—more than two-thirds of them women and children—were shipped off to the killing center of Auschwitz. Fourteen men and one woman returned alive. About 7,000 Roman Jews —that is, seven out of eight—were able to elude their hunters by going into hiding. More than 4,000, with the knowledge and approval of the Pope, found refuge in the numerous monasteries and houses of religious orders in Rome,[143] and a few dozen were sheltered in the Vatican itself. The rest were hidden by their Italian neighbors, among whom the anti-Jewish policy of the fascists had never been popular. But for the Germans, overwhelmingly relieved at having averted a public protest by the Pope, the fact that a few thousand Jews had escaped the net was of minor significance. On October 28 Ambassador Weizsäcker was able to report:

> Although under pressure from all sides, the Pope has not let himself be drawn into any demonstrative censure of the deportation of Jews from Rome. Although he must expect that his attitude will be criticized by our enemies and exploited by the Protestant and Anglo-Saxon countries in their propaganda against Catholicism, he has done everything he could in this delicate matter not to strain relations with the German government and German circles in Rome. As there is probably no reason to expect other German actions against the Jews of Rome, we can consider that a question so disturbing to German–Vatican relations has been liquidated.
>
> In any case, an indication for this state of affairs can be seen in the Vatican's attitude. *L'Osservatore Romano* has in fact prominently published in its issue of October 25-26 an official communiqué on the Pope's charitable activities. The communiqué, in the Vatican's distinctive style, that is, very vague and complicated, declares that all men, without distinction of nationality, race or religion, benefit from the Pope's paternal solicitude. The continual and varied activities of Pius XII have probably increased lately because of the greater sufferings of so many unfortunates.
>
> There is less reason to object to the terms of this message . . . as only a very small number of people will recognize in it a special allusion to the Jewish question.[144]

When an Italian law of December 1, 1943, provided for the internment of all Jews in concentration camps and for the confiscation of their property, *L'Osservatore Romano* criticized these measures as too harsh. But Weizsäcker reassured Berlin that these "commentaries are not official. They have not been broadcast by the Vatican radio."[145] During the following months searches for Jews took place periodically. The Pope, continuing acts of charity, maintained his silence.

The criticism levelled against Pius XII for his failure to protest the massacre of the Jews of Europe, including those in his own diocese of Rome, is composed of two main parts. It has been argued first, most recently by Hochhuth, that the Pope could have saved numerous lives, if not halted the machinery of destruction, had he chosen to take a public stand and had he confronted the Germans with the threats of an interdict or the excommunication of Hitler, Goebbels and other leading Nazis belonging to the Catholic faith. As examples of the effectiveness of public protests it is possible to cite the resolute reaction of the German episcopate to the euthanasia program. In a number of other instances, notably in Slovakia, Hungary and Rumania, the forceful intervention of the Papal Nuncios, who threatened the Quisling governments with a public condemnation by the Pope, was able, albeit temporarily, to stop the deportations.[146] At the very least, it has been suggested, a public denunciation of the mass murders by Pius XII, broadcast widely over the Vatican radio and read from the pulpits by his bishops, would have revealed to Jews and Christians alike what deportation to the east entailed. The Pope would have been believed, whereas the broadcasts of the Allies were often shrugged off as war propaganda. Many of the deportees, who accepted the assurances of the Germans that they were merely being resettled, might thus have been warned and given an impetus to escape. Many more Christians might have helped and sheltered Jews, and many more lives might have been saved.

There exists, of course, no way of definitively proving or disproving these arguments. Whether a Papal decree of excommunication against Hitler would have dissuaded the Führer from carrying out his plan to destroy the Jews is very doubtful. A revocation of the Concordat by the Holy See would have bothered Hitler still less. However, a flaming protest against the massacre of the Jews, coupled with the imposition of the interdict upon all of Germany or the excommunication of all Catholics in any way involved with the apparatus of the Final Solution, would have been a far more formidable and effective weapon. It certainly would have warned many who were deceived by the Germans' promises of good treatment. Yet this was precisely the kind of action which the Pope could not take without risking the allegiance of the German Catholics. Given the indifference of the German population toward the fate of the Jews, and the highly ambivalent attitude of the German hierarchy toward Nazi anti-Semitism, a forceful stand by the Supreme Pontiff on the Jewish question might well have led to a large-scale desertion from the Church. When Dr. Edoardo Senatro, the correspondent of *L'Osservatore Romano* in Berlin, asked Pius XII whether he would not protest the extermination of the Jews, the Pope is reported to have answered, "Dear friend, do not forget that millions of Catholics serve in the German armies. Shall I bring them into conflicts of conscience?"[147] The Pope knew that the German Catholics were not prepared to suffer martyrdom for their Church; still less were they willing to incur the wrath of their Nazi rulers for the sake of the Jews whom their own bishops for years had castigated as a harmful influence in German life. In the final analysis, then, as Poliakov has also concluded, "the Vatican's silence only reflected the deep feeling of the Catholic masses of Europe"[148] —those of Germany and eastern Europe in particular. The failure of the Pope was a measure of the Church's failure to convert her gospel of brotherly love and human dignity into living reality.

Some writers have suggested that a public protest by the Pope would not only have been unsuccessful in helping the Jews, but might have caused additional damage—to the Jews, to the *Mischlinge,* the Church, the territorial integrity of the Vatican and the Catholics in all of Nazi-occupied Europe. It is tempting to dismiss this argument by asking what worse fate could have befallen European Jewry than the disaster that did overtake it. Since the condition of the Jews could hardly have become worse, and might have changed for the better, as a result of a Papal denunciation, one could ask why the Church did not risk the well-being and safety of the Catholics and of the Vatican. Why did she not at least attempt to help the Jews?

The Catholic bishops of Holland tried this gamble. In July 1942, together with the Protestant Church, they sent a telegram of protest against the deportation of the Dutch Jews to the German *Reichskommissar* and threatened to make their protest public unless the deportations were halted. The Germans responded by offering to exempt from deportation non-Aryans converted to Christianity before 1941 if the churches would remain silent. The Dutch Reformed Church agreed to the bargain, but the Catholic Archbishop of Utrecht refused, and issued a pastoral letter in which he denounced the wrong done to the Jews. The Germans retaliated by seizing and deporting all the Catholic non-Aryans they could find, among them the noted philosopher Edith Stein.[149] Once the inability of the Pope to move the masses of the faithful into a decisive struggle against the Nazis is accepted as a fact, there is thus some basis for the contention that a public protest, along with any good that would have come of it, might have made some things worse, if not for the Jews, at least for the *Mischlinge* and the Catholics themselves.

The silence of the Pope had other, perhaps still weightier, reasons. As Mr. Tittmann was told by highly placed officials of the Curia, the Holy See did not want to jeopardize its neutrality by condemning German atrocities. The Vatican wanted to preserve its good name with the Germans, as well as with the Western Allies, and the Pope was unwilling to risk later charges that he had been partial and had contributed to a German defeat. Moreover, as already discussed in an earlier context, the Vatican did not wish to undermine and weaken Germany's struggle against Russia. In the late summer of 1943 the Papal Secretary of State, Luigi Maglione, termed the fate of Europe dependent upon a victorious resistance of Germany at the Eastern Front,[150] and Father Leiber, one of the secretaries of Pius XII, recalls that the late Pope always looked upon Russian Bolshevism as more dangerous than German National Socialism.[151] Hitler, therefore, had to be treated with some forebearance.

Finally, one is inclined to conclude that the Pope and his advisors—influenced by the long tradition of moderate anti-Semitism so widely accepted in Vatican circles—did not view the plight of the Jews with a real sense of urgency and moral outrage. For this assertion no documentation is possible, but it is a conclusion difficult to avoid. Pius XII broke his policy of strict neutrality during World War II to express concern over the German violation of the neutrality of Holland, Belgium and Luxembourg in May 1940. When some German Catholics criticized him for this action, the Pope wrote the German bishops that neutrality was not synonymous "with indifference and apathy where moral and humane considerations demanded a candid word."[152] All things told, did not the murder of several million Jews demand a similarly "candid word"?

The discussion whether a Papal denunciation would have helped or harmed the Jews leaves untouched the one question that perhaps is the most compelling. It concerns the moral integrity of the Church, the performance of the Church as a guardian of the moral law. This second point at issue involves the Pope, the Bishop of Rome and Head of the Church, as much as all the other bishops called upon to provide moral leadership for their flock. In his first encyclical to the world, issued in October 1939, Pius XII described his duties as the Deputy of Christ in these words:

> As vicar of Him who in a decisive hour pronounced before the highest earthly authority of that day the great words: "For this I was born, and for this I came into the world: that I should give testimony to the truth. Every one that is of the truth heareth my voice" (St. John xviii, 37), we feel we owe no greater debt to our office and to our time than to testify to the truth with Apostolic firmness: "To give testimony to the truth." This duty necessarily entails the exposition and confutation of errors and human faults; for these must be made known before it is possible to tend and to heal them. "You shall know the truth and the truth shall make you free" (St. John viii, 32). In the fulfillment of this our duty we shall not let ourselves be influenced by earthly considerations nor be held back by mistrust or opposition, by rebuffs or lack of appreciation of our words, nor yet by fear of misconceptions and misinterpretations.[153]

Similarly the German bishops repeatedly affirmed their duty boldly to preach the word of God and fearlessly to condemn injustice. "The bishop," stressed Cardinal Faulhaber in 1936, "no longer would be the servant of God if he were to speak to please men or remain silent out of fear of men."[154] "I am aware," declared Bishop Galen in a sermon delivered in July 1941, "that as bishop, as harbinger and defender of the legal and moral order desired by God, which grants everyone basic rights and liberties not to be invaded by human demands, I am called upon . . . courageously to represent the authority of the law and to brand as an injustice crying to heaven the condemnation of defenseless innocents."[155] But these noble sentiments remained an empty formula in the face of the Jewish tragedy.

There were those within the Church cognizant of this failure. Writing under the impact of German atrocities in Poland and the defeat of France in June 1940, Cardinal Eugène Tisserant, a high official of the Vatican library, complained to Cardinal Suhard, Archbishop of Paris, that "our superiors do not want to understand the real nature of this conflict." He had pleaded with Pius XII, Tisserant said, to issue an encyclical on the duty of the individual to follow the dictates of his conscience rather than blindly execute all orders, no matter how criminal.

> I fear that history will reproach the Holy See with having practiced a policy of selfish convenience and not much else. This is extremely sad, especially for those [of us] who have lived under Pius XI. Everyone [here] is confident that, after Rome has been declared an open city, members of the Curia will not have to suffer any harm; that is a disgrace.[156]

Criticism of the Church's failure to offer unequivocal moral guidance could be heard also in Germany. The Jesuit Alfred Delp, a member of the German resistance, addressed a conference of priests at Fulda in 1943 and decried the fact that the Church had neglected to stand up for human dignity, the precondition of any Christian existence. "Has the Church," he asked, "forgotten to say 'Thou shalt not,' has the Church lost sight of the commandments, or is she silent because she is convinced of the hopelessness of her clear and firm preaching? Has the 'imprudence' of John the Baptist died out or has the Church forgotten man and his fundamental rights?"[157] The decisive question, Delp asserted on another occasion, is whether the Christians will be able and willing to stand up, not only for the Church and the Christian, but for man himself. The preoccupation with the question of the success or failure of bearing moral witness was in itself already a sign of moral corruption.[158] The silence of the Church on what was being done to the Poles and Jews and on the horrors committed in the concentration camps, Delp told a gathering of Bavarian churchmen in October 1943, threatened the acceptance of the Church by the new Germany that would arise after the downfall of the Nazi regime.[159] But Father Delp was an exceptional figure, whose vision transcended the institutional concerns of the Church. His counsel was not heeded.

Catholic theologians have long debated the dividing line between "Christian prudence" and "un-Christian cowardice." This line is often hard to locate, and no amount of casuistry about silence in the face of crime that is permissible in order to prevent worse will alleviate the arduous task of searching for it. Situations exist where moral guilt is incurred by omission. Silence has its limits, and that also holds true, as another German Jesuit had reminded his Church as early as 1935, for the silence "to prevent worse." "For ultimately," wrote Father Pribilla, "the worst that could really happen is that truth and justice would no longer find spokesmen and martyrs on earth."[160] When Hitler set out on his murderous campaign against the Jews of Europe truth and justice found few defenders. The Deputy of Christ and the German episcopate were not among them. Their role gives a special relevance to the question the young girl in Max Frisch's *Andorra* asks her priest: "Where were you, Father Benedict, when they took away our brother like a beast to the slaughter, like a beast to the slaughter, where were you?"[161] This question still waits for an answer.

The Problem of Resistance 11

The concentration camp Dachau, when reached by American troops on April 26, 1945, held 326 German Catholic priests. A still larger number had passed through the camp, had died in it of starvation or disease, or had been murdered there. Soon thereafter Pope Pius XII invoked these and other acts of persecution to show that the Catholic Church in Germany had strongly resisted the Nazi regime. In his letter to the Bavarian bishops in August 1945 the Pope paid tribute to "those millions of Catholics, men and women of every class" who, loyal to their bishops, had fought against the demonic powers that ruled Germany.[1] The German bishops, too, ever since the downfall of the Third Reich, have expressed their admiration for Catholics like Provost Lichtenberg, Father Delp and others who died resisting the Nazis, and they have linked the Church to these martyrs. Yet there was a time when resistance to the Nazi state was not only discouraged by the Church, but condemned. Catholics who actively fought against the Hitler regime were rebels not only against the state, but against their ecclesiastical authorities as well.

1. The Bishops Condemn Revolt

From the beginning until the end of Hitler's rule the bishops never tired of admonishing the faithful to accept his government as the legitimate authority to whom obedience had to be rendered. The episcopate did teach that in cases of laws violating God's commands Catholics had the duty to obey God rather than man, but this principle was rarely applied to a concrete case of Nazi wrongdoing. Moreover, the bishops repeatedly castigated those who on account of immoral, if not criminal, laws and deeds might seek to oppose the state. The joint pastoral letter of August 1935, quoted earlier (p. 129), is just one of the many instances where the bishops exhorted Catholics not to become involved with those planning to resist Nazi rule. Individual members of the episcopate also frequently warned against any revolutionary action, which was condemned as being in opposition to Catholic teaching. "Good Catholics have always been good patriots," declared Bishop Rackl of Eichstätt in a typical sermon in May 1936. "Surely not good Catholics staged the revolution of 1918, Catholic soldiers indeed have not been deserters, and good Catholics will never be on the side of revolutionaries, no matter how badly things are going."[2]

When a Swiss Catholic in June 1936 was reported to have asked children to pray for Hitler's death, and the German press thereupon accused all Catholics of being in sympathy with sedition, Cardinal Faulhaber declared in a sermon:

> A lunatic abroad has had an attack of madness—does this justify wholesale suspicion of the German Catholics? You all are witnesses for the fact that on all Sundays and holidays at the main service we pray in all churches for the Führer as we have promised in the Concordat. And now one can read in big headlines of the papers at the street corners, "They pray for Hitler's death!" We feel offended on account of this questioning of our loyalty to the state. We will today give an answer, a Christian answer: Catholic men, we will now pray together a paternoster for the life of the Führer. This is our answer.[3]

After the unsuccessful assassination attempt upon Hitler in Munich on November 8, 1939, Cardinal Bertram, in the name of the German episcopate, and Cardinal Faulhaber for the Bavarian bishops sent telegrams of congratulations to Hitler.[4] The Catholic press all over Germany, in response to instructions of the *Reichspressekammer,* spoke of the miraculous working of providence that had protected the Führer. And on November 12 in the Cathedral of Munich a *Te Deum* was sung "in order to thank the Divine Providence in the name of the archdiocese for the Führer's fortunate escape from the criminal attempt made upon his life."[5] It is noteworthy that back in February 1919 Faulhaber had refused to order the ringing of bells and the showing of flags of mourning after Kurt Eisner, the Socialist Prime Minister of Bavaria, had been assassinated by a Catholic nobleman.[6]

In his justly celebrated sermons of July and August 1941 Bishop Galen courageously condemned the power of the Gestapo which subjected perfectly loyal citizens to arbitrary arrest and kept them in concentration camps without an ordinary court trial. But none of these misdeeds were seen by Galen as a justification for opposing the Hitler regime as such. He went out of his way to make clear that he was opposed to any forceful resistance to the state, or to any weakening of the German war effort:

> We Christians make no revolution. We will continue to do our duty in obedience to God, out of love for people and fatherland. Our soldiers will fight and die for Germany, but not for those who . . . disgrace the German name before God and man. We will continue to fight against the external enemy; against the enemy in our midst who tortures and beats us, we cannot fight with arms and there remains only one weapon: strong tenacious, obstinate perseverance.[7]

When later that year the anti-Nazi underground, or perhaps the Gestapo seeking to ruin the Bishop, circulated a bogus sermon in which Galen was quoted as calling for the elimination of the godless regime of injustice that oppressed Germany, the Bishop of Münster disowned this sermon and let it be known that it stood "in glaring contradiction" to his own views and attitudes.[8] It is reported by all of Galen's associates that the "Lion of Münster" was indeed resolutely opposed to any and all attempts to depose the Nazi regime by force or to cause a German defeat.

It might be argued that the German episcopate not only acted prudently in dissociating the Church from any violent tactics, but that the bishops were also bound by traditional Catholic teaching which, in recent centuries at least, had frequently condemned revolutions and tyrannicide. We will have an occasion to take up the more theoretical aspects of this question in the final chapter; but it is appropriate to indicate here that Catholic theologians were, and still are, by no means in agreement on the morality of resisting tyranny.

In a number of instances in recent history the Church has sanctioned armed rebellion. The Mexican hierarchy in 1927 approved of and blessed the revolt of the *Cristeros,* bands of peasants so called because of their rallying cry, *"Viva Cristo Rey,"* and frequently led by Catholic priests.[9] Pope Pius XI, in his encyclical *Firmissimam Constantiam* of March 28, 1937, on conditions in Mexico, distinguished between just and unjust insurrections and left the door open for defensive violence against constituted powers that "arise against justice and truth even to destroying the very foundations of authority . . . [and] make use of public power to bring it to ruin."[10] After the majority of the Spanish hierarchy had sided with the rebellion of General Franco and had called for a crusade against Communism and for Christianity and justice, Pius XI gave his blessing to "those who have assumed the difficult and dangerous task of defending and restoring the rights and honor of God and of religion."[11] And after Franco, generously helped by Hitler and Mussolini, had succeeded in defeating the Loyalists, Pius XII sent the Spanish Catholics his expressions of "immense joy" and "fatherly congratulations for the gift of peace and victory with which God has deigned to crown the Christian heroism of your faith and charity, proved through such great and generous sufferings."[12] Clearly some rebellions were acceptable and could receive the blessing of the Church.

If the German bishops had wanted to sanction active resistance to Hitler, there were thus many precedents for such a stand. The fact that they consistently opposed such resistance will therefore have to be explained on grounds other than the inhibiting effects of Christian theology. In the first few years of Hitler's reign the bishops probably had hopes that the Nazi state would relinquish its anti-Catholic policies if the Catholics only showed sufficient willingness to co-operate and support the Third Reich. Later, when this hope was disappointed, the episcopate had committed the Church to a course of loyal obedience which it would have been very difficult to reverse. Most of the bishops moreover were conservatives and out of sympathy with any policy likely to lead to an open clash between Church and State. Once the war had broken out they considered it their patriotic duty to support the German war effort.

The apparent hopelessness of any successful resistance to Hitler's machinery of terror may also have played a role. But the net effect of the episcopate's exhortations to obedience and their warnings against any seditious activity was, of course, to discourage *any* spirit of opposition and to burden the conscience of those, such as the men of the military resistance group, who felt impelled to resist the Nazi regime. A popular uprising, no doubt, had little chance of success, but the military dissidents were in a stronger position and their cause was by no means a lost one from the start. Bishops are not expected to be plotters and leaders of insurrections, but they could alternatively have explained to their followers what, according to Catholic teaching, are the rights of the individual against an unjust political regime, and then left it to each believer how to act upon this moral guidance. At the very least, the episcopate could have elected to adopt a policy of discreet silence on the entire subject of disobedience and rebellion.

2. The Force of Public Opinion

There can be little doubt that the bishops grossly underestimated the strength of their position, especially during the war period. The reports of the provincial administrators and of the Gestapo, Hitler's table talk and the diaries of his henchmen give abundant testimony to the Church's popularity and to the political risks the Nazis saw in proceeding against the episcopate. In the few important instances when the strength of popular feeling led the bishops to take a resolute stand, the regime was forced to back down. The cessation of the euthanasia program has already been mentioned in this connection and there were a number of other such occurrences.   ,

The joint pastoral letter of the Bavarian bishops protesting the highly unpopular dismissal of all nuns teaching in the public schools, scheduled to be read on June 21, 1936, had been forbidden by the Bavarian Political Police. On June 20 orders had been issued to take into custody all priests who dared to read the pastoral letter in violation of the ban. But when Vicar General Buchwieser of Munich (in charge of the archdiocese in the temporary absence of Cardinal Faulhaber) instructed the clergy to read the pronouncement despite this order, the government yielded. The same evening the Bavarian Minister of the Interior countermanded the earlier order by instructions merely to record the names of priests who read the pastoral letter. Afterwards a number of provincial administrators reported that in the event of arrests the population would not have accepted these measures without resistance, and that disturbances would probably have resulted. "The priest," the *Regierungspräsident* of Upper Bavaria wrote, "is still a person enjoying the greatest respect and that is true especially in rural districts. Even the currency and immorality trials have been unable to change this fact to any substantial degree. When the priest yet appears as a martyr for his convictions, he is defended even by people who normally have little to do with the Church."[13]

Two other examples of the efficacy of public protests are provided by the abortive attempts to remove the crucifixes from public buildings that took place in the predominantly Catholic states of Oldenburg and Bavaria in 1936 and 1941 respectively. On November 4, 1936, the Minister of Religion and Education in Oldenburg had ordered the removal of all religious symbols such as crucifixes from public buildings by December 15. The order caused tremendous agitation. Local officials everywhere were put under pressure to threaten to resign their posts unless the order was revoked; special prayers were ordered by Bishop Galen. Delegations from all corners of the state converged upon the town of Oldenburg, the seat of the state government, to protest the ordinance. On November 25 the *Gauleiter* and *Reichsstatthalter* of Oldenburg addressed a mass meeting where he was heckled throughout his address. At the end he declared that a wise government must know when a mistake has been made and that the order of November 4 stood revoked. Bishop Galen ordered special services of thanks to be held, and in a pastoral letter expressed the hope that this courageous conduct of the people of Oldenburg would be followed by other Christians everywhere.[14]

The same strength of religious feelings was revealed five years later in Bavaria. An order of April 23, 1941, by the *Gauleiter* and Minister of Education and Religious Affairs, Adolf Wagner, had prohibited the opening of the school day by a prayer, and suggested the gradual removal of all crucifixes. Whenever an attempt was made to enforce this ruling, unrest and resistance were obvious. Parents refused to send their children to school, and in many places demonstrations took place that led to the restoration of the crucifixes. In one small town 500 aroused men and women overpowered the mayor and recovered the crucifixes he had hidden. In another place where the local priest had been arrested for preaching a sermon strongly critical of the removal of the crucifixes, fifty women informed the mayor that unless the priest were released, they would cease to work and deliver produce and would surrender the medals earned for having given birth to a large number of children.[15] On July 26 Faulhaber, in the name of the Bavarian bishops, added his voice to this storm of largely spontaneous protest. "The German soldier," he wrote Wagner, "is honored publicly by being called a crusader against Bolshevism. This title of honor would not be deserved, if at the same time at home war is declared on the cross."[16] A month later the Bavarian government yielded. On August 28 the ordinance in question was revoked.

To be sure, not all protests led to such results. After the arrest in June 1937 of the Jesuit Rupert Mayer, a highly popular preacher in Munich, Cardinal Faulhaber delivered a sermon in which he most vigorously condemned the action of the authorities,[17] but Father Mayer was not released until December, only to be arrested again about a week later. Despite Mayer's great popularity in Munich, he remained in custody or under house arrest for most of the war period. It should also be said that none of these cases of successful opposition involved essential parts of the Nazi program. One would not, therefore, be justified in deducing from these episodes that a similar outburst of popular sentiment would have dissuaded Hitler from his plan to exterminate the Jews of Europe.

Nevertheless, it seems clear that public opinion was a force to be reckoned with, even amidst the terror of the Gestapo. On November 1, 1941, Ulrich von Hassell, the former German Ambassador in Rome and one of the continuing conspirators against Hitler, recorded in his diary: "Just as Bishop Galen has exercised not only a powerful and direct moral influence throughout Germany, but also certain indirect influence, it has been demonstrated that an energetic protest often does have an effect."[18]

3. The Church and the German Resistance

Unfortunately we have only spotty information on the hierarchy's attitudes to the plans and actions of the military resistance group. At least two members of the espiscopate seem to have been told by Carl Goerdeler, the spirited though somewhat careless civilian leader of the generals' plot, about the plans for revolt. They were Cardinal Faulhaber and Bishop Preysing.[19] Count Claus von Stauffenberg, the man who planted the bomb on July 20, 1944, also visited Preysing.[20]   In neither case do we know how much concrete information was actually given the two churchmen. According to one report Bishop Preysing, in the event of a successful uprising, was to have become a Papal Legate with special powers in order to supersede Nuncio Orsenigo, who was considered compromised by his pro-Fascist and pro-Nazi views. Joseph Müller, the contact between the plotting generals and the Vatican, tells of having approached Preysing at the Pope's request in 1942 and 1943, and to have obtained his consent. The idea of Preysing's appointment supposedly came from Monsignor Kaas.[21] However, no corroboration is available, and Walter Adolph, a close associate of the late Bishop of Berlin, casts doubt upon its accuracy.[22]

In December 1943 a Catholic chaplain, the Jesuit Hermann Wehrle, was asked by a young officer of Stauffenberg's staff, Major Leonrod, whether his knowledge of the plan to kill Hitler placed him in the state of sin. Wehrle consulted the article on tyrannicide in the *Lexikon für Theologie und Kirche* and then told Leonrod that the killing of a legitimate ruler by a private individual was forbidden, but that knowledge alone was not sinful. He advised Leonrod not to participate in the plot.[23] The question had been posed under the seal of secrecy, but when the episode came to light in the trial of the plotters after the July 20 affair, Wehrle was indicted and condemned to death for complicity. In a sermon preached in 1946 Cardinal Faulhaber praised the chaplain as a fighter against Nazi tyranny.[24]

After the failure of the plot, Faulhaber was questioned by the

Gestapo about his talk with Goerdeler and is said to have expressed the most vigorous condemnation of the assassination attempt and to have affirmed his loyalty to Hitler.[25] Two close colleagues of the Cardinal agree that Faulhaber was probably opposed to this act of tyrannicide. He was an aristocrat in his thinking, they recall, and against "political murder."[26] No information is available about the reaction of the other bishops.

In contrast to November 1939, this time no telegrams of congratulations seem to have been sent to Hitler, and a report of the propaganda office of Münster complained, "It is typical for the attitude of the clergy that no priest, including the bishops, has found a word of indignation for the treasonable assassination attempt or expressed thanks for . . . the preservation of the Führer."[27] A Gestapo agent in Cologne reported that some clergymen decried the plot and had expressed feelings of shame "that something like this could happen among us. Some found it strange that the bishops had not commented at all." One pro-Nazi priest told the agent that the majority of the clergy regretted the failure of the assassination attempt.[28] But all this is highly fragmentary evidence that does not allow us to make generalizations about the response of the Church. Mother Gallin in her study of the German resistance movement concludes that the bishops "offered no encouragement or support to any plans for a revolution by which the Nazis would have been removed from power. Revolution was specifically rejected and denounced by them on several occasions."[29] This conclusion can certainly be accepted.

A number of eminent Catholics were members of resistance groups. Augustinus Rösch, the provincial of the Society of Jesus in Bavaria, and the Jesuit Alfred Delp belonged to the Kreisau Circle, a group of men led by Count Helmuth von Moltke. This group had met since the summer of 1940 to discuss the political, economic and spiritual foundations of the new Germany that would arise after the downfall of the Third Reich. Father Rösch narrowly escaped with his life after July 20, 1944. The brilliant, thirty-eight-year-old Delp, a convert to Catholicism and a former editor of the Jesuit monthly *Stimmen der Zeit,* was hanged on February 2, 1945; his ashes were scattered to the winds. Both men apparently knew nothing of the plan to assassinate Hitler and, had they known, would probably not have approved of it.[30] The Goerdeler–Beck group responsible for the plot included several well-known Catholics, among them the former labor leaders Bernhard Letterhaus and Jakob Kaiser. Stauffenberg himself was a Catholic, though he did not regularly practice his religion.

A large number of Catholic priests were either executed or died in prisons and concentration camps. Many of them had run afoul of ordinances such as those that forbade listening to foreign broadcasts, or were severely punished for other trivial offenses. But some were martyrs to their convictions. Dr. Max Josef Metzger, a life-long pacifist and founder of the *Una Sancta* movement, was sentenced to death and executed on April 17, 1944, for having had "seditious" contacts with the Bishop of Upsala in Sweden. Father Alfons Maria Wachsmann of Berlin was condemned for having undermined the morale of the armed forces. The same charge took the lives of Josef Losch, a parish priest in Bavaria, and of three clergymen in Lübeck. The martyrdom of Provost Lichtenberg and Franz Reinisch has been mentioned earlier, and there were still others who sealed their testimony to human dignity with their blood.[31] And yet, it is sad to record, these courageous few were no more representative of the Church than Goerdeler was of the German bureaucracy, or General Beck of the military.

If by resistance to Nazi rule we mean not criticism of certain specific measures, but opposition to the regime as such, then the Church as an institution did not resist. A good number of individual Catholics of extraordinary courage and moral integrity, on the other hand, who disregarded the constant exhortations to loyal obedience in the pronouncements of their spiritual superiors, belong on the honor roll of the resistance. Men like Letterhaus and Delp were part of that "other Germany," which has done so much to safeguard and restore the honor of the German name, because they were prepared to flout the official line of their Church and listen instead to the voice of their consciences. The Church fought for her confessional schools, her press and organizations, her monasteries; she clashed with the government on some issues of moral teaching, such as sterilization and euthanasia. But at no time did the Church challenge the legitimacy of the Nazi regime or give her explicit or implicit approval to the various attempts to bring about its downfall. While thousands of anti-Nazis were beaten into pulp in the concentration camps, the Church talked of supporting the moral renewal brought about by the Hitler government. This line of co-operation was never abandoned.

It has been said that the bishops exercised restraint in their protests in order not to aggravate the tribulations of the lower clergy, who had to bear the brunt of the Church's persecution. It is true that the regime frequently punished those who read a certain pastoral letter but shied away from laying hands on the bishop who had composed it. Bishop Galen is said to have become far less outspoken after 1943, when three priests in Lübeck were executed, one of the accusations having been that they had distributed copies of Galen's sermons to soldiers. We also know that bishops like Galen and Preysing felt hindered by their more conciliatory colleagues, with whom they frequently disagreed in matters of tactics, but to whom they deferred in order not to jeopardize the shaky unity of the episcopate. Some bishops, like Ehrenfried of Würzburg, were convinced monarchists; others, like Faulhaber, were aristocrats, anchored in the politics of an imperial Germany that had long passed away. Most of them were ardent patriots and entrapped in a legalistic approach that had some relevance to the Wilhelmian *Rechtsstaat,* but was sadly unsuited to the realities of life in Hitler's dictatorship. In this basically conservative group, men like Galen and Preysing, advocating a more resistant stand, could not prevail.

It is doubtful anyway whether the masses of the faithful would have been prepared to follow a more radical leadership. Most of the Catholics, like human beings everywhere, were not heroes and merely wanted to live in peace. These were the simple people, regular churchgoers, who might be willing to send an unsigned postcard to the authorities like this one found in the files of the Bavarian government: "We regard the campaign against Jewish Bolshevism as a crusade. With the name of the Savior on their lips thousands of soldiers now sacrifice their lives. We protest against the removal of the crucifixes from the schools. The school prayer should also continue."[32] With such "resisters" nothing much could be done to check the crimes of the Nazi regime.

A small minority, sometimes organized in informal groups led by priests, rejected the official irenical line of the Church. Many of these Catholics had belonged to the Catholic youth movement. Some had a loose connection with the Catholic periodical *Hochland,* and with the Catholic writer Theodor Haecker; others may have been influenced by the sonnets of the Catholic poet Reinhold Schneider that circulated clandestinely all over Germany during the war years. Most of these men and women did not plot revolts, but they did maintain their spiritual integrity. The nationalistic pronouncements of the episcopate bewildered and distressed them; every critical note in a pastoral letter or sermon was eagerly welcomed. The personal courage of a Galen inspired and fortified them; the silence of the Church in the face of the most revolting crimes created a crisis of confidence in their spiritual superiors which, for some, still exists today.[33]

For these Catholics the bishops' struggle to save the Catholic organizations and to defend other rights guaranteed by the Concordat meant relatively little; the progress of the liturgical movement seeking the more active and intelligent participation of the faithful in the holy mysteries and prayers of the Church was more important to them than the fate of the Church's functional machinery. For these few the Church was free as long as she fearlessly adhered to her gospel of human dignity and love; and she became enslaved, no matter how many millions continued to attend services, when the Church chose a course of compromise with evil.

Had German Catholicism from the start adhered to a policy of resolute opposition to the Nazi regime, world history might well have taken a different course. Even if this struggle had ultimately failed to defeat Hitler and prevent all of his many crimes, it would in this view have raised the moral prestige of the Church immeasureably. The human cost of such resistance would undeniably have been great, but these sacrifices would have been made for the greatest of all causes. With the home front unreliable, Hitler might not have dared going to war and literally millions of lives would have been saved.

There is no reason, of course, to single out for criticism the Catholic Church. The German Catholics were part and parcel of a milieu that, with few notable exceptions, lacked a sufficient leavening of political sophistication and moral backbone to see through the patriotic shibboleths of the Hitler regime. But there has spread a legend of resistance on the part of the Church at large in Germany that badly needs historical corrective. The fact is, as the Catholic historian Friedrich Heer has aptly put it, "that Christian resistance to Hitler during the Third Reich from the beginning had the character of the unique, . . . the undesirable. . . . In 1945 the situation was so critical that only a gigantic attempt at concealment was regarded as able to save and restore the face of official Christianity in Germany."[34]

This concealment has been so bold and successful that in Germany, unlike France after the deposition of the Vichy regime, not a single bishop had to resign his office. Quite the contrary, Bishop Berning, who had served until the downfall of Hitler in Göring's Prussian State Council, in 1949 was given the honorary title of Archbishop. Herr von Papen was made Papal Privy Chamberlain in 1959.

Such rewards for men deeply involved with the Nazi regime represent a mockery of heroic figures like Delp and Reinisch, who died fighting Hitler. The erection of shrines and churches consecrated to the memory of church martyrs during the Nazi era, of which the Church Maria Regina Martyrum in Berlin is a beautiful example, indicates a belated act of tribute. Still to come is an honest confrontation with the mistakes necessitating their martyrdom.

Church
and Totalitarianism **III**

Catholic Political Ideology: The Unity of Theory and Practice 12

The behavior of the Catholic Church under Nazi rule was related to a number of specifically German conditions. The Church shared the widely prevailing sense of nationalism and patriotism; she was affected by the same excessive respect for authority that did so much to hinder the Resistance. More importantly, the bishops, many of the lower clergy and their parishioners concurred in certain Nazi aims. They welcomed the Nazis' anti-Communism as a counterpoise to the liberal, anti-clerical and atheistic currents of the Weimar republic. They were attracted by the National Socialist call for a strong state, a new German Reich that would again be a world power and able to solve the country's pressing economic and social problems. Some churchmen expected that the increase in the power of the state and the introduction of the leadership principle would result also in a strengthening of the authority of the Church.

In a mood of naïve trust and wishful thinking about Hitler's promises of religious peace, and anxious to protect the Church's organizations, schools and newspapers, the German bishops supported the signing of the Concordat. After this pact had been concluded the course of accommodation was fixed. In order not to jeopardize those provisions of the Concordat which the Nazi regime chose to honor it was regarded as imperative to placate the Nazis.

Had Hitler pursued a policy similar to that of Mussolini's peaceful coexistence with the Church, it is more than likely that the German episcopate, like its counterpart in Italy, would have become even more identified with the Nazi government and movement than they actually did. But German National Socialism was truly totalitarian in its aspirations, intent upon dominating all aspects of life, and hence ill-inclined to accept partners. The conflict between Church and State was therefore probably unavoidable no matter what the policy of the hierarchy and the Holy See.

Only very gradually and rather late did the bishops begin to realize that Hitler's regime was intent upon destroying the Church. Even then they thought that they could ward off the encroachments of the Nazis by protesting against violations of the Concordat and combining these protests with affirmations of loyalty to the state. The Church's opposition was carefully circumscribed; it was rooted in her concern for her institutional interests rather than in a belief in freedom and justice for all men. In this the German episcopate followed a policy very much in keeping with the Church's traditional mode of operation and thought.

With this summary we leave behind the specific German elements underlying the conduct of the German Church. We turn to our concluding task, an explanation on a higher level that involves the Catholic Church as a world-wide institution, and its political and moral theories.

1. The Church and Democracy

"In any crucial situation," Sidney Hook once observed, "the behavior of the Catholic Church may be more reliably predicted by reference to its concrete interests as a political organization than by reference to its timeless dogmas."[1] One may go a step further and say that these dogmas are sufficiently flexible and ambiguous so that the Church can accommodate a variety of political conditions running the gamut from democracy to totalitarian dictatorship. Some of this ambiguity can be attributed to the highly abstract theological and metaphysical foundations of Catholic political theory, but much is a matter of design that serves to pave the way for the Church's adjustment to different situations.

Some Catholic political theorists, Jacques Maritain for example, have sought to show that the natural law ethic of the Church necessarily leads to the affirmation of the natural rights of man and thence to the defense of democracy as the only political system able to guarantee such rights. Some day, perhaps, the Church will put the stamp of orthodoxy upon these ideas. Today, however, when still many political forms other than democracy are alive and functioning, the Church has not made Maritain's espousal of democracy official. Papal teachings on politics, which we can consider authoritative even if they are not expressly delivered as *ex cathedra* pronouncements, still adhere to a more elusive doctrine, and this finding holds true for the nineteenth-century pope, Leo XIII, as well as for the recent reform pope, John XXIII.

Contemporary Catholic political doctrine owes a great debt to Pope Leo XIII. His election to the Chair of Peter in 1878 marked a decisive turning away from the essentially negative, if not reactionary, policies and ideas of his predecessors in the first three quarters of the nineteenth century. Most European states in 1878 were still monarchies, but Leo XIII perceived that new forces were in the making and he understood that the Church could not blindly oppose them. In a number of encyclicals he reformulated Catholic thought on the state in such a way as to prepare for the acceptance of democracy.

Abandoning the principle taught by St. Thomas Aquinas and most later theologians that monarchy was the best form of government, Leo XIII maintained that the Church was essentially indifferent to the various modes of ruling provided the general welfare and the interests of the Church were insured:

> Of the various forms of government the Church does not reject any that are fitted to procure the welfare of the subject; she wishes only—and nature itself requires—that they should be constituted without involving wrong to any one, and especially without violating the rights of the Church.[2]

Two years later, in 1890, Leo XIII again pointed out that "the Church, the guardian always of her own right and most observant of that of others, holds that it is not her province to decide which is the best amongst many diverse forms of government, and the civil institutions of Christian states, and amid the various kinds of state rule she does not disapprove of any, provided the respect due to religion and the observance of good morals be upheld."[3]

Leo XIII's successors, presiding over a Church still composed of a variety of political currents—monarchy and liberalism, democracy and fascism—have continued to teach Leo's ideas. "Universally known is the fact," declared Pope Pius XI in 1933, "that the Catholic Church is never bound to one form of government more than to another, provided the divine rights of God and of Christian conscience are safe. She does not find any difficulty in adapting herself to various civil institutions, be they monarchic or republican, aristocratic or democratic."[4]

The adaptation to authoritarian and dictatorial regimes was facilitated by the Church's hierarchical constitution and the affinity for authoritarian ideas produced by its makeup. Catholicism, wrote the historian Christopher Dawson in 1936, "is by no means hostile to the authoritarian ideal of the State. Against the liberal doctrines of the divine right of majorities and the unrestrained freedom of opinion the Church has always maintained the principles of authority and hierarchy and a high conception of the prerogatives of the State." Catholic social ideals set forth in the encyclicals of Leo XIII and Pius XI, Dawson argued, "have far more affinity with those of Fascism than with those of either Liberalism or Socialism." Catholic political ideas "correspond much more closely, at least in theory, with the Fascist conception of the functions of the 'leader' and the vocational hierarchy of the Fascist State than they do with the system of parliamentary democratic party government. . . ."[5]

As long as Fascist movements served as a bulwark against Communism, the Church was willing to accept the loss of political liberties that followed their accession to power. Atheistic Communism has for a century been the Church's number one enemy. This uncompromising hostility drew strength from the personal experiences of Popes Pius XI and XII. At the end of World War I, as Papal Nuncios in Poland and Germany, respectively, the two men had had experience with the anti-religious fervor of Communist regimes, and what they saw and heard in Warsaw, Munich and Berlin colored their political outlook and influenced their subsequent policies as heads of the Church. Both of these Popes were preoccupied with the threat of Communism, and therefore showed considerable benevolence to both Fascist Italy and Nazi Germany. The French Fascist movement, *Action Française,* was eventually condemned by the Vatican, but, in the words of one Catholic writer, this was done "not merely because there was ground for condemnation, but because it estimated that the degree of success possible for the movement was great enough permanently to damage the essential Catholic interests in democratic France, but not great enough to protect them in the long run."[6] On July 7, 1939, soon after the election of Pacelli to the Papacy, the ban was lifted.[7] Pius XII, even more than his predecessor, was convinced of the usefulness of anti-Communist right-wing movements.

At the end of World War II, cognizant of the fact that the support of dictatorial, if not outright criminal regimes such as those of Mussolini and Hitler, had done much to injure the moral prestige of Catholicism, the Church began to assume a more sympathetic attitude toward democracy. Pius XII, who throughout World War II had steered a course of careful neutrality, in December 1944, when the defeat of the Axis powers was imminent, acknowledged "that a democratic form of government is considered by many today to be a natural postulate of reason itself."[8] After the downfall of the Nazi regime, Pope Pius in October 1945 declared that totalitarianism cannot satisfy "the vital exigencies of any human community" since "it allows the state power to assume an undue extension" and forces "all legitimate manifestations of life—personal, local and professional—into a mechanical unity or collectivity under the stamp of nation, race or class." Short of totalitarianism, even the so-called authoritarian regimes, the Pope went on, pervert the essential nature of state power by splitting the nation into rulers and ruled, and by excluding the citizens from effective participation in forming the will of society. True democracy, on the other hand, holding the Christian faith as the principle of civil life, satisfies the requirements of a sound community, though "the same applies, or could apply, under the same conditions, also to the other legitimate forms of government [monarchy, aristocracy, etc.]."[9]

The benevolence toward popular forms of government became even more pronounced under Pius' successor, Pope John XXIII. In his encyclical *Pacem in Terris* (Peace on Earth) issued on April 10, 1963, Pope John, like Leo XIII seventy years earlier, reaffirmed that even though authority comes from God, men have the right to choose their rulers. "It is thus clear that the doctrine which we have set forth is fully consonant with any truly democratic regime." The old neutrality toward the forms of government was not yet repudiated, but John XXIII did proclaim that the rule of law and the principle of constitutionalism were preferred modes of government. The separation of the state's functions into legislative, judicial and executive branches, the Pope declared, is "in keeping with the innate demands of human nature."[10] Pope John's lengthy discussion of human rights, including "the right to take an active part in public affairs," also pointed toward an eventual acceptance of democracy by the Church as the form of government judged best for all who have reached a degree of political maturity.

The timing of this gradual political reorientation is significant; it shows that the Church is following rather than leading. As a perceptive Catholic sociologist has noted in connection with the social encyclicals of the modern popes, the Church respects "the majesty of facts," she ratifies the gains scored by others. Once a liberating movement has broken certain chains, the Church will incorporate the newly gained liberties into her ethic of natural law. She will then recognize them, as previously she had recognized the validity of the chains.[11] Whereas in earlier centuries monarchy was held to be the best and most natural form of government, now the rule of law and the separation of functions are viewed as consonant with the demands of human nature.

The indifference of Catholic political philosophy to the forms of government has been justified by the abuses to which all political systems are exposed and "because the political form of government as such does not actually guarantee the best realization of the common good."[12] One can readily assent to this proposition. It shows the same realism, reminiscent of Aristotle, as is displayed in Pope John's statement in *Pacem in Terris* that "it is impossible to determine, once and for all, what is the most suitable form of government, or how civil authorities can most effectively fulfil their respective functions, . . . great weight has to be given to the historical background and circumstances of given political communities, circumstances which will vary at different times and in different places."[13] But the validity of one premise does not prove a conclusion. While it may be impossible to substantiate the assertion that democracy, as practiced for example in the United States or Great Britain, represents an ideal form of government to be followed by all other nations everywhere and at any time, it is certainly possible, negatively, to rule out some forms of government from consideration. The Nazi regime's policies of genocide, for example, were an integral part of National Socialist doctrine; these policies represented a logical outgrowth of a system of government refusing to recognize human equality and dignity. Quite apart from the question of what is the best mode of government, it is therefore not at all difficult to show that certain totalitarian regimes by their very nature are in open violation of the basic moral principles of the Judaeo-Christian tradition. This judgment the Church avoided making until Nazi and Fascist totalitarianism, containing and supported by large numbers of Catholics, had disappeared from the map of history.

As soon as one of these totalitarian regimes attacks the rights of the Church, the Church will protest. But until these regimes are actually overthrown, the Church will hesitate to utter the ban and she will seek an accommodation to protect her own interests as an institution. In such situations, of which the encounter with the Third Reich was a good example, the doctrine of the Church's indifference to the forms of government is highly useful. Thus the German bishops were able to assert that the Catholic religion was no more opposed to the Nazi form of government than to any other. And when the Hitler government reacted with anger to the statement of *L'Osservatore Romano* in July 1933, that the conclusion of the Concordat between Germany and the Holy See did not entail the recognition of a specific political doctrine, the bishops were able to explain: "The assertion of *L'Osservatore Romano* that the conclusion of the Concordat did not express assent to the National Socialist state does by no means signify a basic rejection of that state. Otherwise the Concordat would never have been concluded. It merely represents the intentional suspension of an evaluation, [a suspension] made necessary by the relations of the Holy See to all other states."[14]

The neutrality of the Church toward the various forms of government is thus an ideological adjunct of church diplomacy;

neutrality is necessitated by the wide-flung interests of the Church. These interests demand flexibility. On the other hand, and more basically, this neutrality derives from the fact that the chief concern of the Church is with the supernatural aspects of human existence. The Church regards herself as the divinely appointed means of man's redemption; to protect her pastoral mission the Church will work with all types of government, and these acts of accommodation, in the form of a concordat or without such a formal tie, rule out ideological intransigence. Given a sufficient *quid pro quo,* the Church will even close an eye to the violation of the common good by such a regime, for the interests of religion are her paramount concern. Or to put it differently: since religion is "the general and supreme good" of the community[15] to which all else must yield, the welfare of the state is measured by the freedom enjoyed by religion. From the standpoint of the Church, as a prominent English Catholic has observed correctly, "political and civil liberties . . . are secondary and only favored in so far as they seem to give some guarantee for the higher liberties."[16] It is for such reasons that Catholic dictators like Franco and Salazar, despite the oppressive character of their regimes, are considered more valuable by the Church than democratic statesmen, eager to secularize the state, no matter how much the latter may contribute to other areas of public life.

The Church, insisted Lord Acton, must be attached to a spirit making for good government: "a country entirely Protestant may have more Catholic elements in its government than one where the population is wholly Catholic."[17] This enlightened point of view has never yet been shared by those guiding the destiny of the Church.

2. The Challenge of Tyranny

The attitude of the contemporary Church to the problem of resistance to tyrannical regimes is marked by the same ambivalence of doctrine and the acceptance of accomplished facts as she shows toward forms of government.

It was not always so. The medieval scholastics, led by St. Thomas Aquinas, and Catholic theologians during the time of the

Counter Reformation, such as Suarez and Mariana, taught the legitimacy of resisting tyranny, including the right of killing a tyrant who had usurped the reigns of government. During these centuries of struggle between *imperium* and *sacerdotium* the doctrines of popular sovereignty and the right of resistance to tyranny were useful tools—to both of the contending parties; the papacy repeatedly absolved subjects from allegiance to heretical rulers, and tyrannicide resolved many a problem in the religious strife of the Reformation.

But these doctrines were forgotten in the eighteenth and nineteenth centuries after the ideas of the Enlightenment and revolutionary anti-clerical forces had attacked the privileges of the Church on many fronts, and absolute monarchies provided the only source of protection. The encyclical letters of Popes Gregory XVI (1831-1846) and the Syllabus of Errors of Pius IX (1864) therefore resolutely condemned any acts of rebellion. Even Leo XIII still castigated revolutionary violence, no matter how great the provocation:

> And if at any time it happen that the power of the state is rashly and tyrannically wielded by Princes, the teaching of the Catholic Church does not allow an insurrection on private authority against them, lest public order be only the more disturbed, and lest society take greater hurt therefrom. And when affairs come to such a pass that there is no other hope of safety, she teaches that relief may be hastened by the merits of Christian patience and by earnest prayers to God.[18]

When in the twentieth century revolutionary movements appeared on the scene which were friendly to the Church, Catholic teaching once more returned to an acceptance of resistance and revolt under certain circumstances. In 1925 Charles Maurras, the leader of the *Action Française,* was tried for having threatened the life of the French Minister of the Interior. Jacques Maritain, then a professor at the Catholic Institute of Paris, testified as a defense witness and argued the thesis "that Maurras' threat must be taken as the extreme measure of legitimate defense of social order."[19] The Mexican bishops in 1927, as already mentioned, supported the revolt of the *Cristeros.* And in 1937, against the background of the Spanish Civil War, in which most members of the Spanish hierarchy sided with the rebel, General Franco, Pope Pius XI drew a distinction between just and unjust insurrections. He upheld "recourse to force" as an act of "self-defense" against those dragging a nation to ruin, with the qualification that the means used might not be intrinsicaly evil and "bring greater harm to the community than the harm they were intended to remedy."[20]

The possibility of success appears to be one of the factors determining the Church's attitude to rebellions. She wants to be on the winning side. This desire is reflected in her recognition of *de facto* governments, even if established through a coup d'état. The acceptance of such regimes, taught Leo XIII, "is not only permissible, but even obligatory, being imposed by the need of the social good. . . . This is all the more imperative because an insurrection stirs up hatred among citizens, provokes civil war and may throw a nation into chaos and anarchy. . . ."[21] Once a regime has demonstrated its ability to remain in power, the Church will come to terms with it in order to restore the possibility of orderly worship, just as she will try to work with a government that is strongly entrenched in power, even if tyrannical.

This realistic acceptance of the political facts of life can, of course, be justified not only by criteria of statecraft, but also on moral grounds. Peace and order are an unquestionable good, and the shedding of blood in an insurrection without chance of success might be considered criminal. But such realism not only makes right the consequence of might; it means, in effect, that the Church in most cases can offer no guidance to her followers on whether they may or may not attempt to overthrow a tyrannical regime. Revolutionary groups can rarely know in advance whether their rebellion will succeed or merely aggravate suffering. Yet, should an attempt to depose a hated tyranny be foregone for that reason? Even in cases where failure is almost sure, rebellion may represent an act of moral protest of the greatest importance. "We must prove to the world and to future generations," declared Major-General Henning von Tresckow in June 1944, "that the men of the German resistance dared to take the decisive step and to hazard their lives upon it. Compared with this object, nothing else matters."[22] Should one deny the moral greatness and heroism of such a man, who is willing to stake his life upon the cleansing of his nation's name?

Catholic theologians today are divided on the question of active resistance, and Papal teaching is insufficiently clear. Pius XI rejected the use of evil means in any recourse to force without indicating what constitutes "evil means." Some theologians distinguish between the killing and the murder of a tyrant, while others would limit the legitimacy of tyrannicide to cases involving usurpers of political power.[23] Recently a French officer, charged with the submachine gun ambush of General De Gaulle in August 1962, defended himself by saying that he had committed an act of tyrannicide, which the Church had approved in certain periods of her history. The French hierarchy promptly disassociated herself from this argument. The Church, an official communiqué explained, denies that it is ever permissible to "put at the service of a cause, even a good one, means that are intrinsically evil."[24] Does this mean that the attempt upon Hitler's life on July 20, 1944, was illicit? Does not such an absolute prohibition of recourse to evil means often lead to consequences that magnify evil? Why is the life of a Hitler more to be preserved than that of the countless innocent victims who might have been saved by the timely killing of such a tyrant?

The ambiguity of the Church's position on the legitimacy of resistance to constituted authority is of considerable advantage, for with it she can sail a flexible course adaptable to the ebb and flow of the tides of circumstances. But such cautious helmsmanship, such waiting on the sidelines of history, leaves the individual Catholic burdened with a decision in the making of which he should have moral guidance from his Church. Often, moreover, his bishops will seek to conform his thinking to what they consider the long-range interests of the Church, and these interests may or may not coincide with those of the people involved. During the time of the Algerian rebellion the French episcopate could not agree upon a common evaluation of the insurrection. "We cannot positively affirm that it is legitimate," stated one bishop, "neither can we condemn it as if it were illegitimate."[25] In the face of such circumspection one is left wondering about the relevance of Catholic political teaching to the dilemmas of modern man.

The Church's political doctrine, in line with the scriptural injunctions to obey the powers that be, grants the presumption of legitimacy to all types of government provided they are firmly in possession of power. The decision on whether and how far to oppose a regime that is or becomes tyrannical will be made by the episcopate of that country primarily in terms of that state's attitude to the rights of religion. If the Church, as in Fascist Italy and essentially also in Nazi Germany, is allowed to pursue her pastoral mission, the bishops will exhort their followers to render willing obedience to the State. But if the Church's rights are assaulted, as happened in Mexico between 1917 and 1936 and in Spain under the republican regime at the outbreak of the Spanish Civil War, if churches are burnt and priests killed, the Church will support even an insurrection, provided the rebels promise to protect her interests and seem to have a chance to prevail against the legitimate government.

3. The Moral Dimension of Politics

The German–Swiss theologian, Hans Küng, has noted that "the Church, being of men, is forever under the temptation to make herself at home in the world, to regard her worldly successes as the coming of the Kingdom of God, to be intent only on making herself secure and powerful and free from opposition and persecution."[26] Here, indeed, is the fundamental dilemma. The Church is in the world to preach the word of God, to continue the work of Christ irrespective of cost, to be a moral force. But the Church also is an institution interested in self-preservation, extension of influence and the enhancement of her mission as organ of salvation. To use the sociological categories of Ernst Troeltsch, Catholicism is a church rather than a sect. It is an example of "that type of organization which is overwhelmingly conservative, . . . becomes an integral part of the existing social order, . . . [and which knows to attain her end] by a process of adaptation and compromise."[27] The Catholic Church, as a church, has usually been unable to separate her ideal aims from her interest in survival and she has often found her own gospel a liability rather than a source of strength. She has therefore from time to time retreated behind the cloister walls, and instead of being the salt of the earth has become a force tragically upholding injustice and tyranny.

On the level of theory the Church has frequently affirmed her right and duty to confront all moral issues. Reformulating the old doctrine of the indirect temporal power of the Church—the authority to pronounce upon the morality of political actions and relations that involve the spiritual or moral life of the believers—Pope Leo XIII proclaimed the duty of the Church "to show forth what things are to be accepted as right, and what to be regarded as worthless." The Church must "make a strong endeavor that the power of the Gospel may pervade the law and institutions of the nations."[28] Some men, declared Pius XII in 1954, "presume to check and set limits to the power of Bishops, (the Roman Pontiff not excepted), as being strictly the shepherds of the flock entrusted to them. They fix their authority, office and watchfulness within certain bounds, which concern strictly religious matters, the statements of the truths of the faith, the regulation of devotional practices, administration of the Sacraments of the Church, and the carrying out of liturgical ceremonies. They wish to restrain the Church from all undertakings which concern life as it is really conducted."

But this belief, Pope Pius went on, is an error. All aspects of man's life pertaining to the moral order, including many political, social and economic problems, are of concern to conscience and the salvation of man, and therefore within the authority and care of the Church.

> Such are: the purpose and limits of temporal authority; the relations between the individual and society, the so-called "totalitarian state," whatever be the principle it is based on; . . . war, its morality, liceity or non-liceity when waged as it is today, and whether a conscientious person may give or withhold his cooperation in it; the moral relationships which bind and rule the various nations.

These and like problems, Pius XII declared, are the province of the Church, the concern of "that authority established by God to see to a just order and to direct the consciences and actions of men along the path to their true and final destiny." The Church has to fulfill this mission "in the front line, in the midst of the struggle that rages between truth and error, virtue and vice. . . ."[29]

The record of the Church, one regrets to conclude, does not bear out these grand aspirations. The policy of accommodation of the German episcopate, the subject of this study, provides but the most recent striking example of the Church's inability to transcend her institutional interests and to be a guardian of human morality.

Whether the Church can ever fully resolve this dilemma is doubtful. The Jesuit theologian Karl Rahner has suggested that Catholic Christianity become a "Church of active members," in effect assuming "the character of a sect."[30] But this call for reform seems unlikely to be heeded. The need to defend the Church as an organization will always provide a powerful inducement to act opportunistically rather than prophetically. In any conflict between the imperatives of religion in the narrow sense—worship, liturgical services, the administration of the sacraments—and the requirements of human morality, the former will usually prevail. Individual churchmen and believers will become martyrs, but the institution will prefer survival.

The Church's hold upon the faithful in many situations is too precarious to risk an open clash with a state trampling upon human dignity and freedom. The situation is worsened when, as in Nazi Germany, the bishops and the clergy are themselves infected with an alien creed. Whenever either of these manifestations is present, many seemingly good reasons can be brought forth to defend the Church's political quietism and her surrender to Caesar.

The Church, "despite the wide reach of her jurisdiction," as the German Catholic scholar E. W. Böckenförde has appropriately observed, "as a *potestas indirecta* is nowhere directly responsible."[31] The German bishops held to the right to pass moral judgment on those measures of the Nazi state which impinged upon the Church's vital interests and certain cardinal points of doctrine—confessional schools, marriage legislation, sterilization and euthanasia—but they fell back upon the indirect nature of their temporal jurisdiction whenever considerations of tactics required a more cautious course. A recent apologist has gone further: the bishops "were not entitled to take a position or participate in the legal and political arena." Hence, he concluded, none could expect them resolutely and from the start to have opposed the National Socialist regime.[32]

To resolve these difficulties the Church periodically relies upon her theory of natural law, defined as an unwritten law of morality that is ascertainable by sound human reason. In his first encyclical to the world in 1939 Pope Pius XII declared, "It is certain that the radical and ultimate cause of the evils which we deplore in modern society is . . . the disregard, so common nowadays, and the forgetfulness of the natural law itself, which has its foundation in God, almighty Creator and Father of all, supreme and absolute Law-giver, all-wise and just Judge of human actions."[33] Many other churchmen and philosophers, too, have since urged a return to natural law in order to remedy the moral decay and ills of contemporary life. But can natural law provide the foundation for such a moral renewal?

Leaving aside the many strictly philosophical problems which this ethical theory raises, it is enough to observe here that natural law is abstract and vague to the point of making its application to concrete cases extremely difficult. It requires an authoritative interpreter, the Church. But this means that the gap between the abstract principles and the case at issue will be closed by answers tied up and almost predetermined by the interests of the Church as an institution. Individual Catholics turning to their Church for moral guidance in such matters as the legitimacy of non-co-operation with or resistance to political authority will receive replies that derive not from the unequivocal commands of natural law, but from the exigencies of Church tactics in a particular situation. The German Catholics in 1937 were told that resistance to the Nazi state was sinful; Spanish Catholics at the same time were urged to support the rebellion of General Franco against the Second Spanish Republic. In World War II Catholics serving in both of the warring factions were assured that they were fighting a just war. The institution of slavery was at one time defended by leading theologians as in consonance with natural law; today, in an age of colonial revolts and assaults upon all forms of discrimination, the Church stands for full equality. All these positions have been justified on the basis of the same natural law premises.

The conclusion is inescapable that this natural law ethic is essentially a shell able to house a great variety of moral responses. It is an instrument of the Church, argued a Catholic scholar, August M. Knoll, which has "the function of rationally articulating the passive and accommodating attitude of the Church and her teachings in all social and political questions."[34] Or, as a Protestant theologian,

John C. Bennett, has expressed it more succinctly, "Natural law plus prudence equals flexibility."[35]

Catholic political teaching relies on scripture, the teaching of the medieval scholastics and Papal pronouncements as a basis for one body of doctrine. As the Russian Communists never fail to support a new tactical move or change of policy by appropriate quotations from Marx and Lenin, so Catholic moral theology always invokes an authoritative source to buttress a new position. In the final analysis, then, this theology, at least as far as its teachings on man and his relationship to the state are concerned, represents an ideology. A student of Soviet politics has suggested some reasons for the transformation of Russian Marxism into ideology, and this explanation is largely applicable also to Catholic political thought:

> No doctrine, however elaborate or sophisticated, can provide answers and guidelines to fit all aspects of historical development. The shaping of events necessarily involves situations that are either unforeseen or dictate a logic of their own, even if initially fitting the theoretical assumptions. Doctrine is then "creatively" extended, new principles are extrapolated from the original set of assumptions, new generalizations crystallize, and, finally, the identity of ideology emerges. Ideology is, in effect, the link between theory and action.[36]

Catholic ideology, unlike Russian Marxism, is not primarily a guide to action, and it certainly is not a revolutionary creed; rather it serves mainly to provide support in the realm of ideas for policies designed to preserve and enhance the strength of the Church and to protect her mission as the channel of divine grace to man. But common to both ideologies is the claim of representing a fully consistent and essentially timeless body of doctrine which is universal in its appeal to all humanity. Both are in a process of constant change which is not so much a sign of corruption as a logical outgrowth of their inherent flexibility and adaptability; both provide a link between theory and practice.

Many of modern man's moral dilemmas are highly complex. No moral code, no matter how detailed or how much supplemented by casuistry, will be able to supply ready answers to all eventualities. In the last analysis, the individual's conscience will have to make the final decision, whether it be a question of assassinating a hated tyrant, of obeying or disobeying criminal orders of a legal superior, or using weapons of mass destruction. Which ethical system will best form man's conscience so as to inculcate a sense of justice and compassion is hard to determine. But one thing can perhaps be said: the conscience of man must remain free of entanglements with the interests of a religious institution. It cannot depend on an ideology.

When thousands of German anti-Nazis were tortured to death in Hitler's concentration camps, when the Polish intelligentsia was slaughtered, when hundreds of thousands of Russians died as a result of being treated as Slavic *Untermenschen,* and when 6,000,000 human beings were murdered for being "non-Aryan," Catholic Church officials in Germany bolstered the regime perpetrating these crimes. The Pope in Rome, the spiritual head and supreme moral teacher of the Roman Catholic Church, remained silent. In the face of these greatest of moral depravities which mankind has been forced to witness in recent centuries, the moral teachings of a Church, dedicated to love and charity, could be heard in no other form but vague generalities. "The problem is," as a forthright American Catholic has asked recently, "whether the Church, in its dealings with the Nazis, compromised its absolute spiritual essence; whether, faced with an absolute evil such as the Germans posed, it was right to think of 'reasons of state'."[37] Should not the answer be: Yes, the Church failed by not bearing witness to her moral essence; in the face of an upsurge of monstrous barbarism it was wrong to be guided by "reasons of state" or "raison d'église"?

"When God is hated, every basis of morality is undermined," Pope Pius XII asserted in 1939. "The denial of the fundamentals of morality had its origin in Europe, in the abandonment of that Christian teaching of which the Chair of Peter is the depository and exponent."[38] The debate over the relevance of an organized religion to human morality is of long standing and will not be ended by such categorical pronouncements. If mankind ever again is faced with moral challenges of the enormity presented by Hitler's regime of brute force, we must hope that it will have better moral guidance. Man, taught the Renaissance humanist Pico della Mirandola, has the power to degenerate into the lower, brutish forms of life. He also has the potential to reach the realms of wisdom and goodness. His destiny rests upon his own choice, and his choice alone. This is man's greatest burden. It is also his proudest distinction and glory.

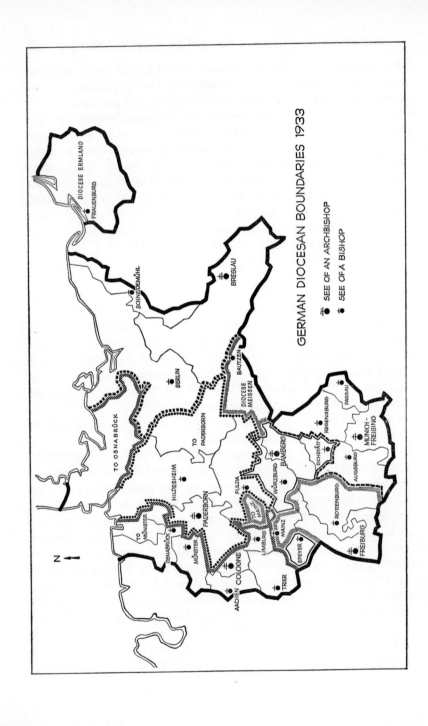

GERMAN DIOCESAN BOUNDARIES 1933

⊞ SEE OF AN ARCHBISHOP
✝ SEE OF A BISHOP

DIOCESE ERMLAND
FRAUENBURG

SCHNEIDEMÜHL

BRESLAU

TO OSNABRÜCK

BERLIN

BAUTZEN

DIOCESE MEISSEN

TO PADERBORN

REGENSBURG

PASSAU

HILDESHEIM

BAMBERG

EICHSTÄTT

MUNICH–FREISING

TO MÜNSTER

PADERBORN

FULDA

WÜRZBURG

AUGSBURG

OSNABRÜCK

MÜNSTER

MAINZ

ROTTENBURG

TO MAINZ

LIMBURG

AACHEN COLOGNE

SPEYER

FREIBURG

TRIER

N ←

Appendix: The German
Catholic Episcopate in September 1933

A. *Church Province Breslau*
   1. Adolf Cardinal Bertram, Archbishop of Breslau
   2. Maximilian Kaller, Bishop of Ermland
   3. Christian Schreiber, Bishop of Berlin
   4. Franz Hartz, Prelate Nullius* of Schneidemühl

B. *Church Province Munich and Freising*
   5. Michael Cardinal Faulhaber, Archbishop of Munich and Freising
   6. Joseph Kumpfmüller, Bishop of Augsburg
   7. Sigismund Felix von Ow-Felldorf, Bishop of Passau
   8. Michael Buchberger, Bishop of Regensburg

C. *Church Province Bamberg*
   9. Jakobus von Hauck, Archbishop of Bamberg
   10. Konrad von Preysing, Bishop of Eichstätt
   11. Ludwig Sebastian, Bishop of Speyer
   12. Matthias Ehrenfried, Bishop of Würzburg

D. *Church Province Cologne*
   13. Karl Joseph Cardinal Schulte, Archbishop of Cologne

* One having independent jurisdiction over a district not subject to a diocesan bishop.

14. Joseph Vogt, Bishop of Aachen
15. Antonius Hilfrich, Bishop of Limburg
16. Clemens August von Galen, Bishop of Münster
17. Wilhelm Berning, Bishop of Osnabrück
18. Franz Rudolf Bornewasser, Bishop of Trier

E. *Church Province Paderborn*
19. Kaspar Klein, Archbishop of Paderborn
20. Joseph Damian Schmitt, Bishop of Fulda
21. Nikolaus Bares, Bishop of Hildesheim

F. *Upper Rhenish Church Province*
22. Konrad Gröber, Archbishop of Freiburg i. Br.
23. Ludwig Maria Hugo, Bishop of Mainz
24. Johannes Baptista Sproll, Bishop of Rottenburg

25. Petrus Legge, Bishop of Meissen (exempt diocese*)

---

* A diocese not under the authority of any archbishop, but immediately subject to the Holy See.

Notes

The main sources of unpublished materials consulted for this study are:

1. *German Diocesan Archives*

   Aachen
   Eichstätt
   Hildesheim
   Limburg/Lahn
   Mainz
   Paderborn
   Passau
   Regensburg
   Trier

   Some of these archives, at the time of consultation by the author, had not yet been arranged. In such cases no specific files are cited.

2. *German and American State Archives*

   Bundesarchiv, Koblenz
   Politisches Archiv des Auswärtigen Amtes, Bonn

Archiv des Bundesministeriums für Justiz, Bonn
Hauptarchiv, Berlin
Bayerisches Geheimes Staatsarchiv, Munich
Bayerisches Allgemeines Staatsarchiv, Munich
Berlin Document Center
National Archives, Washington, D.C.

3. *Others*

Institut für Zeitgeschichte, Munich
Katholisches Judaeologisches Institut, Jetzendorf/Ilm
Wiener Library, London
YIVO Institute for Jewish Research, New York

The following abbreviations have been used:

AB   Amtsblatt
BA   Bundesarchiv
BGS   Bayerisches Geheimes Staatsarchiv
DA   Diocesan Archives
NA   National Archives
PA   Politisches Archiv des Auswärtigen Amtes

All diocesan gazettes are cited as AB *(Amtsblatt). The full titles are:*

Amtsblatt für die Diözese Augsburg
Amtsblatt für die Erzdiözese Bamberg
Amtsblatt des Bischöflichen Ordinariats Berlin
Amtsblatt für die Erzdiözese Freiburg
Amtsblatt des Bistums Limburg
Amtsblatt für die Erzdiözese München und Freising
Kirchlicher Anzeiger für die Diözese Hildesheim
Kirchlicher Anzeiger für die Erzdiözese Köln
Kirchlicher Amtsanzeiger für die Diözese Trier
Kirchliches Amtsblatt des Erzbischöflichen Ordinariats Breslau
Kirchliches Amtsblatt für das Bistum Ermland
Kirchliches Amtsblatt für die Erzdiözese Paderborn
Kirchliches Amtsblatt für die Diözese Münster
Kirchliches Amtsblatt für die Diözese Osnabrück
Kirchliches Amtsblatt für die Diözese Rottenburg
Oberhirtliches Verordnungsblatt für die Diözese Passau

Oberhirtliches Verordnungsblatt Speyer
Pastoralblatt des Bistums Eichstätt
Würzburger Diözesanblatt

Chapter 1

1. Among these was the *Katholische Jungmännerverband* (Association of Catholic Young Men) with about 390,000 members; the *Katholische Gesellenvereine* (Catholic Journeymen's Association) founded around 1845 by Adolf Kolping and now having 130,000 members; the *Deutsche Jugendkraft* (German Youth-Strength), a sports organization, with 250,000 members, and several others.

2. Karl Bachem, *Vorgeschichte, Geschichte und Politik der Deutschen Zentrumspartei*, vol. VIII (Cologne, 1931), p. 362.

3. The relevant part of the Cardinal's sermon was reprinted in the *Münchener Katholische Kirchenzeitung*, no. 31, July 31, 1932, p. 332.

4. Bachem, *op. cit.*, p. 259.

5. The figure of 60 per cent is that of Karl Dietrich Bracher, *Die Auflösung der Weimarer Republik*, 3rd rev. ed. (Villingen, 1960), p. 91, (hereafter cited as Bracher, *Auflösung*), who surmises that the percentage was highest among women and practicing Catholics.

6. *Der Rütlischwur*, I (1924), no. 1, p. 4.

7. J. Roth, *Katholizismus und Judenfrage* (Munich, 1923).

8. Gildis Engelhard, *Abt Schachleiter der deutsche Kämpfer* (Munich, 1941), pp. 26-33.

9. Michael Faulhaber, *Deutsches Ehrgefühl und katholisches Gewissen* (Munich, 1925), p. 13.

10. The complete German text of the party program can be found in Walther Hofer, ed., *Der Nationalsozialismus: Dokumente 1933-1945* (Frankfurt a.M., 1957) doc. 14, pp. 28-31 (hereafter cited as Hofer, *Nationalsozialismus*). I have used the English translation in Michael Oakeshott, ed., *The Social and Political Doctrines of Contemporary Europe* (New York, 1953), pp. 192-193.

11. In the largely Catholic town of Regensburg the Nazi vote increased from 4.1 to 16 per cent of all those cast. In the more rural constituency of Freising, also in Bavaria, the increase was from 4.9 to 12.2 per cent. These figures are taken from the detailed analysis of electoral developments between 1928 and 1932 in Bracher, *Auflösung*, 648-656.

12. Alfred Rosenberg, *Der Mythus des 20. Jahrhunderts* (Munich, 1934), p. 603.

13. Bracher, *Auflösung*, 647. The Catholic population of Breslau constituted close to a third of all the inhabitants of the city.

14. Adolf Bertram, *Die Stellung der katholischen Kirche zu Radikalismus und Nationalismus: Ein offenes Wort in ernster Stunde am Jahresschlusse 1930* (Breslau, 1930), pp. 7-8. The complete statement also appeared in the important organ of the Center party in Berlin, the daily newspaper *Germania* on December 31, 1930, and lengthy excerpts were brought by Jakob Nötges, S.J., *Nationalsozialismus und Katholizismus* (Cologne, 1931), a book highly recommended by the episcopate as late as May 1933.

15. The full text of both the inquiry of September 27, 1930, by the *Gauleitung's* press department and the reply of Dr. Mayer of September 30 is given in Alfons Wild, *Nationalsozialismus und Religion: Kann ein Katholik Nationalsozialist sein?* (Augsburg, 1930), pp. 10-11. This pamphlet reprinted a series of articles in the *Augsburger Postzeitung*, one of the best-known Catholic newspapers in Germany, of which Wild was editor-in-chief. Both documents are reprinted in the recently published collection by Hans Müller, *Kirche und Nationalsozialismus: Dokumente 1930-1935* (Munich, 1963), docs. 1-2, pp. 13-15 (hereafter cited as Müller, *Kirche und NS*).

16. Nötges, *op. cit.*, pp. 107-108.

17. *Ecclesiastica: Archiv für zeitgenössische Kirchengeschichte*, XI (1931), p. 138.

18. Cardinal Bertram's letter of December 2, 1930 on this issue and the response of the German bishops are discussed by Paul Schnitzer, "Die katholische Kirche und der Nationalsozialismus bis 1933" (unpublished Staatsexamenarbeit, University of Frankfurt a.M., 1960).

19. Undated mimeographed statement, DA Regensburg.

20. "Nationalsozialismus und Seelsorge: Pastorale Anweisung für den Klerus," special supplement to *AB Munich*, no. 4, February 10, 1931. The complete statement, subscribed to by the Archbishop of Munich and Freising and the Bishops of Augsburg, Passau, Regensburg, the Archbishop of Bamberg and the Bishops of Eichstätt, Speyer, Würzburg, is also to be found in *Ecclesiastica*, XI (1931), 117ff. A somewhat careless translation into English is given by James Donohoe, *Hitler's Conservative Opponents in Bavaria 1930-1945* (Leiden, 1961), pp. 32-34.

21. Wilhelm Corsten, ed., *Kölner Aktenstücke zur Lage der Katholischen Kirche in Deutschland 1933-1945* (Cologne, 1949), doc. 1, p. 1 (hereafter cited as Corsten, *Kölner Aktenstücke*). The statement was signed by the Archbishop of Cologne and the Bishops of Münster, Osnabrück, Trier, Limburg/Lahn and the Apostolic Administrator of Aachen.

22. Müller, *Kirche und NS*, doc. 8, p. 33.

23. *Ibid.*, p. 30. The lengthy pronouncement was signed by the Archbishop of Paderborn and the Bishops of Fulda and Hildesheim.

24. *Ibid.*, doc. 9, p. 36.

25. "Winke betr. Aufgaben der Seelsorger gegenüber glaubensfeindlichen Vereinigungen" in Wilhelm Corsten, ed., *Sammlung kirchlicher Erlasse:*

Verordnungen und Bekanntmachungen für die Erzdiözese Köln
(Cologne, 1929), p. 619.
26. Mimeographed, DA Aachen, folder "Fuldaer Konferenz 1931."
27. Göring's visit at the Vatican took place in early May 1931. The
Bavarian ambassador to the Holy See reported about it in a note to
the Bavarian premier, Heinrich Held, of May 11, 1931, which is reproduced by Ernst Deuerlein, *Das Reichskonkordat* (Düsseldorf, 1956),
pp. 294-295, n. 343.
28. Armin Roth, a district leader of the NSDAP in the Rhineland, for
example, in July 1931 resigned from the Party for that reason. Cf. his
Nationalsozialismus und Katholische Kirche (Munich, 1931).
29. DA Aachen, folder "Fuldaer Konferenz 1931."
30. *Protokoll der Verhandlungen der Fuldaer Bischofskonferenz vom 3.
bis zum 5. August 1931.* Als Manuskript gedruckt. Appendix 3, p. 24.
Unfortunately, none of these minutes are detailed enough to allow
us to know how individual bishops cast their vote.
31. Cf. Johannes Stark, *Nationalsozialismus und Katholische Kirche*
(Munich, 1931), p. 50.
32. Johannes Stark, *Nationalsozialismus und Katholische Kirche. II. Teil:
Antwort auf Kundgebungen der deutschen Bischöfe* (Munich, 1931),
p. 4.
33. Müller, *Kirche und NS*, 31.
34. Corsten, *Kölner Aktenstücke*, 2.
35. Müller, *Kirche und NS*, 36.
36. See, for example, the program of the *Katholischer Jungmännerverband
Deutschlands,* approved in a new version on June 22, 1931, in which
it said: "Im Herzen des Jungvolks muss der rechte Reichsgedanke
lebendig werden, muss der echte deutsche Wille leben. . . ."Cf. also
Friedrich Muckermann, S.J., "Die Reichsidee bei der katholischen
Jugend," *Der Gral,* XXVI (1932), 662-664.
37. The German original is more expressive of the flavor of the statement:
"Wir sind national bis auf die Knochen, deutsch durch und durch,
bereit zu jedem Opfer für Volk und Vaterland." *Leuchtturm: Monats-
schrift der Neudeutschen Jugend,* XXVI (1932), 65.
38. Zentralstelle des Volksvereins für das katholische Deutschland, *Der
Nationalsozialismus und die deutschen Katholiken* (M.-Gladbach,
[1931]), p. 48.
39. This saying was used by Bishop Buchberger of Regensburg in an article
"Wir Katholiken in den Kämpfen und Gefahren der Zeit," *Schönere
Zukunft,* VII/2 (1932), 976, where he argued that "socialism could not
be fought by socialism, not even when this socialism appears combined
with an exaggerated nationalism."
40. Cf. Erhard Schlund, O.F.M., "Religion, Christentum, Kirche und
Nationalsozialismus," *Gelbe Hefte,* VIII (1931), 115.
41. Friedrich Muckermann, S.J., "Die positive Überwindung des Nationalsozialismus," *Der Gral,* XXVI (1932), 269.

42. Nötges, *op. cit.*, p. 210.

43. Cf. Johannes Steiner, ed., *Propheten wider das Dritte Reich: Aus den Schriften des Dr. Fritz Gerlich und des Paters Ingbert Naab* (Munich, 1946); Erwein Freiherr von Aretin, *Fritz Michael Gerlich: Ein Märtyrer unserer Tage* (Munich, 1949). Dr. Gerlich was murdered on June 30, 1934. Father Naab escaped to Strasbourg, where he died in March 1935.

44. Cf. Anton Scharnagl, *Die völkische Weltanschauung und wir Katholiken* (Munich, 1932); Wilhelm Gerdemann und Heinrich Winfried, *Christenkreuz oder Hakenkreuz?* (Cologne, 1931); Hans Rost, *Christus nicht Hitler* (Westheim bei Augsburg, 1932).

45. Graf Clemens von Galen, *Die Pest des Laizismus* (Münster, 1932), pp. 40-56.

46. Pastoral letter for Lent 1920, quoted in Heinrich Lutz, *Demokratie im Zwielicht: Der Weg der deutschen Katholiken aus dem Kaiserreich in die Republik 1914-1925* (Munich, 1963), p. 82.

47. The phrase is that of Ernst Wolfgang Böckenförde in his important article "Der deutsche Katholizismus im Jahre 1933: Eine kritische Betrachtung," *Hochland,* LIII (1961), 233.

48. "Oberhirtliches Mahnwort zu den Reichstagswahlen," in Müller, *Kirche und NS,* doc. 14, p. 41.

49. Hans Kuth, "Quo vadis? Gedanken und Betrachtungen eines alten Katholiken," *Gelbe Hefte,* VIII (1932), 702-709.

50. *Protokoll der Verhandlungen der Fuldaer Bischofskonferenz vom 17. bis 19. August 1932.* Als Manuskript gedruckt. Appendix 2, p. 20.

51. Cf. Heinrich Brüning, "Ein Brief," *Deutsche Rundschau,* LXX (1947), 5; Josef Becker, "Brüning, Prälat Kaas und das Problem einer Regierungsbeteiligung der NSDAP 1930-1932," *Historische Zeitschrift,* CIVC (1963), 81-83, 89, 96.

52. Rudolf Morsey, "Die deutsche Zentrumspartei," in Erich Matthias and Rudolf Morsey, eds., *Das Ende der Parteien 1933* (Düsseldorf, 1960), p. 320 (hereafter cited as Morsey, *Zentrumspartei*). The story of the complicated negotiations is told in detail on pp. 315-324.

53. *Der Gerade Weg,* no. 37, September 11, 1932, in Steiner, *op. cit.*, p. 479.

54. Corsten, *Kölner Aktenstücke,* doc. 2, p. 3.

55. Wilhelm Maria Senn, *Halt. Katholizismus und Nationalsozialismus: Meine zweite Rede an den deutschen Katholizismus und—nach Rom* (Munich, 1932), p. 9.

56. *AB Munich,* no. 1, January 26, 1933, p. 1.

57. Konrad Heiden, *Der Führer: Hitler's Rise to Power,* trans. Ralph Manheim (Boston, 1944), p. 456. The enthronization of Dr. Gröber had taken place on June 20, 1932.

58. Walter Dirks, "Die Katholiken und die Diktatur." The article appeared at the end of the year 1932 in the periodical *Deutsche Republik.* It is reprinted in *Werkhefte: Zeitschrift für Probleme der Gesellschaft und des Katholizismus,* XVI (1962), 474-476.

Chapter 2

1. Norman H. Baynes, ed., *The Speeches of Adolf Hitler* (London, 1942), I, pp. 369-370.

2. Hjalmar Schacht, *My First Seventy-Six Years*, trans. Diana Pyke (London, 1955), p. 358.

3. Cf. Hitler's talk with Bishop Berning on April 26, 1933, U.S. Department of State, *Documents on German Foreign Policy 1918-1945*, Ser. C, vol. I (Washington, D.C., 1957), Doc. 188, p. 348; Franz von Papen, *Memoirs*, trans. Brian Connell (London, 1952), p. 261. On July 4, 1942, Hitler told his companions at the Supreme Army Headquarters that it had been a great mistake for Rosenberg to be drawn into polemics with the Catholic Church. Cf. *Hitler's Secret Conversations 1941-1944*, trans. Norman Cameron and R. H. Stevens (New York, 1953), p. 450.

4. H. Rauschning. *The Voice of Destruction* (New York, 1940), pp. 49-50.

5. Adolf Hitler, *Mein Kampf*, trans. under auspices of Alvin Johnson (New York, 1940), p. 366.

6. Rauschning, *op. cit.*, p. 53.

7. Cf. Rudolf Morsey, "Hitlers Verhandlungen mit der Zentrumsführung am 31. Januar 1933;" *Vierteljahrshefte für Zeitgeschichte*, IX (1961), pp. 182-194, and Morsey, *Zentrumspartei*, 339-344.

8. This was reported from Rome by the *Neue Zürcher Zeitung* on February 3. Cf. *ibid.*, p. 343, n. 26.

9. George N. Shuster, *Like a Mighty Army: Hitler versus Established Religion* (New York, 1935), p. 188.

10. Robert Leiber, S.J., "Pius XII†," *Stimmen der Zeit*, CLXIII (1958-1959), pp. 95-96.

11. Cf. Morsey, *Zentrumspartei*, 346.

12. In German: "Bolschewismus kann auch werden unter *nationalem* Vorzeichen." This "Bekenntnis und Mahnruf katholischer Volksverbände" was widely publicized in the Catholic press. It is reprinted in Müller, *Kirche und NS*, doc. 20, pp. 59-62.

13. Bertram to the bishops of the Fulda Conference, February 11, 1933, DA Limburg, 565/5 A.

14. Full text in Corsten, *Kölner Aktenstücke*, doc. 4, pp. 3-4; Müller, *Kirche und NS*, doc. 22, pp. 63-64.

15. Letter dated February 20, 1933, signature illegible, DA Trier, 59/26.

16. Full text in Müller, *Kirche und NS*, doc. 23, pp. 64-65. The Bishops of Würzburg and Trier also came out openly for the Catholic parties. Cf. E. F. J. Müller, ed., *Der katholische Episkopat in der nationalen Revolution Deutschlands: Dokumente und Materialien* (Fribourg, 1934), pp. 13-15 (hereafter cited as Müller, *Katholische Episkopat*).

17. *AB Munich*, no. 5, February 21, 1933, pp. 57-64.

18. Karl Speckner, *Die Wächter der Kirche: Ein Buch vom deutschen Episkopat* (Munich, n.d.), p. 29.

19. NA Washington, Micro-copy 580, roll 40. The document is part of the collection of the U.S. Document Center in Berlin, folder 243 I. Lossau's group appeared in public under the name *Katholische Vereinigung für nationale Politik*. Both groups had been in existence since the summer of 1932. Their numerical strength was probably small.

20. See the detailed analysis of election returns in Bavaria in Karl Dietrich Bracher, Wolfgang Sauer and Gerhard Schulz, *Die nationalsozialistische Machtergreifung*. 2nd rev. ed. (Cologne, 1962), pp. 117/2-121 (hereafter cited as Bracher-Sauer-Schulz, *NS Machtergreifung*).

21. BA Koblenz, R 43 II/1460, quoted by Morsey, *Zentrumspartei*, 354.

22. *Niederschrift der Konferenz der bayerischen Bischöfe in Regensburg am 20. April 1933*, p. 1 (DA Eichstätt).

23. Such stories were printed by the Roman News Agency *La Corrispondenza* on March 13; the Roman correspondent of the Paris paper *Le Temps* reported the rumors in an article published on March 16, and the Catholic *L'Avvenire d'Italia* on March 17. A number of German papers reprinted these accounts. Cf. Morsey, *Zentrumspartei*, 357, n. 28.

24. Alfons Nobel, *Der Katholik im neuen Reich* (Augsburg, 1933), p. 20.

25. To the question whether the bishops could have counted on the support of German Catholicism had they wanted to oppose the Nazis early in 1933, the answer of practically all observers is negative. Cf. Hans Buchheim, "Der deutsche Katholizismus im Jahre 1933: Eine Auseinandersetzung mit Ernst-Wolfgang Böckenförde," *Hochland*, LIII (1961), 510; Carl Amery, *Die Kapitulation oder Deutscher Katholizismus heute* (Reinbek bei Hamburg, 1963), pp. 32-33; Heinrich Portmann, *Kardinal von Galen: Ein Gottesmann seiner Zeit* (Münster, 1948), p. 89. This observation, of course, leaves unanswered the question to what extent the bishops themselves had contributed to this state of affairs by their ambivalent attitude to Nazism before 1933.

26. The full text of Bertram's letter of March 10, 1933, to Hindenburg is given by Hans Schlömer, *Die deutschen Bischöfe und der Nationalsozialismus: Zur Vorgeschichte der bischöflichen Erklärung vom 28. März 1933*. Als Manuskript gedruckt (distributed by the Katholische Nachrichtenagentur, n.d.), pp. 2-3.

27. *Ibid.*, p. 3. Original in BA Koblenz, R 43 II/174.

28. Bertram to the members of the Fulda Conference, March 19, 1933, DA Limburg, 561/2 A. The text of this circular was first published by Hans Müller in *Werkhefte*, XV (1961), pp. 260-261; it is reprinted in his *Kirche und NS*, doc. 28, pp. 73-75.

29. *Ibid.*, p. 75.

30. Cf. Bertram's letter to the episcopate of March 24, 1933, *ibid.*, doc. 29, p. 76.

31. The negotiations are discussed in detail by Morsey, *Zentrumspartei*, 358-363.

32. *Augsburger Postzeitung*, March 22, 1933, cited by Schlömer, *op. cit.*, p. 8.
33. Baynes, *op cit.*, I, pp. 371-372. I have used a more literal translation of the last few words further below, cf. n. 41. Morsey, *Zentrumspartei*, 429-431, gives in adjoining columns the Center party's demands and Hitler's public response.
34. Buchheim, *op cit.*, p. 503. Buchheim, in his *Glaubenskrise im Dritten Reich* (Stuttgart, 1953), p. 82, points out that the sentence about the rights of the churches in education was omitted from later official versions of Hitler's speech. It also was absent from the authorized translation. Cf. Ernst Christian Helmreich, *Religious Education in German Schools: An Historical Approach* (Cambridge, Mass., 1959), p. 334, n. 3.
35. Allan Bullock, *Hitler: A Study in Tyranny* (London, 1952), p. 245.
36. Bertram to the members of the Fulda Conference and Cardinal Faulhaber, March 24, 1933, DA Limburg, 561/2 A, printed by Müller, *Kirche und NS*, doc. 29, p. 76.
37. Bertram to the German bishops, March 25, 1933, *ibid.*, doc. 31 pp. 78-79.
38. Rudolf Morsey, ed., "Tagebuch 7.-20. April 1933 Ludwig Kaas†: Aus dem Nachlass von Prälat Ludwig Kaas," *Stimmen der Zeit*, CLXVI (1960), p. 426.
39. Bergen to the Foreign Ministry, March 16, 1933, BA Koblenz, R 43 II/174.
40. Robert Leiber, S.J., "Reichskonkordat und Ende der Zentrumspartei," *Stimmen der Zeit*, CLXVII (1960-61), p. 217.
41. "Weiter zu pflegen und auszugestalten" is the phrase in the German original. Cf. Morsey, *Zentrumspartei*, 363, n. 59.
42. Bertram to the German bishops, March 27, 1933, Müller, *Kirche und NS*, doc. 32, pp. 79-80.
43. Memo of Vicar General Riemer of Passau, April 1, 1933, DA Passau.
44. Cardinal Bertram's draft of March 24 in the files of the DA Limburg, 561/2 A, contains the handwritten suggested changes of Bishop Hilfrich of Limburg. Some of his suggestions were adopted. We do not know the authorship of the other changes. Hans Müller in his *Kirche und NS*, doc. 30, pp. 76-78, prints the draft and the final version side by side. I have noted the more important changes below.
45. Bertram had suggested "gratefully recognized." Bishop Hilfrich crossed out the expression of thanks.
46. Hilfrich, in the place of Bertram's formulation, which was kept, had suggested, "The episcopate trusts that the whole movement will conduct itself in accordance with these programmatic declarations." The important clause "Without repealing the condemnation . . ." was added at the suggestion of another bishop.
47. This short but important paragraph also represented an addition to Bertram's draft. It is symptomatic of the boldness with which some

Catholic writers after 1945 have falsified important documents from the Nazi period that this passage is omitted by Auxiliary Bishop Johann Neuhäusler, without the customary indication of an ellipsis, from the otherwise complete text of the declaration, set in quotation marks, in his book *Kreuz und Hakenkreuz* (Munich, 1946), II, pp. 50-51. Böckenförde, in his second *Hochland* essay, "Der Deutsche Katholizismus im Jahre 1933: Stellungnahme zu einer Diskussion," CIV (1962), 232, surmises that this sentence originated with Archbishop Gröber, who on March 25 had warned the Catholic youth organizations in his archdiocese against any conduct that might be interpreted as jeopardizing the public peace and order (*Kölnische Volkszeitung,* no. 81, March 25, 1933, p. 2).

48. Müller, *Kirche und NS,* p. 78. The declaration is also to be found in Corsten, *Kölner Aktenstücke,* doc. 6, pp. 4-5.

49. Cardinal Bertram's draft of March 25 is given by Schlömer, *op. cit.* pp. 11-12. The instructions were publicized in various diocesan gazettes. Cf. *AB Paderborn* of April 13, 1933, p. 30, also reprinted in Müller, *Kirche und NS,* doc. 33, pp. 80-81.

50. *AB Passau,* no. 7, April 12, 1933, supplement, pp. 3-4. The instructions are also to be found in Jakob Lenz, ed., *Sammlung kirchlicher Erlasse für die Diözese Passau* (Pasau, 1935), pp. 667-671.

51. BGS Munich, MA 1946/C1.

52. Cf. Müller, *Der katholische Episkopat,* 34; Waldemar Gurian, *Der Kampf um die Kirche im Dritten Reich* (Luzern, 1936), p. 93 (hereafter cited as Gurian, *Kampf;* the English edition is entitled *Hitler and the Christians* and was published in New York also in 1936); Paul Mikat, "Zur Kundgebung der Fuldaer Bischofskonferenz über die Nationalsozialistische Bewegung vom 28. März 1933," *Jahrbuch des Instituts für Christliche Sozialwissenschaft,* III (1962), 230, n. 51.

53. The unsigned lead article in the Catholic journal *Die Hilfe,* VIII (1933), 220, spoke of a "unilaterally declared peace"; cited by Morsey, *Zentrumspartei,* 369.

54. Nobel, *op cit.,* pp. 21-22.

55. Cf. Morsey, *Zentrumspartei,* 370.

56. Signed by the chairman August Weber, the declaration appeared in the *Kölnische Volkszeitung,* no. 88, April 1, 1933. It is reprinted in Müller, *Kirche und NS,* doc. 36, pp. 86-87.

57. "Kundgebung der Katholischen Arbeiterbewegung Deutschlands," *ibid.,* doc. 39, pp. 91-93.

58. Cf. Heinrich Roth, ed, *Katholische Jugend in der NS-Zeit unter besonderer Berücksichtigung des Katholischen Jungmännerverbandes: Daten und Dokumente* (Düsseldorf, 1959), p. 57 (hereafter cited as Roth, *Katholische Jugend*).

59. Müller, *Kirche und NS,* doc. 38, p. 90.

60. Cf. Helmreich, *op. cit.,* p. 155; Bracher-Sauer-Schulz, *NS Machtergreifung,* 328.

61. Cf. the minutes of the Prussian cabinet meeting on February 22, 1933, Hauptarchiv, Berlin, Rep. 90, Sitzungsprotokolle 1933.

62. Nikolaus Hilling, "Die kirchenpolitische Gesetzgebung des National-sozialismus von 1933-1945," *Archiv für katholisches Kirchenrecht,* CXXIV (1949-50), 6.

63. *AB Passau,* no. 10, May 6, 1933, pp. 50-51.

64. Cf. Jakob Overmans, S.J., "Um Demokratie" and Max Pribilla, S.J., "Verfassungstreue;" both in *Stimmen der Zeit,* CXXV (1933), 18-26 and 57-61 respectively.

65. Franziskus Stratmann, O.P., "Der Christ und sein politischer Gegner," *Der Friedenskämpfer,* IX (1933), 89.

66. Cf. Hans Müller, "Zur Interpretation der Kundgebung der Fuldaer Bischofskonferenz vom 28. März 1933," *Werkhefte,* XVI (1962), 199; Müller, *Kirche und NS,* doc. 35, pp. 84-85.

67. Hans Buchheim in his *Hochland* critique of Böckenförde (August 1961, p. 512) interprets this section of the bishops' declaration as being directed against the illegal terror of the S.A. Böckenförde in his reply (*Hochland,* February 1962, pp. 231-232) to my mind has convincingly shown that the passage was addressed to Catholics. See also Müller, *Werkhefte,* XVI (1962), 197-199.

68. No. 16, April 19, 1933, p. 243.

69. Bertram to Hindenburg, April 6, 1933. BA Koblenz, R 43 II/954, printed by Müller, *Kirche und NS,* doc. 40, pp. 93-94.

70. The statement of April 11, 1933, is reprinted in Corsten, *Kölner Aktenstücke,* doc. 7, p. 5.

71. The proclamation of Bertram was published on April 13, that of Gröber on April 15, 1933. They are both to be found in Müller, *Kirche und NS,* docs. 42-43, pp. 96-97.

72. See the correspondence between Himmler and Pohl of January 1938 over the exclusion of Gröber in folders 243 I and 245, NA Washington, Microcopy 580, rolls 40 and 42 respectively. For the meaning of "promoting membership" in the S.S. see the article of Hans Buchheim, "Fördernde Mitgliedschaft bei der SS" in *Gutachten des Instituts für Zeitgeschichte* (Munich, 1958), p. 350.

73. Kogon soon became disillusioned and as a convinced anti-Nazi was imprisoned in the concentration camp at Buchenwald, about which he wrote the classic work, *Der S.S. Staat.*

74. Text of the appeal in BA Koblenz, R 43 II/174.

75. Franz von Papen, *Appell an das deutsche Gewissen: Reden zur nationalen Revolution,* New series (Oldenburg, 1933), p. 71.

76. BA Koblenz, R 43 II/174.

77. *Kölnische Volkszeitung,* no. 107, April 21, 1933, cited by Morsey, *Zentrumspartei,* 379.

78. BGS Munich, MA 1957/VII-1-7-I.

79. "Protokoll der Konferenz der Diözesanvertreter in Berlin, 25. und 26. April 1933," Mimeographed, DA Limburg, 561/2 A. The minutes are

printed in Müller, *Kirche und NS*, doc. 48, pp. 104-120, and this pagination is used here.

80. *Ibid.*, p. 106.
81. *Ibid.*, p. 107.
82. *Ibid.*
83. *Ibid.*, pp. 108-109.
84. *Ibid.*, pp. 109-110.
85. *Ibid.*, p. 114.
86. *Ibid.*, pp. 115-116.
87. *Ibid.*, p. 117. We have two accounts of this parley. One in the minutes of the conference that had suggested these meetings with various ministers, and the other in the files of the German Foreign Office. Both are rather similar in content and may well be based on a jointly agreed-upon draft.
88. The governmental memo about the meeting begins its account at this point. The German text is to be found in PA Bonn, II, Vatikan, Politik 17, Bd. 2. An English translation is given in *Documents on German Foreign Policy*, Ser. C, vol. I, Doc. 188, pp. 347-348. For the most part, I have used the report of Berning and Steinmann to the above-mentioned conference, for it is somewhat more detailed and also gives us their reactions to Hitler's comments.
89. This is the wording of the official memo (English version, p. 348). Berning reports Hitler saying, "For this reason I have turned against Ludendorff and broken company with him, and for the same reason I reject the book of Rosenberg" (Müller, *Kirche und NS*, 118).
90. *Ibid.*, pp. 119-120.
91. Bertram to Hitler, April 16, 1933, BA Koblenz, R 43 II/954. The same file contains a letter of April 24 by Cardinal Faulhaber to Hitler, which in the name of the Bavarian Bishops' Conference puts forth much the same arguments in defense of the Catholic youth organizations. Both are to be found in Müller, *Kirche und NS*, docs. 44-45, pp. 97-100.
92. Hitler to Bertram, April 28, 1933, *Documents on German Foreign Policy*, Ser. C, vol. I, Doc. 196, p. 361. The German original is in PA Bonn, Pol. II 316/2, printed in Müller, *Kirche und NS*, doc. 50, pp. 122-125.
93. Bertram to Hitler, May 6, 1933, BA Koblenz, R 43 II/954, reproduced in Müller, *Kirche und NS*, doc. 54, pp. 127-130.
94. Copy of address in DA Passau.
95. *AB Munich*, no. 8, May 5, 1933, p. 101. The pastoral letter is reprinted in Müller, *Kirche und NS*, doc. 56, pp. 130-136.
96. *AB Osnabrück*, no. 41, May 16, 1933; *AB Münster*, no. 10, May 22, 1933; *AB Cologne*, May 26, 1933; *AB Paderborn*, May 29, 1933. Reprinted in Corsten, *Kölner Aktenstücke*, doc. 8, p. 5, and Müller, *Kirche und NS*, doc. 60, p. 139.

97. Letter of Father Erhard Schlund, O.F.M., to Vicar General Riemer of Passau, May 27, 1933, DA Passau.
98. Roth, *Katholische Jugend*, 59.

Chapter 3

1. See Ernst Deuerlein, *Das Reichskonkordat: Beiträge zur Vorgeschichte, Abschluss und Vollzug des Konkordats zwischen dem Heiligen Stuhl und dem Deutschen Reich vom 20. Juli 1933* (Düsseldorf, 1956), pp. 1-105 (hereafter cited as Deuerlein, *Reichskonkordat*); Rudolf Morsey, "Zur Vorgeschichte des Reichskonkordates aus den Jahren 1920 und 1921," *Zeitschrift der Savigny-Stiftung für Rechtsgeschichte,* Kanonistische Abteilung, CXXV (1958), 237-267, and the same author's "Zur Problematik und Geschichte des Reichskonkordats," *Neue Politische Literatur,* V (1960), 1-30; Georg Schreiber, *Zwischen Demokratie und Diktatur* (Münster, 1949), especially pp. 75-95 and 114-143.
2. The full text of these three concordats can be found in Hans Liermann, *Kirchen und Staat,* vol. I (Munich, 1954) or in Joseph Wenner, *Reichskonkordat und Länderkonkordate,* 6th rev. ed. (Paderborn, 1957).
3. BGS Munich, Ges. Päpstl. Stuhl 1008, No. 720-723, full text printed in Kupper, "Zur Geschichte des Reichskonkordats," *Stimmen der Zeit,* CLXXI (1962), 31-32.
4. On the friendship between Kaas and Pacelli, see also Arthur Wynen, *Ludwig Kaas: Aus seinem Leben und Wirken* (Trier, 1953), which book, however, is inaccurate in a number of important details.
5. Memorandum by the Holy See of April 23, 1931, PA Bonn, Vatikan No. 8b Militärseelsorge, Bd. 3, full text given by Kupper, *Stimmen der Zeit,* CLXXI (1962), 33.
6. Schleicher to Klein, July 13, 1932, *ibid.,* pp. 35-37.
7. The contents of this letter is summarized by Kupper, *ibid.,* pp. 28-29.
8. Pro memoria of the Holy See, October 25, 1932, PA Bonn, II Vatikan Pol. 16, Bd. 4; printed by Deuerlein, *Reichskonkordat,* 89-90, and Kupper, *op. cit.,* pp. 37-38.
9. Pacelli to Papen, October 29, 1932, *ibid.,* pp. 39-40.
10. The account of Orsenigo's visit to Papen is based on a report of Bergen from the Vatican dated October 28, 1932. This report, as well as the undated memo of Von Bülow, are printed by Kupper, *ibid.,* pp. 39-40.
11. Both documents, dated November 25, 1932, are given by Kupper, *ibid.,* pp. 40-42.
12. The draft note of the Ministry of Interior is printed by Kupper, *ibid.,* pp. 42-44.
13. *Ibid.,* pp. 47-50.
14. Menshausen to Bergen, March 3, 1933, PA Bonn, Botschaft Vatikan,

Militärseelsorge 8b, Bd. 4. Menshausen speaks of discussing the matter "with the great and good friend," but from the context it is clear that this friend is Kaas. Eupen-Malmedy is referred to as "E.M."

15. Notation of Menshausen of May 2, 1933 on another draft submitted by the Ministry of Defense, quoted in Kupper, *Stimmen der Zeit,* CLXXI (1962), 30-31.

16. PA Bonn, Politik 2 No. 1 Vatikan, Geheim; NA Washington, Microcopy T-120, roll 2902, frames E460619-20.

17. Memo of Menshausen of April 7, 1933, *Documents on German Foreign Policy,* Ser. C, vol. I, doc. 145, pp. 266-268.

18. *Memoirs,* 278.

19. Papen to Bergen, April 7, 1934, *Documents on German Foreign Policy,* C, II, doc. 383, p. 715 (because of a misprint the date mentioned at the end of the quoted passage is erroneously given as January 1932).

20. See e.g., the beginning of the encyclical *Mit Brennender Sorge* of Pope Pius XI issued in March, 1937 or the address of Pope Pius XII to the College of Cardinals on June 2, 1945, both in Corsten, *Kölner Aktenstücke,* at pp. 175 and 316 respectively.

21. See his articles cited earlier in *Stimmen der Zeit,* CLXIII (1958-59), 81-100, and CLXVII (1960-61), 213-223. Kupper (*ibid.,* CLXIII, 285) also reports on a lengthy talk with Father Leiber dealing with this question. This writer in several attempts found Father Leiber unwilling to meet for a conversation or to reply to or even to acknowledge letters of inquiry.

22. See n. 17, *supra.*

23. Quoted in Deuerlein, *Reichskonkordat,* 110. The German phrase "in seinem Auftrage" could also be translated as "on his behalf."

24. Unpublished deposition "Zur Rechtsgültigkeit des Reichskonkordats," June 15, 1956, quoted in Alfons Kupper, "Zur Geschichte des Reichskonkordats," *Stimmen der Zeit,* CLXIII (1958-59), 282-283.

25. See Kupper, *ibid.,* p. 283, and Karl Otmar Freiherr von Aretin, "Das Ende der Zentrumspartei und der Abschluss des Reichskonkordats am 20. Juli 1933," *Frankfurter Hefte,* XVII (1962), 242.

26. II Besetzte Gebiete 414/6, Pol. Angelegenheiten Eupen Malmedy; NA Washington, Microcopy T-120, roll 3364, frames E596087-88.

27. BA Koblenz, R 43 I/1461, cited by Morsey, *Zentrumspartei,* 355-356.

28. Cf. *ibid.,* pp. 363-364, n. 59.

29. Memo of Von Bülow, April 4, 1933, PA Bonn, Büro des Reichsaussenministers, Eupen-Malmedy, Bd. 2.

30. Cf. Schlömer, *op. cit.,* p. 16.

31. Morsey, *Zentrumspartei,* 372.

32. Diary entry of Kaas on April 8, 1933, quoted by Morsey, *Stimmen der Zeit,* CLXVI (1960), 426.

33. This point is also made by Karl Aretin, *op. cit.,* p. 241.

34. BA Koblenz, R 43 II/174, quoted in Morsey, *Zentrumspartei,* 371.

35. See n. 17, *supra*.

36. *Ibid.*, p. 268. The above hypothesis as to who, in the spring of 1933, took the initiative for the start of new negotiations for a concordat agrees with the conjectures of Rudolf Morsey when in 1960 he published portions of Kaas's diary in *Stimmen der Zeit*, CLXVI (1960), 425. Dr. Morsey told me on January 25, 1962, that he was no longer sure of this hypothesis and that he was more inclined now to accept Papen's authorship. That the first move was made by the Vatican is also the conclusion of Walter Conrad, adviser on church matters in the Ministry of the Interior until February 1934. See his *Der Kampf um die Kanzeln: Erinnerungen und Dokumente aus der Hitlerzeit* (Berlin, 1957), p. 34.

37. Note of Menshausen of April 7, see n. 17 *supra*.

38. *Ibid.*

39. Cf. Morsey, *Zentrumspartei*, 375, n. 44.

40. Morsey, *Stimmen der Zeit*, CLXVI (1960), 426.

41. *Ibid.*, p. 427.

42. See on this point the suggestive remarks of Karl Aretin, *op. cit.*, pp. 237-239.

43. Clive to Foreign Minister, April 22, 1933, *Documents on British Foreign Policy: 1919-1939*, Ser. II, vol. V (London, 1956), doc. 85, p. 156.

44. Oral communication to Kupper, *Stimmen der Zeit*, CLXIII (1959), 289.

45. There is the possibility that Kaas was in danger of arrest because of his involvement with the recently bankrupted Kölner Görreshaus Company, Cf. Morsey, *Zentrumspartei*, 371, n. 26 and literature cited there.

46. Papen, *Memoirs*, 279.

47. BGS Munich, MA 1957/VII-1-7, Bd. 1.

48. *Ibid.*

49. Cf. Morsey, *Zentrumspartei*, 375, n. 44; Kupper, *Stimmen der Zeit*, CLXIII (1959), 286.

50. Bergen to the Foreign Ministry, April 18, 1933, *Documents on German Foreign Policy*, C, I, doc. 162, p. 298.

51. The German text of these communications has been published by Morsey, "Briefe zum Reichskonkordat: Ludwig Kaas—Franz von Papen," *Stimmen der Zeit*, CLXVII (1960-61), 11-30.

52. Papen to Bergen, May 26, 1933, *Documents on German Foreign Policy*, C, I, doc. 263, pp. 491-492.

53. *Protokoll der Verhandlungen der Bischofskonferenz in Fulda vom 30. Mai bis 1. Juni 1933*. Als Manuskript gedruckt, p. 3.

54. Telegram of Papen to Bergen of June 16, 1933, *Documents on German Foreign Policy*, C, I, doc. 319, p. 574.

55. Handwritten addition to Papen's telegram to Bergen of June 23, 1933, *ibid.*, doc. 333, p. 594. On June 6 Bergen informed the Foreign Ministry that he had learned of the intention of the episcopate to

dispatch Cardinal Bertram to Rome, but this information may have been erroneous (*ibid.*, p. 573).

56. Papen to Bergen, June 16, 1933, *ibid.*, doc. 319, p. 573.
57. Cf. Morsey, *Zentrumspartei,* 396-397.
58. Faulhaber to the Bavarian Council of Ministers, July 5, 1933, BGS Munich, MA 1957/VII-1-8-I.
59. See for example the report in the London *Times* of June 13, 1933 on the disturbances at the *Gesellentag* in Munich.
60. Bergen to the Foreign Ministry, June 30, 1933, *Documents on German Foreign Policy,* C, I, doc. 341, p. 611.
61. Bergen to Neurath, July 3, 1933, *ibid.*, doc. 351, p. 635.
62. Deuerlein, *Reichskonkordat,* 255, reports Archbishop Gröber relaying this information of the Center party's leader's objections to the Concordat. Cf. Morsey, *Zentrumspartei,* 406, n. 9.
63. Report of Papen to the Cabinet on July 14, 1933, *Documents on German Foreign Policy,* C, I, doc. 362, p. 652.
64. Bergen to Neurath, July 3, 1933, *ibid.*, doc. 351, p. 635.
65. Papen to Hitler, July 2, 1933, *ibid.*, doc. 347, pp. 623-624.
66. Telegram of H. Rumbold to Sir J. Simon of June 30, 1933, *Documents on British Foreign Policy,* II, V, doc. 227, p. 383.
67. Cf. Morsey, *Zentrumspartei,* 397.
68. Entry for July 7, 1933, quoted in *ibid.*, p. 443.
69. *Stimmen der Zeit,* CLXVII (1960-61), 222; Karl Dietrich Bracher, "Nationalsozialistische Machtergreifung und Reichskonkordat: Ein Gutachten," in Friedrich Giese et. al., eds., *Der Konkordatsprozess* (Munich, 1958), III, 999 (hereafter cited as Bracher, *Gutachten*).
70. Papen to Neurath, July 3, 1933, *Documents on German Foreign Policy,* C, I, doc. 350, p. 634.
71. Letter of Papen to Hitler of July 2, 1933, *ibid.*, doc. 347, p. 624.
72. Oral communication of Joos to Morsey (*Zentrumspartei,* 398).
73. The draft Concordat with Neurath's changes is to be found in *Documents on German Foreign Policy,* C, I, doc. 348, pp. 625-633.
74. A description of the talks of July 6-8, based on a set of notes made by Buttmann, can be found in Deuerlein, *Reichskonkordat,* 117-119.
75. Bergen to the Foreign Ministry, July 8, 1933, *Documents on German Foreign Policy,* C, I, doc. 356, p. 642.
76. Both the statement that was finally issued and the earlier draft of Buttmann are given by Conrad, *op. cit.*, pp. 42-43.
77. Papen, *Memoirs,* 281.
78. Minutes of the Cabinet meeting of July 14, 1933, *Documents on German Foreign Policy,* C, I, doc. 362, p. 652. On July 4 Mussolini had received Ulrich von Hassell, the German Ambassador in Rome, and had charged him "to say to the Chancellor that in Germany's present isolated position it would be, in his opinion, an immense moral victory to persuade the Vatican to conclude a concordat. One would

thereby win over Catholic opinion throughout the world" (*ibid.*, doc. 352, p. 636).

79. *Ibid.*, doc. 362, pp. 652-653.
80. Cf. Kupper, *Stimmen der Zeit*, CLXIII (1959), 362-363. Kupper, by mistake, refers to Rust as *Reichsminister*. This title he assumed only on April 30, 1934.
81. The text of this written understanding is given by Conrad, *op. cit.*, pp. 44-45.
82. I am using throughout the English translation of Sidney Z. Ehler and John B. Morrall, who reproduce the text of the Concordat in their anthology, *Church and State Through the Centuries* (London, 1954), pp. 487-496. Their translation is smoother than that to be found in *Documents on German Foreign Policy*, C, I, doc. 371, pp. 669-679. For the German text see Deuerlein, *Reichskonkordat*, 332-346, where the 1933 text is printed alongside the corresponding provisions of the first draft of a Reichskonkordat, the so-called "Delbrück-Entwurf."
83. Cf. Rudolf Jestaedt, "Das Reichskonkordat vom 20. Juli 1933 in der nationalsozialistischen Staats- und Verwaltungspraxis unter besonderer Berücksichtigung des Artikels 1," *Archiv für Kirchenrecht*, CXXIV (1949-50), 370-374.
84. Cf. Joseph H. Kaiser, *Die politische Klausel der Konkordate* (Berlin, 1949), pp. 29-72.
85. *Memoirs*, 280. See also the discussion in Helmreich, *op. cit.*, pp. 157-159.
86. Werner Weber, "Das Reichskonkordat in der deutschen Rechtsentwicklung," *Zeitschrift der Akademie für deutsches Recht*, V (1938), 535.
87. Complete text of the Annex in *Documents on German Foreign Policy*, C, I, doc. 371, pp. 678-679.
88. Kaas to Papen, June 11, 1933, printed by Morsey, *Stimmen der Zeit*, CLXVII (1960-61), 29.
89. *Documents on German Foreign Policy*, series D, vol. VII, doc. 432, p. 426.
90. One of the very few persons to hear of the existence of a secret annex was the English Catholic writer William Teeling. He did not know its content, but in his book *Crisis for Christianity* (London, 1939) he speculated that this secret clause stood in the way of the renunciation of the Concordat by both Hitler and the Vatican.
91. The text of the talk was published under the title "Zum Reichskonkordat" in the quarterly of the Catholic academicians' association, *Der katholische Gedanke*, VI (1933), 331-336.
92. *Völkischer Beobachter*, no. 205 of July 23, 1933, cited by *Ecclesiastica*, XIII (1933), 325.
93. Note of July 27, 1933, cited by Kupper, *Stimmen der Zeit*, CLXIII (1959), 366, n. 45.
94. "Ancora a Proposito del Concordato tra la Santa Sede a la Germania,"

Osservatore Romano, no. 174, July 27, 1933; quoted in Deuerlein, *Reichskonkordat*, 128. The full original text of both articles is given on pp. 304-306.

95. *Augsburger Postzeitung*, no. 173, July 30, 1933, cited *ibid.*, p. 131. The authorship of Buttmann is revealed in a letter of Menshausen to Klee of July 29, 1933. Cf. Kupper, *Stimmen der Zeit*, CLXIII (1959), 366.

96. Report of Mr. Kirkpatrick of August 19, 1933. *Documents on British Foreign Policy*, II, V, doc. 342, p. 524.

97. The Foreign Ministry here played the mediator between the Ministry of the Interior and the Vatican. Cf. Kupper, *Stimmen der Zeit*, CLXIII (1959), 367-370.

98. Pacelli's complaints were embodied in a "Short Note" to be found in *Documents on German Foreign Policy*, C, I, doc. 418, p. 785.

99. Bertram to Pacelli, September 2, 1933, DA Passau; also printed in Müller, *Kirche und NS*, doc. 87, 185-186.

100. *Ibid.*, pp. 186-190.

101. *Documents on German Foreign Policy*, C, I, doc. 422, p. 789.

102. Pacelli to Bertram, September 10, 1933, DA Passau.

103. Sermon in the Cathedral of Munich on February 14, 1937, "Das Reichskonkordat—Ja oder Nein?" in *Münchener Kardinalspredigten*, 3rd series (Munich, 1937), pp. 4-5.

104. Gerhard Ritter, *The German Resistance*, trans. R. T. Clark (London, 1958), p. 54.

105. Amery, *op. cit.*, p. 32.

106. Leiber, *Stimmen der Zeit*, CLXVII (1960-61), 220-221.

107. Bracher, *Gutachten*, 1021.

108. Waldemar Gurian, "Hitler's Undeclared War on the Catholic Church," *Foreign Affairs*, XVI (1938), 268.

109. On February 17, 1938, quoted in Deuerlein, *Reichskonkordat*, 238.

110. For a brief summary of the issues in this so-called *Konkordatsprozess* of 1955-1957 see Helmreich, *op. cit.*, pp. 239-240. Bracher's *Gutachten*, referred to earlier, was prepared for this trial.

111. *Rückblick und Ausschau: Hirtenschreiben vom 8. Mai 1945* (Konstanz, 1945), p. 9.

112. Conrad Gröber, ed., *Handbuch der religiösen Gegenwartsfragen* (Freiburg i. Br., 1937), p. 362.

Chapter 4

1. Hans Müller, "Die Fuldaer Bischofskonferenz vom 30. Mai 1933," *Werkhefte*, XVII (1963), 185. Müller has had access to a handwritten set of minutes in the archdiocesan archives in Breslau (Wroclaw) which is a little more detailed than the usually cryptic printed minutes.

2. Text in Müller, *Kirche und NS*, doc. 62, pp. 143-150.

3. *Ibid.*, doc. 61, pp. 139-142, and doc. 63, pp. 150-152.
4. *Ibid.*, pp. 140-141.
5. *Ibid.*, pp. 150-152.
6. *Ibid.*, doc. 64, p. 153.
7. Neuhäusler, who edits the joint pastoral letter in a way that completely changes its meaning, leaves out the words "On the other hand" and does so, again, without the customary use of the ellipsis (*op. cit.*, p. 53). This hides the existence of the preceding part of that section, which he omits. Hans Müller (in a review article "Zur Behandlung des Kirchenkampfes in der Nachkriegsliteratur," *Politische Studien*, XII [1961], 474-481), has counted twenty-one cuts in Neuhäusler's reproduction of the text of this pastoral letter: ten of these passages very clearly are omitted because they do not fit the thesis of Neuhäusler's book; nine times omissions in the text are not indicated; in five instances the wording is actually altered. Typical of the unsatisfactory character of much American scholarship in this area, C. J. Friedrich and Z. K. Brzezinski in their standard work *Totalitarian Dictatorship and Autocracy* (Cambridge, Mass., 1956), repeatedly rely on Neuhäusler's data and recommend the work as "the most detailed story of individual and group efforts of Catholics to resist the Nazification of the Church" (p. 324, n. 124).
8. Müller, *Kirche und NS*, 154.
9. *Ibid.*, pp. 155-156.
10. *Ibid.*, sec. 4, p. 156.
11. *Ibid.*, secs. 5 and 6, p. 157.
12. *Ibid.*, secs. 7 and 9, pp. 158-159.
13. *Ibid.*, p. 160.
14. Robert D'Harcourt, *The German Catholics*, trans. Reginald J. Dingle (London, 1939), p. 84.
15. *Protokoll der Verhandlungen der Bischofskonferenz in Fulda vom 30. Mai bis 1. Juni 1933*, appendix 2, p. 18.
16. Report of June 21, 1933, BGS Munich, MA 1957/VII-1-7-I.
17. Manuscript entitled "Rechtsstaat," p. 2, Nachlass Schiffer, Hauptarchiv Berlin quoted in Böckenförde, *Hochland*, LIV (1962), 236.
18. Reported in *Kölnische Volkszeitung*, no. 171, June 27, 1933, quoted in Müller, *Katholische Episkopat*, 78.
19. BA Koblenz, R 43 II/174.
20. Report in *Münchener Katholische Kirchenzeitung*, no. 27, July 2, 1933. p. 282.
21. A summary report on this conversation that took place on May 27, 1933, is to be found in BGS Munich, MA 1957/VII-1-30.
22. Count Quadt-Isny, a leading member of the Bavarian People's party and Minister of Economic Affairs in the new Bavarian government, on May 25 was able to report to the Bavarian premier, Ludwig Siebert, that the Cardinal had promised to ask for the resignation of Muhler (BGS Munich, MA 1957/VII-1-8-I).

23. Letter of Siebert, June 18, 1933, *ibid.* The suspension was lifted by Rome in September. The Bavarian ambassador to the Holy See reported on September 5 that this had been done mainly on account of Faulhaber's intervention (BGS Munich, MA 1957/VII-1-33).
24. Wagner to Faulhaber, June 11, 1933, BGS Munich, MA 1957/VII-1-8-I.
25. Faulhaber to Hitler, Siebert, Wagner, Himmler, June 12, 1933, *ibid.*
26. Faulhaber to Wagner, June 12, 1933, *ibid.*
27. *Saarbrücker Landes-Zeitung,* July 2, 1933, clipping in DA Passau.
28. *AB Speyer,* no. 9, June 29, 1933, pp. 81-82. The instruction was dated June 24, 1933.
29. *AB Freiburg,* no. 17, June 30, 1933, p. 85.
30. See Müller, *Katholische Episkopat,* 79; *AB Passau,* no. 16, July 7, 1933; report on the "Paderborner Stadtkonferenz" of July 19, 1933, DA Paderborn, XXII, 4.
31. On the last days of the party see Karl Schwend, "Die Bayerische Volkspartei" in Matthias and Morsey, eds., *Das Ende der Parteien,* pp. 504-509.
32. These negotiations are described by Morsey, *Zentrumspartei,* 399-403.
33. BA Koblenz, R 43 II/176.
34. Morsey, *Zentrumspartei,* 406. According to Monsignor Schreiber (*op. cit.,* p. 22, n. 10), Bishop Berning's acceptance of service in Göring's government had the approval of Pope Pius XI.
35. Bertram to Hitler, July 22, 1933, BA Koblenz, R 43 II/176; full text printed by Kupper, *Stimmen der Zeit,* CLXIII (1959), 367, and Müller, *Kirche und NS,* doc. 76, pp. 169-170.
36. Faulhaber to Hitler, July 24, 1933, *ibid.,* doc. 77, p. 170.
37. *Ibid.,* p. 171.
38. *Schulthess' Europäischer Geschichtskalender,* LXXVI (1933), 186 (hereafter cited as *Schulthess*); also reprinted in Müller, *Kirche und Ns,* doc. 78, p. 171.
39. *Germania,* no. 222, August 14, 1933.
40. *Ibid.,* no. 229, August 21, 1933; full text in Müller, *Kirche und NS,* doc. 85, pp. 181-184.
41. *Völkischer Beobachter,* no. 236, August 24, 1933.
42. *Germania,* no. 275, October 6, 1933.
43. The plan of the *Gauleitung* was submitted for Hitler's approval on August 23 (BA Koblenz, R 43 II/174). The *Katholische Kirchenblatt für das Bistum Berlin* on September 24 carried a detailed report on the special service. Both the plan and the report are printed by Müller, *Kirche und NS,* docs. 93-94, pp. 200-206.
44. BA Koblenz, R 43 II/176.
45. *Die Wacht,* XIX (1933), 260ff., quoted in Müller, *Kirche und NS,* doc. 88, p. 192.
46. *Ibid.,* doc. 84, pp. 180-181.
47. "Wir Neudeutschen bejahen also die Totalität unseres Staates und die Totalität unserer Religion. Unser tiefstes Problem und Anliegen ist,

beide Totalitäten richtig zu einen und ineinanderzufügen. . . ." Complete text in *ibid.*, doc. 83, pp. 177-180 (quoted passage at p. 179).

48. Bergen to Papen, June 1, 1933. *Documents on German Foreign Policy,* C, I, doc. 278, p. 507.

49. Germania, no. 255, September 16, 1933, and *Badischer Beobachter,* no. 254, September 22, 1933, cited by Müller, *Katolische Episkopat,* 76-77.

50. *Badischer Beobachter,* no. 272, October 10, 1933, *ibid.*, pp. 72-73.

51. "Kardinal Bertram an die Theologiestudenten," *Ostdeutsches Pastoralblatt,* LIII (1933), 170.

52. Joseph Lortz, *Katholischer Zugang zum Nationalsozialismus kirchengeschichtlich gesehen* (Münster, 1933), pp. 9-15.

53. *Ibid.*, p. 26. Lortz provided the example by joining the Nazi party on May 1, 1933. After the war Lortz claimed to have left the Party in 1936, but his file at the Berlin Document Center has no record of this step.

54. Michael Schmaus, *Begegnungen zwischen katholischem Christentum und nationalsozialistischer Weltanschauung,* 2nd ed. (Münster, 1934), pp. 7, 23, 42.

55. *Ibid.*, p. 29. Professor Schmaus, too, eventually came to regret his earlier confidence in Hitler. Today he heads the theological faculty of the University of Munich.

56. Bookjacket of Lortz, *op. cit.*

57. Karl Adam, "Deutsches Volkstum und katholisches Christentum," *Theologische Quartalschrift,* CXIV (1933), 59.

58. *Ibid.*, p. 42. This article is missing from the bibliography of Adam's works in the *Festschrift* published in 1952 on occasion of his seventy-fifth birthday (*Abhandlungen über Theologie und Kirche: Festschrift für Karl Adam,* edited by Marcel Reding).

59. Theodor Brauer, *Der Katholik im neuen Reich: Seine Aufgaben und sein Anteil* (Munich, 1933), pp. 32 and 77.

60. Carl Eschweiler, "Die Kirche im neuen Reich," *Deutsches Volkstum,* XV (1933), 454.

61. *Mitteilungen zur Weltanschaulichen Lage,* II (1936), 1. Eschweiler had joined the Nazi party on May 1, 1933, and remained a member until his death (Berlin Document Center, file "Karl Eschweiler").

62. Axel Emmerich, "Katholizismus ohne Politik," *Zeit und Volk,* I (1933), 5. Emmerich gave up the editorship after the tenth number, emigrated and soon became a convinced anti-Nazi. Cf. Edgar Alexander, *Der Mythus Hitler* (Zürich, 1937).

63. Jakob Hommes, "Katholisches Staats- und Kulturdenken und Nationalsozialismus," *Deutsches Volk,* I (1933), 285-288. See also his *Lebens-und Bildungsphilosophie als völkische und katholische Aufgabe* (Freiburg, 1934), where he characterized the new nationalist movement as "the return to natural law and God" (p. 135). Hommes joined the Nazi party on May 1, 1933, but declared his exit on November 27 of that year—

for religious reasons *only* (Berlin Document Center, file "Jakob Hommes"). Today he is professor of philosophy in Regensburg.

64. Professor Max Bierbaum of Münster in an interview on February 9, 1962.

65. "Erlass der Reichsparteileitung der NSDAP" of October 3, 1933, *Mitteilungsblatt* (AKD), no. 1, November 22, 1933.

66. Papen to Bertram, October 3, 1933, copy in DA Passau.

67. Bertram to Papen, October 7, 1933, copy in DA Passau.

68. Bertram to Graf von Praschma, November 13, 1933, copy in DA Aachen, file 30138.

69. Under the headline "Das Wort der kirchlichen Autorität," the statement of Archbishop Gröber, issued on November 19, 1933, was published in the first number of the *Mitteilungsblatt* of the AKD.

70. Papen to Bergen, April 7, 1934. *Documents on German Foreign Policy*, C, II, doc. 383, p. 720.

71. Bornewasser to Bertram, November 24, 1933, DA Trier, file 59/13.

72. Cf. the two collections of Papen's speeches published under the title *Appell an das deutsche Gewissen:Reden zur nationalen Revolution* (Oldenburg, 1933) and his *Der 12. November 1933 und die deutschen Katholiken* (Münster, 1933) published in the series "Reich und Kirche."

73. Report in the *Münchener Katholische Kirchenzeitung*, no. 47, November 19, 1933, p. 511.

74. Erwein von Aretin, *Krone und Ketten: Erinnerungen eines bayerischen Edelmannes* (Munich, 1955), p. 316.

75. Michael Kardinal Faulhaber, *Judaism, Christianity and Germany*, trans. George D. Smith (London, 1934), pp. 55-56.

76. *AB Passau*, no. 26, December 1, 1933, p. 127.

77. *Münchener Katholische Kirchenzeitung*, no. 50, December 10, 1933, p. 541.

78. Ludwig Koch, S.J., "Die Kraft der Symbole," *Stimmen der Zeit*, CXXVI (1933-34), 272.

79. Letter of Vicar General Mayer to the Reverend Danz in Darmstadt, November 10, 1933, DA Mainz, file "Fall Gemeinder."

80. Report of Mayer to the chancery of Munich, February 7, 1934, *ibid.*

Chapter 5

1. Bertram to the German bishops, August 1, 1933, DA Passau, Nachlass Ow-Felldorf, printed also in Müller, *Kirche und NS*, doc. 81, pp. 175-176.

2. Bergen to the Foreign Ministry, October 16, 1933, *Documents on German Foreign Policy*, C, II, doc. 3, pp. 3-4.

3. Kaas to Hackelsberger, October 21, 1933, cited by Rudolf Morsey, "Vatikanische Proteste," *Rheinischer Merkur*, no. 47, November 23, 1962, p. 11.

4. *Pro memoria* of the Papal Secretariat of State, October 19, 1933, *Documents on German Foreign Policy*, C, II, doc. 17, pp. 24-28.

5. The order, dated July 30, 1933, is reproduced in the volume *The Persecution of the Catholic Church in the Third Reich: Facts and Documents translated from the German* (London, 1940), p. 89 (hereafter cited as *Persecution*). The author of this volume is supposed to have been Walter Mariaux, S.J., another of Pacelli's advisors on German probems.

6. *Dokumente betreffend die Verhandlungen zwischen dem Hl. Stuhl und der Deutschen Reichsregierung über die Ausführung des Reichskonkordates.* Vol. I: September 5, 1933-April 20, 1934. Geheim. Als Manuskript gedruckt und lediglich für den dienstlichen Gebrauch der Hochwürdigsten Ordinarien bestimmt. Doc. 7 and 9, pp. 26, 32-33 (hereafter cited as *Dokumente*).

7. Papen to Bergen, November 11, 1933, *Documents on German Foreign Policy*, C, II, doc. 64, pp. 113-114.

8. Faulhaber to Bertram and Berning, November 25, 1933, DA Passau, Nachlass Ow-Felldorf.

9. Bertram to the German bishops, November 22, 1933, DA Regensburg, Geheimakten 1933-35.

10. Roth, *Katholische Jugend,* 146.

11. Marginal notation on Papen's note to Bergen of November 11, 1933, see n. 7, *supra.*

12. Bertram to the German bishops, November 27, 1933, DA Hildesheim.

13. Memos on talks between Buttmann and Pacelli, December 18 and 19, 1933, *Documents on German Foreign Policy*, C, II, docs. 133-136, pp. 239-249.

14. Memorandum of the Reich government to the Holy See, January 11, 1934, *ibid.,* doc. 177, pp. 340-344.

15. Memo of Menshausen, February 8, 1934, NA Washington, T-120, roll 3310, frames E580279-283.

16. Riemer to Abbott Maier, March 13, 1934, BA Koblenz, NS 10/81.

17. Schirach to Papen, February 20, 1934, *Documents on German Foreign Policy*, C, II, doc. 272, p. 519.

18. Bergen to Neurath, March 29, 1934, *ibid.,* doc. 370, p. 693.

19. Pacelli to Bertram, April 20, 1934, *Dokumente,* I, doc. 22, pp. 135-146. See also Deuerlein, *Reichskonkordat,* 151-152, who relies primarily on the private papers of Buttmann.

20. The text of the telegram is mentioned by Galen in a speech at Werden on June 17, 1934. See Müller, *Kirche und NS,* doc. 144, p. 288.

21. Joint pastoral letter of June 7, 1934, Corsten, *Kölner Aktenstücke,* doc. 34, p. 30.

22. *Ibid.,* p. 33.

23. Memo of Menshausen, June 30, 1934, *Documents on German Foreign Policy*, C, III, doc. 50, p. 110.

24. *Verhandlungen der Vertreter der Fuldaer Plenar-Bischofskonferenz*

im Reichsinnenministerium vom 25. bis 30. Juni 1934. Streng geheim. Mimeographed, pp. 10-11, DA Passau. This report was drawn up by Bishop Berning.

25. Memo of Menshausen, see n. 23, *supra.*
26. Bertram to the German bishops, June 27, 1934, DA Regensburg; printed by Müller, *Kirche und NS*, doc. 149, p. 291.
27. Frick to the Foreign Ministry, July 7, 1934 (copy of letter to the Reich Chancellery), BA Koblenz, R 43 II/176a.
28. Memo of Menshausen, see n. 23, *supra.*
29. Bergen to Foreign Ministry, July 31, 1934, NA Washington, T-120, roll 2903, frame E461000.
30. "Auszug aus eingegangenen bischöflichen Gutachten zum Ergebnis der Verhandlungen vom 25. bis 30. Juni 1934," mimeographed, 6 pp., DA Passau.
31. Galen comment on the June negotiations, August 5, 1934, copy in DA Passau.
32. Full text in note of Frick to Lammers, August 4, 1934, *Documents on German Foreign Policy*, C, III, doc. 147, pp. 291-292.
33. Note of Pacelli to the German government, September 2, 1934, *ibid.,* doc. 195, pp. 387-390.
34. Counselor Renthe-Fink (Dept. II of the Foreign Ministry) to the German Embassy at the Holy See, September 21, 1934, *ibid.,* doc. 216, pp. 423-424.
35. Köpke (Director of Dept. II of the Foreign Ministry) to the German Embassy at the Holy See, September 21, 1934, *ibid.,* doc. 215, pp. 422-423.
36. Bergen to the Foreign Ministry, October 12, 1934, *ibid.,* doc. 245, p. 478.
37. Faulhaber to Buchberger, December 16, 1934, DA Regensburg.
38. Köpke to the German Embassy at the Holy See, January 31, 1935, *Documents on German Foreign Policy*, C, III, doc. 470, p. 890.
39. Quoted in *Persecution*, 87.
40. "Hirtenwort an die katholischen Arbeiter- und Arbeiterinnenvereine," *AB Munich*, no. 12, June 4, 1935, supplement. This pastoral letter was later adopted by other dioceses. It is reprinted by Müller, *Kirche und NS*, doc. 191, pp. 350-355.
41. Wilhelm Frick at a party rally in Münster, July 7, 1935, *Völkischer Beobachter* (Munich edition), no. 189, July 8, 1935, p. 1, quoted in Hofer, *Nationalsozialismus*, doc. 65, p. 128.
42. "Runderlass an die Herren Oberpräsidenten, Regierungspräsidenten etc.," July 16, 1935, copy in DA Limburg, 561/2 B.
43. The text of the Prussian decree, dated July 23, 1935, is given by Müller, *Kirche und NS*, doc. 193, pp. 360-361.
44. *Denkschrift der katholischen kirchlichen Verbände an den hochwürdigsten Episkopat*, p. 22. The entire mimeographed memorandum is 31 pages long. I have consulted it in the DA Passau.

45. "Hirtenwort . . . an die katholischen Vereine und Verbände," released on August 23, 1935, Corsten, *Kölner Aktenstücke,* doc. 82, p. 79.
46. Pastoral letter to the German Catholics "Stehet fest im Glauben!" August 20, 1935, *ibid.,* doc. 80, p. 76.
47. Schulte to Berning, June 7, 1935, *ibid.,* doc. 69, pp. 63-64.
48. Report of Berning, July 1, 1935, DA Passau.
49. "Denkschrift der deutschen Bischöfe an Hitler," August 20, 1935. Full text in Müller, *Kirche und NS,* doc. 198, pp. 364-389; the section dealing with the Catholic organizations is on pp. 383-386.
50. Kerrl to the German bishops, September 9, 1935, DA Hildesheim, file "Katholische Vereine und Organisationen."
51. Bertram to Kerrl, October 29, 1935, copy in DA Passau.
52. *Protokoll der Verhandlungen der ausserordentlichen Plenar-Konferenz der deutschen Bischöfe in Fulda am 8. und 9. Januar 1936.* Als Manuskript gedruckt, p. 4.
53. See, e.g., the pastoral letter of Schulte of March 30, 1936, Corsten, *Kölner Aktenstücke, doc.* 104, pp. 123-124.
54. Complete text, *ibid.,* doc. 106, pp. 125-126.
55. *Mit brennender Sorge,* March 14, 1937, Ehler and Morrall, *op. cit.,* pp. 533-534.
56. Quoted in *Persecution,* pp. 111-112.
57. Faulhaber to ? [a state authority not mentioned in the document], January 29, 1938, copy in DA Passau.
58. Joint pastoral letter of the Bavarian bishops, read on February 6, 1938, DA Passau. An English translation is given by Donohoe, *op. cit.,* pp. 58-60.
59. *Protokoll der Verhandlungen der Plenar-Konferenz der deutschen Bischöfe vom 29. bis 31. August 1933.* Als Manuskript gedruckt, p. 10.
60. *Ecclesiastica,* XIII (1933), p. 420. Full text also in Müller, *Kirche und NS,* doc. 68, pp. 164-165.
61. The complete text of the laws is given in *Reichsgesetzblatt,* I (1933), 713, and in *Ecclesiastica,* XIII (1933), 393-396.
62. Memorandum of the Holy See to the Foreign Ministry, January 31, 1934, *Dokumente,* I, doc. 14, p. 73.
63. The statement of Amann of April 27, 1935 is quoted by Karl Aloys Altmeyer, *Katholische Presse unter NS-Diktatur* (Berlin, 1962), doc. 61, p. 59 (hereafter cited as Altmeyer, *Katholische Presse*). Altmeyer also gives excerpts from the ordinance of April 24 in doc. 54, pp. 54-55.
64. Bertram to Hitler, Frick and Goebbels, May 5, 1935, *ibid.,* doc. 65, pp. 61-64.
65. Müller, *Kirche und NS,* doc. 200, p. 393.
66. Steinmann "an die katholische-kirchliche Presse Deutschlands," December 16, 1933, mimeographed copy in possession of author; excerpt in Altmeyer, *Katholische Presse,* doc. 88, p. 84.
67. Bertram to Goebbels, January 24, 1934, YIVO, Berlin Collection G-100.

68. Goebbels to Bertram, March 5, 1934, Altmeyer, *Katholische Presse,* doc. 94, p. 87.
69. Report of Bishop Preysing, the episcopate's press referee, May 12, 1936, *ibid.,* doc. 108, pp. 95-98.
70. *Münchener Katholische Kirchenzeitung,* no. 16, April 21, 1935, p. 246.
71. Excerpts from Amann's order, dated July 12, 1935, in Altmeyer, *Katholische Presse,* doc. 105, pp. 92-93.
72. Excerpts from a clarifying letter of Adolph, July 27, 1935, *ibid.,* doc. 106, p. 93.
73. Report of January 8, 1936, BGS Munich, MA 1946/ C15.
74. Discussion of Adolph with representatives of the *Reichspressekammer,* January 17, 1936, excerpts in Altmeyer, *Katholische Presse,* doc. 110, p. 104.
75. Goebbels to Amann, February 14, 1935, printed *ibid.* doc. 115, p. 109.
76. Amann to the *Fachschaft der katholisch-kirchlichen Presse,* February 19, 1936, BA Koblenz, NS Splitter 180; excerpts in Altmeyer, *Katholische Presse,* doc. 116, pp. 109-111.
77. Bertram to Goebbels and Kerrl, February 28, 1936, YIVO, Berlin Collection G-100; printed in Altmeyer, *Katholische Presse,* doc. 125, pp. 115-116; Preysing to Goebbels and Kerrl, March 18, 1936, *ibid.,* doc. 127, p. 117.
78. Bertram to the German bishops, March 23, 1936, excerpts *ibid.,* doc. 132, p. 119.
79. Amann to Adolph, July 1, 1936, printed *ibid.,* doc. 146, p. 130.
80. Excerpts from Preysing's letters to Goebbels on July 18 and September 7, 1936 are given by Altmeyer, *Katholische Presse,* docs. 147 and 148, pp. 130-132.
81. Willi to all diocesan chanceries, July 4, 1936, DA Mainz, M XVII; also Altmeyer, *Katholische Presse,* doc. 149, p. 133.
82. *Protokoll der Verhandlungen der Plenar-Konferenz der deutschen Bischöfe vom 18. bis 20. August 1936,* p. 23.
83. Bertram to Goebbels, September 7, 1936, YIVO, Berlin Collection G-100; excerpts in Altmeyer, *Katholische Presse,* doc. 155, pp. 136-139.
84. Order of October 1, 1936, *ibid.,* doc. 161, pp. 142-143.
85. Bertram to Kerrl, October 12, 1936, excerpt *ibid.,* doc. 164, p. 144.
86. *Protokoll der Verhandlungen der Plenar-Konferenz der deutschen Bischöfe* vom 12. und 13. Januar 1937. Als Manuskript gedruckt, p. 7.
87. Bertram to the German bishops, March 30, 1937, excerpt in Altmeyer, *Katholische Presse,* doc. 173, pp. 150-151.
88. Galen to the clergy of Münster, March 5, 1937, DA Paderborn, XXII, 4.
89. Mertens to Moser, October 26, 1937, DA Mainz, M XVII.
90. Mertens to Moser, January 27, 1938, *ibid.*
91. *Martinus-Blatt,* no. 17, April 23, 1939, p. 9.
92. Gordon Zahn, "The German Catholic Press and Hitler's Wars," *Cross Currents,* X (1960), 344.

93. Interview with Dr. Emil Janik, May 8, 1962. See also his article "Bindeglied zwischen Bischof und Volk in schwerer Zeit: Ein Gang durch die ersten 20 Jahre des Passauer Bistumsblattes," *Passauer Bistumsblatt*, no. 27, July 1, 1956, pp. 2-6.

94. Cf. Karl Aloys Altmeyer, "Der Episkopat und die katholische Presse im Dritten Reich," *Herder-Korrespondenz*, XIV (1959-60), 374-381.

95. Preysing about "Die Lage der katholisch-kirchlichen Presse: Sommer 1938," *Protokoll der Plenar-Konferenz der deutschen Bischöfe in Fulda vom 17.-19. August 1938*. Als Manuskript gedruckt, p. 31. The report is reprinted in Bischöfliches Ordinariat Berlin, ed., *Dokumente aus dem Kampf der katholischen Kirche im Bistum Berlin gegen den Nationalsozialismus* (Berlin, 1946), pp. 40-48.

96. From a report of Bishop Preysing made on March 2, 1940; excerpt in Altmeyer, *Katholische Presse,* doc. 212, pp. 179-181.

97. Riemer to Amann, April 25, 1939, DA Passau, file "Bistumsblatt."

98. *Der Deutsche Weg,* April 1936, reprinted in *Der Christliche Ständestaat,* III (1936), 359.

99. Circular of Willi to the Catholic press, September 11, 1939, DA Trier, B III 14, 8 Bd. 12; excerpts in Altmeyer, *Katholische Presse,* doc. 214, pp. 182-183.

100. Reichspropagandaamt Cologne-Aachen, "Strictly confidential" instruction of November 9, 1939, DA Aachen, 30219.

101. Instruction of December 12, 1939, *ibid.;* excerpt in Altmeyer, *Katholische Presse,* doc. 216, p. 183.

102. Reichspropagandaamt Cologne-Aachen, instruction of March 14, 1940, DA Aachen, 30219.

103. *St. Konradsblatt,* no. 14, April 7, 1940, p. 68.

104. "Der Krieg des Geldes gegen uns," *Passauer Bistumsblatt,* no. 15, April 14, 1940, p. 3.

105. Mauritius Volk, O.S.B., "Plutokratismus," *Haec Loquere et Exhortare,* XXXIV (1940), 145.

106. Janik to the Propaganda Ministry, September 24, 1940, DA Passau, file "Bistumsblatt."

107. Riemer to Wienken, December 10, 1940, *ibid.*

108. Report of Berning to the German bishops, February 3, 1941, DA Mainz, 4/9; excerpts in Altmeyer, *Katholische Presse,* doc. 228, p. 189.

109. "Geleitwort" by Bishop Berning, *Mitteilungen und Ratschläge für die Katholisch-kirchliche Presse,* no. 1, February 5, 1941, p. 1, DA Mainz, 4/9.

110. DA Passau, file "Bistumsblatt"; excerpt in Altmeyer, *Katholische Presse,* doc. 230, p. 190.

111. Bormann to Goebbels, March 1, 1941, NA Washington, T-454, roll 62, frames 364-365.

112. Diocesan chancery Regensburg to chancery Passau, May 20, 1941, DA Passau, file "Bistumsblatt."

113. Brauchitsch to Keitel, April 26, 1941, NA Washington, T-77, roll 1040, frame 6513406.
114. *Regensburger Bistumsblatt*, no. 22, May 31, 1941, p. 1.
115. Wienken to Bertram, July 2, 1943, excerpt in Altmeyer, *Katholische Presse*, doc. 241, p. 195.
116. Kerrl to Bertram, October 22, 1935, copy in DA Passau.
117. Berning to the German bishops, July 25, 1941, DA Mainz, P XVI.
118. I have consulted two large files of these supplements in the DA Mainz.
119. Altmeyer, *Herder-Korrespondenz*, XIV (1959-60), 380.
120. "Ein Bischofswort an die Lesergemeinde," *Passauer Bistumsblatt*, no. 22, May 30, 1941, p. 2.
121. Bishop Machens of Hildesheim, for example, in a pastoral letter entitled "Remain loyal to the church paper" and read to the faithful on January 1, 1937, called the *Katholisches Kirchenblatt für das Bistum Hildesheim* "my weekly letter to you" (DA Hildesheim, III F/2,II).

Chapter 6

1. Corsten, *Kölner Aktenstücke*, doc. 21, p. 19.
2. *Protokoll der Verhandlungen der Plenar-Konferenz der deutschen Bischöfe in Fulda am 5., 6. und 7. Juni 1934*. Als Manuskript gedruckt, p. 4.
3. Joint pastoral letter of June 7, 1934, Corsten, *Kölner Aktenstücke*, doc. 34, pp. 29-32.
4. Order of July 3, 1934, BGS Munich, MA 1957/III-11-4, Bd. II.
5. Bertram to Frick, July 16, 1934, copy in DA Passau; printed in Müller, *Kirche und NS*, doc. 151, pp. 292-293.
6. Wilhelm Neuss, *Kampf gegen den Mythus des 20. Jahrhunderts* (Cologne, 1947), pp. 18-24.
7. *Studien zum Mythus des XX. Jahrhunderts: Amtliche Beilage zum Kirchlichen Amtsblatt für die Diözese Münster*, p. iii.
8. According to the *AB Munich* of August 28, 1935, the condemnatory decree was dated July 19, 1935.
9. "Denkschrift der deutschen Bischöfe an Hitler," August 20, 1935, Müller, *Kirche und NS*, doc. 198, especially pp. 367-376.
10. Joint pastoral letter "Stehet fest im Glauben!" August 20, 1935, Müller, *Kirche und NS*, doc. 200, pp. 391-393.
11. Report of December 5, 1934, printed in Bernhard Vollmer, ed., *Volksopposition im Polizeistaat* (Stuttgart, 1957), pp. 128-129.
12. Report of July 5, 1935, *ibid.*, p. 251.
13. Order of December 2, 1935, NA Washington, T-580, roll 113, folder 35.
14. Himmler order of September 20, 1935, *ibid.*, T-175, roll 149, frame 2677453.

15. Schachleiter to Kerrl, October 28, October 29, November 3, 1935, Von Detten to Schachleiter, November 25, 1935, NA Washington, T-77, roll 641, frames 1836719-724.
16. Joint pastoral letter of January 9, 1936, Corsten, *Kölner Aktenstücke,* doc. 94, pp. 108-109.
17. *AB Munich,* no. 30, November 25, 1936, supplement.
18. See, e.g., Bergen's note to Neurath, January 4, 1936, *Documents on German Foreign Policy,* C, IV, doc. 482, pp. 964-966, and Brüning's evaluation in 1935 in Henry Graf Kessler, *Tagebücher 1918-1937* (Frankfurt a.M., 1961), p. 742.
19. For a description of the way in which the reading of the encyclical was secretly prepared, see Simon Hirt, ed., *Mit Brennender Sorge* (Freiburg, Br., 1946), pp. 91-93. The original German text is given there on pp. 1-24. In the discussion that follows I have used the English translation in Ehler and Morrall, *op. cit.,* pp. 519-539.
20. Foreign Ministry to the Papal Secretary of State, April 12, 1937, *Documents on German Foreign Policy,* D, I, doc. 646, pp. 951-954.
21. Foreign Ministry to the German Embassy at the Holy See, April 7, 1937, *ibid.,* doc. 642, p. 945.
22. Cf. *ibid.,* docs. 691, 693, 708, 710; Leiber, *Stimmen der Zeit,* CLXIII (1958-1959), 97.
23. Cf. Edgar Alexander, *Der Mythus Hitler* (Zürich, 1937), p. 9; E.E.Y. Hales, *The Catholic Church in the Modern World* (Garden City, L.I., 1958), p. 273.
24. Michael de la Bedoyère, *Christian Crisis* (London, 1940), p. 100.
25. Pacelli to Bergen, April 30, 1937, *Documents on German Foreign Policy* D, I, doc. 649, pp. 964-965.
26. These figures are based on a report of the "Zentralstelle für kirchliche Statistik," Cologne, issued on August 8, 1944 (DA Passau). The complete figures are as follows:

Year	Number of Withdrawals	Returns
1933	31,987	13,407
1934	26,376	9,872
1935	34,347	6,569
1936	46,687	5,039
1937	108,054	3,897
1938	88,715	3,811
1939	88,335	3,596
1940	51,799	3,196
1941	52,560	2,932
1942	38,367	3.580

27. Bergen to the Foreign Ministry, April 1, 1937, *Documents on German Foreign Policy,* D, I, doc. 640, p. 942.

28. Conrad Gröber, *Nationalkirche? Ein aufklärendes Wort zur Wahrung des konfessionellen Friedens* (Freiburg, Br., 1934), pp. 63-66.

29. Wilhelm Berning, *Katholische Kirche und Deutsches Volkstum* (Munich, 1934), p. 9.

30. Berning to Hitler, May 5, 1934, BA Koblenz, R 43 II/175.

31. *Hirtenbriefe der deutschen, österreichischen und deutsch-schweizerischen Bischöfe 1934* (Paderborn, 1934), p. 162.

32. *Ibid.*, p. 89.

33. Konrad Algermissen, "Christentum und Germanentum," *Theologie und Glaube*, XXVI (1934), 302.

34. Anton Stonner, *Nationale Erziehung und Religionsunterricht* (Regensburg, 1934), pp. 148, 153, 157. Stonner's book appeared with the *Imprimatur* (dated March 21, 1934) and was warmly praised by many diocesan gazettes. For a searching critique of Stonner's ideas, see Hugo Diwald, "Sophistik des 'Brückenbauens': Kritische Betrachtungen zu Anton Stonners Buch . . ." *Der Christliche Ständestaat*, I (1934), no. 29, pp. 13-16.

35. Jakob Hommes, *Lebens- und Bildungsphilosophie als völkische und katholische Aufgabe* (Freiburg, Br., 1934), p. 152.

36. Franz Taeschner, *Der Totalitätsanspruch des Nationalsozialismus und der deutsche Katholizismus* (Münster, 1934), pp. 38, 51.

37. Desiderius Breitenstein, O.F.M., *Geist oder Blut?* (Paderborn, 1934), p. 45 *(Imprimatur, August 10, 1934).*

38. Speckner, *Wächter der Kirche,* 10 *(Imprimatur, Munich, October 23, 1934).*

39. *Germania,* no. 261, September 21, 1934, quoted in *Ecclesiastica,* XV (1935), 179.

40. Kuno Brombacher, *Deutschland und der Glaube* (Breslau, 1935), p. 17. Brombacher had been a member of the Nazi party since 1931 (Berlin Document Center, file "Kuno Brombacher").

41. Kuno Brombacher and Emil Ritter, eds., *Sendschreiben katholischer Deutscher an ihre Volks- und Glaubensgenossen* (Münster, 1936) p. 77.

42. Joseph Lortz to Galen, June 22, 1945, DA Münster, duplicate file.

43. The *Katholisch-nationalkirchliche Bewegung* published the periodical *Der romfreie Katholik.* In 1941 this publication was suspended with the rest of the confessional press.

44. Erzbischöfliches Ordinariat Breslau, *Diözesansynode des Erzbistums Breslau 1935* (Breslau, 1936), pp. 12-13.

45. "Mitteilungen für den Klerus der Diözese Würzburg," December 14, 1937, DA Passau.

46. Monatsbericht XIII (June 1936), NA Washington, T-181, roll 164, frame E1530860.

47. "Katholische Grundsätze für den Religionsunterricht in unserer Zeit," *AB Freiburg,* no. 9, March 4, 1936, p. 61.

48. Article "Rasse" in Conrad Gröber, ed., *Handbuch der religiösen*

Gegenwartsfragen (Freiburg, Br., 1937), pp. 536-537 (hereafter cited as Gröber, *Handbuch*).

49. Sermon on December 31, 1936, in *Münchener Kardinalspredigten,* 1st series (Munich, 1936), p. 11.

50. Article "Aufklärung," Gröber, *Handbuch,* 68-69.

51. Article "Recht," *ibid.,* p. 540.

52. Article "Politik," *ibid.,* pp. 520-521.

53. Article "Ehre," *ibid.,* p. 149.

54. Pastoral letter of February 6, 1935, *AB Regensburg,* no. 3, February 11, 1935, p. 18.

55. Sermon on November 8, 1936 in *Münchener Kardinalspredigten,* 1st series, p. 5.

56. "Ein deutscher Katholik: Albert Leo Schlageters heldenmütiges Leben und Sterben," *Klerusblatt,* XVI (1935), p. 395.

57. Order of August 5, 1937, DA Trier, 14,8, Bd. 11.

58. Otto Schilling, "Das moralische Recht des deutschen Volkes auf Kolonien," *Theologische Quartalschrift,* CXV (1934), 397-404.

59. Article "Völkerfriede," Gröber, *Handbuch,* 631.

60. *Deutsche Briefe,* no. 107, October 9, 1936, p. 1.

61. In 1936 the *Reichsverband* received 139,150 Reichsmark (PA Bonn, Kult. VIa, 27, 2).

62. Alois Hudal, *Die Grundlagen des Nationalsozialismus: Eine ideengeschichtliche Untersuchung von katholischer Warte* (Leipzig and Vienna, 1937), p. 13.

63. "Der politische Katholizismus," (no date given but apparently from the year 1937), NA Washington, T-175, roll 281, frames 2774908-912.

64. Ernst Fürth, "Mehr Würde: Kritische Gedanken über Methoden zeitgenössischer Apologetik im deutschen Raum," *Der Christliche Ständestaat,* III (1936), 901-905.

65. See n. 63, *supra.*

66. Reported by the American ambassador in Rome, July 14, 1933, *Foreign Relations of the United States: Diplomatic Papers 1933* (Washington, D.C., 1949), II, 299 (hereafter cited as *U.S. Diplomatic papers*).

67. Pastoral letter of February 20, 1938, *Würzburger Diözesan-Blatt,* no. 4, February 23, 1938, p. 37.

68. "Runderlass an die Herren Oberpräsidenten, Regierungspräsidenten etc.," July 16, 1935, copy in DA Limburg, 561/2 B.

69. "Die religiöse Lage in Deutschland: Feststellungen und Klarstellungen," *L'Osservatore Romano,* no. 181, August 4, 1935; German translation in Corsten, *Kölner Aktenstücke,* doc. 84, pp. 80-83.

70. Sermon on December 31, 1935, *AB Munich,* supplement to no. 1, January 15, 1936, p. 1.

71. Article "Politik," Gröber, *Handbuch,* 522.

72. The Fulda Bishops' Conference of August 1935 to the German clergy, *AB Munich,* supplement to no. 17, August 29, 1935, pp. 207-208.

73. Speech at Marburg on June 17, 1934, full text in International Military Tribunal, *Trial of the Major War Criminals* (Nuremberg, 1949), XL, 543-558 (hereafter cited as IMT).

74. Pastoral letter of February 1, 1934, *AB Munich,* no. 2, February 6, 1934, p. 23.

75. Pastoral letter of the Bavarian bishops read on June 21, 1936, *AB Regensburg,* no. 10, August 4, 1936, p. 86.

76. Speech to a conference of deans, October 28, 1935, *AB Münster,* supplement to no. 23 of October 23, 1935, p. 1.

77. Memorandum of the Holy See to the German government, January 29, 1936, *Dokumente,* III, doc. 14, p. 69.

78. Walter Adolph, *Erich Klausener* (Berlin, 1955), p. 106.

79. Chancery Berlin to all the diocesan chanceries of Germany, July 13, 1934, DA Passau.

80. Wolker to the diocesan presidents of the DJK, July 7, 1934, DA Passau.

81. Bares to Hitler, July 12, 1934, copy in DA Passau.

82. Bares to Hitler, November 21, 1934, copy in DA Passau.

83. Dietrich von Hildebrand, "Die letzte Maske fällt!" *Der Christliche Ständestaat,* vol. I, no. 31 (July 8, 1934), 5.

84. Stefan Kirchmann [Waldemar Gurian], *St. Ambrosius und die deutschen Bischöfe* (Lucerne, n.d. [1934]).

85. Sermon at Xanten on February 9, 1936, quoted in Heinrich Portmann, *Kardinal von Galen* (Münster, 1948), pp. 101-102.

86. Alfons Erb, *Bernhard Lichtenberg: Domprobst von St. Hedwig zu Berlin* (Berlin, 1949), p. 41.

87. Memorandum of the German episcopate to Hitler, August 20, 1935, Müller, *Kirche und NS,* 388.

88. Bertram to the head office of the Gestapo in Berlin, July 22, 1938, copy in DA Limburg, 561/6.

89. On the basis of an article in the *Kölnische Volkszeitung* (dateline KZ Papenburg, July 1, 1936), reported by Waldemar Gurian's *Deutsche Briefe,* no. 93, July 10, 1936, p. 2.

90. *Der Deutsche Weg* of July 28, 1936, quoted in *Deutsche Briefe,* no. 97, July 31, 1936, p. 6.

91. [Friedrich Muckermann, S.J.], "Vatikan und Nationalsozialismus," *Der Deutsche Weg,* no. 20, December 23, 1934, reprinted in Müller, *Kirche und NS,* doc. 167, p. 321.

92. *Deutsche Briefe,* no. 46, August 16, 1935, p. 5.

93. Gurian, *Hitler and the Christians,* 162.

94. Buchberger to Bertram, June 23, 1935, copy in DA Regensburg.

95. See n. 76, *supra.*

96. Teeling, *op. cit.,* p. 304.

97. "Vom innerkirchlichen Problem der Abwehr des Nationalsozialismus," *Der Deutsche Weg,* no. 11, March 13, 1938, pp. 1-2.

98. Max Pribilla, S.J., "Charakter," *Stimmen der Zeit,* CXXVIII (1935), 305.

Chapter 7

1. Cuno Horkenbach, ed., *Das Deutsche Reich von 1918 bis heute* (Berlin, 1935), p. 418. Also printed in Müller, *Kirche und NS,* doc. 100, p. 212.
2. *Ibid.,* doc. 109, p. 220.
3. *Documents on German Foreign Policy,* C, II, doc. 17, pp. 23-28.
4. Gröber to Bertram, October 27, 1933, copy in DA Trier, 59/13; printed by Müller, *Kirche und NS,* doc. 103, p. 214.
5. Bertram to the German bishops, October 30, 1933, DA Trier, 59/13; text printed in Müller, *Kirche und NS,* doc. 104, pp. 216-217.
6. Vicar General Riemer to Faulhaber, January 13, 1934, DA Passau.
7. Statement of November 1, 1933, in *Rheinisches Volksblatt,* no. 255, November 6, 1933, copy in BGS Munich MA 1957/VII-1-15-I.
8. Circular letter of Gröber and Berning, no date, received on November 6, DA Mainz, SXXIV.
9. This circular letter is dated November 5, but the envelope carries a postal cancellation stamp of November 4, DA Limburg, 561/2 A; printed by Müller, *Kirche und NS,* doc. 105, p. 217.
10. *AB Freiburg,* no. 28, November 9, 1933, p. 133.
11. *AB Breslau,* no. 16, November 8, 1933, cited by Müller, *Katholische Episkopat,* 81.
12. Statement of November 8, 1933 in *Rheinisches Volksblatt,* no. 258, November 9, 1933, copy in BGS Munich, MA 1957/VII-1-15-I.
13. *AB Passau,* no. 25, November 10, 1933; printed in Müller, *Kirche und NS,* doc. 107, p. 219.
14. Cf. Bracher-Sauer-Schulz, *NS Machtergreifung,* 358-368.
15. Interview on November 8, 1933 with a representative of the official WTB news agency, *ibid.,* p. 351, n. 441.
16. BGS Munich, MA 1957/VII-15-I.
17. Report on the meeting of November 14, 1933, *ibid.*
18. *Documents on German Foreign Policy,* C, II, doc. 133, p. 240.
19. Faulhaber to the Bavarian State Chancellery, November 18, 1933, copy in DA Limburg, 561/2 A, printed in Müller, *Kirche und NS,* doc. 112, pp. 221-224.
20. Sarah Wambaugh, *The Saar Plebiscite* (Cambridge, Mass., 1940), pp. 12, 15, 60-61. Miss Wambaugh was a member of the Plebiscite Commission and her account of the vote and its background is the best available.
21. *Le Matin,* November 10, 1922 in *Münchener Katholische Kirchenzeitung,* no. 51, December 17, 1933, p. 549.
22. Wambaugh, *op. cit.,* pp. 83-84; "Die Katholische Kirche und die Saarabstimmung," *Ecclesiastica,* XV (1935), 210-211.
23. François Charles-Roux, *Huit Ans au Vatican: 1932-1940* (Paris, 1947), p. 100.
24. Telegram of Bergen to the Foreign Ministry, November 7, 1933, NA

Washington, T-120, roll. 3296, frame E574730 (II, Vat., Pol. 24, Saargebiet).

25. Bergen to the Foreign Ministry, November 22, 1933, *ibid.*, E574741.
26. Report of Bornewasser to Bergen about his negotiations in Rome, written November 20, 1933, *Documents on German Foreign Policy*, C, II, doc. 96, pp. 167-171.
27. Memo of Papen (dated December 8, 1933) on his talk with Testa on December 7, 1933, *ibid.*, doc. 114, pp. 195-196.
28. *Germania*, no. 326, November 26, 1933, quoted in *Ecclesiastica*, XV (1935), 211. Testa was considered pro-German also by Schreiber (*op. cit.*, p. 92).
29. Bornewasser to Papen, March 30, 1934, copy in DA Trier, B III 2, 13, Bd. 1.
30. Bornewasser to Reichert, April 3, 1934, copy in DA Trier, B III 2, 13, Bd. 2. The release was published a few days later. See, e.g., *Westdeutscher Beobachter*, no. 152, April 9, 1934.
31. Wambaugh, *op. cit.*, p. 207.
32. *Ecclesiastica*, XV (1935), 214.
33. Note of the Plebiscite Commission to the Secretariat of the League of Nations, August 24, 1934, *ibid.*, pp. 214-215.
34. Memo of Voigt, July 18, 1934, PA Bonn, II, Besetzte Gebiete, Saargebiet, Bd. 4, Kirchliche Fragen.
35. Bergen to Foreign Ministry, August 4, 1934, NA Washintgon, T-120, roll 3296, frame E574773.
36. Bornewasser to Pacelli, August 22, 1934, copy in DA Trier, 59/48.
37. Bornewasser to Hitler, August 27, 1934, BA Koblenz, R 43 II/175.
38. Bornewasser to Kaas, August 27, 1934, copy in DA Trier, 59/48.
39. Memo of Braun von Stumm, October 12, 1934, NA Washington, T-120, roll 3295, frames E574707-710.
40. Bürckel to Neurath, October 17, 1934, *Documents on German Foreign Policy*, C, III, doc. 255, pp. 495-498.
41. Köpke to Bergen, October 23, 1934, NA Washington, T-120, roll 3296, frames E574814-820.
42. Bergen to Köpke, October 31, 1934, *Documents on German Foreign Policy*, C, III, doc. 286, pp. 552-554.
43. Report of Müller, November 7, 1934, NA Washington, T-120, roll 3296, frames E574830-840.
44. Summary report on meeting between Bornewasser and Müller, November 17, 1934, DA Trier, 59/48.
45. *AB Trier*, no. 21, November 15, 1934; full text also in *Ecclesiastica*, XV (1935), 215, and Müller, *Kirche und NS*, doc. 163, p. 314.
46. *Deutsche Front*, no. 206, November 17, 1934; *Neue Saar Post*, no. 192, November 17, 1934, both quoted in *Ecclesiastica*, XV (1935), 215.
47. Wambaugh, *op. cit.*, pp. 271-272.
48. *AB Trier*, no. 23, December 5, 1934; full text also in *Ecclesiastica*, XV (1935), 215, and Müller, *Kirche und NS*, doc. 164, p. 315.

49. *Generalanzeiger,* no. 327, December 4, 1934, quoted in *Ecclesiastica,* XV (1935), 215.
50. Bornewasser to the *Dechanten* (deans) of the Saar, December 5, 1934, copy in DA Trier, 59/48; printed in Müller, *Kirche und NS,* doc. 165, pp. 315-316.
51. See n. 44, *supra.*
52. Frick to Bornewasser, December 6, 1934, DA Trier, 59/48.
53. Müller to Bornewasser, December 14, 1934; Bornewasser to Müller, December 19, 1934, DA Trier, 59/48.
54. Müller to Bornewasser, December 19, 1934; Bornewasser to Müller, December 24, 1934, DA Trier, 59/48.
55. Josef Himmelreich to Bornewasser, January 10, 1935, DA Trier, 59/48.
56. Bornewasser to Bürckel, December 31, 1934, DA Trier, 59/48.
57. *AB Cologne,* no. 1, January 1, 1935, p. 1, reprinted in Müller, *Kirche und NS,* doc. 168, p. 328. It is typical of the attempt of some Catholic writers to distort the Church's role in the Third Reich that Corsten fails to publicize this declaration in his *Kölner Aktenstücke,* a collection of documents practically all taken from the *AB Cologne.*
58. Faulhaber to Schulte, December 28, 1934, copy in DA Passau.
59. Faulhaber to the Bavarian bishops, December 30, 1934, DA Passau.
60. *AB Munich,* no. 1, January 4, 1935, p. 2.
61. Bornewasser to the *Dechanten* of the Saar, September 27, 1934, copy in DA Trier, B III 4, 35.
62. Bornewasser to Bürckel, December 1, 1934, copy in DA Trier, 59/48.
63. Cf. Wambaugh, *op. cit.,* pp. 272-273.
64. The declaration was published by the *Saarbrücker Landes-Zeitung* on January 3, 1935. I have used a clipping in DA Trier, 59/48. The German text is also reprinted by Wambaugh, *op. cit.,* p. 289, n. 200, and by Müller, *Kirche und NS,* doc. 170, p. 329.
65. "Feststellungen!" *Neue Saar Post,* no. 3, January 4, 1935, clipping in DA Trier, 59/48.
66. *Neue Saar Post,* no. 8, January 9, 1935, quoted in *Ecclesiastica,* XV (1935), 212. The exact date of this telegram is not known.
67. Bergen to the Foreign Ministry, January 6, 1935, NA Washington, T-120, roll 3296, frame E574844.
68. Alan E. Rodhe (President of the Plebiscite Commission) to Bornewasser, January 5, 1935, DA Trier, 59/48. The identical note was sent to the Bishop of Speyer (Wambaugh, *op. cit.,* pp. 289-290). It was published in the *Völkischer Beobachter* on January 8, 1935 and is reprinted from there by Müller, *Kirche und NS,* doc. 171, p. 330.
69. The note of President Rodhe in the files of DA Trier bears the handwritten notation "Not answered."
70. *L' Osservatore Romano,* no. 6, January 7-8, 1935, quoted in Wambaugh, *op. cit.,* p. 292.
71. Bornewasser's statement "In Sachen der Saarabstimmung" was dated

January 11, 1935 (DA Trier, B III 2, 13, Bd. 2). It was published by the press on January 12, just one day before the plebiscite.

72. *L' Osservatore Romano*, no. 7, January 9, 1935 and no. 11, January 13, 1935, quoted in *Ecclesiastica*, XV (1935), 212-213.

73. Father Anton Fontain in the *Saarbrücker Zeitung* on January 8, 1935, cited by Wambaugh, *op. cit.*, p. 292.

74. "Aufruf an die katholische Saarjugend," *Junge Front*, no. 2, January 13, 1935, complete text in Müller, *Kirche und NS*, doc. 173, pp. 331-332.

75. Detailed electoral statistics are given by Wambaugh, *op. cit.*, pp. 469-472.

76. *Saarbrücker Landes-Zeitung*, no. 16, January 17, 1935, quoted in *Ecclesiastica*, XV (1935), 217-218.

77. *Saarbrücker Landes-Zeitung*, no. 21, January 21, 1935, quoted in *ibid.*

78. Reported in *Augsburger Postzeitung*, no. 24, January 29, 1935, quoted in *ibid.*

79. *Saarbrücker Landes-Zeitung*, no. 16, January 17, 1935, quoted in *ibid.*

80. *AB Paderborn*, no. 2, quoted in Müller, *Kirche und NS*, doc. 174, p. 333.

81. Order of January 10, 1935, DA Passau.

82. See the corresponding orders, e.g., in *AB Münster*, no. 5, March 1, 1935, p. 31; *AB Limburg*, no. 5, March 21, 1935, p. 25.

83. Bornewasser at the "Papstfeier" in Trier, January 27, 1935, *Germania*, no. 32, January 31, 1935, quoted in *Ecclesiastica*, XV (1935), 218.

84. Cf. Bornewasser to Gürtner, May 22, 1937, copy in DA Passau.

85. Goebbels in the Kroll Opera House of Berlin on January 6, 1935, *Kölnische Volkszeitung*, no. 7, January 7, 1935, quoted in *Ecclesiastica*, XV (1935), 216.

86. *Sonntagsblatt für die Diözese Speyer*, no. 3, n.d., quoted in *Münchener Katholische Kirchenzeitung*, no. 4, January 27, 1935, p. 58.

87. Pacelli to Sebastian, April 22, 1935, copy in DA Trier, 59/49.

88. William L. Shirer in his *Rise and Fall of the Third Reich* (New York, 1962), pp. 391-399, gives a vivid account of these days.

89. *AB Freiburg*, no. 3, January 20, 1936, p. 11.

90. Corsten, *Kölner Aktenstücke*, doc. 100a, p. 118. Corsten argues that this telegram was "a public appeal to the Armed Forces for protection against the Nazi terror" (*ibid.*, p. 118, n.1).

91. *AB Münster*, no. 7, March 12, 1936, p. 44.

92. Quoted in *Klerusblatt*, XVII (1936), 194.

93. Albert Stohr (Bishop of Mainz) to Pacelli, May 5, 1936, DA Mainz, XIIIᵃK; editor of *Nationalblatt* (Trier), acting in the name of the *Reichspressestelle*, to Dr. Michel (private secretary to Bornewasser), March 12, 1936, DA Trier, 59/32. Some bishops are also supposed to have sent telegrams of congratulation to Hitler (cf. the report of Gestapo Aachen of April 6, 1936 in Vollmer, *op. cit.*, p. 37), but none have been found.

94. Bertram to the German bishops, March 16, 1936, DA Limburg, 561/5 A.
95. Faulhaber to the Bavarian bishops, March 15, 1936, DA Passau.
96. Preysing to all (?) German bishops, March 17, 1936, DA Passau.
97. Stohr to Preysing, March 18, 1936, copy in DA Limburg, 561/5 A.
98. Telegram of Bertram to Hilfrich (Bishop of Limburg), March 19, 1936, DA Limburg, 561/5 A; Faulhaber to the Bishops of Regensburg, Augsburg and Passau, March 20, 1936, DA Passau.
99. Full text in Corsten, *Kölner Aktenstücke*, doc. 103, p. 123.
100. *AB Munich*, no. 8, March 21, 1936, p. 71; *AB Passau*, March 23, 1936 (special number, no page given).
101. *AB Münster*, no. 8, March 27, 1936, p. 51; *AB Freiburg*, no. 12, March 24, 1936, p. 73; *AB Regensburg*, no. 5, March 25, 1936, p. 50.
102. "Erklärung zur Abstimmung vom 29. März 1936," issued March 20, copy in DA Limburg, 561/5 A.
103. Sermon in Gelsenkirchen-Buer, March 22, 1936, copy in DA Limburg, 561/5 A.
104. Gröber to the *Reichsstatthalter* of Baden, March 27, 1936, copy in DA Limburg, 561/3 B.
105. Shirer, *op. cit.*, p. 405.
106. Monthly report for March 1936, in Vollmer, *op. cit.*, pp. 370-371.
107. Monthly report of the Bavarian Political Police of April 1, 1936, BGS Munich, MA 1946/C14.
108. Circular of Bavarian Political Police, March 11, 1936, NA Washington, T-580, roll 102, file 6.
109. Copies of this order were sent to all Catholic bishops and the text of the ordinance was frequently published in the diocesan gazettes. See, e.g., *AB Münster*, no. 10, April 17, 1936, p. 63.
110. Quoted in T. L. Jarman, *The Rise and Fall of Nazi Germany* (New York, 1956), p. 205.
111. Kurt G. W. Ludecke, *I Knew Hitler* (London, 1938), p. 422, quoted *ibid.*, p. 204.
112. Corsten, *Kölner Aktenstücke*, doc. 112, pp. 131-132.
113. Dodd to the Secretary of State, September 2, 1936, *U.S. Diplomatic Papers 1936*, II, 173-174.
114. Cf. Pius XI, *The Pope on the Spanish Terror* (London, 1936).
115. Bischöfliches Generalvikariat Trier, *Kirche und Bolschewismus* (n.p., 1937).
116. *Passauer Bistumsblatt*, no. 19, November 1, 1936, p. 2.
117. Faulhaber's report on the meeting was composed on November 5, 1936, and sent out by messenger. The account of the talk that follows is based on Faulhaber's 9-page summary which I have consulted in the DA Limburg, 561/2 C.
118. Interview with Dr. Michael Höck, former editor of the *Münchener Katholische Kirchenzeitung*, June 3, 1962.

119. Dodd to the Department of State, December 17, 1936, *U.S. Diplomatic Papers 1936*, II, 176.
120. *Niederschrift über die Beratungen der bayerischen Bischöfe auf der Konferenz in Regensburg am 24. und 25. November 1936*, p. 1 (DA Regensburg).
121. "Hirtenwort der bayerischen Bischöfe," December 6, 1936, p. 5 (mimeographed); the pastoral letter is reprinted by Konrad Hofmann, ed., *Zeugnis und Kampf des deutschen Episkopats* (Freiburg, Br., 1946), pp. 52-57.
122. Monthly report of the Gestapo of Munich, January 1, 1937, BGS Munich, MA 1946/C19.
123. Faulhaber to the German bishops, December 23, 1936, DA Regensburg.
124. "Hirtenwort der deutschen Bischöfe über die Abwehr des Bolschewismus," December 24, 1936, Corsten, *Kölner Aktenstücke,* doc. 130, pp. 156-161.
125. Faulhaber to Kerrl, December 29, 1936, copy in DA Passau.
126. "Wir Stehen zum Kreuz," *Der Deutsche Weg,* IV (January 16, 1937), p. 1.
127. "Staat und Kirche," *Kulturkampf,* no. 43, January 8, 1937, p. 1.
128. Quoted in Shirer, *op. cit.,* p. 394.
129. A description of how this statement came into existence is given by Erika Weinzierl-Fischer, "Österreichs Katholiken und der Nationalsozialismus," *Wort und Wahrheit,* XVIII (1963), 509-511.
130. The text of the declaration of March 18 and Innitzer's letter to Bürckel are reproduced in *Schulthess,* LXXIX (1938), 80-81.
131. The memo about a talk between the Bavarian Minister of the Interior, Adolf Wagner, and Cardinal Faulhaber on March 7, 1934, notes that the latter upon entering and leaving gave a "flawless Hitler salute conforming to the rules" (BA Koblenz, EAB 251-a/301). Bishop Berning's letters to the authorities were frequently signed "Mit deutschem Gruss und Hitler Heil"—see, e.g., his letter to Buttmann of February 1, 1935, (BGS Munich, VII-1-8-I) and to Rust of May 22, 1935 (copy in DA Passau).
132. Faulhaber to the Bavarian bishops, April 6, 1938, DA Regensburg.
133. Order of Kerrl of March 30, 1938, *AB Munich,* no. 7, April 4, 1938, p. 29.
134. Bertram to the German bishops, January 3, 1935, DA Limburg, 561/22.
135. Faulhaber to Rösch, January 21, 1935, copy in DA Eichstätt.
136. Faulhaber to Kerrl, March 23, 1936, copy in DA Passau.
137. Copy in DA Limburg, 561/22.
138. Faulhaber to the Bavarian bishops, April 4, 1938, DA Regensburg.
139. Buchberger to Faulhaber, April 5, 1938, DA Regensburg.
140. Faulhaber order to the clergy, April 6, 1938, copy in DA Limburg, 561/22.
141. Buchberger order of April 7, 1938, DA Regensburg.
142. *AB Passau,* no. 9, April 8, 1938, p. 46.

143. On October 11, 1937, in a letter that began with "My Führer!", Eberle had asked to be received by Hitler and this talk took place on December 6. On March 18, 1938, Eberle reported to Hitler that his proposals for peace submitted to the German cardinals and Pacelli had fallen on deaf ears (BA Koblenz, R 43 II/155a). See also the memoirs of the man who had helped Eberle to be received by Hitler, the former *Gauleiter* of Swabia, Karl Wahl, ". . . es ist das deutsche Herz:" *Erlebnisse und Erkenntnisse eines ehemaligen Gauleiters* (Augsburg, 1954), pp. 136-138.

144. Eberle to Faulhaber, April 3, 1938, copy in BA Koblenz, R 43 II/155a.

145. See n. 140, *supra*.

146. Dietz to all (?) German bishops, April 4, 1938, DA Regensburg.

147. Order of the *Fachschaft der katholisch-kirchlichen Presse in der Reichspressekammer*, March 30, 1938, DA Passau, file "Bistumsblatt."

148. *Passauer Bistumsblatt: Mitteilungsblatt des Bischöflichen Stuhles,* vol. III, no. 15 (April 10, 1938), p. 3.

149. Preysing to the editor of the *Katholisches Kirchenblatt für das Bistum Berlin,* March 27, 1938, copy in DA Passau.

150. Preysing to all parishes of the diocese of Berlin, March 31, 1938, copy in DA Limburg, 561/2 E.

151. Riemer to all parishes of the diocese of Passau, April 4, 1938, DA Passau, file "Bistumsblatt," printed in Altmeyer, *Katholische Presse,* doc. 200, p. 168.

152. Report of the *Regierungspräsident* of Lower Bavaria and the Upper Palatinate, May 6, 1938, BGS Munich, MA 1946/C26.

153. The statement of the two curates from Grafenau is dated April 13, 1938, and is found in the files of DA Passau.

154. Substitute Vicar General Weber Haselmair to "X," July 20, 1938. The text of this letter and the necessary background information was put at my disposal by the priest involved in this incident. In his interest, I have decided to omit his name.

155. Sproll to Bertram, September 8, 1938, copy in DA Passau.

156. Bergen to Foreign Ministry, June 10, 1938, *Documents on German Foreign Policy,* D, I, doc. 713, p. 1044.

157. This decision was taken at a conference of Kerrl and several other officials with Woermann of the Foreign Ministry on August 15, 1938. Cf. *ibid.,* doc. 725, pp. 1055-1056. The ban on Sproll's residence in Würtemberg was never rescinded and he did not return to Rottenburg until June 12, 1945.

158. Bertram to the German bishops, October 1, 1938, DA Aachen, 30076.

159. *Martinus-Blatt,* no. 41, October 9, 1938, p. 11. I have used the English translation in Nathaniel Micklem, *National Socialism and the Roman Catholic Church* (London, 1938), p. 229.

160. "Hirtenwort an die Sudetendeutschen," October 3, 1938, *AB Breslau,* no. 14, October 7, 1938, p. 118.

161. "Oberhirtlicher Erlass," October 5, 1938, *AB Bamberg*, No. 61, October 6, 1938.
162. *Münchener Katholische Kirchenzeitung*, no. 42, October 16, 1938, p. 669.
163. "Zum 30. Januar: Der Christliche Deutsche kennt die Treue," *Passauer Bistumsblatt*, no. 5, January 29, 1939, p. 3. This editorial was written by Dr. Emil Janik, the clerical editor appointed by the Bishop of Passau, and today again in the same office.
164. Bergen to the Foreign Ministry, March 22, 1939, *Documents on German Foreign Policy*, D, VI, doc. 65, p. 74.
165. The text of this note, dated March 6, is reproduced by Alberto Giovannetti, *Der Vatikan und der Krieg*, trans. Antonius Funke (Cologne, 1961), pp. 36-37.
166. "Heilige Kraft des Reiches," *Der Neue Wille*, no. 7, March 19, 1939, p. 7.
167. *Schulthess*, LXXX (1939), 86-87.
168. Bertram to the German bishops, March 27, 1939, DA Aachen, 30076.
169. Orders to this effect, phrased in identical language, can be found in the gazettes of the following dioceses: Breslau, Münster, Cologne, Hildesheim, Mainz, Munich, Bamberg, Passau, Würzburg, Freiburg, Trier, Rottenburg. They appear to be based upon a draft perhaps suggested by Bertram.
170. Copy in DA Mainz, 1/1.
171. See n. 169, *supra*.
172. *AB Mainz*, no. 7, April 17, 1939.
173. See n. 169, *supra*.
174. *Mitteilungsblatt* (of the AKD), no. 5, March 15, 1934.
175. "Beflaggung der Kirchen und kirchlichen Gebäude," February 22, 1934, *AB Osnabrück*, no. 5, February 23, 1934, p. 31; reprinted in Müller, *Kirche und NS*, doc. 119, p. 245.
176. "Beflaggung von Gotteshäusern und kirchlichen Gebäuden," September 27, 1935, *AB Münster*, no. 21, September 28, 1935, p. 142.
177. Faulhaber to Frick, October 5, 1935, copy in DA Limburg, 561/22.
178. Bertram to Frick, November 4, 1935, copy in DA Passau.
179. *Protokoll der Verhandlungen der Plenar-Konferenz der deutschen Bischöfe vom 18. bis 20. August, 1936.* Als Manuskript gedruckt, p. 11.
180. Order of diocesan chancery Mainz, December 21, 1937 (copy in possession of the author). This refusal was carried out at the suggestion of Bishop Preysing and Cardinal Bertram (cf. letter of Schulte to Hilfrich, December 3, 1937, DA Limburg, 561/22).
181. Memo of Weizsäcker, April 11, 1939, PA Bonn, Staatssekretär, Vatikan, Bd. 1, recording the wish of Orsenigo personally to transmit the congratulations of Pius XII.
182. "Der Führer Adolf Hitler 50 Jahre alt: Zum 20. April 1939," *Passauer Bistumsblatt*, no. 16, April 16, 1939, p. 3.

183. "Zum 20. April," by J. S., *Klerusblatt*, no. 15, April 12, 1939, pp. 221-222.

184. Conrad Gröber, *Kirche, Vaterland und Vaterlandsliebe: Zeitgemässe Erwägungen und Erwiderungen* (Freiburg, Br., 1935), p. 120.

Chapter 8

1. Michael Faulhaber, *Der Krieg im Lichte des Evangeliums* (Munich, n.d. [1915]), p. 4.

2. Sermon on December 31, 1935, *AB Freiburg*, no. 3, January 20, 1936, p. 12.

3. *Protokoll der Verhandlungen der Plenar-Konferenz der deutschen Bischöfe vom 12.-13. Januar 1937*. Als Manuskript gedruckt, p. 11.

4. L. Börst, *Die Theologen der Erzdiözese München-Freising im Weltkrieg 1914-18* (Munich, 1938), p. 1.

5. Johann Albert Aich, ed., *"Im Dienste zweier Könige": Das Heldenbuch der Kriegstheologen* (Breslau, 1937), p. 31.

6. Gröber, *Kirche, Vaterland und Vaterlandsliebe*, 103-104.

7. Instructions of Vicar General Riemer to all the parishes of the diocese, September 29, 1938, DA Passau.

8. William L. Shirer, *Rise and Fall of the Third Reich* (New York, 1962), pp. 648, 664-665, 691.

9. Bertram to the German bishops, July 17, 1939, DA Regensburg; Vicar General Offenstein of Hildesheim to the clergy of the diocese, August 25, 1939, DA Hildesheim.

10. A mimeographed report about the conference (probably a substitute for minutes) is found in BA Koblenz, R 43 II/177a.

11. "Gemeinsames Wort der deutschen Bischöfe," *Martinus-Blatt*, no. 38, September 17, 1939.

12. Pastoral letter of September 8, 1939, *AB Rottenburg*, September 8, 1939, p. 223.

13. Pastoral letter of September 4, 1939, *AB Freiburg*, no. 26, September 5, 1939, p. 123.

14. Pastoral letter of September 15, 1939, *AB Berlin*, no. 10, September 15, 1939, p. 53. For the full text or excerpts from other pastoral letters see Konrad Hofmann, ed., *Seelsorge und kirchliche Verwaltung im Krieg* (Freiburg, Br., 1940), pp. 3-15 (hereinafter cited as Hofmann, *Seelsorge im Krieg*).

15. Kerrl to all church authorities, September 30, 1939, DA Mainz, K/1.

16. Bertram to the German bishops, October 1, 1939, DA Limburg, 561/22.

17. Martin Broszat, *Nationalsozialistische Polenpolitik 1939 bis 1945* (Stuttgart, 1961), pp. 45 and 159-160.

18. Pastoral letter of November 20, 1939, *AB Cologne*, no. 27, December 1, 1939, p. 166.

19. Dr. Janik, "Für unser deutsches Lebensrecht," *Passauer Bistumsblatt,* no. 42, October 15, 1939, p. 3.
20. F. X. Gerstner, "Bereit sein ist Alles," *Klerusblatt,* no. 39, September 27, 1939, p. 509.
21. "Das Recht auf Freiheit," *Katholisches Kirchenblatt für das Bistum Hildesheim,* no. 9, March 3, 1940, p. 1.
22. W. K., "Das Recht des deutschen Volkes auf Lebensraum," *Bistumsblatt Erzdiözese Breslau,* no. 7, February 18, 1940, p. 44.
23. The full text of the three telegrams can be found in Harry C. Koenig, ed., *Principles for Peace* (Washington, D.C., 1943), pp. 668-669.
24. *Der romfreie Katholik,* no. 11, June 2, 1940, p. 4; *Der Neue Wille,* no. 22.
25. "Zum deutschen Sieg," June 25, 1940, *AB Cologne,* no. 14, July 1, 1940, p. 103.
26. "Bischofswort aus Anlass der Beendigung des Krieges mit Frankreich," June 25, 1940, *AB Trier,* July 1, 1940, p. 141.
27. *AB Würzburg,* no. 15, July 31, 1940, p. 100; *AB Limburg,* no. 10, August 13, 1940, p. 58; etc.
28. "Kriegsbeginn vor einem Jahr," *St. Konradsblatt,* no. 35, September 1, 1940, p. 174.
29. Cf. the report of Heydrich to Ribbentrop of September 10, 1940, PA Bonn, Inland IIg, 45.
30. Cf. Matthes Ziegler, *Was sagen die Weltkirchen zu diesem Krieg? Zeugnisse und Urteile.* Als Manuskript gedruckt (Berlin, 1940), p. 152.
31. Bertram to the German bishops, October 10, 1940, DA Mainz, K/3.
32. *AB Breslau,* no. 21, November 14, 1940, p. 164.
33. *AB Osnabrück,* no. 21, December 12, 1940, p. 119; *AB Trier,* December 31, 1940.
34. Pastoral letter of November 8, 1940, *AB Osnabrück,* no. 20, November 13, 1940, p. 110.
35. Pastoral letter of February 8, 1941, *AB Freiburg,* no. 5, February 12, 1941, pp. 355 and 366.
36. In an undated report, probably to the Reich Chancellery, BA Koblenz, R 43 II/178a.
37. Pastoral letter of January 25, 1941, *AB Ermland,* no. 2, February 1, 1941, pp. 13-14.
38. Sermon on December 31, 1936, Faulhaber, *Münchener Kardinalspredigten,* 2nd series, p. 14.
39. Joint pastoral letter of June 26, 1941, Corsten, *Kölner Aktenstücke,* doc. 209, p. 253.
40. Kerrl to Bertram, August 4, 1941, copy in BA Koblenz, R 43 II/173a.
41. Pastoral letter of September 24, 1941, *AB Eichstätt,* September 25, 1941, p. 71.
42. Inaugural sermon on October 19, 1941, *Klerusblatt,* XXII (1941), 377.

43. Pastoral letter of September 21, 1941, *AB Augsburg*, no. 22, September 22, 1941, p. 256.

44. "Kanzelerklärung zur Abnahme der Glocken," *AB Munich*, December 23, 1941, p. 162.

45. See, e.g., his sermon of July 20, 1941, Portmann, *Kardinal von Galen*, 54.

46. Heinrich Portmann, ed., *Der Bischof von Münster* (Münster, 1946), p. 85.

47. Pastoral letter of March 15, 1942, *AB Münster*, no. 6, March 12, 1942, p. 49.

48. Order of May 10, 1942, *AB Breslau*, no. 9, May 22, 1942, p. 58.

49. Pastoral letter for Lent 1942, *AB Paderborn*, no. 3, February 11, 1942, p. 17.

50. Cf. several such reports in BA Koblenz, EAP 250-a/4 and NS Splitter/ 10; BGS Munich, MA 1946/C37.

51. Bertram to the Ministry of Ecclesiastical Affairs, October 23, 1943. BA Koblenz, R 43 II/178a.

52. Pastoral letter of January 1, 1945, *AB Paderborn*, no. 1, January 16, 1945, p. 2.

53. Quoted in Max Bierbaum, ed., *Nicht Lob Nicht Furcht* (Münster, 1958), pp. 256-257.

54. Gordon C. Zahn, *German Catholics and Hitler's Wars* (New York, 1962), p. 203, (hereinafter cited as Zahn, *German Catholics*).

55. Address on November 13, 1960, quoted *ibid.*, p. 181.

56. Undated report in DA Trier, B III 3, 17.

57. Josef Perau, *Priester im Heere Hitlers: Erinnerungen 1940-1945* (Essen, 1962), p. 53.

58. See, e.g., Bertram to Kerrl, October 22, 1941, and Bertram to Lammers, October 4, 1943, copies of both in DA Mainz, 1/1.

59. Corsten, *Kölner Aktenstücke*, doc. 227, p. 301.

60. Sermon of Galen on July 4, 1943, Bierbaum, *op. cit.*, p. 235; sermon of Frings on December 25, 1943, Corsten, *Kölner Aktenstücke*, doc. 232, p. 310.

61. Both the theologian in question and the source of this information, a highly placed churchman, by request of the latter must remain unnamed.

62. Heinrich Kreutzberg, *Franz Reinisch: Ein Märtyrer unserer Zeit* (Limburg/Lahn, 1953), p. 86.

63. Zahn, *German Catholics*, 147; Josef Fleischer, "Reichskonkordat und Wehrpflichtgesetz" (unpublished manuscript), p. 4.

64. The text of the apology, dated December 15, 1939, is to be found in DA Regensburg.

65. Edward A. Shils and Morris Janowitz, "Cohesion and Disintegration in the Wehrmacht in World War II," *Public Opinion Quarterly*, XII (1948), 303.

66. Matthias Laros, *Was ist zu Tun?* (Dülmen/Westf., 1940), p. 3. Except

for two changes in wording, I have used the translation of Zahn, *German Catholics,* 57.

67. Zahn, *German Catholics,* 187.
68. Faulhaber report of November 5, 1936, DA Limburg, 561/2 C.
69. PA Bonn, II, Vat., Pol. 16, 5.
70. *Ibid.; Acta Apostolica Sedis,* XXX (1935), 367ff. The statutes are reprinted in Werner Weber, *Die deutschen Konkordate und Kirchenverträge der Gegenwart* (Göttingen, 1962), pp. 33-37.
71. Menshausen to Bergen, July 16, 1935, PA Bonn, II, Vat., Pol. 16, 5.
72. Memo to Menshausen, January 15, 1936, PA Bonn, II, Vat., Pol. 16, Geheimakten, Kath. Militärseelsorge; interview with Father Georg Werthmann, the former Vicar General of Rarkowski, June 13, 1962.
73. Memo of Menshausen, September 16, 1935, PA Bonn, II, Vat., Pol. 16, 5.
74. Report on a conference of representatives of the Foreign Ministry, Ministry of Ecclesiastical Affairs, War Ministry on February 6, 1936, PA Bonn, II, Vat., Pol. 16, Geheimakten, Kath. Militärseelsorge.
75. Helm (for Hess) to Blomberg, April 24, 1936, *ibid.*
76. *Katholisches Kirchenblatt für das Bistum Berlin,* no. 9, February 27, 1938, p. 10.
77. Interview with Vicar General Georg Werthmann, June 14, 1962.
78. Pastoral letter of September 1, 1939, *Verordnungsblatt des Katholischen Feldbischofs der Wehrmacht,* vol. III (1939), no. 2, p. 5 (hereinafter cited as *Verordnungsblatt*). I have used the English translation of Zahn, *German Catholics,* 145, though here and in later quotations I have translated German terms like *Volk* into English.
79. Pastoral letter of October 16, 1939, *Verordnungsblatt,* III (1939), no. 3, p. 9.
80. Pastoral letter of September 1940, reprinted in *Klerusblatt,* nos. 4-5, October 23 and 30, 1940, pp. 25 and 34.
81. Pastoral letter "Zu dem grossen Entscheidungskampf im Osten," July 29, 1941, *Verordnungsblatt,* V (1941), no. 6, pp. 2-4.
82. *Katholisches Feldgesangbuch* (Berlin, 1939), p. 10.
83. W. Reibert, *Der Dienstunterricht im Heere* (Berlin, 1939), p. 29.
84. "Erklärung der Fuldaer Bischofskonferenz bezüglich der vorgeschriebenen staatsbürgerlichen Eidesleistung," August 1935, Corsten, *Kölner Aktenstücke,* doc. 83, pp. 79-80.
85. *Katholisches Feldgesangbuch,* 9.
86. Pastoral letter of August 1942, copy in DA Mainz, K/3.
87. *Katholisches Feldgesangbuch,* 20.
88. Heinrich Böll, "Brief an einen jungen Katholiken," *Erzählungen, Hörspiele, Aufsätze* (Cologne, 1961), pp. 381-382.
89. Rarkowski, "Frühling unseres Volkes," *Glaube und Kampf,* April 7, 1940, pp. 1-2, quoted in Zahn, *German Catholics,* 160.
90. Cf. Giovannetti, *op. cit.,* pp. 47-109. In October 1939 Pius XII agreed to act as an intermediary between the military conspirators against

Hitler (represented by Dr. Joseph Müller) and Great Britain, but the generals failed to act and nothing came of the projected peace. Cf. John W. Wheeler-Bennett, *The Nemesis of Power: The German Army in Politics 1918-1945* (London, 1953), pp. 490-493.

91. Osborne to Halifax, September 1, 1939, *Documents on British Foreign Policy*, Third Series, vol. VII (1939), doc. 687, p. 495.

92. Bergen to the Foreign Ministry, October 14, 1939, PA Bonn, Staatssekretär, Vatikan, Bd. 1.

93. Emil Maurice Guerry, *L'Eglise Catholique en France sous l'Occupation* (Paris, 1947), p. 9.

94. Ziegler, *op. cit.*, pp. 74-83.

95. Ives de la Brière, *Le Droit de Juste Guerre* (Paris, 1938), p. 82.

96. Gordon Zahn, "Social Science and the Theology of War," William J. Nagle, ed., *The State of the Question: Morality and Modern Warfare* (Baltimore, 1960), p. 118.

97. Quoted in Ziegler, *op. cit.*, pp. 109-112.

98. Message of April 24, 1940, Giovannetti, *op. cit.*, p. 300.

99. Pastoral letter "Asperis Commoti Anxietatibus" of December 8, 1939, Hofmann, *Seelsorge im Krieg*, 144.

100. Encyclical letter *Summi Pontificatus* of October 20, 1939, *International Conciliation*, no. 355 (December 1939), p. 577.

101. Order of Gestapo Munich, November 7, 1939, NA Washington, T-175, roll 250, frame 2741860.

102. *Münchener Katholische Kirchenzeitung*, no. 47, November 19, 1939, p. 584; memo of Weizsäcker, November 14, 1939, PA Bonn, Staatssekretär, Vatikan, Bd. 1.

103. Giovannetti, *op. cit.*, p. 147; Koenig, *op. cit.*, p. 634.

104. Ziegler, *op. cit.*, p. 25.

105. Menshausen to the Foreign Ministry, PA Bonn, Staatssekretär, Vatikan, Bd. 1.

106. Bergen to the Foreign Ministry, October 10, 1939, *ibid.*

107. *The Persecution of the Catholic Church in German-Occupied Poland* (New York, 1941), pp. 116-117.

108. Bergen to the Foreign Ministry, January 29, 1940, PA Bonn, Staatssekretär, Vatikan, Bd. 1.

109. Mackensen (German ambassador in Italy) to the Foreign Ministry, May 13, 1940, *ibid.*, Bd. 2. Mackensen had the information from the Italian ambassador at the Holy See, Dino Alfieri, who had delivered Mussolini's rebuke.

110. Bergen to the Foreign Ministry, May 11, 1940, *ibid.*

111. Pius XII to the German bishops, August 6, 1940, copy in DA Regensburg. According to the marginal comment of Bishop Buchberger of Regensburg, this "teacher of theology" was Karl Adam, the theologian from Tübingen. In December 1939 Professor Adam had delivered a lecture at Aachen in which he had taken the Church to task for showing insufficient patriotic zeal. German Catholicism, he had argued,

should be German "to the core" (Die geistige Lage des deutschen Katholizismus," lecture on December 10, 1939, DA Limburg 561/2 E). At an undetermined later time and place Adam must also have criticized the three telegrams of Pope Pius and thus drawn the latter's rebuke.

112. "Hier spricht Deutschland," October 6, 1940, "Vatikan-Funkspiegel" no. 00396, PA Bonn, Pol. Verschluss, 23.
113. Interview with Father Georg Werthmann, June 14, 1962.
114. Giovannetti, *op. cit.*, pp. 300-301.
115. "Das Schweigen des Papstes," September 3, 1940, "Vatikan-Funkspiegel" no. 00355, PA Bonn, Pol. Verschluss, 23.
116. See, e.g., "Seltsame Neutralitätspolitik des Vatikans," *Mitteilungen zur Weltanschaulichen Lage,* vol. VI, no. 5 (May 31, 1940).
117. Bertram to the German bishops, February 5, 1941, DA Aachen, 30076.
118. Pius XII to Galen, February 16, 1941, quoted in Bierbaum, *Nicht Lob Nicht Furcht,* 231.
119. Bergen to the Foreign Ministry, June 24, 1941, PA Bonn, Staatssekretär, Vatikan, Bd. 2.
120. Gurian, *Foreign Affairs,* XVI (1938), 270.
121. Pius XII to the German Catholics, January 3, 1943, copy in DA Trier, B III 3, 44.
122. Bertram to the German bishops, July 31, 1943, summarizing content of Maglione's letter of January 9, 1943, DA Trier, B III 3, 44.
123. Weizsäcker to the Foreign Ministry, September 23, 1943, PA Bonn, Staatssekretär, Vatikan, Bd. 4.
124. Report of a German undercover agent about his stay in Rome, July 15-29, 1943, PA Bonn, Inland IIg, 45.
125. Pius XII during a reception for the diplomatic corps, February 18, 1946, Bruno Wuestenberg and Joseph Zabkar, eds., *Der Papst an die Deutschen* (Frankfurt a.M., 1956), p. 124.
126. Tittmann to the U.S. State Dept., October 27, 1941, Dept. of State Papers, 851.00/2416.
127. Cf. Giovannetti, *op. cit.*, pp. 131-134; several protest notes are to be found in the Nuremberg documents, e.g., 3263-PS and 3264-PS in IMT, 32, 93-105. After June 1942 the German government rejected the jurisdiction of the Holy See over the newly acquired territories in the east and elsewhere on the grounds that the Concordat of 1933 was valid for the *Altreich* only (cf. NA Washington, T-454, roll 22, frames 813-819).
128. Cf. PA Bonn, Staatssekretär, Vatikan, Bd. 2.
129. Giovannetti, *op. cit.*, p. 223.
130. Gaetano Salvemini and George LaPiana, *What to Do With Italy* (New York, 1943), p. 128.
131. See n. 111, *supra.*
132. Maglione to the Pallotine Fathers, August 18, 1943, quoted in Kreutzberg, *op. cit.*, p. 170.

133. *AB Eichstätt*, no. 17, September 21, 1939.

134. Bishop Machens to the clergy of the diocese, February 7, 1940, DA Hildesheim.

135. Edict of Kerrl, January 6, 1940, Joseph Engert, ed., *Klerus-Kalender 1941* (Würzburg, n.d.), p. 111.

136. Memo of conversation between Ribbentrop and Pius XII on March 11, 1940, *Documents on German Foreign Policy*, D, VIII, doc. 668, p. 897.

137. Relayed by the Minister of the Interior to the *Reichsstatthälter* etc. on July 24, 1940, BGS Munich, MA 1957/VII-1-8-III.

138. *Hitler's Secret Conversations*, July 4, 1942, pp. 449-451. See also entries for December 13, 1941, p. 117, and February 8, 1942, p. 247, and Hitler's statements reported by Rosenberg in Robert M. W. Kempner, ed., "Der Kampf gegen die Kirche: Aus unveröffentlichten Tagebüchern Alfred Rosenbergs," *Der Monat*, I (1949), 34 and 38.

139. Rosenberg to Bormann, October 23, 1944, and Bormann to Rosenberg, October 27, 1944, NA Washington, T-454, roll 7, frames 4913123-124 and 4913117.

140. Cf. OKH, "Gedanken zur Heeresseelsorge," September 23, 1940, *ibid.*, T-78, roll 281, frame 6229351.

141. Goebbels to the *Gauleiters*, etc., August 13, 1940, *ibid.*, roll 267, frames 6215135-136.

142. Hilling, *Archiv für Katholisches Kirchenrecht*, CXXIV (1949-1950), 19. This order was revoked by Bormann on February 15, 1945 (NA Washington, T-580, roll 42, file 245).

143. A list of confiscated monasteries is given by Neuhäusler, *op. cit.*, I, 149-155.

144. Order of April 23, 1941, BGS Munich, MA 1957/VIII-1-8-III.

145. Bormann to the *Gauleiters*, June 7, 1941, IMT, XXXV, doc. 075-D, pp. 9-13.

146. See, in particular, the reports of the *Regierungspräsidenten* for May and June 1941, BGS Munich, MA 1946/C33.

147. The *Führerbefehl* was relayed by Bormann to the *Gauleiters* on July 31, 1941, BA Koblenz, R 43 II/1271.

148. Papen, *Memoirs*, 482.

149. Kerrl to Lammers, August 23, 1941, BA Koblenz, R 43 II/1272.

150. IMT, XXVIII, 447.

151. Order of Heydrich re. "Behandlung der konfessionellen Gegner," October 24, 1941, NA Washington, T-175, roll 409, frame 2932603.

152. Heydrich to the Foreign Ministry, November 1941, PA Bonn, IIg, 44. The text of the bogus program is reproduced in Stewart W. Herman, *It's Your Souls We Want* (New York, 1943), pp. 297-300. It is accepted as genuine by Shirer, *op. cit.*, p. 332.

153. Order of January 27, 1942, copy in BA Koblenz, 251-a/302.

154. Order of April 26, 1943, NA Washington, T-580, roll 42, file 245.

155. Copies of letters 2-4, 6-8 of the *Pfarrer-Notbund* can be found in DA Mainz, 10/2. That this "organization" was the work of the Gestapo can

be learnt from a memo of June 25, 1943, in the files of the Foreign Ministry, PA Bonn, Inland I-D, Kirche 1.
156. Bormann to Göring, December 20, 1939, NA Washington, T-454, roll 8, frame 4914562.
157. Circular letter no. 53/41, *ibid.*, T-81, roll 676, frame 5485216.
158. Memo about talks held on December 4 and 16, 1941, *ibid.*, roll 673, RPL 172.
159. "Meldungen aus dem Reich," June 5, 1942, *ibid.*, T-175, roll 271, frames 2766979-7001.
160. Order of Bormann, March 18, 1942, BA Koblenz, EAP 251-a/302. The text of the letter is reproduced in Rosenberg's *Mitteilungen zur Weltanschaulichen Lage*, no. 3, March 15, 1942, pp. 14-15.
161. Gröber to the "Ministerrat für Reichsverteidigung" February 19, 1940, BA Koblenz, R 43 II/173.
162. Bertram to Hitler, April 10, 1940, copy in DA Passau.
163. Pastoral letter of the Cologne and Paderborn church provinces, March 20, 1942, Corsten, *Kölner Aktenstücke*, doc. 214, p. 261.
164. Sermon of Landersdorfer, December 31, 1941, DA Passau, file "Hirtenworte."
165. *The Goebbels Diaries 1942-1943*, ed. and trans. Louis P. Lochner (Garden City, N.Y., 1948), p. 382.

Chapter 9

1. *Völkischer Beobachter,* no. 181, August 7, 1929, quoted in Ingbert Naab, *Ist Hitler ein Christ?* (Munich, 1931), p. 22.
2. *Protokoll der Verhandlungen der Bischofskonferenz in Fulda vom 30. Mai bis 1. Juni 1933,* p. 11 and appendix 6.
3. *Reichsgesetzblatt 1933,* I, 529-531.
4. *Protokoll der Verhandlungen der Plenar-Konferenz der deutschen Bischöfe vom 29. bis 31. August 1933,* p. 12.
5. Bertram to Frick, September 12, 1933, copy in DA Passau.
6. Bertram to the German bishops, October 23, 1933, DA Passau.
7. Instruction of October 15, 1933, *Archiv für Katholisches Kirchenrecht,* CXIII (1933), 656.
8. Report of Gröber and Berning, November 3, 1933, DA Mainz, S XXIV.
9. Bertram to the German bishops, December 12, 1933; Papen to Bertram, December 18, 1933; Bertram to the German bishops, January 5, 1934— all in DA Trier, 59/24.
10. Announcement read in the archdiocese of Cologne, Corsten, *Kölner Aktenstücke,* doc. 19, pp. 17-18.
11. *AB Münster,* no. 2, January 31, 1934, p. 6.
12. Faulhaber to Frick, February 7, 1934, copy in DA Trier, 59/24.
13. The full text of these regulations, reprinted from the *Reichsgesetzblatt* of December 7, 1933, can be found in *Ecclesiastica,* XIV (1934), 29-30.
14. Bertram to the German bishops, January 23, 1935, DA Passau.

15. Cf. *Münchener Katholische Kirchenzeitung*, no. 49, December 2, 1934. p. 714; *Ecclesiastica*, XIV (1934), 345-346, n. 4. Both Barion and Eschweiler had joined the Nazi party in May 1933 (Berlin Document Center, files "Hans Barion" and "Carl Eschweiler").

16. *Sterilisierung und Seelsorge* (Beuron, 1935).

17. *Niederschrift über die Konferenz der Bischöfe der Kölner Kirchenprovinz am 27. und 28. März 1935 in Bensberg bei Köln* (typed), p. 6.

18. *Hauptarchiv* Berlin, Rep. 320, no. 585, Heft 1.

19. Norman St. John-Stevas, *Life, Death and the Law* (Bloomington, Ind., 1961), p. 174.

20. Pacelli to Bergen, July 10, 1935 (copy in BA Koblenz, R 43 II/176a) and November 16, 1935, *Dokumente*, III, doc. 12, pp. 34-37.

21. *Niederschrift über die Konferenz der Bischöfe der Kölner Kirchenprovinz am 18./19. Februar 1934 im Priesterseminar zu Bensberg bei Köln* (mimeographed), p. 9. The other church provinces adhered to the same position.

22. *Protokoll der Verhandlungen der Plenar-Konferenz der deutschen Bischöfe in Fulda am 5., 6. und 7. Juni 1934*, p. 6; expert opinion of Professor Wehr, Trier, December 4, 1935, DA Trier, 59/23.

23. Decision of July 24, 1940, copy in DA Mainz, 1/1.

24. Pastoral letter of January 4, 1935, quoted in *Ecclesiastica*, XV (1935), 50.

25. Instructions of Vicar General Riemer of Passau, January 15, 1936, DA Passau.

26. Alice Platen-Hallermund, *Die Tötung Geisteskranker in Deutschland* (Frankfurt a.M., 1948), pp. 63-73. See also *Trials of War Criminals before the Nuernberg Military Tribunals under Control Council Law No. 10,* Case no. 1: "The Medical Case" (Washington, D.C., n.d.) generally.

27. Cf. Gerald Reitlinger, *The SS: Alibi of a Nation* (London, 1956), p. 275.

28. Bertram to Lammers, August 11, 1940, copy in DA Regensburg.

29. Faulhaber to Lammers, November 6, 1940, quoted in Neuhäusler, *op. cit.*, II, 359-363.

30. Portmann, *Bischof Graf von Galen*, 66-76.

31. Cf. *Nazi Conspiracy and Aggression* (Washington, D.C., 1946), VI, doc. 3701-PS, pp. 405-410.

32. *Hitler's Secret Conversations*, October 25, 1941, p. 74, and July 4, 1942, p. 451.

33. Bertram to Frick, March 6, 1943, copy in DA Limburg, 561/20.

34. Léon Poliakov, *Harvest of Hate* (London, 1956), p. 283.

Chapter 10

1. The literature on the subject is too voluminous to be listed here. See, most recently, Ludwig von Hertling, S.J., "Die Schuld des jüdischen Volkes am Tode Christi," *Stimmen der Zeit*, CLXXI (1962), 16-25.

2. For an empirical study of this problem see Bernhard E. Olson, *Faith and Prejudice* (New Haven, 1963) and the earlier work of Paul Déman, N.D.S., "La Catéchèse chrétienne et le peuple de la Bible," *Cahiers Sioniens,* VI (1952), special number 3-4.

3. Jules Isaac, *Jésus et Israël* (Paris, 1948), p. 508.

4. Cf. Eleonore Sterling, *Er ist wie du: Aus der Frühgeschichte des Antisemitismus in Deutschland (1815-1850)* (Munich, 1956).

5. *Historisch-Politische Blätter,* I (1860), 593, quoted in Emil Ritter, ed., *Katholisch-konservatives Erbgut: Eine Auslese für die Gegenwart* (Freiburg, Br., 1934), p. 239.

6. Konrad Martin, *Blicke ins talmudische Judentum,* abridged ed. by Josef Rebbert (Paderborn, 1876), p. 44.

7. Paul Wilhelm von Keppler, *Wanderfahrten and Wallfahrten im Orient,* 7th ed. (Freiburg, Br., 1912), p. 313.

8. Paul W. Massing, *Rehearsal for Destruction: A Study of Political Anti-Semitism in Imperial Germany* (New York, 1949), p. 17.

9. Matthias Erzberger, *Christliche oder sozialdemokratische Gewerkschaften?* (Stuttgart, 1898), pp. 29-30, quoted in Klaus Epstein, *Matthias Erzberger and the Dilemma of German Democracy* (Princeton, 1959), p. 402.

10. Hans Rost, *Gedanken and Wahrheiten zur Judenfrage* (Trier, 1907), p. 89.

11. Erhard Schlund, O.F.M., *Katholizismus und Vaterland* (Munich, 1923), pp. 32-33.

12. Gustav Gundlach, S.J., "Antisemitismus," *Lexikon für Theologie und Kirche,* 2nd rev. ed. (Freiburg, Br., 1930), I, 504. The new edition of this work, published after the downfall of Nazism, has replaced this article by one that condemns all types of anti-Semitism.

13. Michael Buchberger, *Gibt es noch eine Rettung?* (Regensburg, n.d. [1931]), pp. 97-98.

14. Dr. Mayer, "Kann ein Katholik Nationalsozialist sein?" in Wild, *op. cit.,* p. 12.

15. Harry Pross, ed., *Die Zerstörung der Deutschen Politik* (Frankfurt a.M., 1959), p. 242.

16. Josef Roth, *Katholizismus und Judenfrage* (Munich, 1923), p. 5.

17. Philipp Haeuser, *Jud und Christ oder Wem gebührt die Weltherrschaft?* (Regensburg, 1923).

18. Wilhelm Maria Senn, *Katholizismus und Nationalsozialismus* (Münster, 1931), p. 80.

19. In 1960 Dr. Franz Rödel, a retired Catholic priest and the organizer of the *Katholisch-Judaeologischen Institut* in Jetzendorf/Ilm, unsuccessfully appealed to the Bavarian Bishops' Conference to abolish the commemoration exercises of Deggendorf and to remove the offensive pictures and inscriptions in the church erected for the miraculous event in question. In a detailed memorandum he exposed the historical falsehoods involved, but nothing came of his plea until a mass circula-

tion magazine, *Der Spiegel,* picked up the incredible story. Only then did the Church authorities move into action and the affair has now been converted into an annual call for forgiveness for the wrongs done to the Jews.

20. Franz Steffen, *Antisemitische und deutschvölkische Bewegung im Lichte des Katholizismus* (Berlin, 1925), p. 88.
21. Felix Langer, *Der "Judenspiegel" des Dr. Justus kritisch beleuchtet* (Leipzig, 1921), p. 30.
22. Muckerman, *Der Gral,* XXVI (1932), 273.
23. Sermon on December 31, 1923, in Faulhaber, *Deutsches Ehrgefühl,* 19.
24. "Der Erzbischof von Köln für den inneren Frieden," *Münchener Katholische Kirchenzeitung,* no. 15, April 10, 1932, p. 170.
25. Memorandum of unknown authorship, *Documents on German Foreign Policy,* C, I, doc. 188, p. 347.
26. Report of Bishop Berning, Müller, *Kirche und NS,* 118.
27. Article "Rasse" in Gröber, *Handbuch der religiösen Gegenwartsfragen,* 536.
28. Sermon of December 31, 1933, in Faulhaber, *Judaism, Christianity and Germany,* 107.
29. Sermon of December 17, 1933, *ibid.,* pp. 68-69.
30. Yves M.-J. Congar, O. P., *Die katholische Kirche und die Rassenfrage,* trans. W. Armbruster (Recklinghausen, 1961), p. 68.
31. *AB Munich,* November 15, 1934, supplement.
32. J. Scherm, "Der alttestamentliche Bibelunterricht: Planungen und Wegweisungen," *Klerusblatt,* XX (1939), 225.
33. Pastoral letter of January 30, 1939, *AB Freiburg,* no. 3, February 8, 1939, p. 15.
34. Pastoral letter for Lent 1939, *AB Limburg,* no. 1, February 6, 1939, pp. 1-8.
35. Article "Marxismus," Gröber, *Handbuch der religiösen Gegenwartsfragen,* 404.
36. Article "Bolschewismus," *ibid.,* p. 86.
37. *Ibid.,* p. 87.
38. Article "Kunst," *ibid.,* p. 372.
39. Waldemar Gurian, "Anti-Semitism in Modern Germany" in Koppel S. Pinson, ed., *Essays on Anti-Semitism* (New York, 1946), p. 235.
40. Lichtenberg to Hitler, December 10, 1935, BA Koblenz, R 43 II/175.
41. *Klerusblatt,* XVI (1935), 817; *Münchener Katholische Kirchenzeitung,* no. 50, December 15, 1935, p. 795. The new evidence was first reported by the *Münsterer Kirchenblatt* of December 1, 1935.
42. Clemens Gahlen, *Der zerbrochene Pfaffenspiegel* (Bocholt, 1938), p. 19.
43. Joseph Schneider, *Wider den Pfaffenspiegel* (Aschaffenburg, 1937), pp. 21 and 65.
44. *AB Regensburg,* no. 2, February 5, 1937, p. 22; Konrad Hofmann, ed., *Hirtenbriefe des Erzbischofs Gröber* (Freiburg, Br., 1947), p. 145.
45. Adam, *Theologische Quartalschrift,* CXIV (1933), 60-62.

46. "Vor 17 Jahren: Marxismus über Deutschland," *Klerusblatt,* XVI (1935), 785-788.
47. F. Schühlein, "Geschichte der Juden," *Lexikon für Theologie und Kirche,* 2nd rev. ed. (Freiburg, Br., 1933), V, 687.
48. Gustav Lehmacher, S.J., "Rassenwerte," *Stimmen der Zeit,* CXXVI (1933), 81.
49. "Verdient die katholische Kirche den Namen 'Judenkirche'?," *Klerusblatt,* XVIII (1937), 542.
50. Theodor Bogler, O.S.B., *Der Glaube von gestern und heute* (Cologne, 1939), p. 150.
51. AKD *Mitteilungsblatt,* no. 6, May 15, 1934, [p. 8].
52. Erwin Roderich Kienitz, *Christliche Ehe: Eine Darstellung des Eherechts und der Ehemoral der katholischen Kirche für Seelsorger und Laien* (Munich, 1938), pp. 47-54.
53. *Denkschrift über die Reform des Deutschen Strafrechtes,* mimeographed, 39 pp., copy in DA Passau.
54. Circular letter of the "Kirchliche Informationsstelle der Bischöflichen Behörden Deutschlands," no. 341, September 16, 1935, DA Eichstätt.
55. This was the complaint of Alfred Richter, "Parteiprogramm der NSDAP und Reichskonkordat: Zum dritten Jahrestag der Unterzeichnung des Reichskonkordats (20. Juli 1933)," *Deutschlands Erneuerung,* XX (1936), 468. The occurrence of such marriages was confirmed to me by the former Vicar General of Hildesheim, Dr. Wilhelm Offenstein, in an interview on February 5, 1962. The German Federal Republic subsequently legalized these illegal marriages.
56. *Deutsche Briefe,* no. 52, September 27, 1935, pp. 6-7.
57. Regierungsrat Münsterer, "Die Regelung des Rassenproblems durch die Nürnberger Gesetze," *Klerusblatt,* XVII (1936), 47.
58. Hudal, *op. cit.,* pp. 75 and 88.
59. Cf. *Niederschrift der Konferenz der bayerischen Bischöfe in München am 21. März 1934,* p. 3.
60. J. Demleitner, "Volksgenealogie," *Klerusblatt,* XV (1934), 503.
61. All of the diocesan archives preserved contain voluminous files of correspondence in connection with the certification of Aryan descent.
62. Bertram to the German bishops, October 14, 1936, DA Eichstätt.
63. Vicar General Buchwieser of Munich to Kerrl, November 18, 1937, copy in DA Eichstätt.
64. Bertram to the "Forschungsabteilung Judenfrage des Reichsinstituts für die Geschichte des neueren Deutschland" in Munich, January 20, 1938, copy in DA Mainz, J XXIII.
65. Bertram to Pacelli, September 2, 1933, copy in DA Passau; printed in Müller, *Kirche und NS,* doc. 87, p. 190.
66. Corsten, *Kölner Aktenstücke,* doc. 17, p. 16.
67. Cf. Report of the "Sonderhilfswerk des St. Raphaelsvereins für Persönlichkeiten die infolge Abstammung oder aus anderen Gründen

ihre Existenz verloren haben," May 31, 1935, DA Mainz, file "St. Raphaelsverein."

68. Neuhäusler, *op. cit.*, II, 389; DA Mainz, V/xvi.

69. *Protokoll der Verwaltungsratssitzung und der Hauptversammlung des St. Raphaelsvereins in Dortmund am Freitag, den 27. August 1937*, mimeo, 12 pp., DA Mainz, file "St. Raphaelsverein"; minutes of the Fulda Bishops' Conference of August 1939, BA Koblenz, R 43 II/177a.

70. *Petrusblatt* (Berlin), no. 16, April 16, 1961, p. 3.

71. BA Koblenz, R 43 II/174.

72. Report of the Gestapo Munich, January 1, 1937, BGS Munich, MA 1946/019.

73. Von einem deutschen, römisch-katholischen Priester, "Die katholische Kirche und die Judenfrage," *Eine heilige Kirche*, XVI (1934), 177.

74. From a report of Heydrich to Göring, November 11, 1938, quoted in Poliakov, *op. cit.*, p. 17.

75. Hugh Martin *et al.*, *Christian Counter-Attack* (New York, 1944), p. 24.

76. Quoted in Erb, *op. cit.*, p. 43.

77. Quoted in Poliakov, *op. cit.*, p. 30.

78. Quoted in Raul Hilberg, *The Destruction of the European Jews* (Chicago, 1961), p. 262.

79. Several such letters can be found in DA Limburg, file "Nichtarier."

80. Bertram to the German bishops, September 17, 1941, DA Limburg, file "Nichtarier."

81. Berning to Bertram, October 27, 1941, copy in DA Limburg, file "Nichtarier."

82. *Ibid.*

83. Hilfrich to Wienken, October 27, 1941, DA Limburg, file "Nichtarier."

84. Wienken to Hilfrich, October 30, 1941, DA Limburg, file "Nichtarier."

85. *Niederschrift über die Konferenz der Bischöfe der Kölner- und Paderborner Kirchenprovinz am 24. und 25. November 1941 in Paderborn*, mimeo, p. 5.

86. Herman, *op. cit.*, p. 234; Bernhard Lösener, "Das Reichsministerium des Inneren und die Judengesetzgebung: Aufzeichnungen," *Vierteljahrshefte für Zeitgeschichte* IX (1961), 310.

87. Inge Scholl, *Die weisse Rose* (Frankfurt a.M., 1961), pp. 126-128.

88. "Augenzeugenbericht zu den Massenvergasungen," *Vierteljahrshefte für Zeitgeschichte*, I (1953), 193. The opening scene of Hochhuth's play *Der Stellvertreter* is based on Gerstein's account, which is considered fully reliable by all students of the subject.

89. Interview with Dr. Gertrud Luckner, March 9, 1962. One such officer, Dr. Alfons Hildenbrand, took special leave from his unit stationed near Minsk in order to report about the massacres he had witnessed to Cardinal Faulhaber. Cf. Thomas Dehler, "Sie zuckten mit der Achsel," Fritz J. Raddatz, ed., *Summa inuria oder Durfte der Papst schweigen?* (Reinbek bei Hamburg, 1963), p. 231.

90. Interview with Dr. Joseph Müller, March 26, 1962.

91. Hilberg, *op. cit.*, p. 267.
92. Bertram to Thierack, November 11, 1942, Archives of the Ministry of Justice, Bonn, R 22 Gr. 5/XXII-2; copy in DA Aachen.
93. Ruth Andreas-Friedrich, *Berlin Underground 1938-1945,* trans. Barrows Mussey (New York, 1947), p. 92; Philip Friedman, *Their Brothers' Keepers* (New York, 1957), p. 93.
94. Cf. the affidavit of Bishop Preysing for Globke, January 18, 1946, printed in *Petrusblatt*, no. 32, August 7, 1960, p. 3.
95. Bertram to Thierack, March 2, 1943, Archives of the Ministry of Justice, R 22 Gr. 5/XXII-2; copy in DA Mainz, 1/1.
96. Preysing to the German bishops, April 16, 1943, DA Limburg, file "Nichtarier."
97. Memo on oral information from Preysing relayed to the Bishop of Limburg etc. on June 26, 1943, by Father Odilo Braun, O.P., DA Limburg, file "Nichtarier." Father Braun, a friend of Alfred Delp, was arrested by the Gestapo in 1944, but escaped with his life.
98. Bertram to the Minister of the Interior and the RSHA, November 17, 1943, copy in DA Limburg, file "Nichtarier."
99. Bertram to Thierack, January 29, 1944, BA Koblenz, R 22 Gr. 5/XXI, la.
100. Pastoral letter of December 12, 1942, Corsten, *Kölner Aktenstücke,* doc. 218, p. 269.
101. Joint pastoral letter of August 19, 1943, *ibid.,* doc. 227, pp. 301-303.
102. Sermons of December 25, 1943, and March 12, 1944, *ibid.,* docs. 232-233, p. 310.
103. Report of October 10, 1943, BGS Munich, MA 1946/C38.
104. From an internal S.S. report, NA Washington, T-580, roll 42, file 245.
105. Erb, *op. cit.*, pp. 46-65. According to the *Freiburger Rundbrief,* I (1948), 16, Bishop Kaller of Ermland asked the permission of the Papal Nuncio to go as a priest to Theresienstadt, a Ghetto city for old people, decorated veterans and other Jews of prominence. This request does not seem to have reached the hands of the Gestapo.
106. For the text of the protests see W. W. Visser't Hooft, ed., *Holländische Kirchendokumente* (Zollikon-Zürich, 1944), pp. 58-60.
107. Werner Warmbrunn, *The Dutch under German Occupation 1940-1945* (Stanford, Cal., 1963), p. 161.
108. Friedman, *op. cit.*, pp. 70-71; C. Leclef, ed., *Le Cardinal van Roey et l'Occupation Allemande en Belgique: Actes et Documents* (Brussels, 1945), ch. 8.
109. Emile Maurice Guerry, *L'Eglise Catholique en France sous l'Occupation* (Paris, 1947), pp. 33-65; Jules Géraud Saliège, *Fürchtet euch nicht: Hirtenbriefe und Ansprachen* (Offenburg, 1949), pp. 150-151; Friedman, *op. cit.*, pp. 49-51.
110. Pastoral letter of March 25, 1941, *AB Freiburg*, no. 9, March 27, 1941, p. 388.
111. The case of a Jewish mother and her son, who were hidden in a

monastery near Berlin, is described by Kurt R. Grossmann, *Die unbesungenen Helden* (Berlin, 1957), p. 153.

112. Cf. Gertrud Ehrle, ed., *Licht über dem Abgrund* (Freiburg, Br., 1951), pp. 118-124.

113. Heinrich Grüber, "Zu Rolf Hochhuth's 'Stellvertreter,' " Raddatz, *op. cit.*, p. 202.

114. Grossmann, *op. cit.*, p. 113; Ernst Schnydrig, "Hilfe für die verfolgten Juden," Zentralvorstand des Deutschen Caritasverbandes, *An der Aufgabe gewachsen* [60th anniversary Festschrift] (Freiburg, Br., 1957), pp. 74-77; interview with Dr. Gertrud Luckner, March 9, 1962.

115. "Thesen christlicher Lehrverkündigung im Hinblick auf umlaufende Irrtümer über das Gottesvolk des Alten Bundes" (Schwalbacher Thesen), *Freiburger Rundbrief*, II (1949-50), no. 8/9, p. 9.

116. BGS Munich, MA 1946/C35.

117. Cf. Hilda Graef, *Leben unter dem Kreuz: Eine Studie über Edith Stein* (Frankfurt a.M., 1954), p. 130.

118. *Acta Apostolica Sedis*, XX (1928), 104, quoted in Luigi Sturzo, *Nationalism and Internationalism* (New York, 1946), p. 46. On the dissolution of the society "Amici Israel" see Franz Rödel, "Der Papst und das 'Erkorene Volk Gottes'," *Abwehrblätter*, XXXVIII (1928), 88-89.

119. Note of the Papal Secretariat of State to the German government, September 9, 1933, *Documents on German Foreign Policy*, C, I, doc. 425, p. 794.

120. *Civiltà Cattolica*, no. 2024, quoted in Daniel Carpi, "The Catholic Church and Italian Jewry under the Fascists (to the Death of Pius XI)," *Yad Washem Studies*, IV (1960), 51.

121. *Ibid.*, pp. 51-52.

122. Cf. Congar, *op. cit.*, p. 69.

123. The statement was first reported by *La Croix*, no. 17060, September 17, 1938. It is accepted as accurate by Sturzo, *op. cit.*, p. 47.

124. No. 288 of December 13, 1938, reported by Bergen, December 13, 1938, PA Bonn, Pol. III, 22.

125. Richard A. Webster, *The Cross and the Fasces: Christian Democracy and Fascism in Italy* (Stanford, Cal., 1960), p. 126.

126. Tardini, *op. cit.*, p. 59.

127. Quoted in Poliakov, *op. cit.*, p. 300.

128. Abetz to the Foreign Ministry, August 28, 1942, PA Bonn, Staatssekretär, Vatikan, Bd. 4.

129. Tittmann to the Secretary of State, July 30, 1942, *U. S. Diplomatic Papers 1942*, III, 772.

130. Taylor to Maglione, September 26, 1942, *ibid.*, p. 776.

131. Tittmann's summary of Holy See statement of October 10, 1942, *ibid.*, p. 777.

132. Tittmann to the Department of State, October 6, 1942, *ibid.*; Titt-

mann dispatch of September 8, 1942, Department of State Papers, 740.00116 European War 1939/573, 1/2.

133. Tittmann to the Department of State, December 22, 1942, Department of State Papers, 740.0016 European War 1939/689.

134. Corsten, *Kölner Aktenstücke*, doc. 220, p. 280. The message was mimeographed and distributed in Germany by the diocesan chanceries. I have seen a copy in DA Eichstätt.

135. Pius XII to the Cardinals, June 2, 1943, excerpts in *AB Munich*, August 12, 1943.

136. Memo of Woermann, PA Bonn, Staatssekretär, Vatikan, Bd. 4.

137. Weizsäcker to Woermann etc., December 5, 1941, quoted in Hilberg, *op. cit.*, p. 441.

138. *The Ciano Diaries: 1939-1943*, ed. by Hugh Gibson (New York, 1946), p. 530.

139. Poliakov, *op. cit.*, pp. 159-160; Hilberg, *op. cit.*, pp. 469-470.

140. Hilberg, *op. cit.*, p. 427

141. Gumbert (of the German Embassay at the Quirinal) to the Foreign Ministry, October 16, 1943, PA Bonn, Inland IIg, 192. Bishop Hudal had signed this letter at the urging of several anti-Nazi officials in the German legations at the Quirinal and Holy See who had composed it. I have used the English translation of Hilberg, *op. cit.*, p. 429.

142. Weizsäcker to the Foreign Ministry, October 17, 1943, PA Bonn, Inland IIg, 192. The translation is that of Poliakov, *op. cit.*, p. 297, n. 16.

143. Cf. Robert Leiber, S.J., "Pius XII und die Juden in Rom 1943-1944," *Stimmen der Zeit*, CLXVII (1960-61), 429-430.

144. Weizsäcker to the Foreign Ministry, October 28, 1943, PA Bonn, Inland IIg, 192. The English translation is that of Poliakov, *op. cit.*, pp. 297-298, n. 16.

145. Weizsäcker to the Foreign Ministry, December 3, 1943, PA Bonn, Pol. III, 22.

146. Cf. Hilberg, *op. cit.*, p. 539; Gerald Reitlinger, *The Final Solution* (New York, 1953), pp. 431-432. The successful intervention of the Papal Nuncio in Rumania was attested to by the former Chief Rabbi of Rumania at the Eichmann trial (cf. *New York Times*, May 24, 1961, p. 12).

147. Statement of Dr. Senatro on March 11, 1963, at a public discussion in Berlin (Raddatz, *op. cit.*, p. 223).

148. Poliakov, *op. cit.*, p. 302.

149. Louis de Jong, "Jews and non-Jews in Nazi-Occupied Holland," Max Beloff, ed., *On the Track of Tyranny* (London, 1960), pp. 148-149.

150. Reported by Weizsäcker, September 23, 1943, PA Bonn, Staatssekretär, Vatikan, Bd. 4.

151. Robert Leiber, S.J., "Der Papst und die Verfolgung der Juden," Raddatz, *op. cit.*, p. 104.

152. Pius XII to the German bishops, August 6, 1940, copy in DA Regensburg.
153. Encyclical letter *Summi Pontificatus,* October 20, 1939, *International Conciliation,* no. 355 (December 1939), 556.
154. Sermon on February 6, 1936, Faulhaber, *Münchener Kardinalspredigten,* 1st series, p. 17.
155. Sermon on July 13, 1941, Heinrich Portmann, ed., *Bischof Galen spricht* (Freiburg, Br., 1946), p. 49.
156. Tisserant to Suhard, June 11, 1940, published from the files of the German Reich Chancellery (BA Koblenz, R 43 II/1440a) by Eberhard Jäckel, "Zur Politik des Heiligen Stuhls im Zweiten Weltkrieg: Ein ergänzendes Dokument," *Geschichte in Wissenschaft und Unterricht,* XV (1964), 45. The letter was found and confiscated by the Germans during a search of the official residence of Cardinal Suhard in Paris.
157. Alfred Delp, S.J., *Zwischen Welt und Gott* (Frankfurt a.M., 1957), p. 97.
158. *Ibid.,* pp. 293 and 233.
159. Report on a talk by Delp at an "Informationskonferenz der bayerischen Ordinariate" in Munich on October 25, 1943, DA Passau.
160. Pribilla, *Stimmen der Zeit,* CXXVIII (1935), 305.
161. Max Frisch, *Andorra* in *Three Plays,* trans. Michael Bulloch (London, 1962), p. 254.

Chapter 11

1. Pius XII to the Bavarian bishops, August 15, 1945, Wuestenberg and Zabkar, *op. cit.,* p. 113.
2. Sermon on May 24, 1936, in Ingolstadt, DA Regensburg.
3. Sermon on June 7, 1936, *AB Munich,* supplement to no. 16, June 12, 1936, p. 7.
4. Cf. *Schönere Zukunft,* no. 11/12, December 10, 1939, p. 139.
5. *Münchener Katholische Kirchenzeitung,* no. 47, November 19, 1939, p. 588.
6. Cf. Karl Forster, "Vom Wirken Michael Kardinal Faulhabers in München," *Der Mönch im Wappen* (Munich, 1960), p. 504.
7. Sermon of July 20, 1941, Portmann, *Bischof Graf von Galen,* 57. It is typical of Neuhäusler's mode of work that he omits the sentence about the continued fight "against the external enemy" without any indication of this ellipsis.
8. Letter to all diocesan chanceries, November 19, 1941, quoted in Portmann, *Der Bischof von Münster,* 203.
9. Ernest Gruening, *Mexico and its Heritage* (New York, 1928), pp. 277-285; Charles S. MacFarland, *Chaos in Mexico* (New York, 1935), pp. 132-133.
10. Encyclical letter *Firmissimam Constantiam,* March 28, 1937, Joseph Husslein, S.J., *Social Wellsprings* (Milwaukee, 1942), II, 385.

11. Pius XI, *To the Spanish Refugees (Discourse of September 14, 1936)* (New York, 1937), p. 20.
12. Radio address "Con immenso gozo," April 16, 1939, *The Tablet,* CLXXIII (1939), 514.
13. Report of July 10, 1936, BGS Munich, MA 1946/C16. The entire episode is described by Neuhäusler, *op. cit.,* II, 104-109.
14. The order of November 4, 1936, and a report on the subsequent proceedings can be found in *AB Trier,* December 10, 1936.
15. These incidents are reported by the provincial administrators, BGS Munich, MA 1946/C34. Many of these reports are published by Heinrich Huber, *Dokumente einer christlichen Widerstandsbewegung* (Munich, 1948).
16. Faulhaber to Wagner, July 26, 1941, copy in DA Passau.
17. Faulhaber's sermon of July 4, 1937 is to be found in Donohoe, *op. cit.,* pp. 84-92.
18. *The Von Hassell Diaries 1938-1944* (Garden City, N.Y., 1947), p. 223.
19. Interview with Dr. Joseph Müller, March 26, 1962; Karl Heinrich Peter, ed., *Spiegelbild einer Verschwörung: Die Kaltenbrunner Berichte* (Stuttgart, 1961), p. 437.
20. Cf. Mary Alice Gallin, *German Resistance to Hitler: Ethical and Religious Factors* (Washington, D.C., 1961), p. 228.
21. Interview with Dr. Joseph Müller, March 26, 1962.
22. Letter to this writer, June 22, 1962.
23. Peter, *Kaltenbrunner Berichte,* 321-324.
24. Gallin, *op. cit.,* p. 228.
25. Peter, *Kaltenbrunner Berichte,* 304.
26. Interview with Dr. Emil Muhler (Munich), March 23, 1962; Gallin, *op. cit.,* p. 228.
27. Report of August 8, 1944, NA Washington, T-580, roll 675, file 528.
28. Report of September 8, 1944, *ibid.,* T-175, roll 464, frame 2983830.
29. Gallin, *op. cit.,* p. 229.
30. *Ibid.,* pp. 226-227.
31. The literature on these men is large. See, especially, Franz Kloidt, *Verräter oder Märtyrer?* (Düsseldorf, 1962) and Walter Adolph, *Im Schatten des Galgens* (Berlin, 1953).
32. Undated and unsigned postcard, BGS Munich, MA 1957/VII-1-8-III.
33. Cf. Amery, *op. cit.,* pp. 44-48.
34. Friedrich Heer, *Offener Humanismus* (Bern, 1962), p. 232.

Chapter 12

1. Sidney Hook, "Integral Humanism," *Reason, Social Myths and Democracy* (New York, 1940), p. 91.
2. Encyclical *Libertas Praestantissimum* (On Human Liberty), June 20, 1888, Etienne Gilson, ed., *The Church Speaks to the Modern World* (Garden City, N.Y., 1954), p. 81.

3. Encyclical *Sapientiae Christianae* (On Christian Citizenship), January 10, 1890, *ibid.*, p. 262.

4. Encyclical *Dilectissimo nobis*, June 3, 1933, Joseph Husslein, S.J., *Social Wellsprings* (Milwaukee, 1942), II, 294.

5. Christopher Dawson, *Religion and the Modern State* (New York, 1936), pp. 135-136.

6. De la Bedoyère, *The Dublin Review*, CC (1937), 248-249.

7. Eugen Weber, *Action Française* (Stanford, Cal., 1962), pp. 249-251.

8. Christmas message 1944, *Selected Letters and Addresses of Pius XII* (London, 1949), p. 305, quoted in Joseph N. Moody, ed., *Church and Society: Catholic Social and Political Thought and Movements 1789-1950* (New York, 1953), p. 70.

9. Allocution to the members of the *Rota Romana*, October 2, 1945, Ehler and Morrall, *op. cit.*, pp. 603-604.

10. Encyclical *Pacem in Terris*, April 10, 1963, (St. Paul Editions), pp. 21 and 27.

11. August M. Knoll, *Katholische Kirche und scholastisches Naturrecht: Zur Frage der Freiheit* (Vienna, 1962), pp. 56-59.

12. Heinrich A. Rommen, *The State in Catholic Thought* (St. Louis, 1955), p. 478.

13. *Pacem in Terris*, April 10, 1963 (St. Paul Editions), p. 26.

14. *Verhandlungen der Vertreter der Fuldaer Plenar-Bischofskonferenz im Reichsinnenministerium vom 25. bis 30. Juni 1933*, p. 27.

15. Leo XIII in *Sapientiae Christianae*, January 10, 1890, Gilson, *op. cit.*, p. 263.

16. Michael de la Bedoyère, "Rome and Reaction," *The Dublin Review*, CC (1937), p. 251.

17. Lord John Emerich Edward Dalberg Acton, "Political Thoughts on the Church," *The History of Freedom and other Essays*, (London, 1907), p. 210.

18. Encyclical *Quod Apostolici Muneris*, December 28, 1878, Husslein, *op. cit.*, I, 19.

19. Cf. Luigi Sturzo, "The Right of Resistance to the State: Echoes of a Discussion in France," *Contemporary Review*, CXXXIV (1928), 312.

20. Encyclical *Firmissimam Constantiam*, March 28, 1937, Ehler and Morrall, *op. cit.*, p. 590. Cf. Luigi Sturzo, "The Right to Rebel," *The Dublin Review*, CCI (1937), 35-36.

21. Encyclical *Au Milieu des Sollicitudes*, February 16, 1892, *The Great Encyclical Letters of Pope Leo XIII* (New York, 1903), p. 258.

22. Quoted in Wheeler-Bennett, *op. cit.*, p. 627.

23. Cf. Bernhard Häring, *Das Gesetz Christi: Moraltheologie* (Freiburg, Br., 1961), III, 177-178; Joseph Mausbach–Gustav Ermecke, *Katholische Moraltheologie*, 10th rev. ed. (Münster, 1961), vol. III, part II, pp. 149-151.

24. Cf. *The New York Times*, September 25, 1962, p. 18.

25. Monsignor Ancel, Auxiliary Bishop of Lyon, in 1959, quoted in William

Bosworth, *Catholicism and Crisis in Modern France* (Princeton, N. J., 1962), p. 81.

26. Hans Küng, *The Council, Reform and Reunion,* trans. Cecily Hastings (New York, 1961), pp. 21-22.

27. Ernst Troeltsch, *The Social Teaching of the Christian Churches,* trans. Olive Wyon (New York, 1960), I, 331 and 339.

28. Encyclical *Sapientiae Christianae,* Gilson, *op. cit.,* pp. 261-264.

29. Allocution of Pius XII on the occasion of ceremonies in honor of the Blessed Virgin, November 2, 1954, Gerard F. Yates, S.J., ed., *Papal Thought on the State* (New York: Appleton-Century-Crofts, Inc., 1958), pp. 136-138. Copyright © 1958, Appleton-Century-Crofts. Reprinted by permission of same.

30. Karl Rahner, S.J., *The Christian Commitment: Essays in Pastoral Theology* (New York, 1963), p. 24.

31. Böckenförde, *Hochland,* LIII (1961), 239.

32. Hofmann, *Zeugnis und Kampf des deutschen Episkopats,* 10.

33. Encyclical *Summi Pontificatus,* October 20, 1939, *International Conciliation,* no. 355 (December 1939), p. 558.

34. Knoll, *op. cit.,* p. 24.

35. John C. Bennett, *Christians and the State* (New York, 1958), p. 268.

36. Zbigniew K. Brzezinski, *Ideology and Power in Soviet Politics* (New York: Frederick A. Praeger, 1962), pp. 97-98. Reprinted by permission of Frederick A. Praeger, Inc.

37. Joseph L. Featherstone, "Did the Church Fail?" *The Commonweal,* LXXIX (February 28, 1964), 650.

38. See n. 33, *supra.*

INDEX

[All index page references beyond page 341 refer to Notes, although for reasons of space the note numbers do not appear. In this way, readers desiring to find the full title of a work cited as "*op. cit.*" can locate it by looking up the first index reference to the author in question after page 341. Authors of books and articles cited several times are included in the index only once for each work. Subentries for the principal figures of this study are arranged in chronological order; other subentries are alphabetical.]